RADIANT BLACK

URL radiant.black

RADIANT BLACK, VOL. 2. First printing. March 2022. Published by Image Comics, Inc. Office of publication: PO BOX 14457, Portland, OR 97293. ISBN: 978-1-5343-2109-0.

RADIANT BLACK

VOLUME	002
TITLE	Team-Up

CREATED BY

WRITER	Kyle Higgins	
ARTIST	Marcelo Costa	
CO-WRITERS	Joe Clark	(CHAPTER 11)
	Meghan Camarena	(CHAPTER 12)
GUEST ARTISTS	Eduardo Ferigato	(CHAPTER 09)
	French Carlomagno	(CHAPTER 12)
GUEST COLORISTS	Natália Marques	(CHAPTERS 07 & 08)
	Igor Monti	(CHAPTER 10)
	Mattia Iacono	(CHAPTERS 11 & 12)
COLOR ASSISTANT	Sabrina Del Grosso	(CHAPTER 10)
LETTERER	Becca Carey	
GUEST LETTERER	Diego Sanches	(CHAPTER 12)
SERIES LOGO	Rich Bloom	
EDITOR & DESIGNER	Michael Busuttil	
PRODUCTION ARTIST	Deanna Phelps	

BLACK MARKET NARRATIVE

CHAPTER SEVEN

TITLE   Radiant[s]

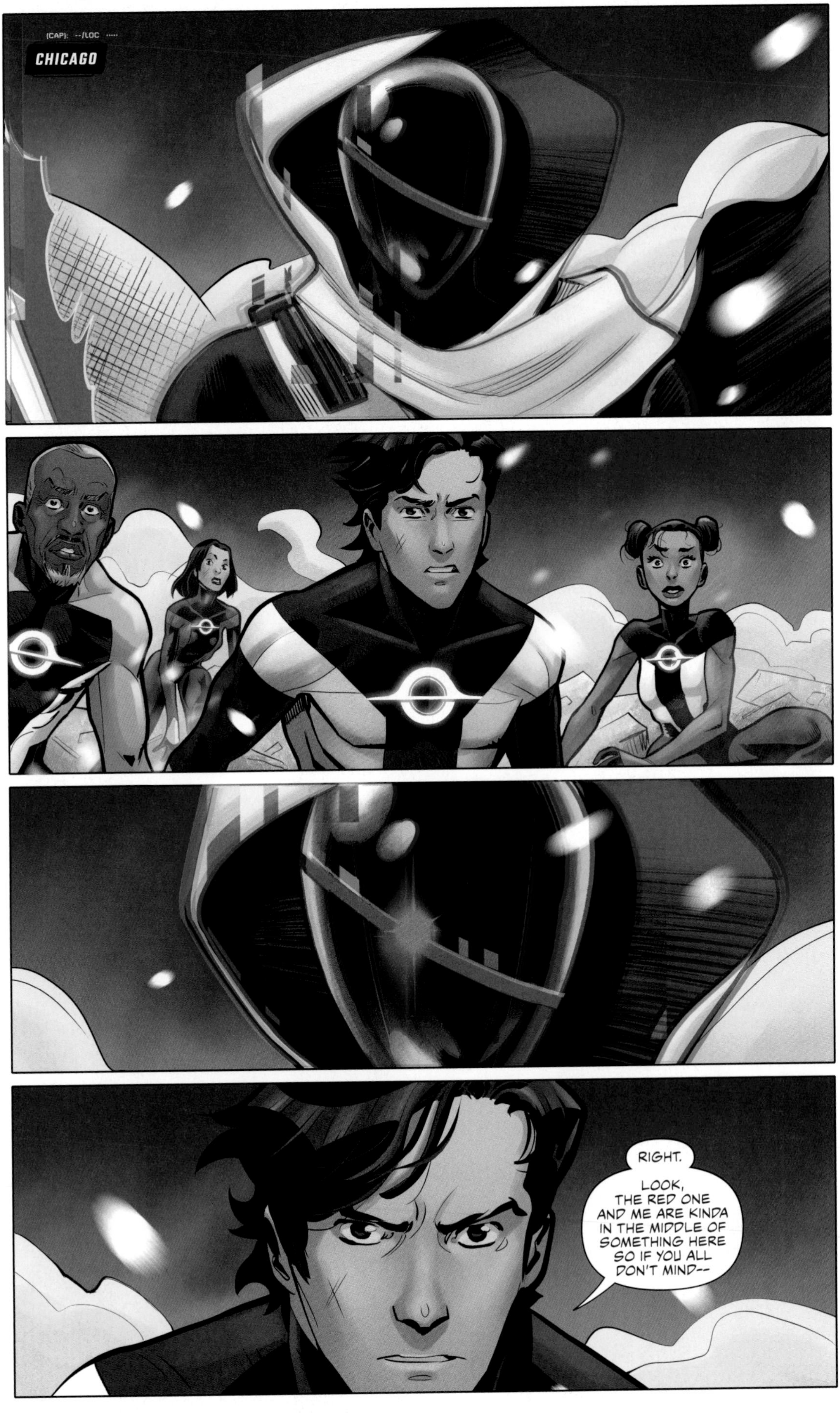

(CAP): --/LOC •••••
CHICAGO
RIGHT.
LOOK, THE RED ONE AND ME ARE KINDA IN THE MIDDLE OF SOMETHING HERE SO IF YOU ALL DON'T MIND--

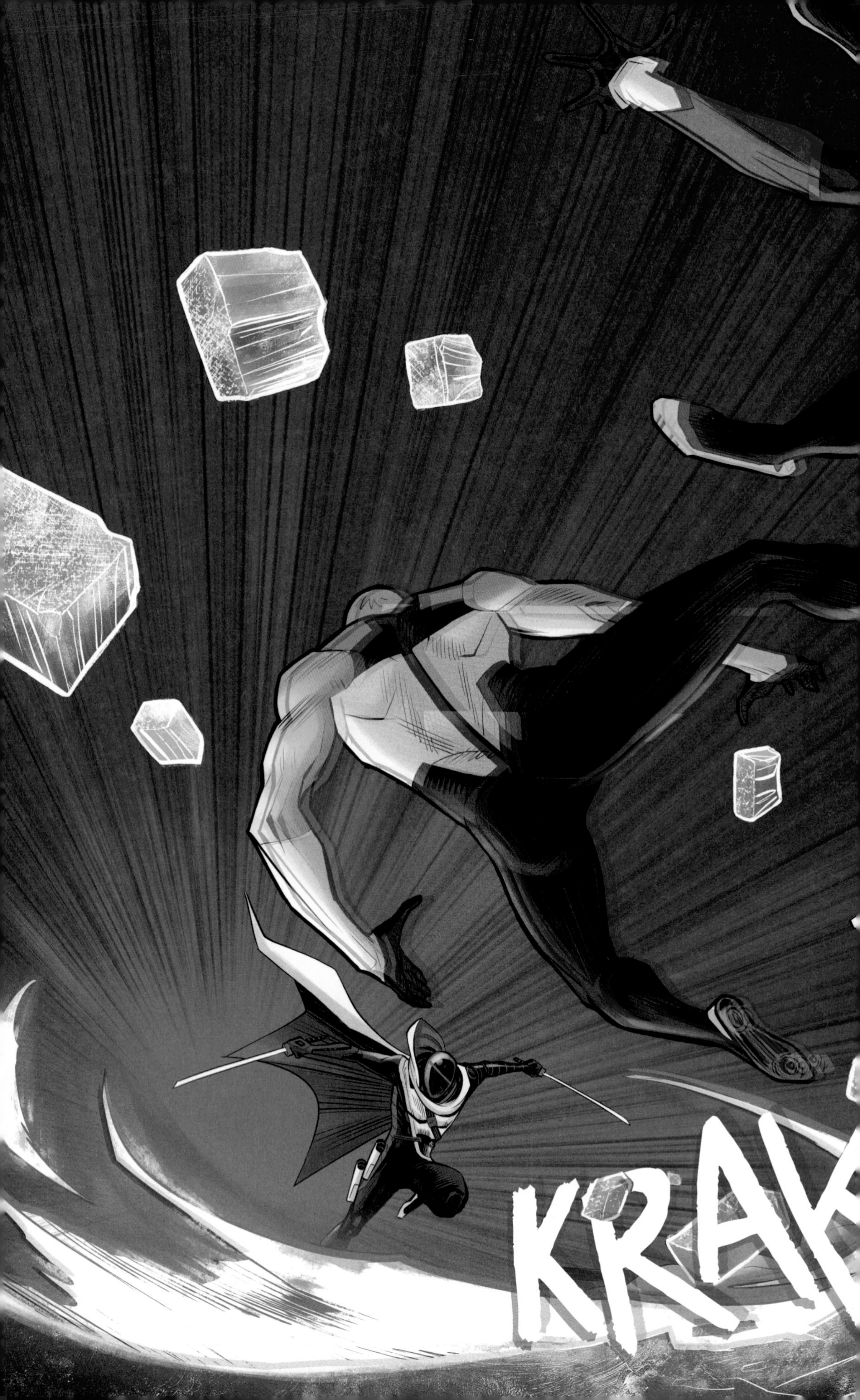
KRAK

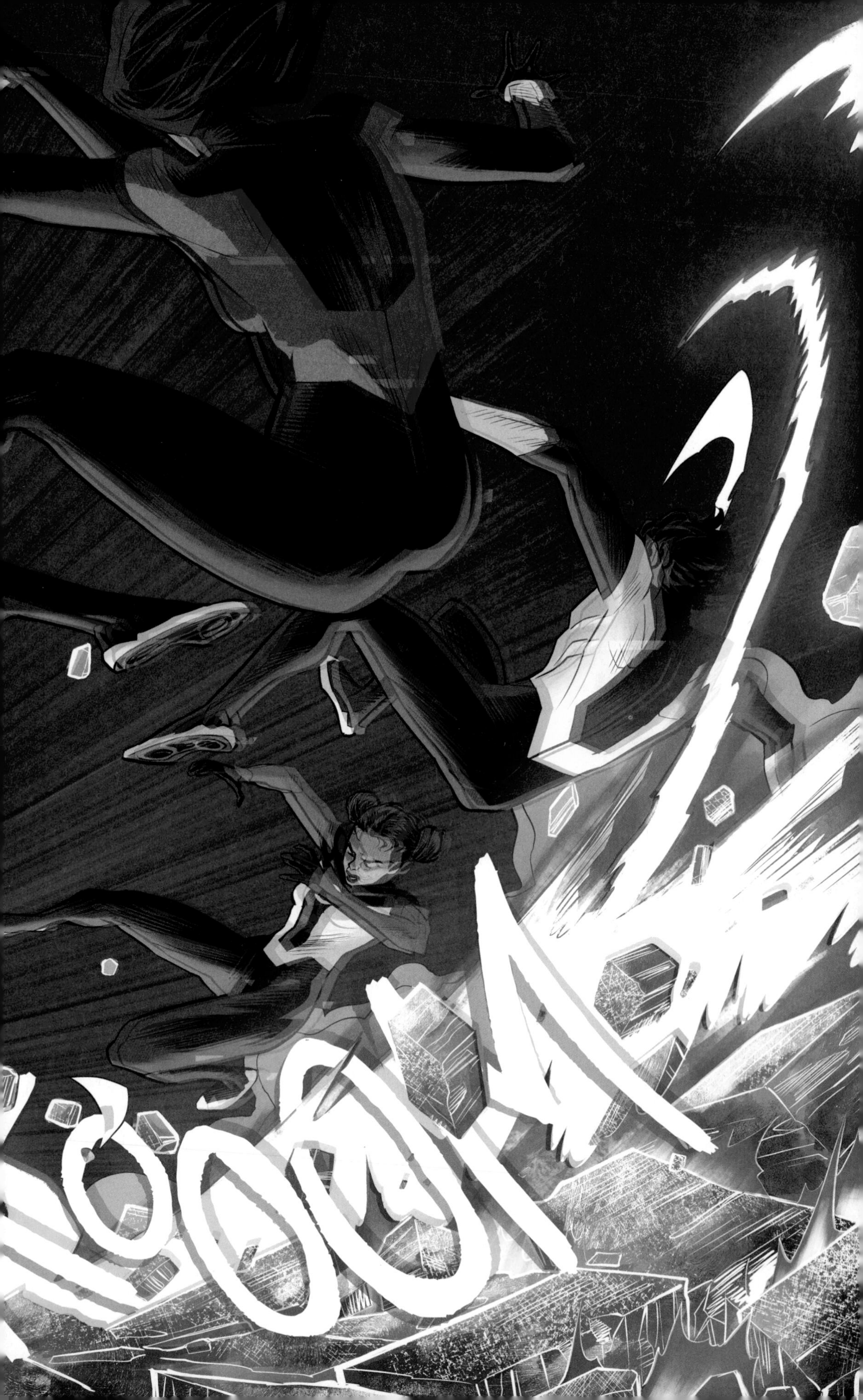

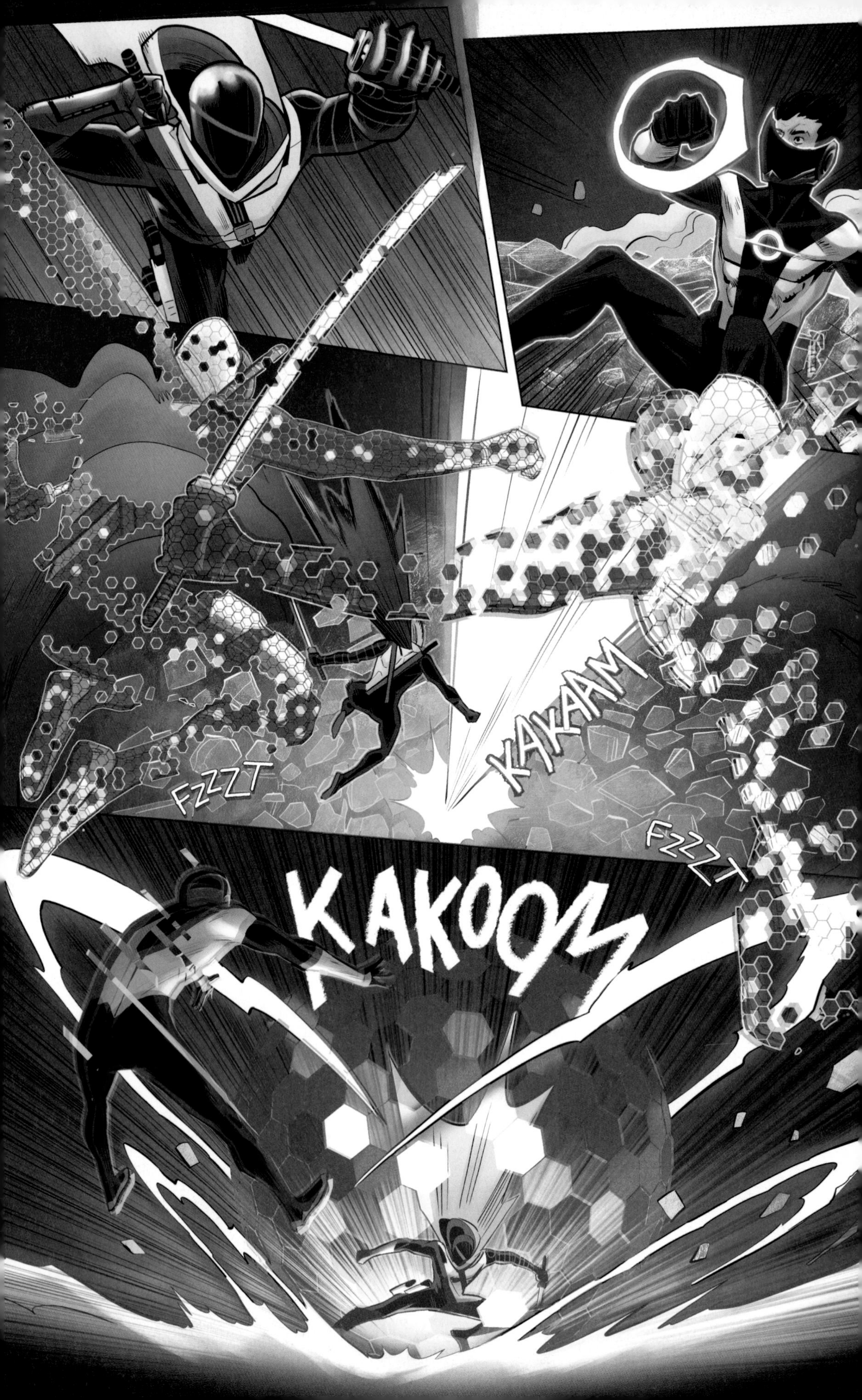
FZZZT
KAKAAM
FZZZT
KAKOOM

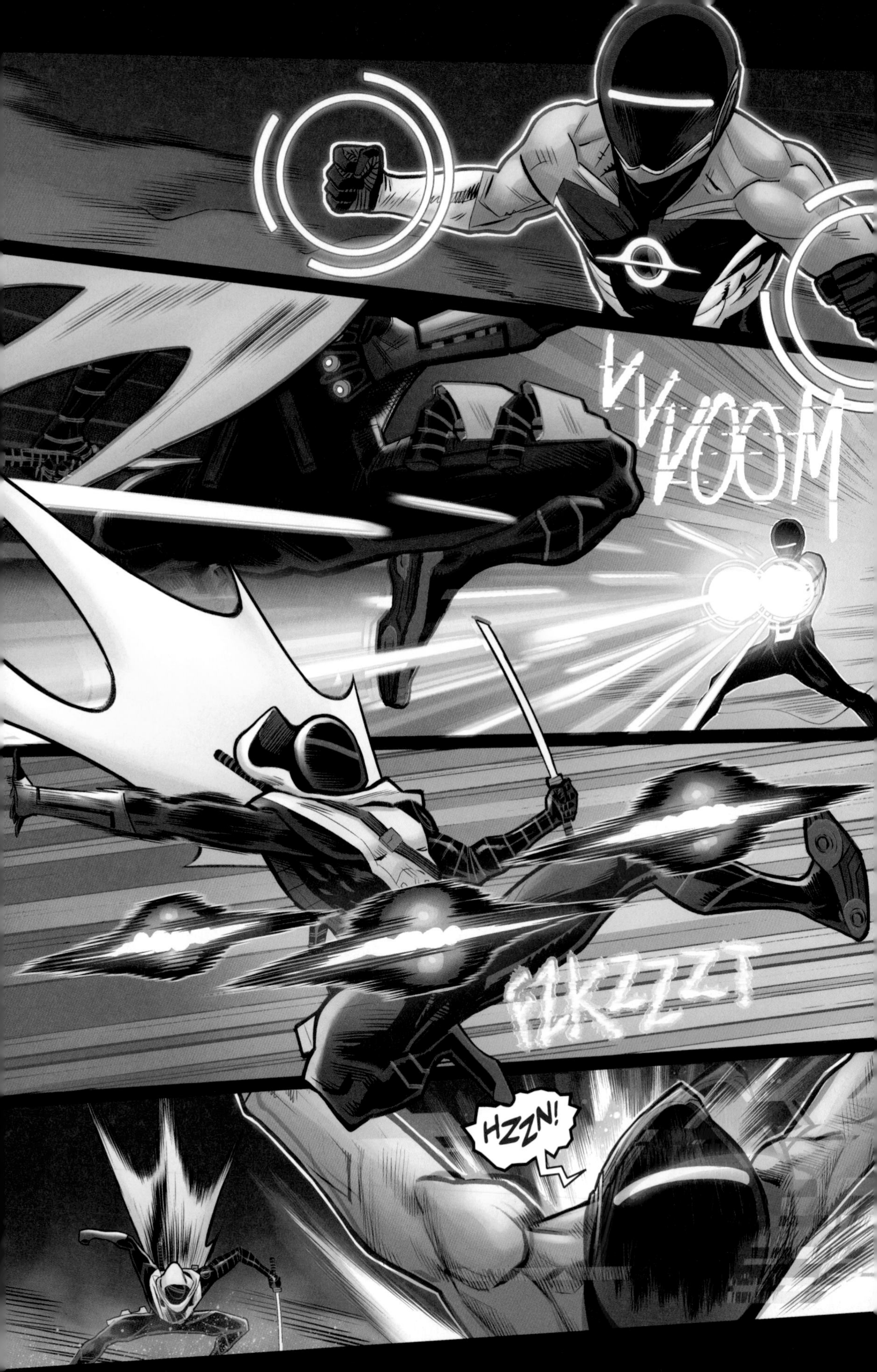
VVVOOM
FZKZZZT
HZZN!

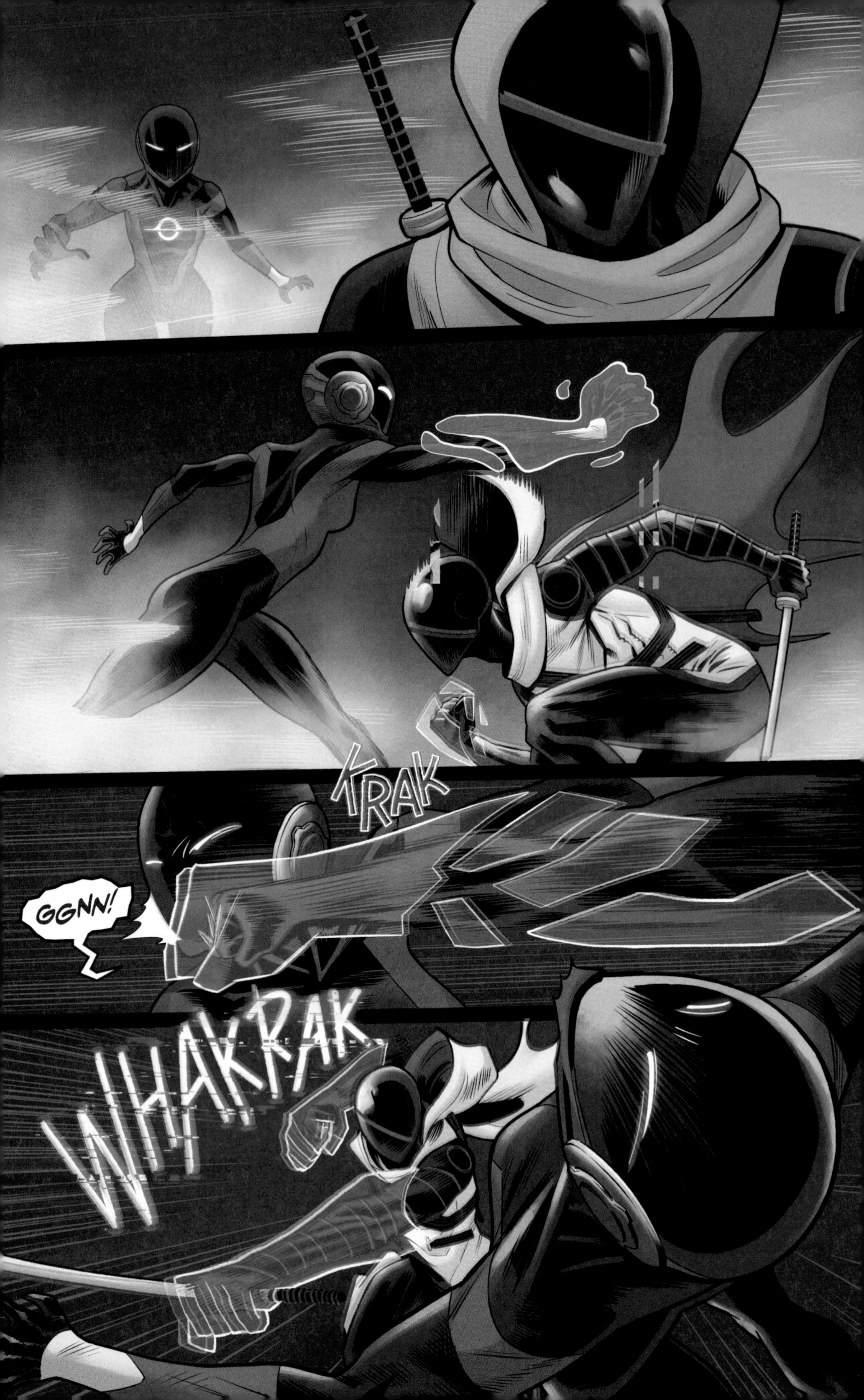
KRAK
GGNN!
WHAKRAK

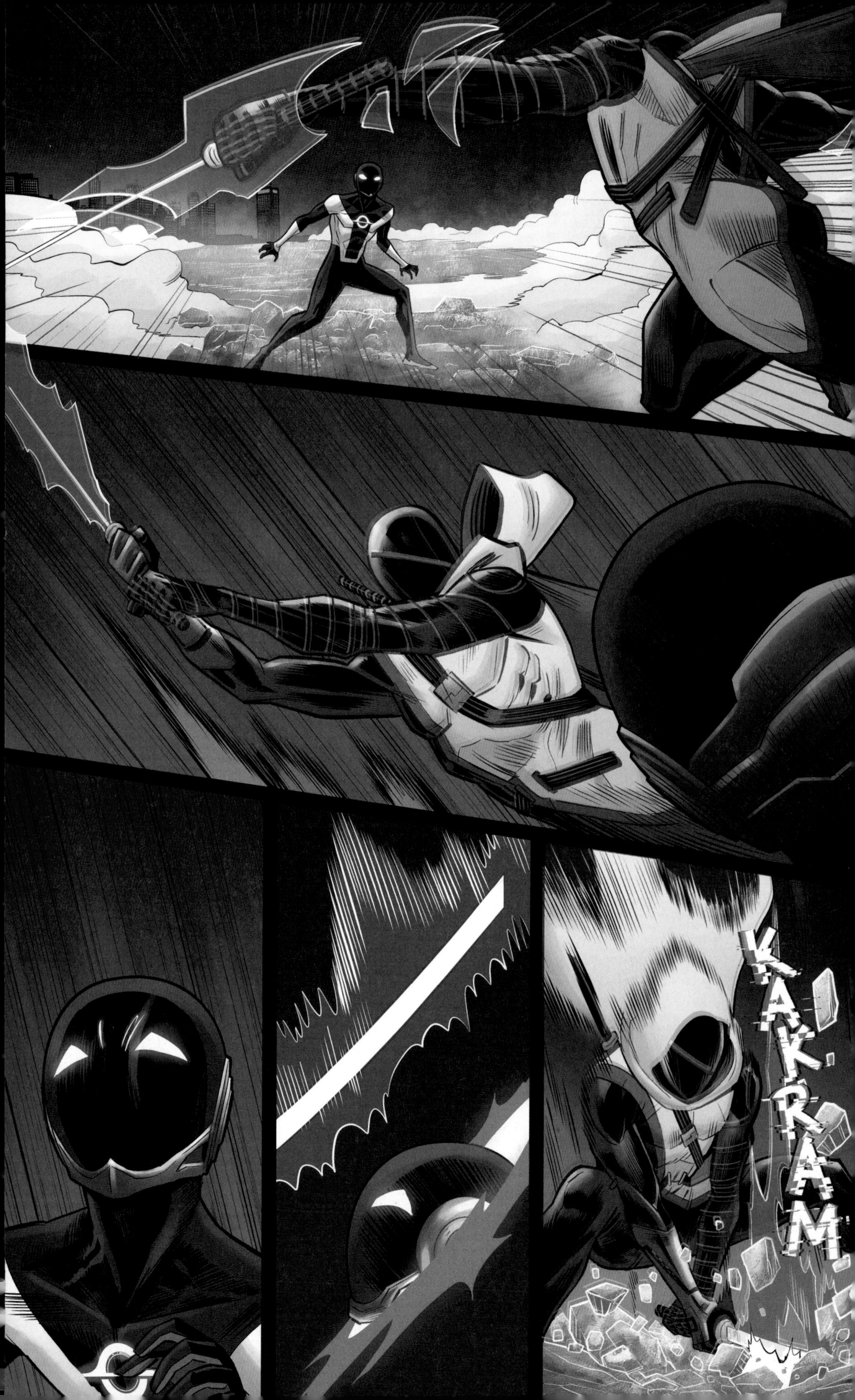
KAKRAM

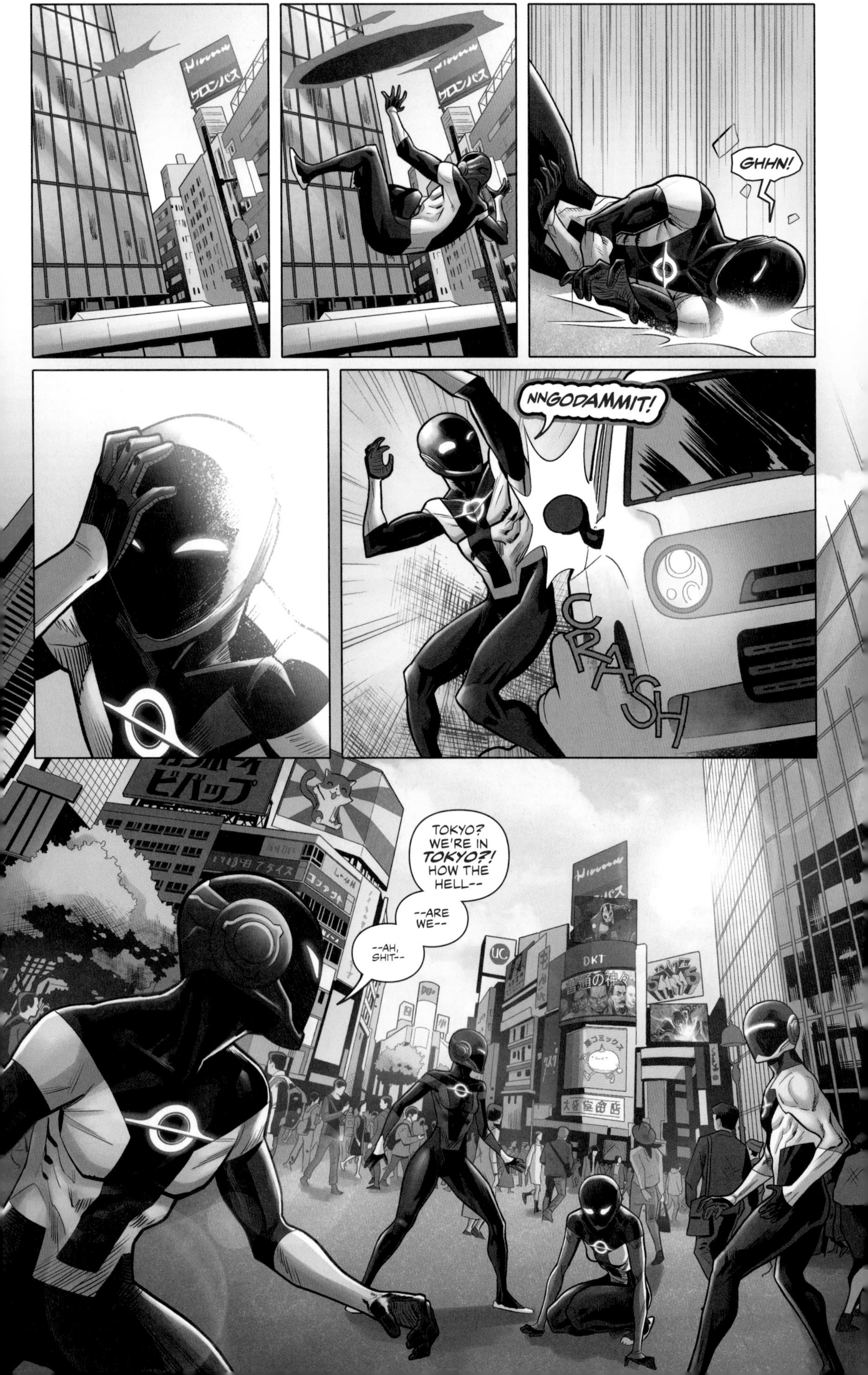
GHHN!
NNGODAMMIT!
CRASH
TOKYO? WE'RE IN TOKYO?! HOW THE HELL--
--ARE WE--
--AH, SHIT--

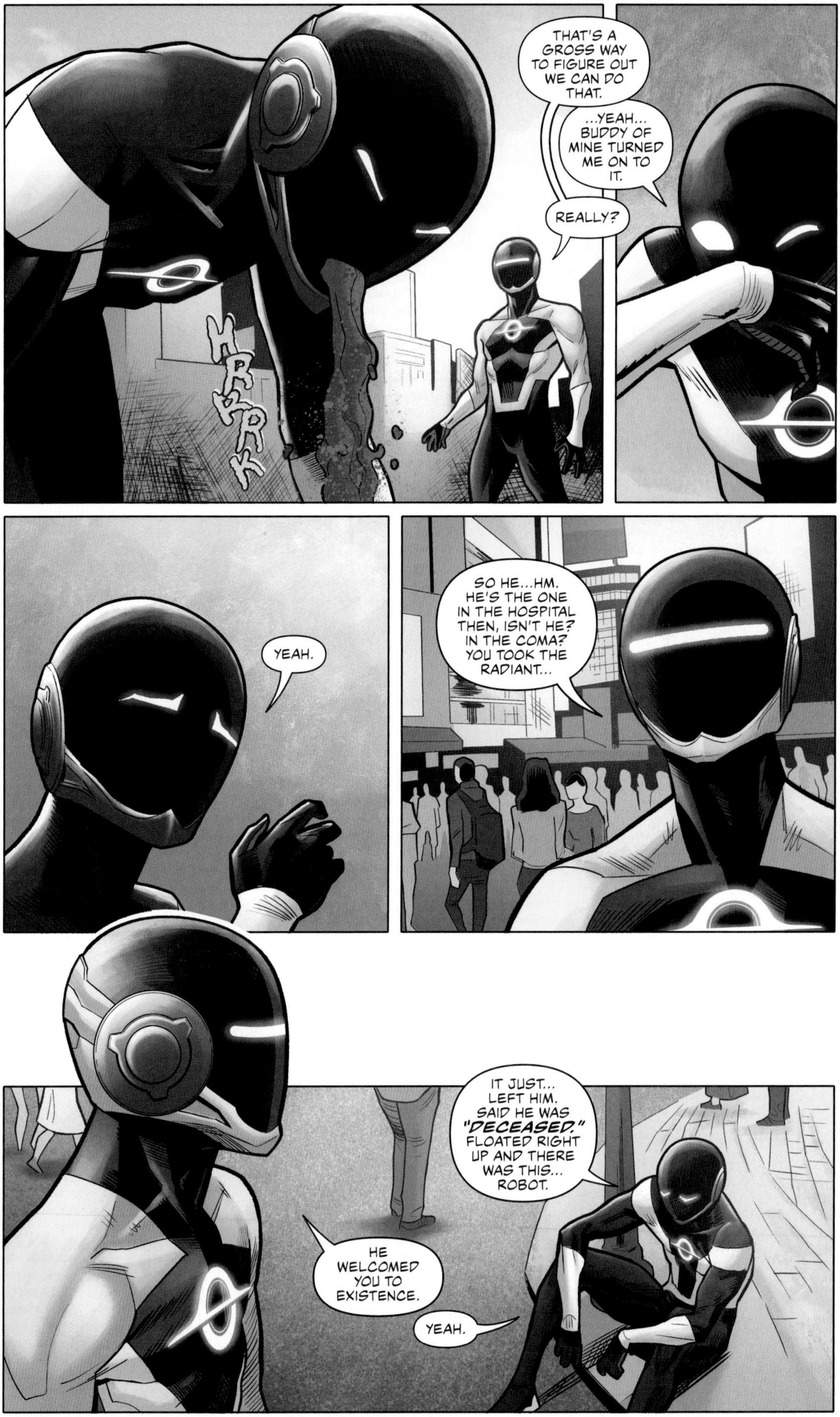
HRRRK
THAT'S A GROSS WAY TO FIGURE OUT WE CAN DO THAT.
...YEAH... BUDDY OF MINE TURNED ME ON TO IT.
REALLY?
SO HE...HM. HE'S THE ONE IN THE HOSPITAL THEN, ISN'T HE? IN THE COMA? YOU TOOK THE RADIANT...
YEAH.
IT JUST... LEFT HIM. SAID HE WAS "DECEASED." FLOATED RIGHT UP AND THERE WAS THIS... ROBOT.
HE WELCOMED YOU TO EXISTENCE.
YEAH.

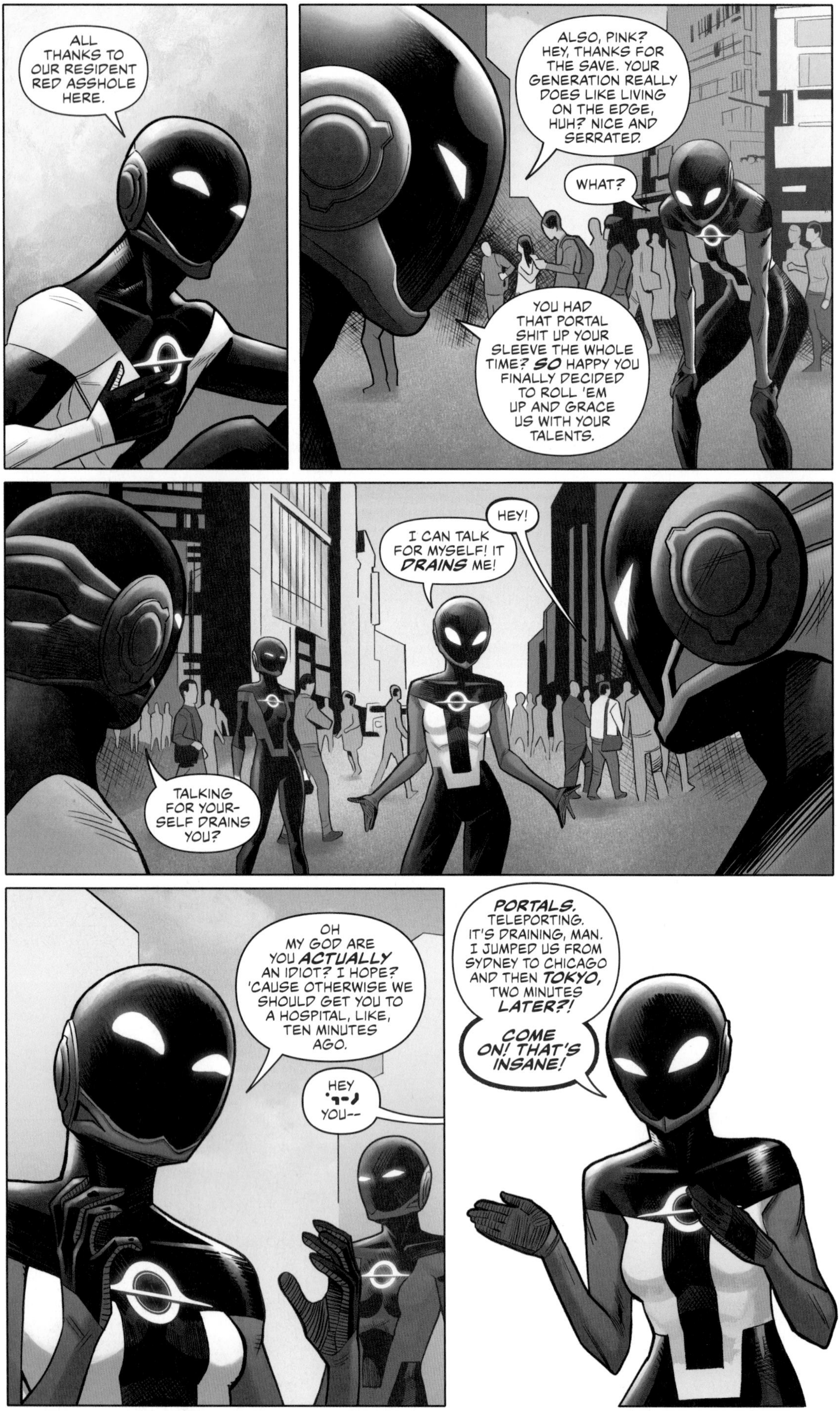
ALL THANKS TO OUR RESIDENT RED ASSHOLE HERE.
ALSO, PINK? HEY, THANKS FOR THE SAVE. YOUR GENERATION REALLY DOES LIKE LIVING ON THE EDGE, HUH? NICE AND SERRATED.
WHAT?
YOU HAD THAT PORTAL SHIT UP YOUR SLEEVE THE WHOLE TIME? SO HAPPY YOU FINALLY DECIDED TO ROLL 'EM UP AND GRACE US WITH YOUR TALENTS.
HEY!
I CAN TALK FOR MYSELF! IT DRAINS ME!
TALKING FOR YOUR-SELF DRAINS YOU?
OH MY GOD ARE YOU ACTUALLY AN IDIOT? I HOPE? 'CAUSE OTHERWISE WE SHOULD GET YOU TO A HOSPITAL, LIKE, TEN MINUTES AGO.
HEY YOU--
PORTALS. TELEPORTING. IT'S DRAINING, MAN. I JUMPED US FROM SYDNEY TO CHICAGO AND THEN TOKYO, TWO MINUTES LATER?!
COME ON! THAT'S INSANE!

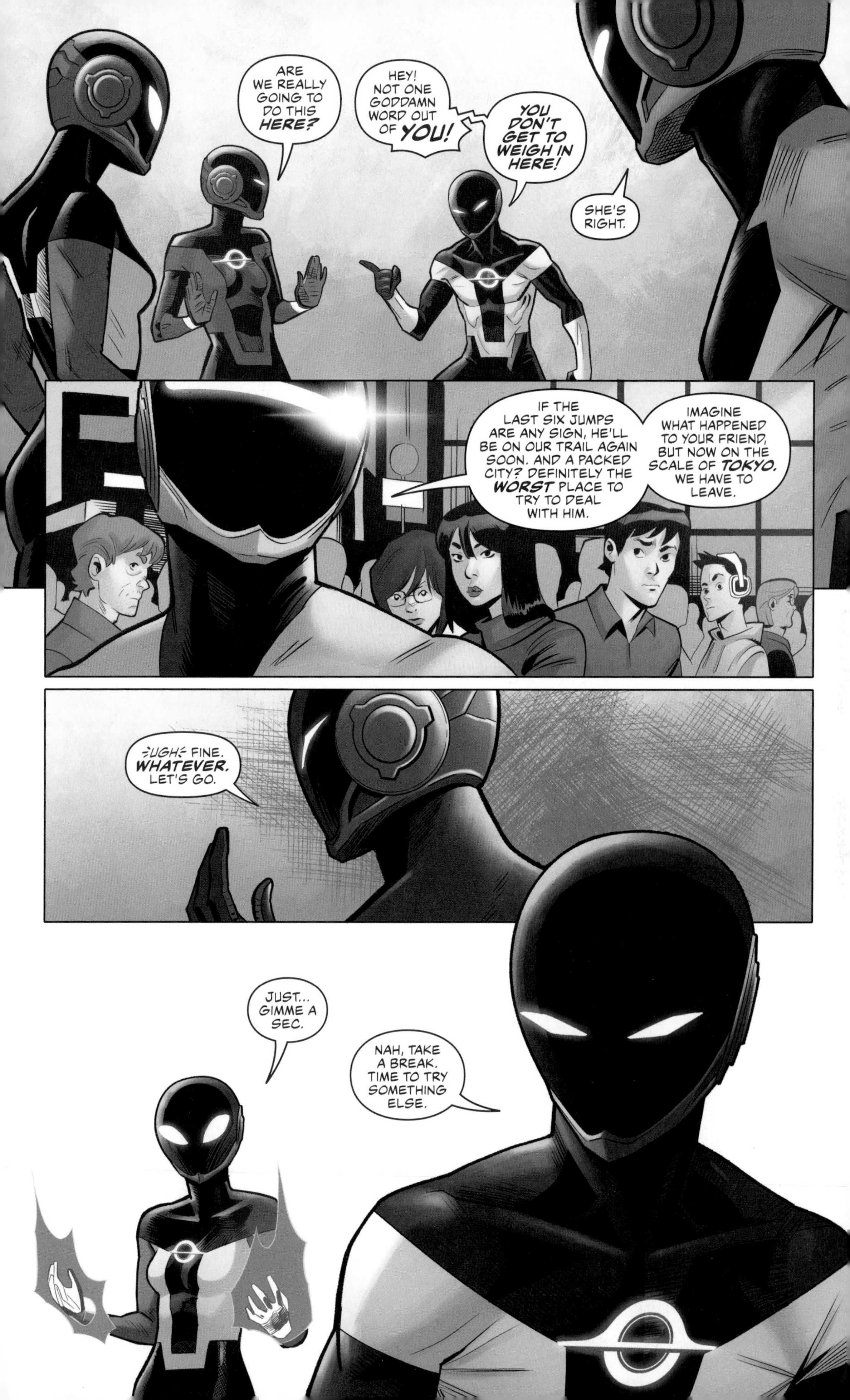
ARE WE REALLY GOING TO DO THIS HERE?
HEY! NOT ONE GODDAMN WORD OUT OF YOU!
YOU DON'T GET TO WEIGH IN HERE!
SHE'S RIGHT.
IF THE LAST SIX JUMPS ARE ANY SIGN, HE'LL BE ON OUR TRAIL AGAIN SOON. AND A PACKED CITY? DEFINITELY THE WORST PLACE TO TRY TO DEAL WITH HIM.
IMAGINE WHAT HAPPENED TO YOUR FRIEND, BUT NOW ON THE SCALE OF TOKYO. WE HAVE TO LEAVE.
UGH FINE. WHATEVER. LET'S GO.
JUST... GIMME A SEC.
NAH, TAKE A BREAK. TIME TO TRY SOMETHING ELSE.

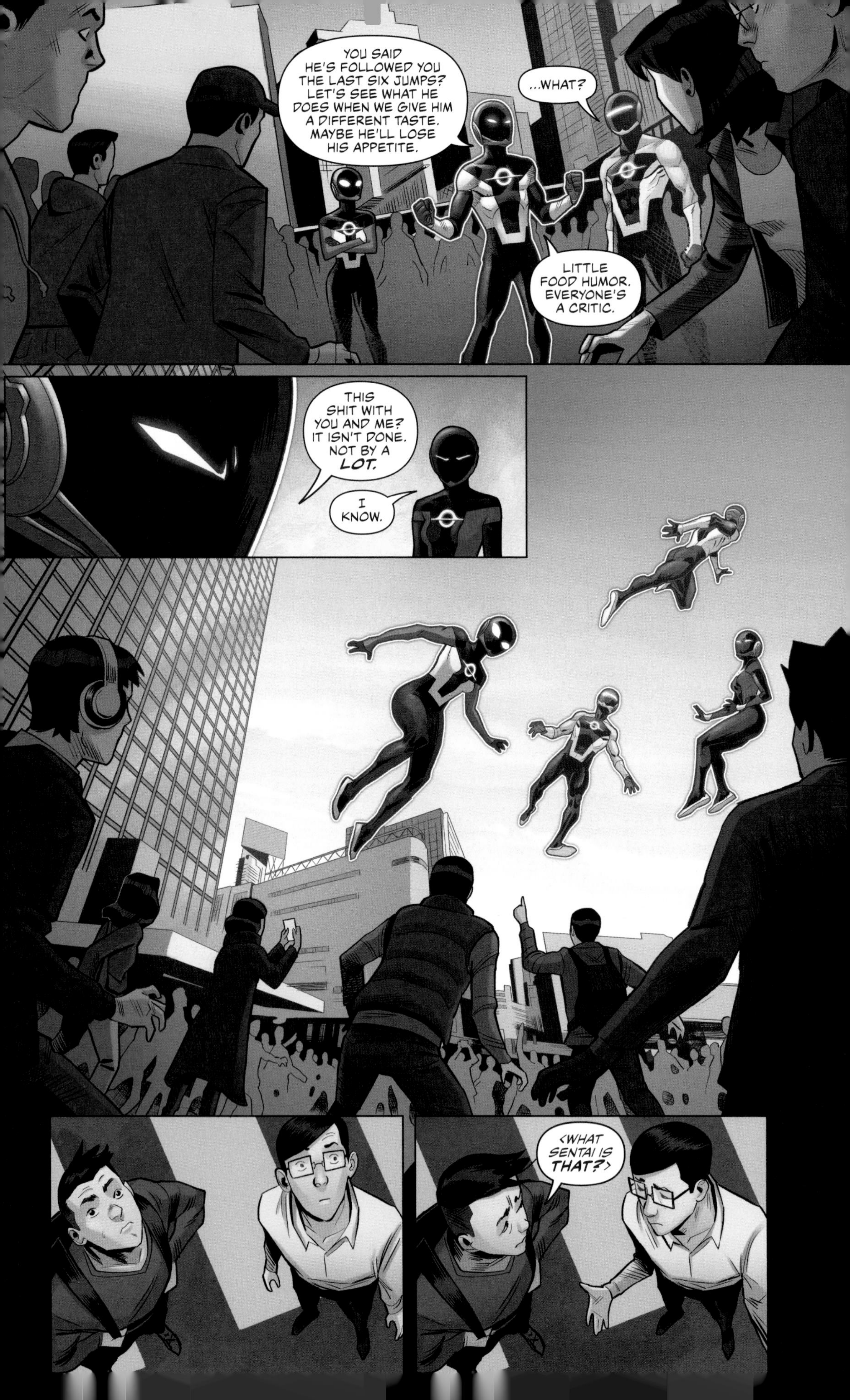
YOU SAID HE'S FOLLOWED YOU THE LAST SIX JUMPS? LET'S SEE WHAT HE DOES WHEN WE GIVE HIM A DIFFERENT TASTE. MAYBE HE'LL LOSE HIS APPETITE.
...WHAT?
LITTLE FOOD HUMOR. EVERYONE'S A CRITIC.
THIS SHIT WITH YOU AND ME? IT ISN'T DONE. NOT BY A LOT.
I KNOW.
<WHAT SENTAI IS THAT?>

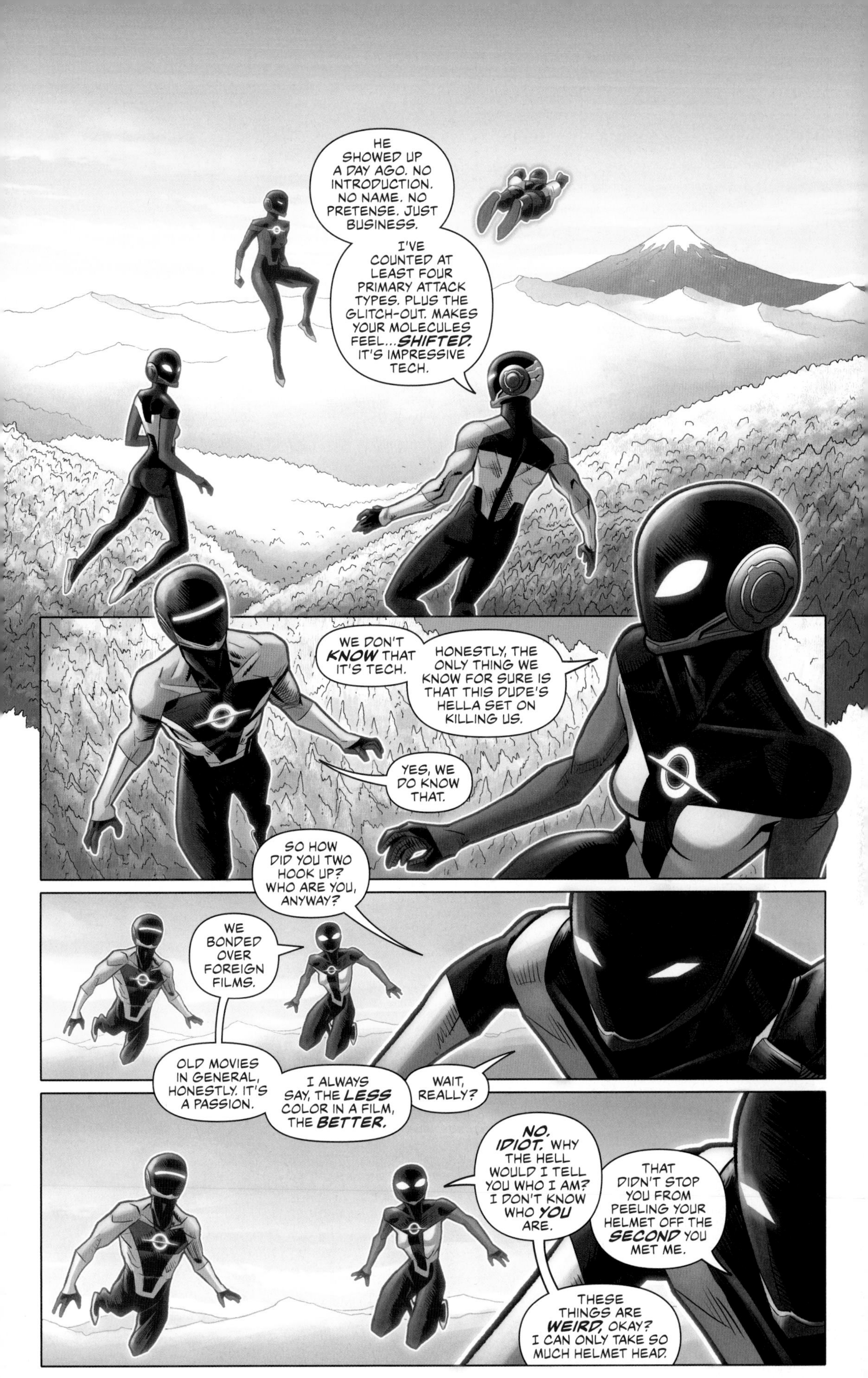
HE SHOWED UP A DAY AGO. NO INTRODUCTION. NO NAME. NO PRETENSE. JUST BUSINESS.
I'VE COUNTED AT LEAST FOUR PRIMARY ATTACK TYPES. PLUS THE GLITCH-OUT. MAKES YOUR MOLECULES FEEL...SHIFTED. IT'S IMPRESSIVE TECH.
WE DON'T KNOW THAT IT'S TECH.
HONESTLY, THE ONLY THING WE KNOW FOR SURE IS THAT THIS DUDE'S HELLA SET ON KILLING US.
YES, WE DO KNOW THAT.
SO HOW DID YOU TWO HOOK UP? WHO ARE YOU, ANYWAY?
WE BONDED OVER FOREIGN FILMS.
OLD MOVIES IN GENERAL, HONESTLY. IT'S A PASSION.
I ALWAYS SAY, THE LESS COLOR IN A FILM, THE BETTER.
WAIT, REALLY?
NO, IDIOT. WHY THE HELL WOULD I TELL YOU WHO I AM? I DON'T KNOW WHO YOU ARE.
THAT DIDN'T STOP YOU FROM PEELING YOUR HELMET OFF THE SECOND YOU MET ME.
THESE THINGS ARE WEIRD, OKAY? I CAN ONLY TAKE SO MUCH HELMET HEAD.

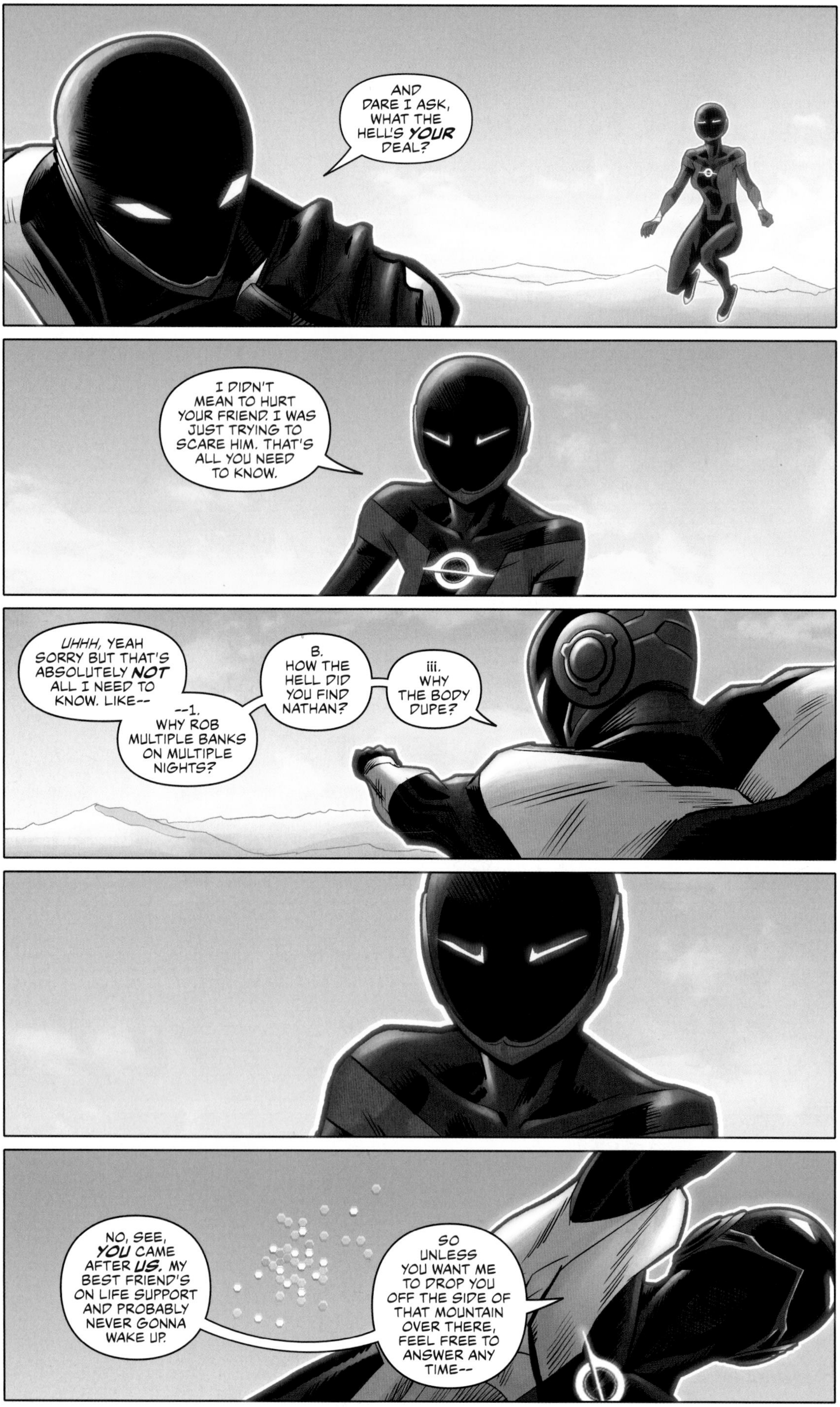
AND DARE I ASK, WHAT THE HELL'S YOUR DEAL?
I DIDN'T MEAN TO HURT YOUR FRIEND. I WAS JUST TRYING TO SCARE HIM. THAT'S ALL YOU NEED TO KNOW.
UHHH, YEAH SORRY BUT THAT'S ABSOLUTELY NOT ALL I NEED TO KNOW. LIKE--
--1. WHY ROB MULTIPLE BANKS ON MULTIPLE NIGHTS?
B. HOW THE HELL DID YOU FIND NATHAN?
iii. WHY THE BODY DUPE?
NO, SEE, YOU CAME AFTER US. MY BEST FRIEND'S ON LIFE SUPPORT AND PROBABLY NEVER GONNA WAKE UP.
SO UNLESS YOU WANT ME TO DROP YOU OFF THE SIDE OF THAT MOUNTAIN OVER THERE, FEEL FREE TO ANSWER ANY TIME--

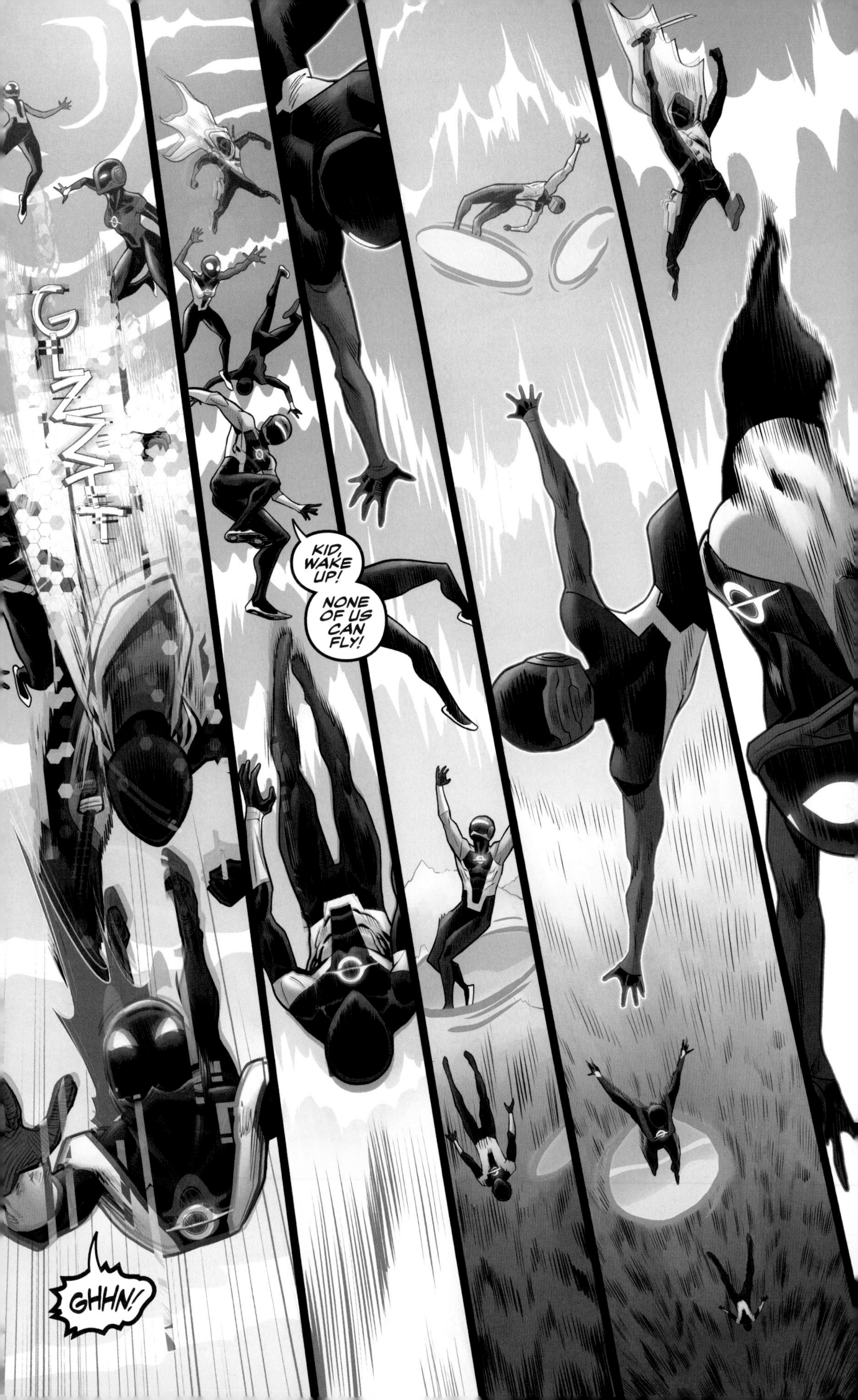
GLZZHT
KID, WAKE UP!
NONE OF US CAN FLY!
GHHN!

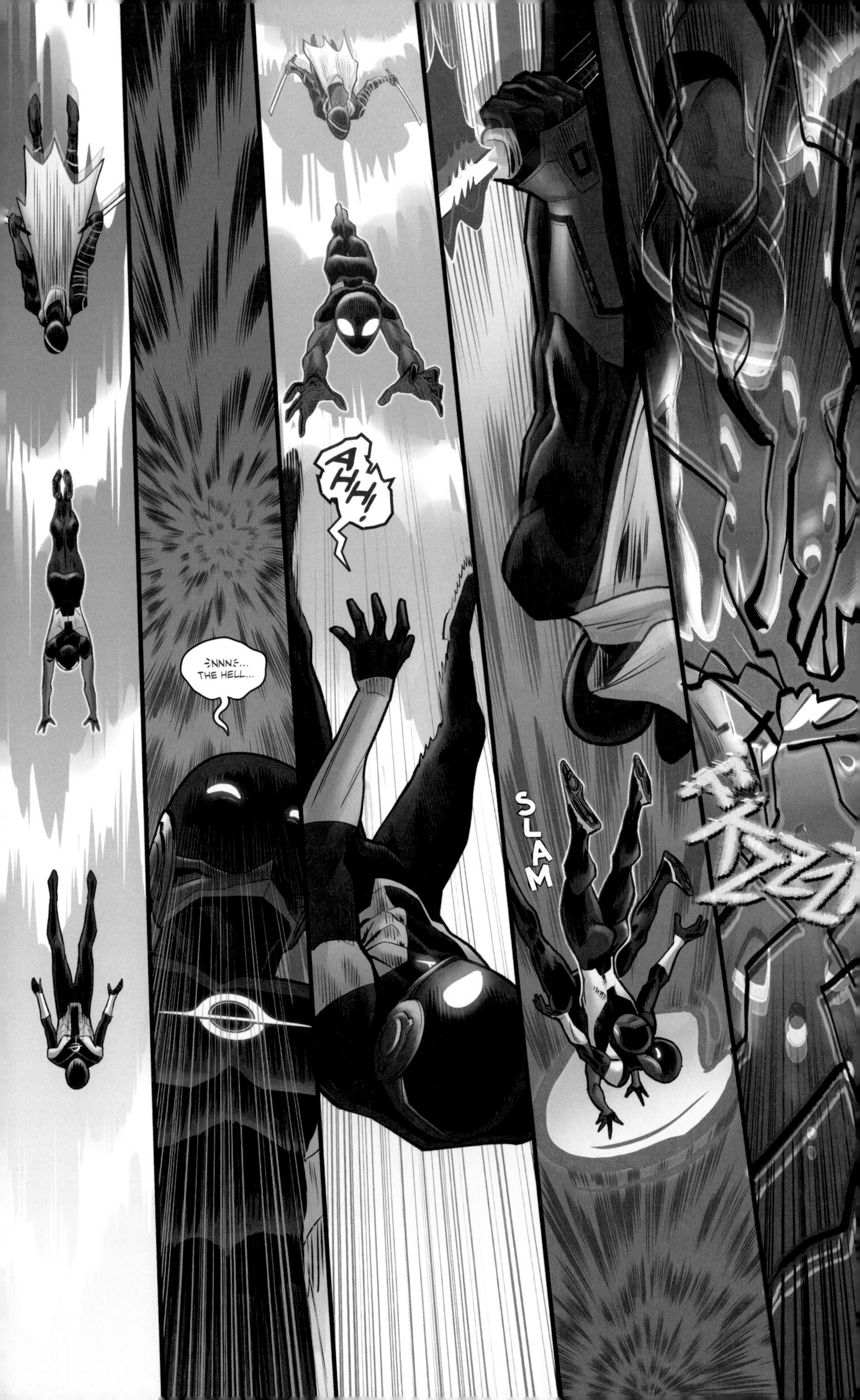
AHH!
NNN... THE HELL...
SLAM

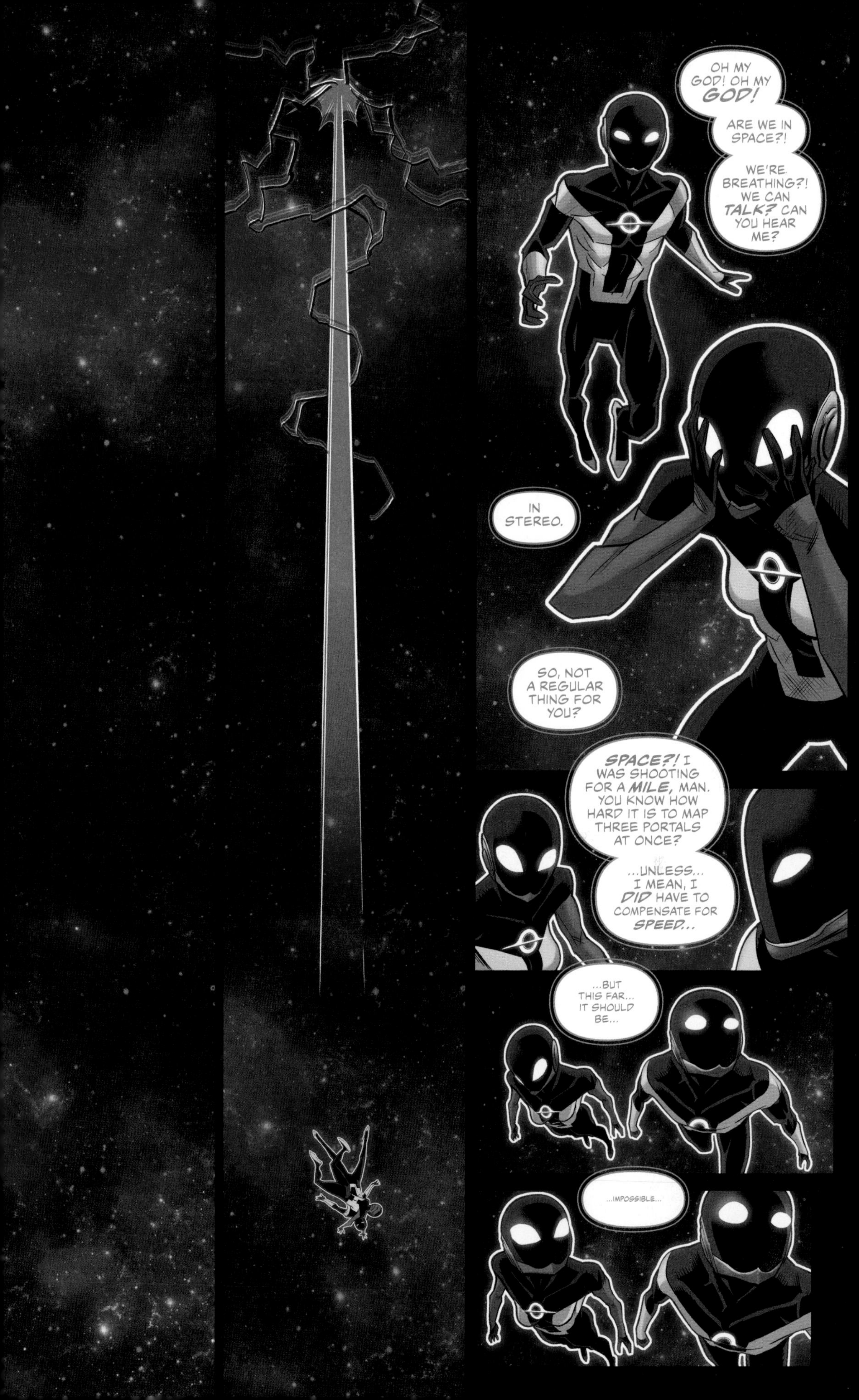
OH MY GOD! OH MY GOD!
ARE WE IN SPACE?!
WE'RE BREATHING?! WE CAN TALK? CAN YOU HEAR ME?
IN STEREO.
SO, NOT A REGULAR THING FOR YOU?
SPACE?! I WAS SHOOTING FOR A MILE, MAN. YOU KNOW HOW HARD IT IS TO MAP THREE PORTALS AT ONCE?
...UNLESS... I MEAN, I DID HAVE TO COMPENSATE FOR SPEED...
...BUT THIS FAR... IT SHOULD BE...
...IMPOSSIBLE...

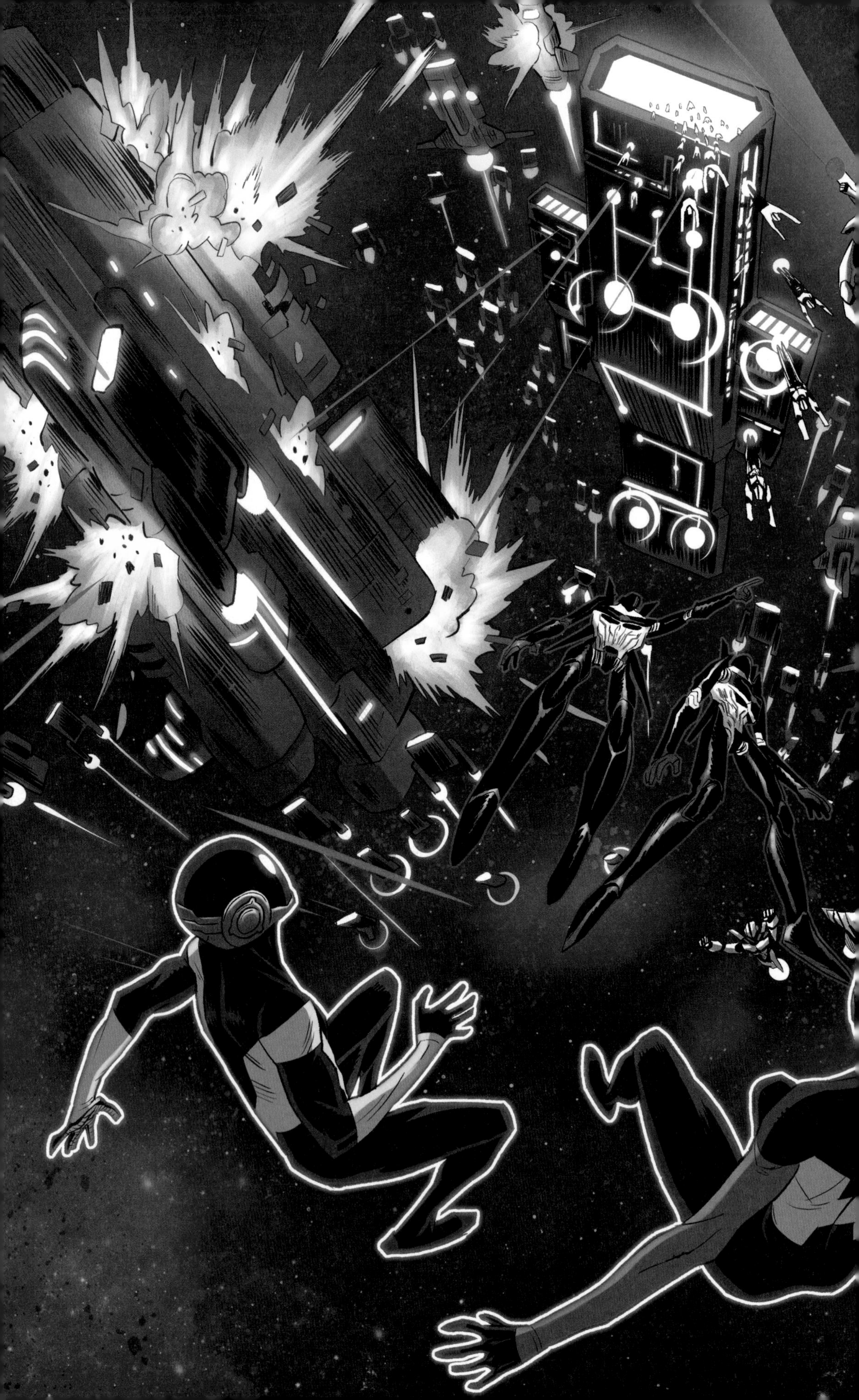

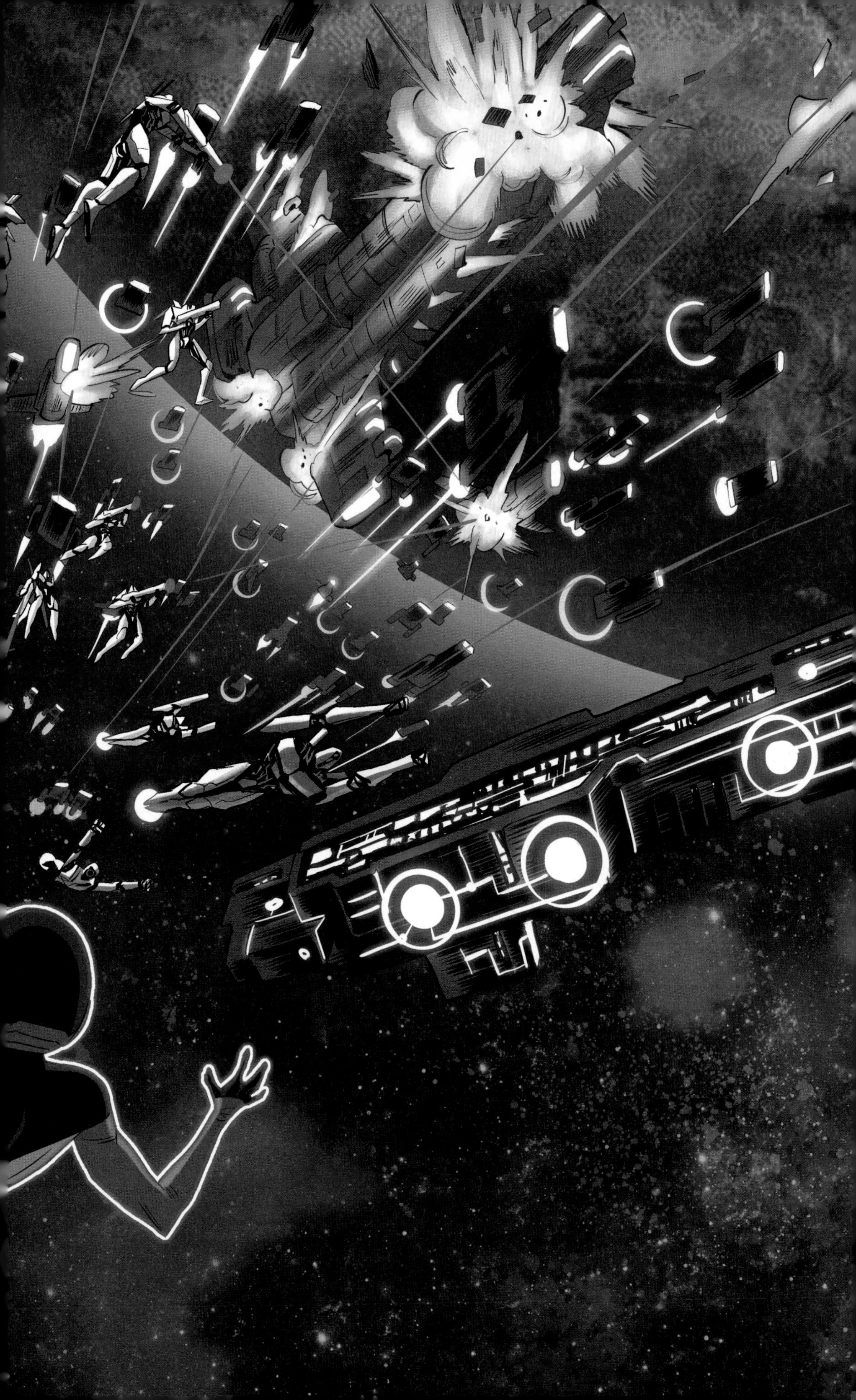

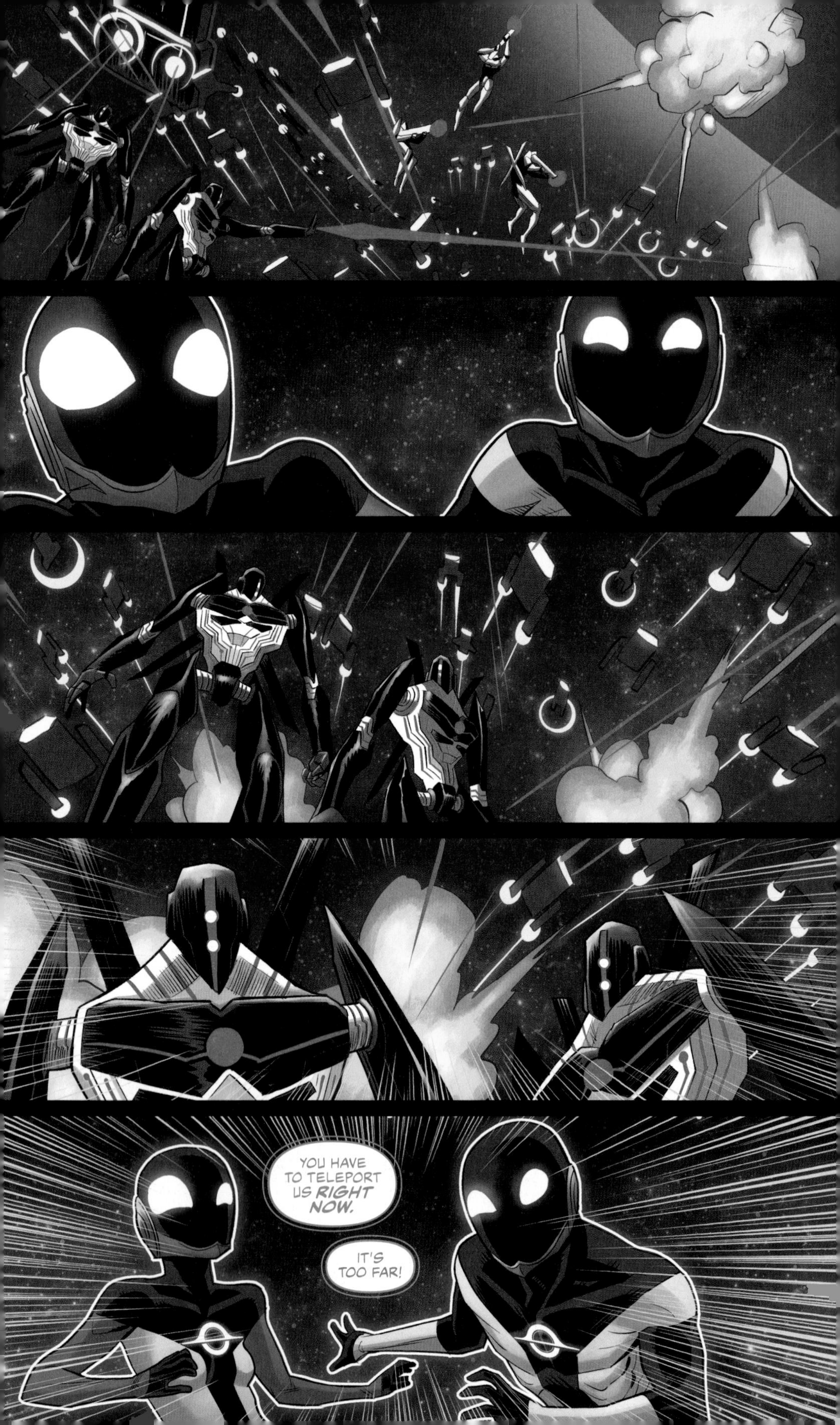
YOU HAVE TO TELEPORT US RIGHT NOW.
IT'S TOO FAR!

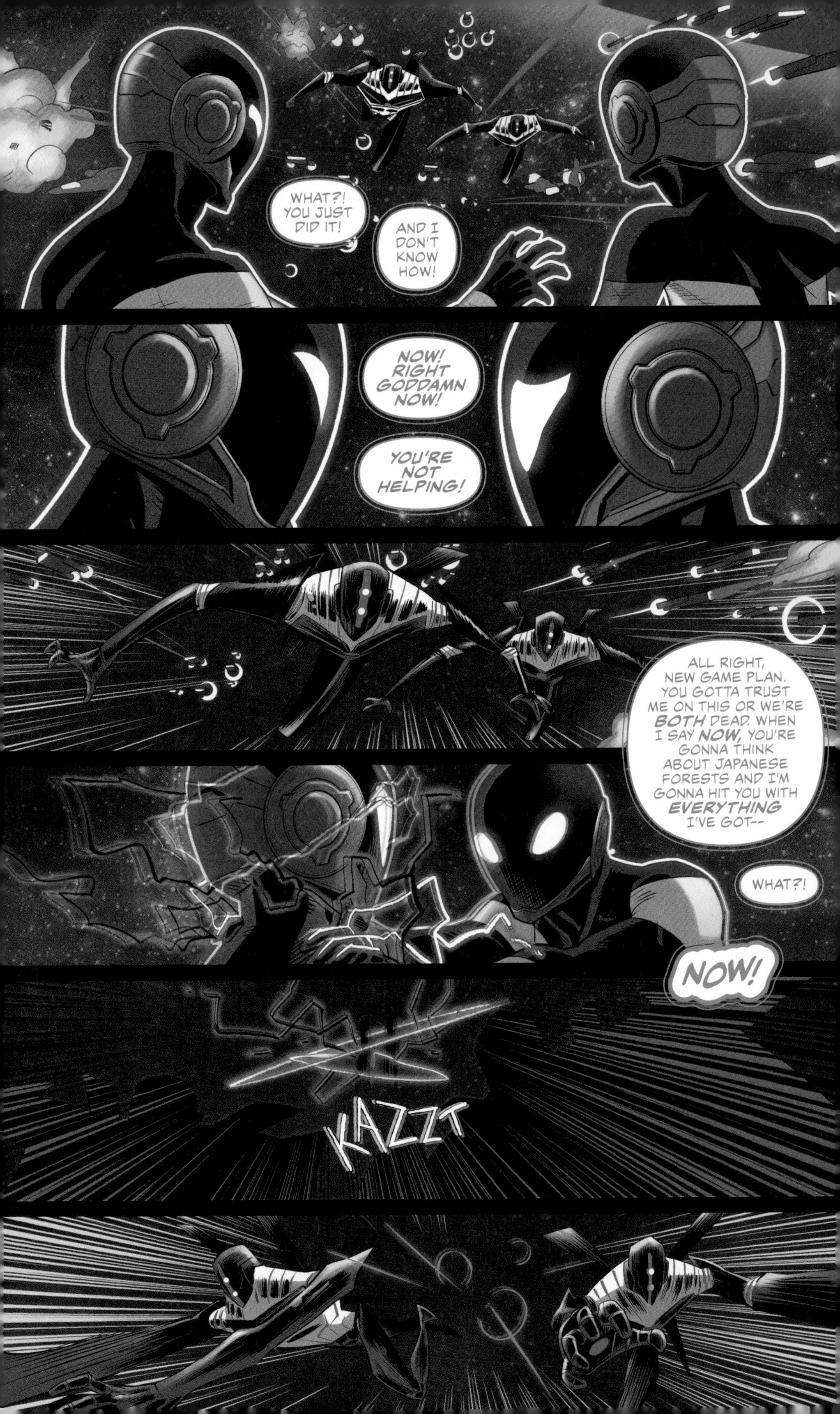
WHAT?! YOU JUST DID IT!
AND I DON'T KNOW HOW!
NOW! RIGHT GODDAMN NOW!
YOU'RE NOT HELPING!
ALL RIGHT, NEW GAME PLAN. YOU GOTTA TRUST ME ON THIS OR WE'RE BOTH DEAD. WHEN I SAY NOW, YOU'RE GONNA THINK ABOUT JAPANESE FORESTS AND I'M GONNA HIT YOU WITH EVERYTHING I'VE GOT--
WHAT?!
NOW!
KAZZT

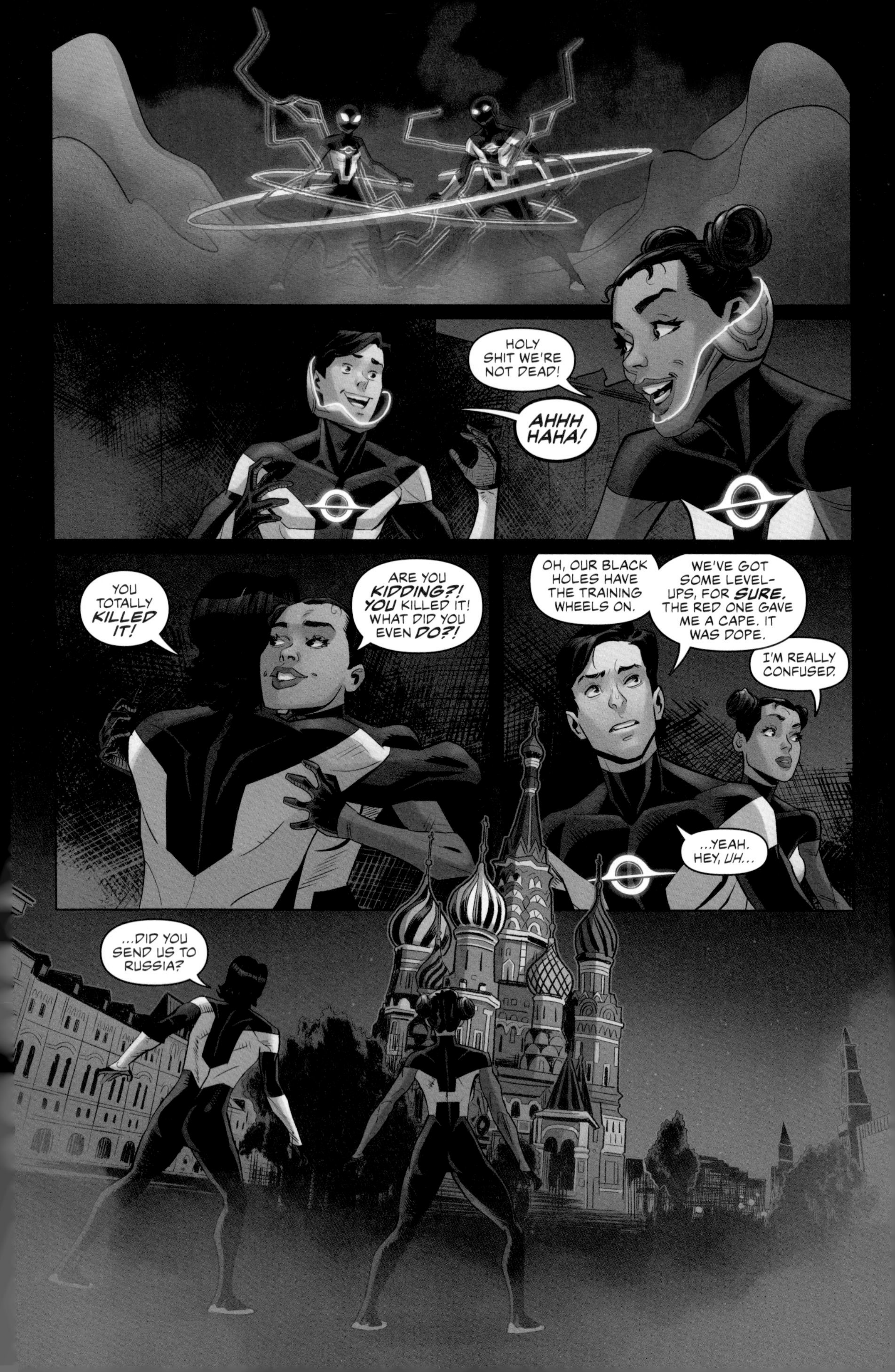

HOLY SHIT WE'RE NOT DEAD!
AHHH HAHA!
YOU TOTALLY KILLED IT!
ARE YOU KIDDING?! YOU KILLED IT! WHAT DID YOU EVEN DO?!
OH, OUR BLACK HOLES HAVE THE TRAINING WHEELS ON.
WE'VE GOT SOME LEVEL-UPS, FOR SURE. THE RED ONE GAVE ME A CAPE. IT WAS DOPE.
I'M REALLY CONFUSED.
...YEAH. HEY, UH...
...DID YOU SEND US TO RUSSIA?

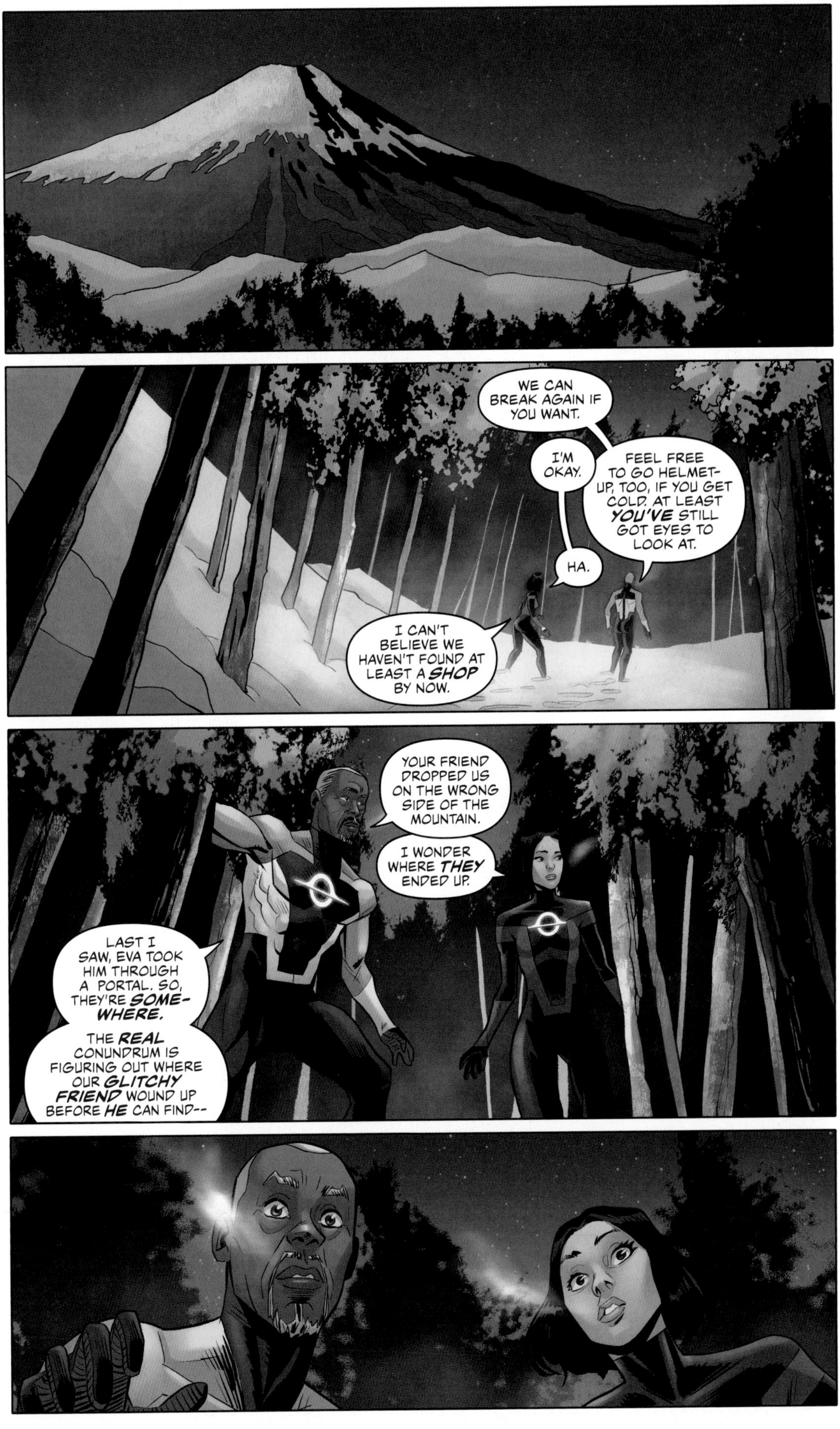

WE CAN BREAK AGAIN IF YOU WANT.
I'M OKAY.
FEEL FREE TO GO HELMET-UP, TOO, IF YOU GET COLD. AT LEAST YOU'VE STILL GOT EYES TO LOOK AT.
HA.
I CAN'T BELIEVE WE HAVEN'T FOUND AT LEAST A SHOP BY NOW.
YOUR FRIEND DROPPED US ON THE WRONG SIDE OF THE MOUNTAIN.
I WONDER WHERE THEY ENDED UP.
LAST I SAW, EVA TOOK HIM THROUGH A PORTAL. SO, THEY'RE SOME-WHERE.
THE REAL CONUNDRUM IS FIGURING OUT WHERE OUR GLITCHY FRIEND WOUND UP BEFORE HE CAN FIND--

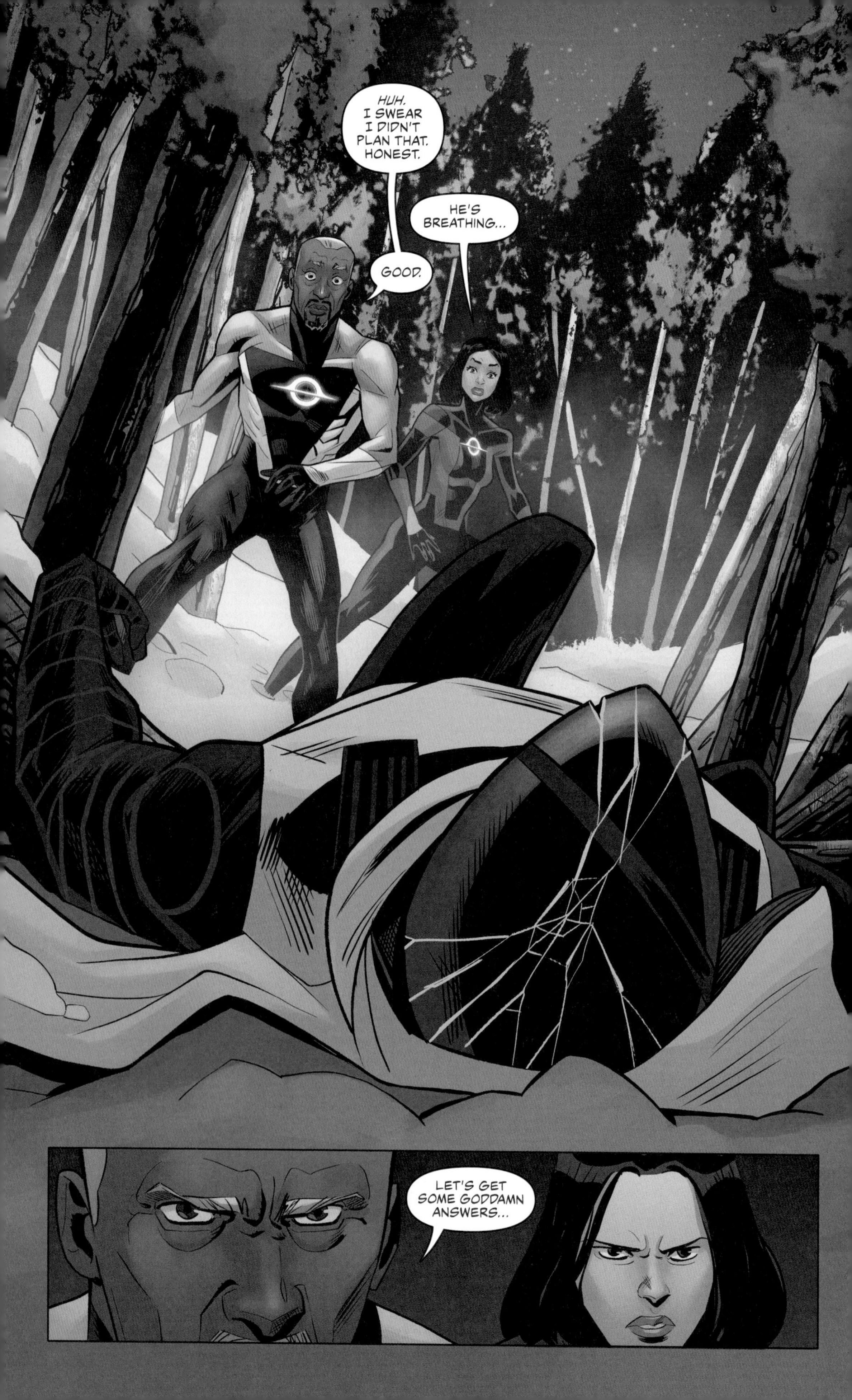
HUH. I SWEAR I DIDN'T PLAN THAT. HONEST.
HE'S BREATHING...
GOOD.
LET'S GET SOME GODDAMN ANSWERS...

CHAPTER EIGHT

TITLE   <001>

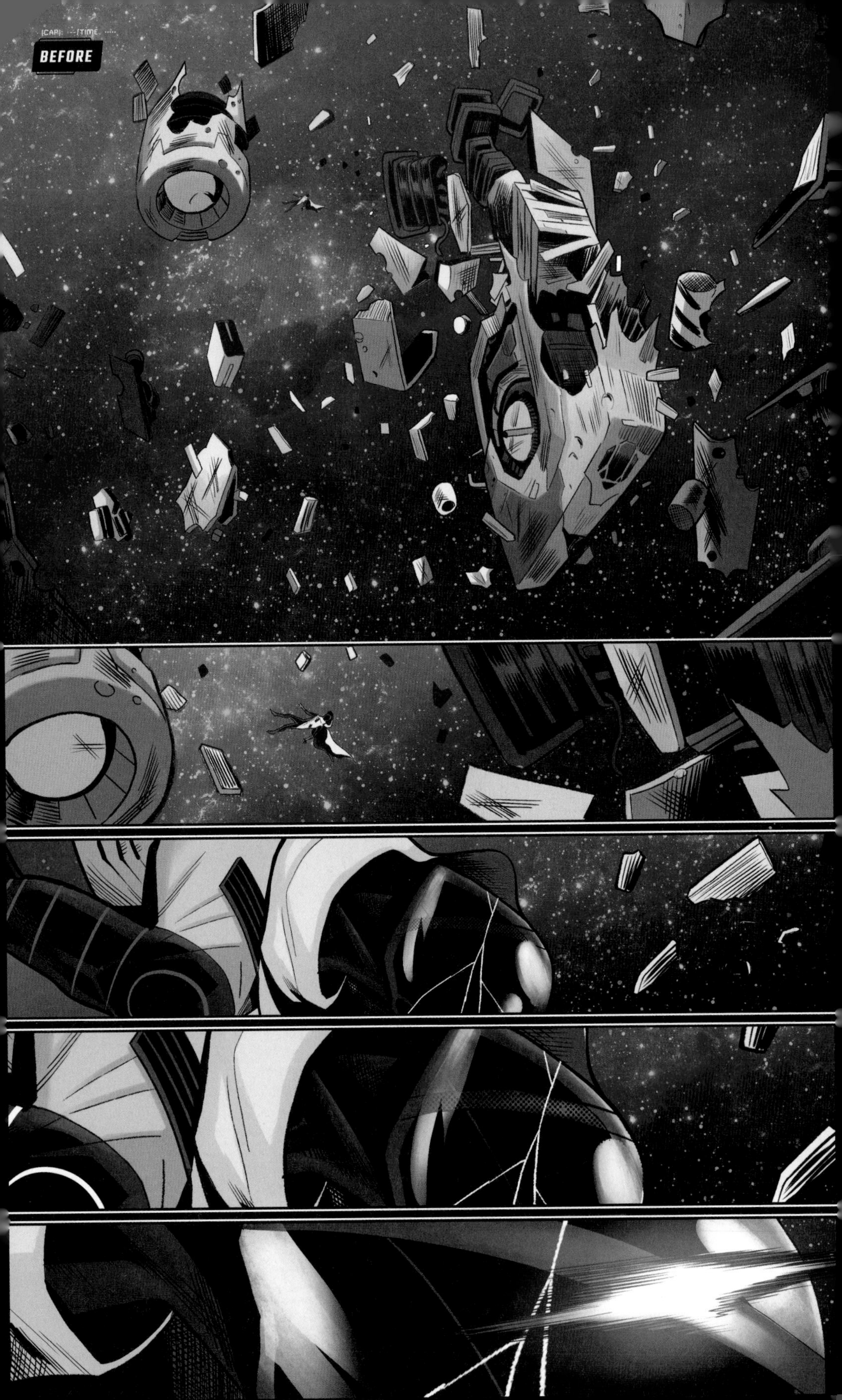
(CAP): --/TIME .....
BEFORE

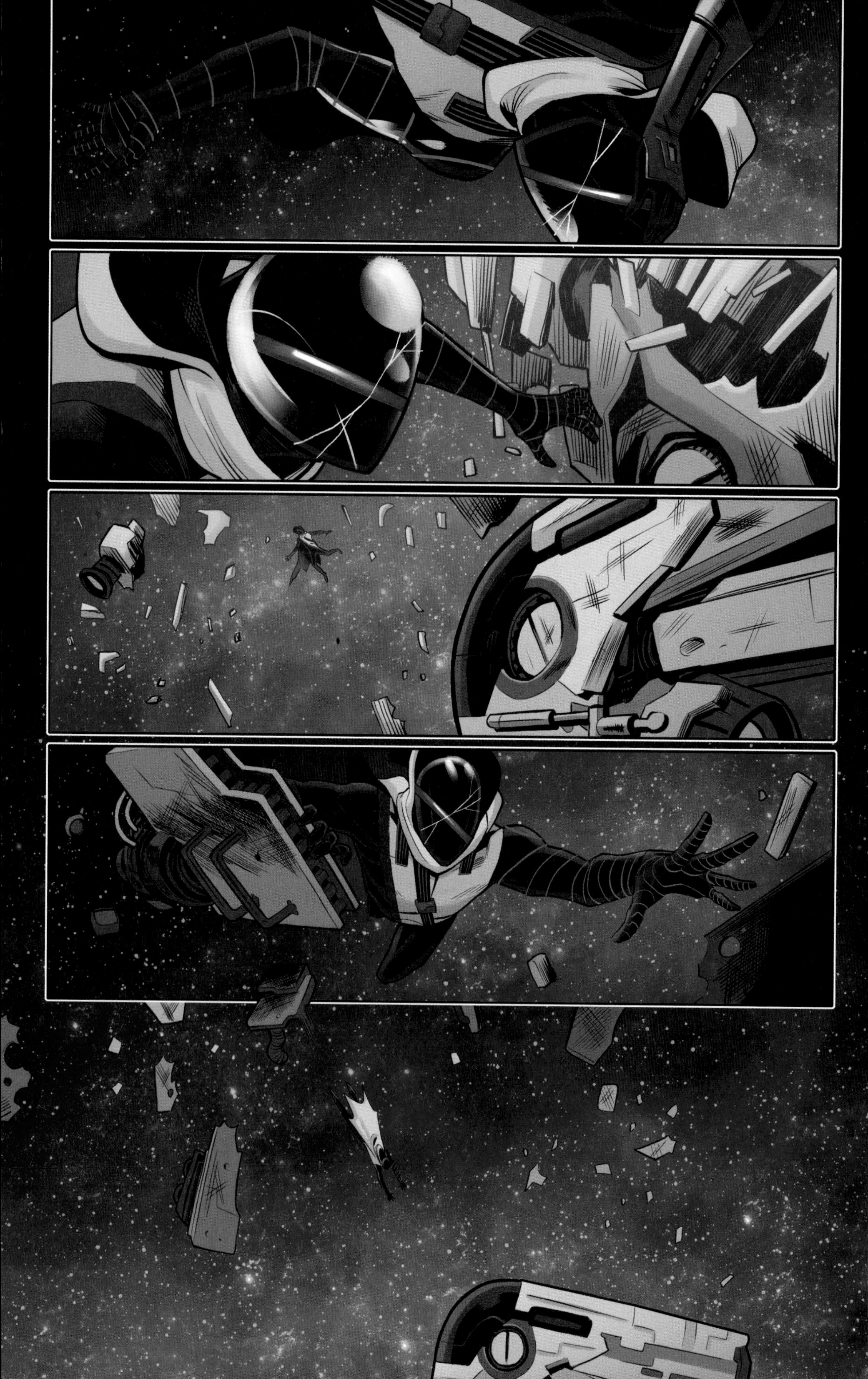

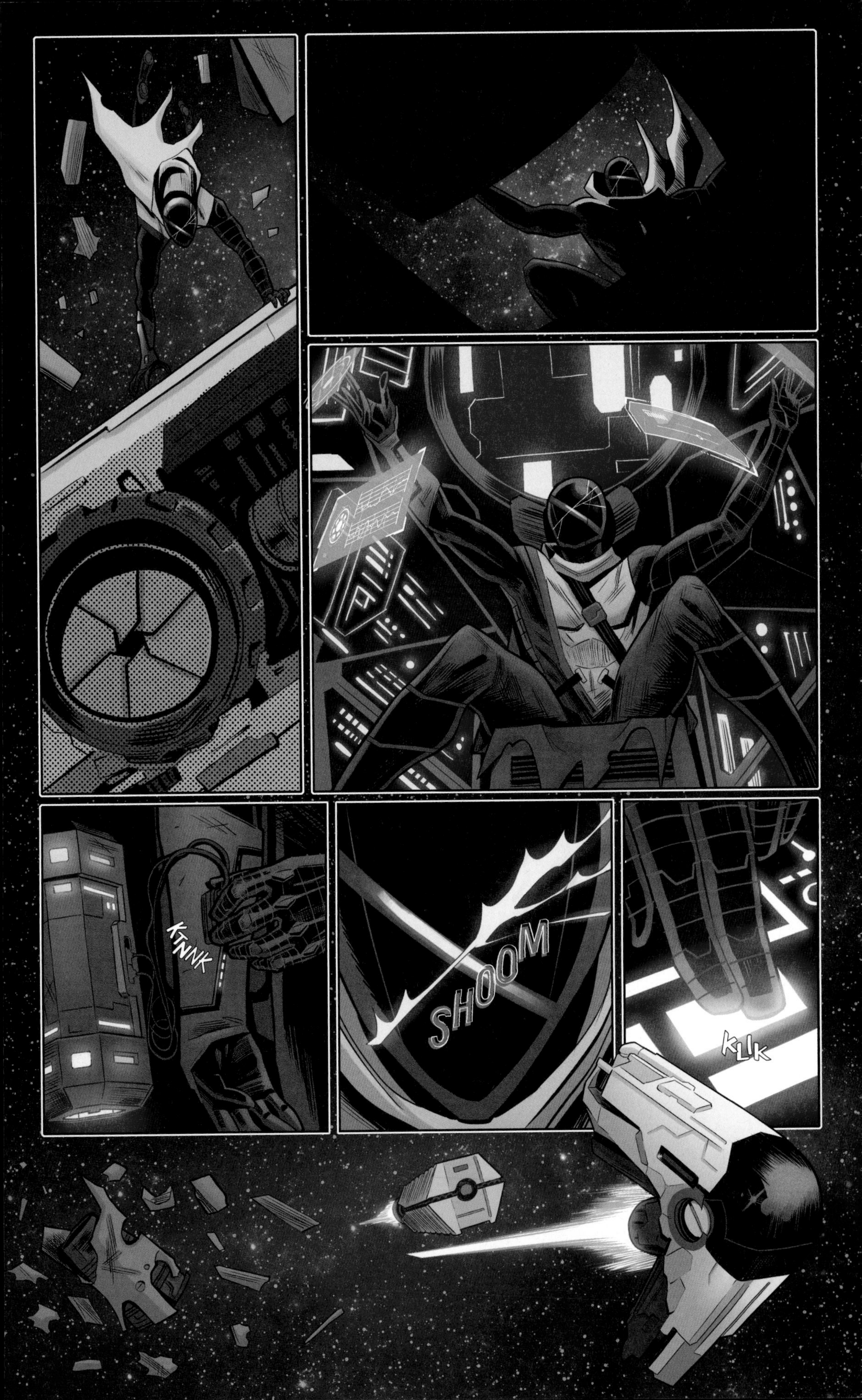
KTNNK
SHOOM
KLIK

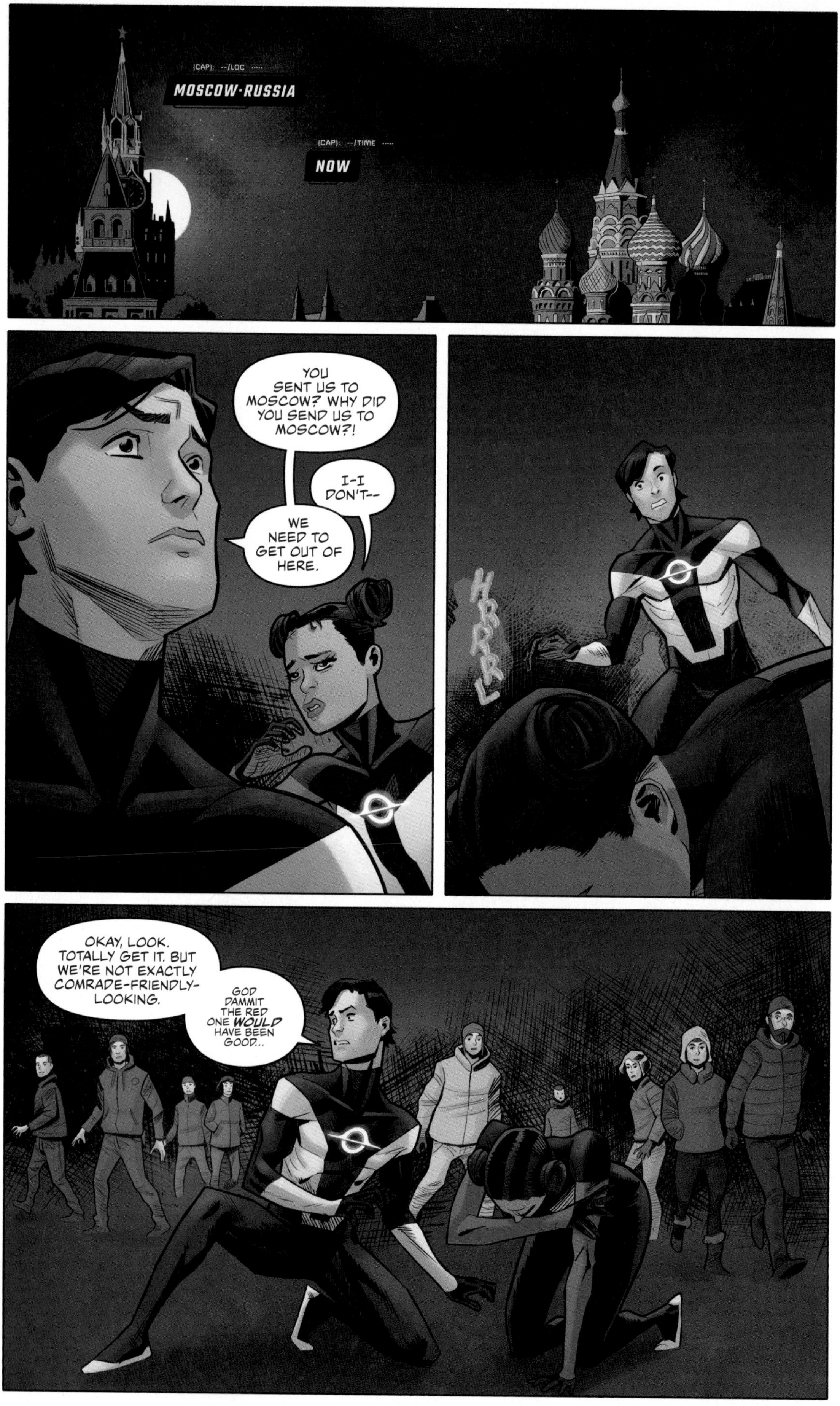
{CAP}: --/LOC .....
MOSCOW·RUSSIA
{CAP}: --/TIME .....
NOW
YOU SENT US TO MOSCOW? WHY DID YOU SEND US TO MOSCOW?!
I-I DON'T--
WE NEED TO GET OUT OF HERE.
HRRRL
OKAY, LOOK. TOTALLY GET IT. BUT WE'RE NOT EXACTLY COMRADE-FRIENDLY-LOOKING.
GOD DAMMIT THE RED ONE ***WOULD*** HAVE BEEN GOOD...

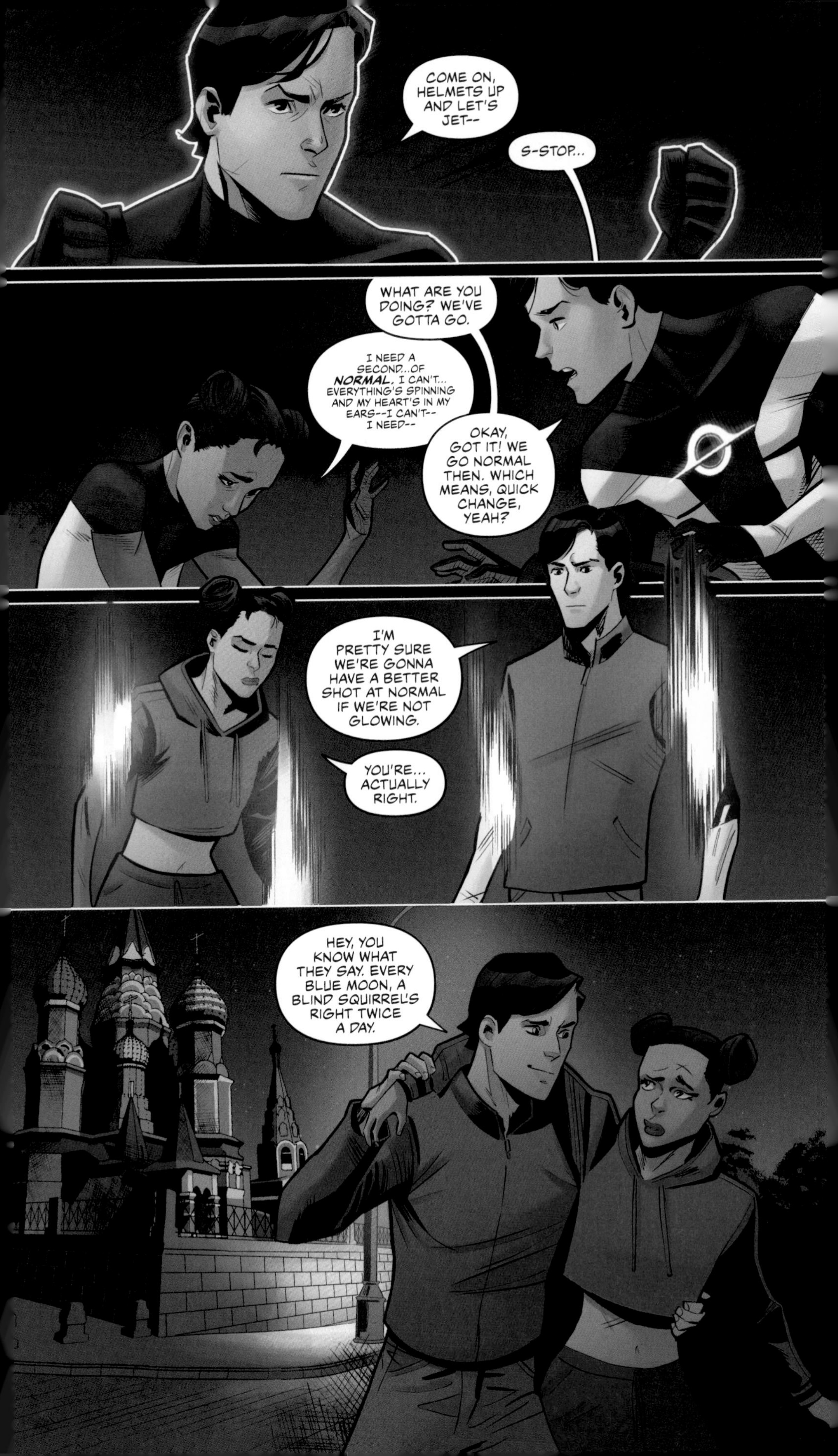
COME ON, HELMETS UP AND LET'S JET--
S-STOP...
WHAT ARE YOU DOING? WE'VE GOTTA GO.
I NEED A SECOND...OF NORMAL. I CAN'T... EVERYTHING'S SPINNING AND MY HEART'S IN MY EARS--I CAN'T-- I NEED--
OKAY, GOT IT! WE GO NORMAL THEN. WHICH MEANS, QUICK CHANGE, YEAH?
I'M PRETTY SURE WE'RE GONNA HAVE A BETTER SHOT AT NORMAL IF WE'RE NOT GLOWING.
YOU'RE... ACTUALLY RIGHT.
HEY, YOU KNOW WHAT THEY SAY. EVERY BLUE MOON, A BLIND SQUIRREL'S RIGHT TWICE A DAY.

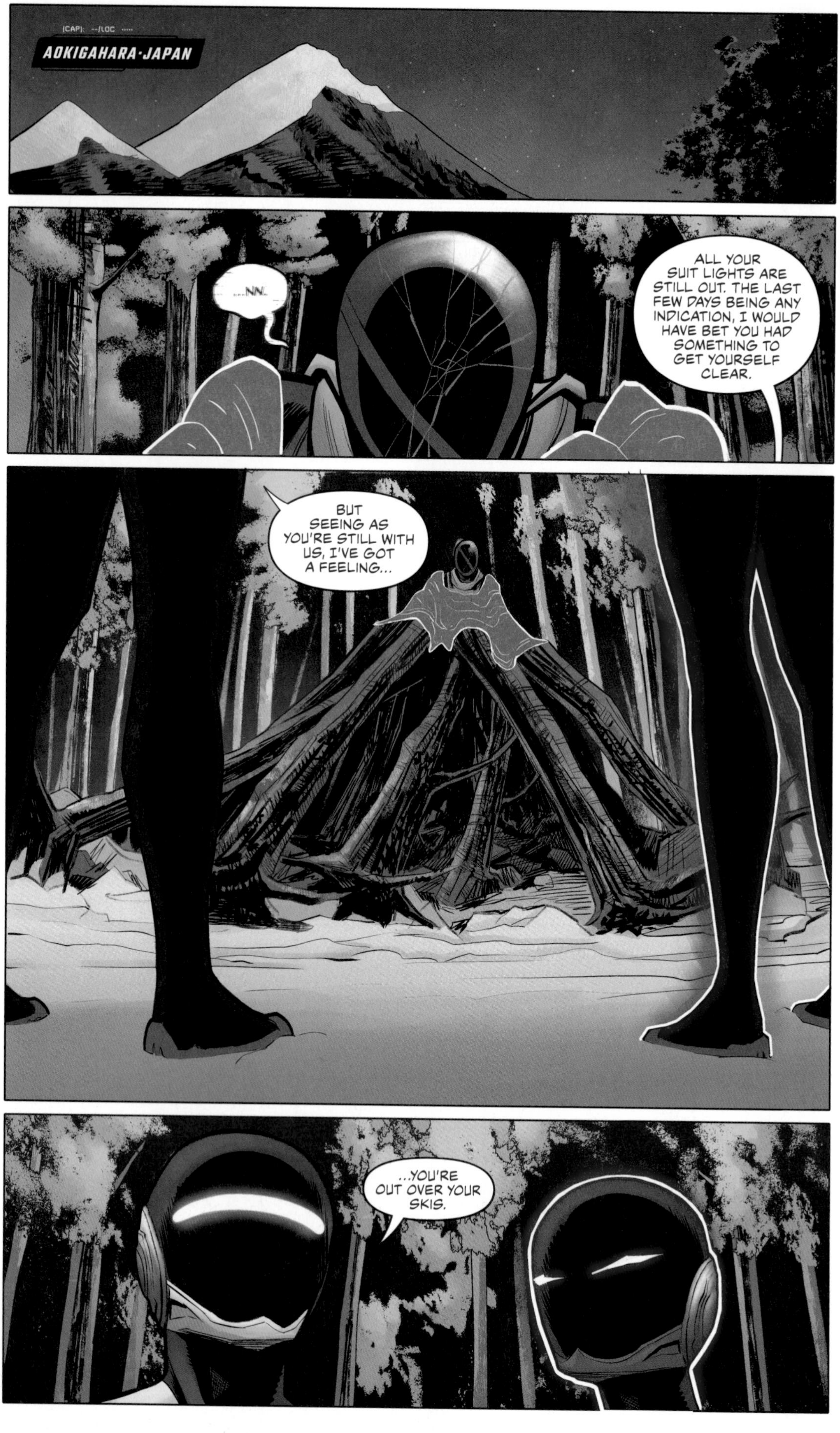
(CAP): --/LOC .....
AOKIGAHARA·JAPAN
...NN.
ALL YOUR SUIT LIGHTS ARE STILL OUT. THE LAST FEW DAYS BEING ANY INDICATION, I WOULD HAVE BET YOU HAD SOMETHING TO GET YOURSELF CLEAR.
BUT SEEING AS YOU'RE STILL WITH US, I'VE GOT A FEELING...
...YOU'RE OUT OVER YOUR SKIS.

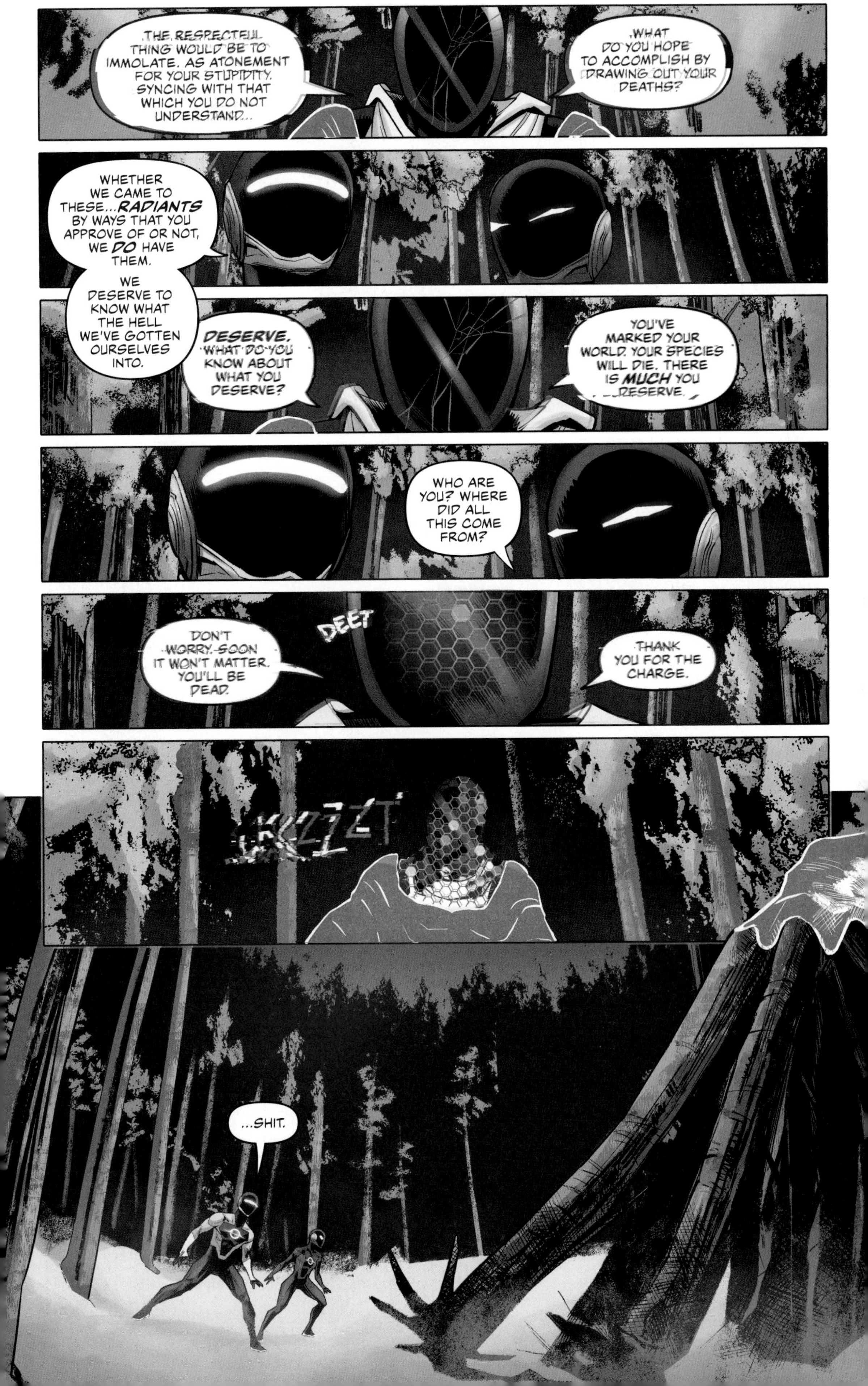
THE RESPECTFUL THING WOULD BE TO IMMOLATE. AS ATONEMENT FOR YOUR STUPIDITY. SYNCING WITH THAT WHICH YOU DO NOT UNDERSTAND...
WHAT DO YOU HOPE TO ACCOMPLISH BY DRAWING OUT YOUR DEATHS?
WHETHER WE CAME TO THESE...RADIANTS BY WAYS THAT YOU APPROVE OF OR NOT, WE DO HAVE THEM.
WE DESERVE TO KNOW WHAT THE HELL WE'VE GOTTEN OURSELVES INTO.
DESERVE. WHAT DO YOU KNOW ABOUT WHAT YOU DESERVE?
YOU'VE MARKED YOUR WORLD. YOUR SPECIES WILL DIE. THERE IS MUCH YOU DESERVE.
WHO ARE YOU? WHERE DID ALL THIS COME FROM?
DEET
DON'T WORRY. SOON IT WON'T MATTER. YOU'LL BE DEAD.
THANK YOU FOR THE CHARGE.
...SHIT.

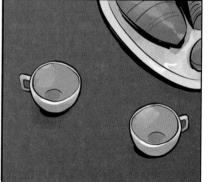

I WAS THINKING I'D GIVE YOU MY JACKET, BUT THEN I SAW THIS *BLANKET* IN A STORE AND NOBODY WAS *LOOKING.*

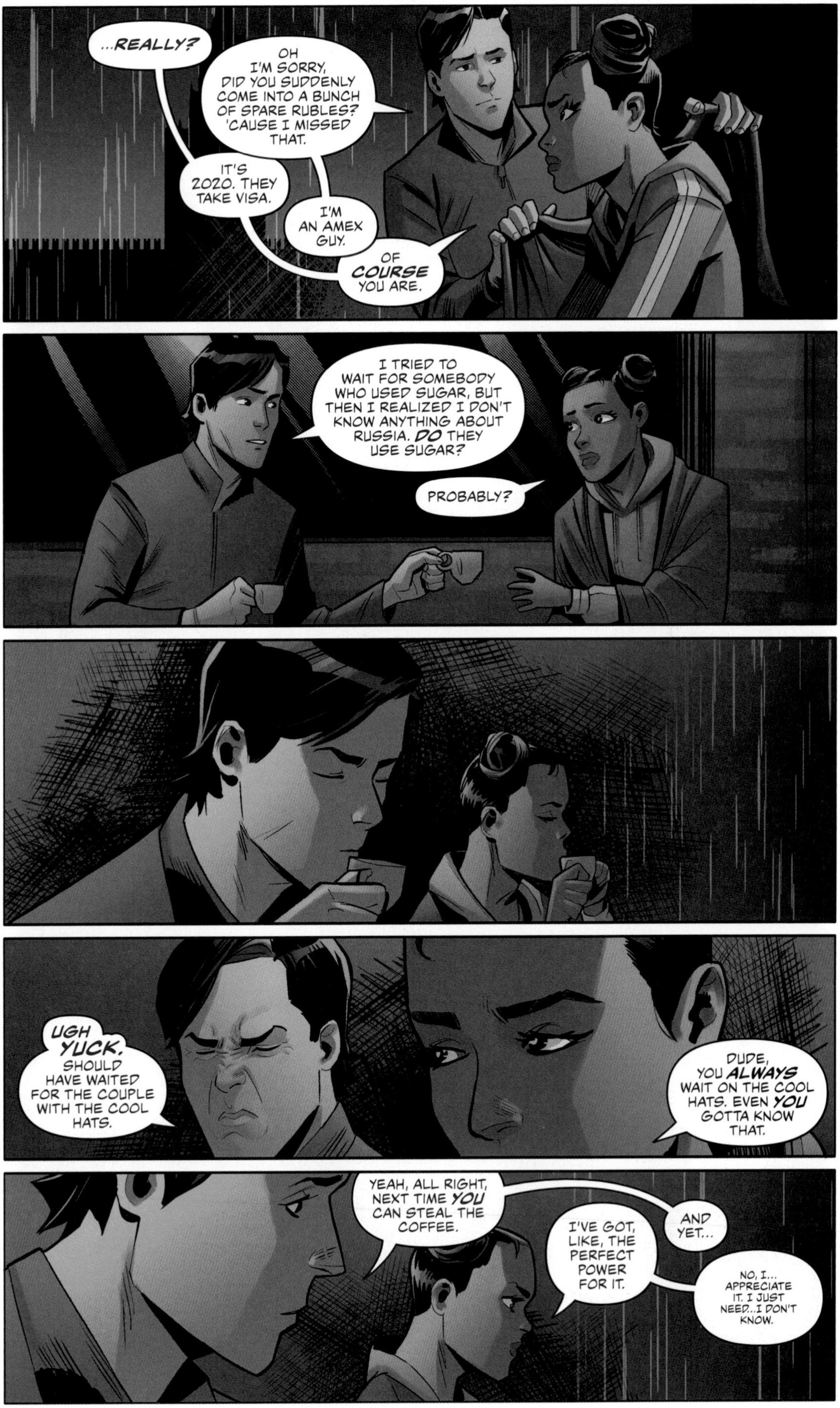
...REALLY?
OH I'M SORRY, DID YOU SUDDENLY COME INTO A BUNCH OF SPARE RUBLES? 'CAUSE I MISSED THAT.
IT'S 2020. THEY TAKE VISA.
I'M AN AMEX GUY.
OF COURSE YOU ARE.
I TRIED TO WAIT FOR SOMEBODY WHO USED SUGAR, BUT THEN I REALIZED I DON'T KNOW ANYTHING ABOUT RUSSIA. DO THEY USE SUGAR?
PROBABLY?
UGH YUCK. SHOULD HAVE WAITED FOR THE COUPLE WITH THE COOL HATS.
DUDE, YOU ALWAYS WAIT ON THE COOL HATS. EVEN YOU GOTTA KNOW THAT.
YEAH, ALL RIGHT, NEXT TIME YOU CAN STEAL THE COFFEE.
AND YET...
I'VE GOT, LIKE, THE PERFECT POWER FOR IT.
NO, I... APPRECIATE IT. I JUST NEED...I DON'T KNOW.

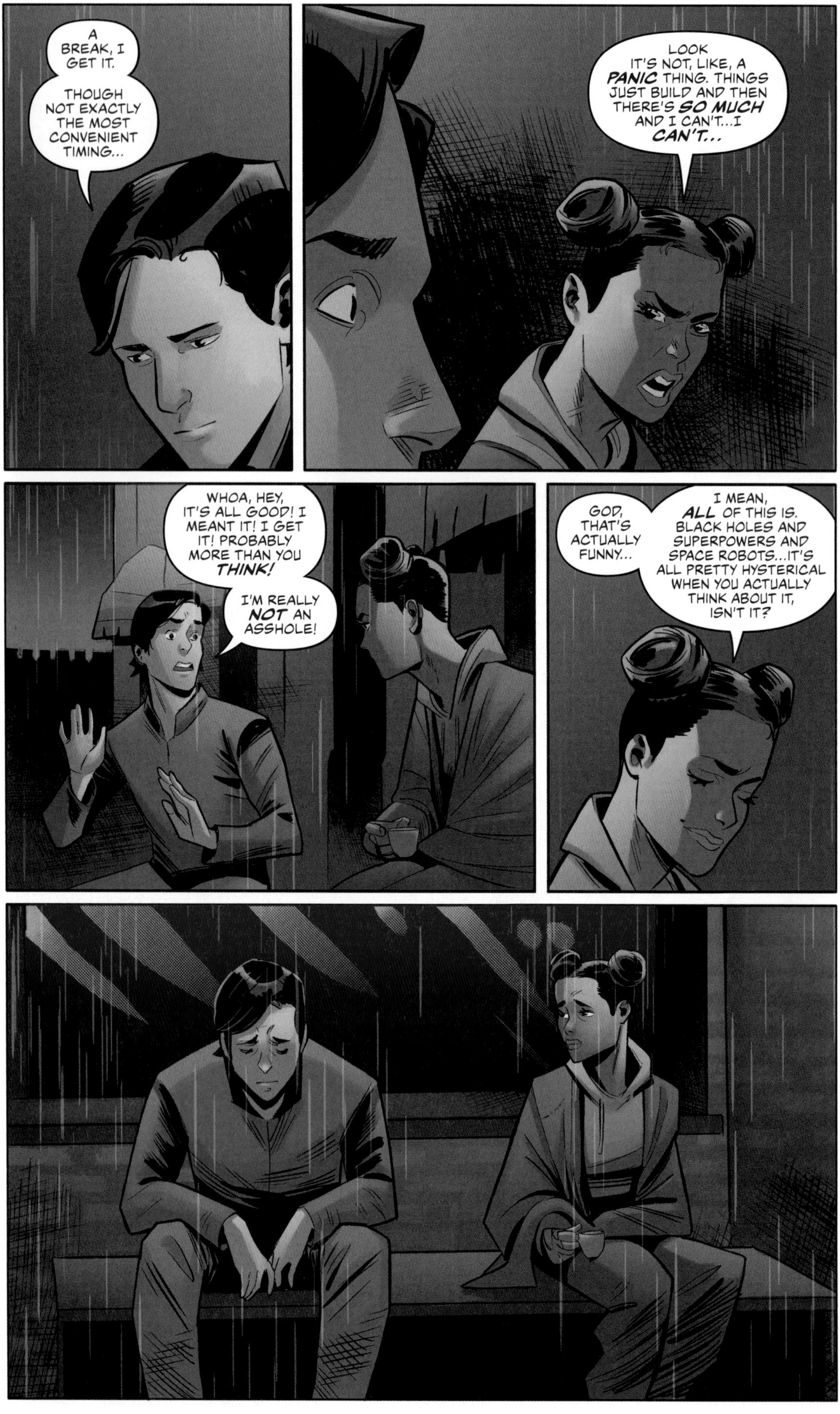
A BREAK, I GET IT.
THOUGH NOT EXACTLY THE MOST CONVENIENT TIMING...
LOOK IT'S NOT, LIKE, A PANIC THING. THINGS JUST BUILD AND THEN THERE'S SO MUCH AND I CAN'T...I CAN'T...
WHOA, HEY, IT'S ALL GOOD! I MEANT IT! I GET IT! PROBABLY MORE THAN YOU THINK!
I'M REALLY NOT AN ASSHOLE!
GOD, THAT'S ACTUALLY FUNNY...
I MEAN, ALL OF THIS IS. BLACK HOLES AND SUPERPOWERS AND SPACE ROBOTS...IT'S ALL PRETTY HYSTERICAL WHEN YOU ACTUALLY THINK ABOUT IT, ISN'T IT?

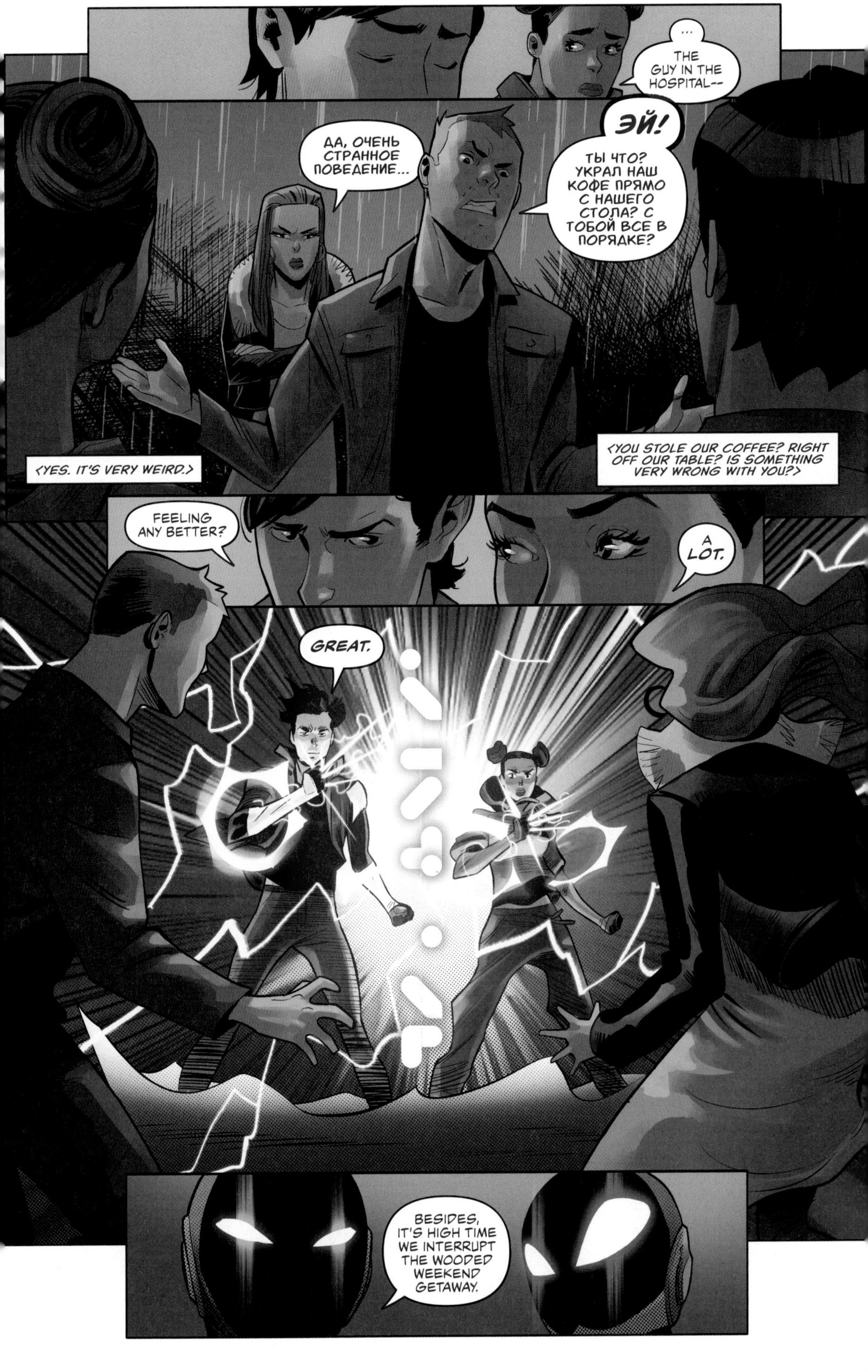
...
THE GUY IN THE HOSPITAL--
ДА, ОЧЕНЬ СТРАННОЕ ПОВЕДЕНИЕ...
ЭЙ!
ТЫ ЧТО? УКРАЛ НАШ КОФЕ ПРЯМО С НАШЕГО СТОЛА? С ТОБОЙ ВСЕ В ПОРЯДКЕ?
<YES. IT'S VERY WEIRD.>
<YOU STOLE OUR COFFEE? RIGHT OFF OUR TABLE? IS SOMETHING VERY WRONG WITH YOU?>
FEELING ANY BETTER?
A LOT.
GREAT.
BESIDES, IT'S HIGH TIME WE INTERRUPT THE WOODED WEEKEND GETAWAY.

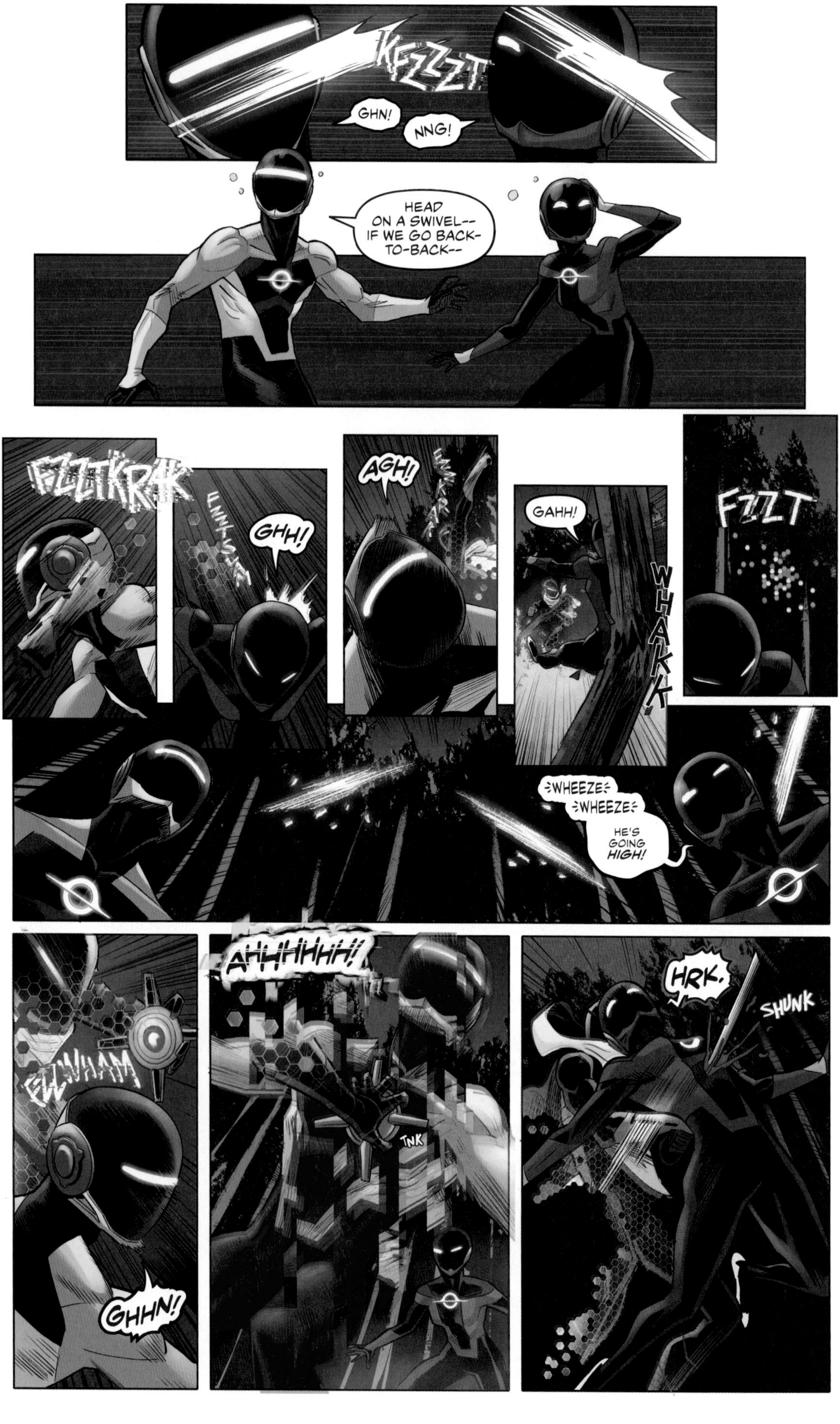
KFZZZT
GHN!
NNG!
HEAD ON A SWIVEL-- IF WE GO BACK-TO-BACK--
FZZZTKRAK
FZZTSWM
GHH!
AGH!
GAHH!
WHAKKK
FZZT
WHEEZE
WHEEZE
HE'S GOING HIGH!
WHAM
GHHN!
AHHHHHH!
TNK
HRK.
SHUNK

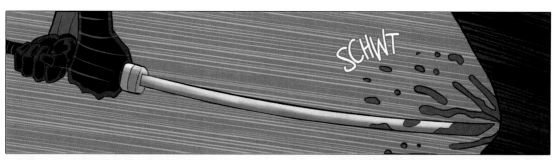

SCHWT

≶GHN≶...
≶GHOD≶

SURVIVAL MODE. ABSORB TO REPAIR. TRY TO STOP THE LOSS OF FLUID. CLEVER.

BUT TOO ADVANCED.

SH

NNK

MAYBE... JUST NEED TO ABSORB...SOMETHING *STRONGER...*

NNNH!

KAKOOM

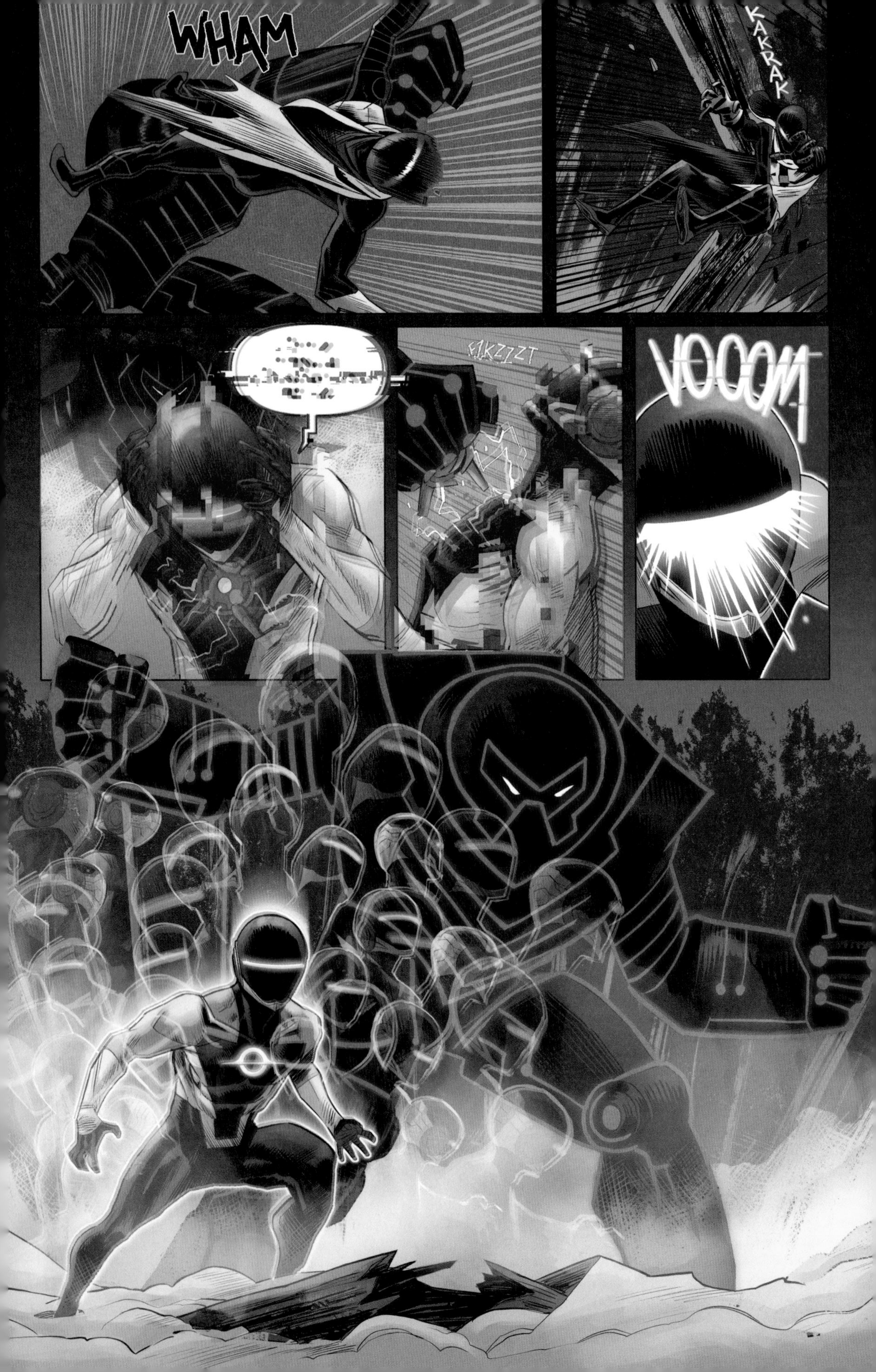
WHAM
KAKRAK
FZKZZZT
VOOOM

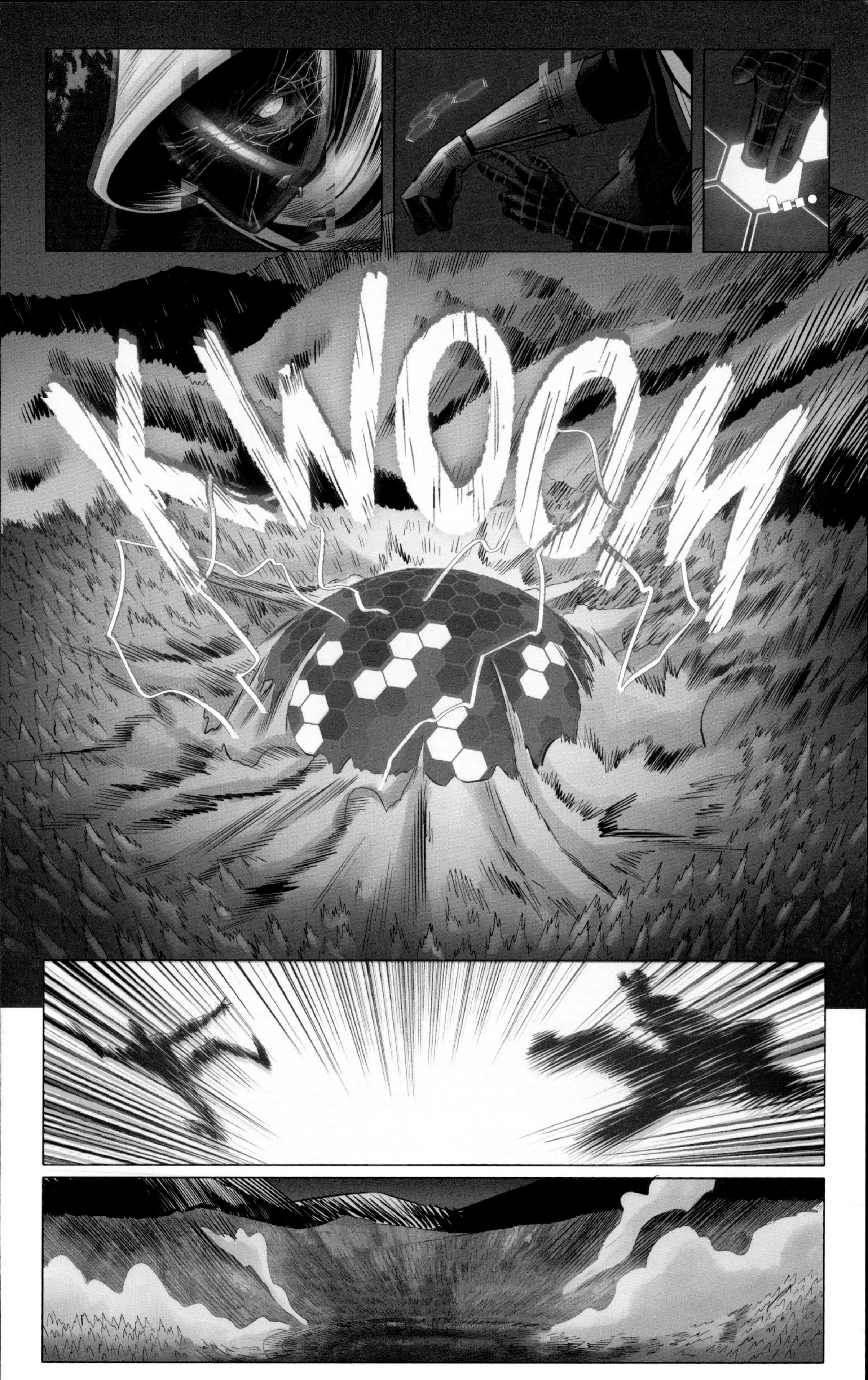
KWOOM

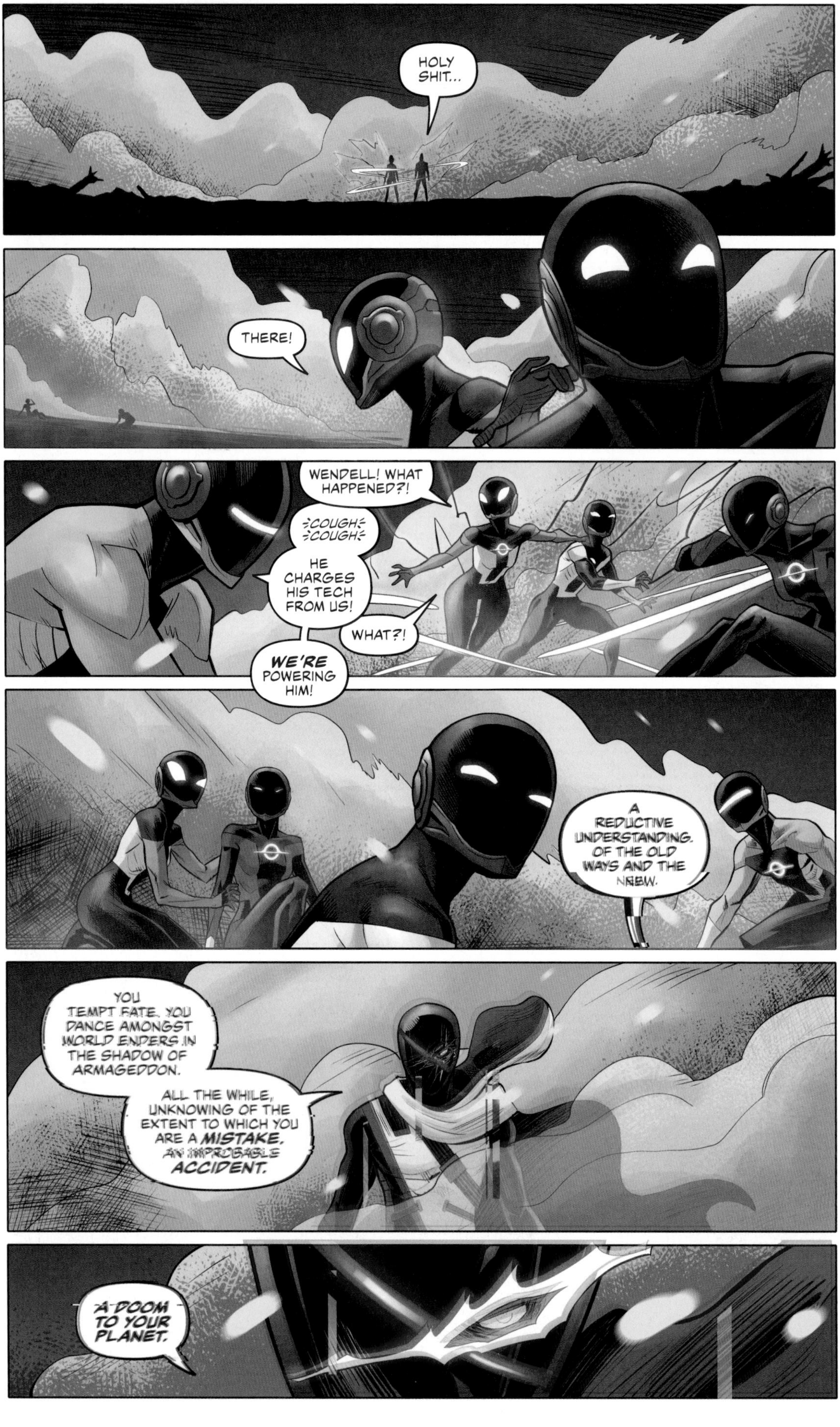

HOLY SHIT...
THERE!
WENDELL! WHAT HAPPENED?!
COUGH COUGH
HE CHARGES HIS TECH FROM US!
WHAT?!
WE'RE POWERING HIM!
A REDUCTIVE UNDERSTANDING OF THE OLD WAYS AND THE NEW.
YOU TEMPT FATE. YOU DANCE AMONGST WORLD ENDERS IN THE SHADOW OF ARMAGEDDON.
ALL THE WHILE, UNKNOWING OF THE EXTENT TO WHICH YOU ARE A MISTAKE. AN IMPROBABLE ACCIDENT.
A DOOM TO YOUR PLANET.

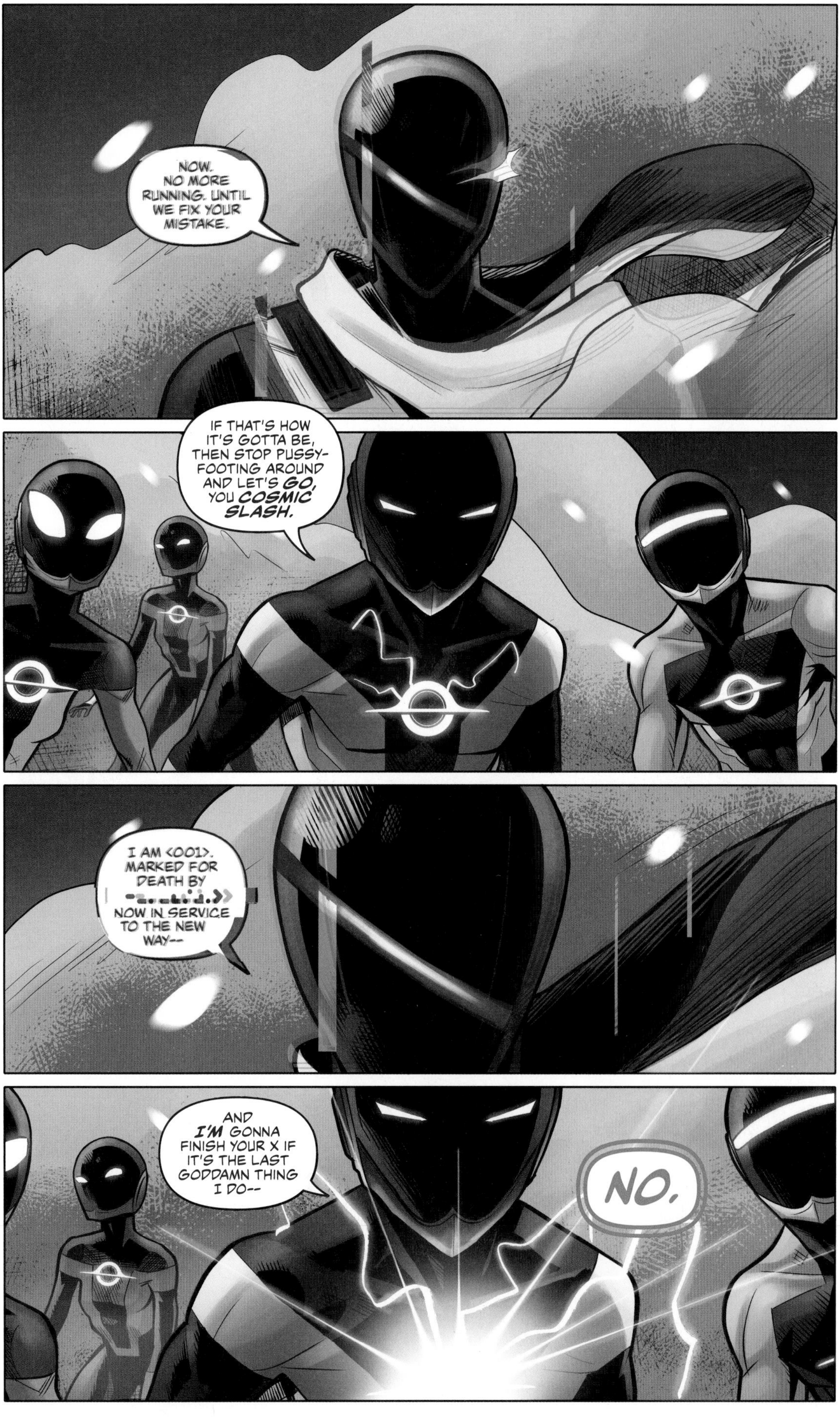
NOW. NO MORE RUNNING. UNTIL WE FIX YOUR MISTAKE.
IF THAT'S HOW IT'S GOTTA BE, THEN STOP PUSSY-FOOTING AROUND AND LET'S GO, YOU COSMIC SLASH.
I AM <001>. MARKED FOR DEATH BY
NOW IN SERVICE TO THE NEW WAY--
AND I'M GONNA FINISH YOUR X IF IT'S THE LAST GODDAMN THING I DO--
NO.

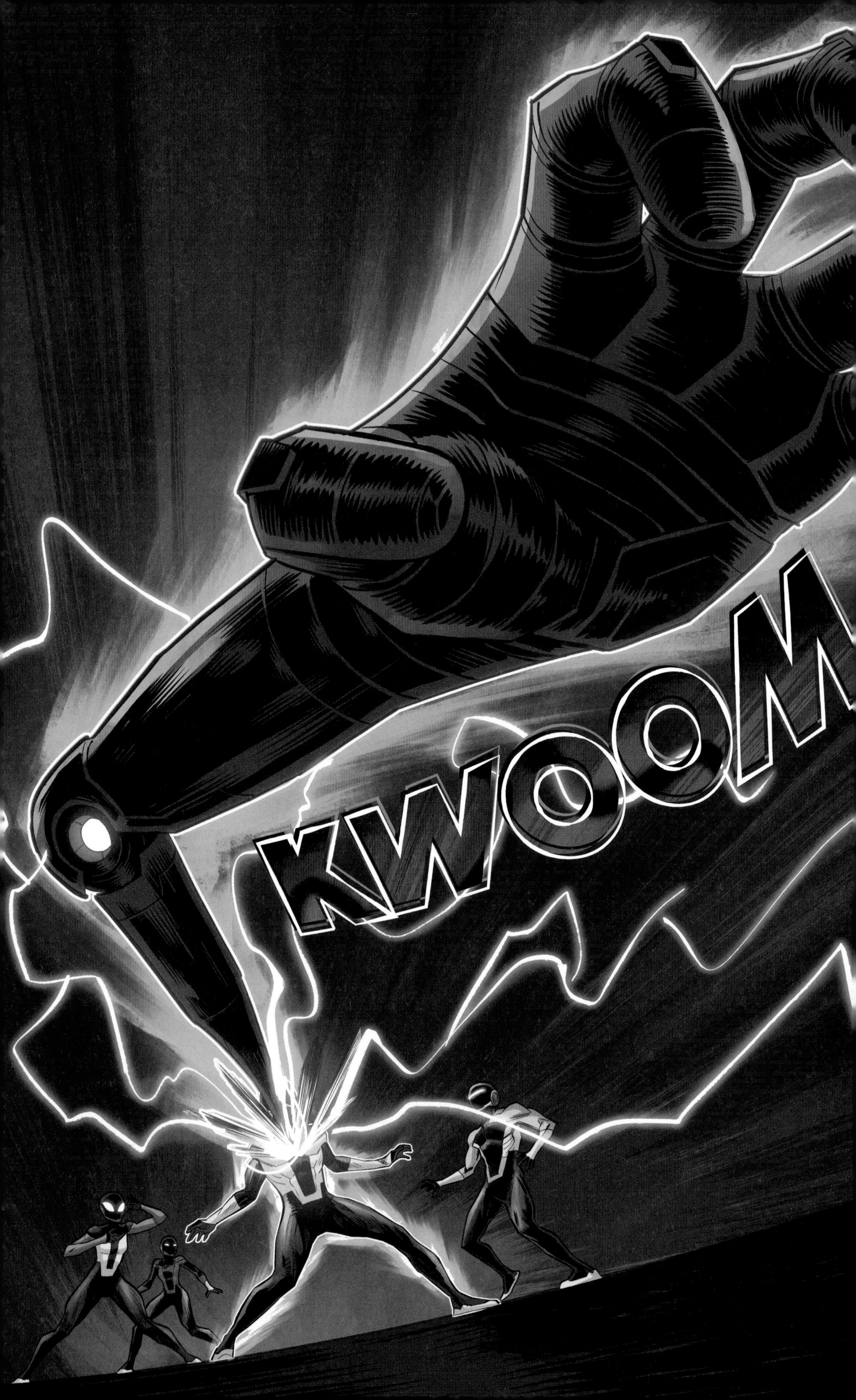
KWOOM

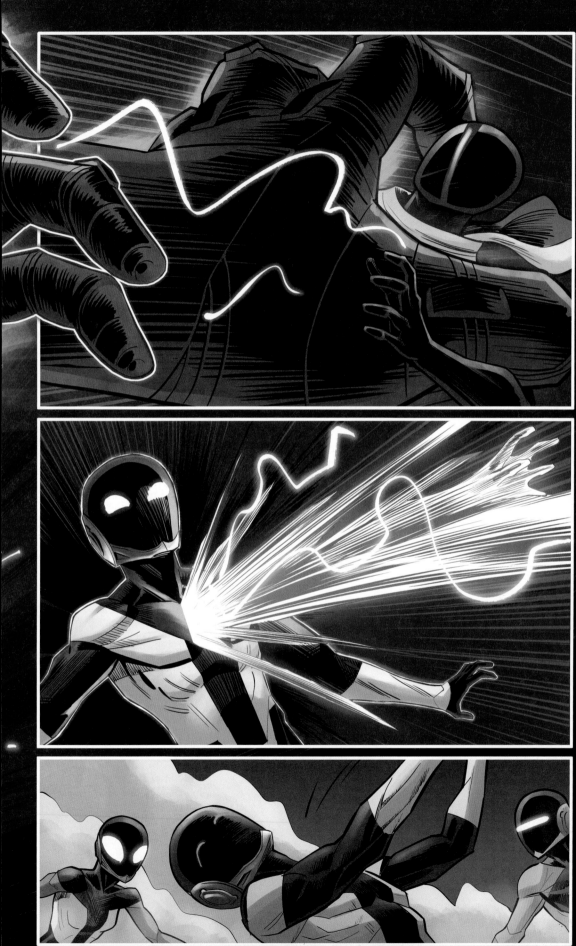

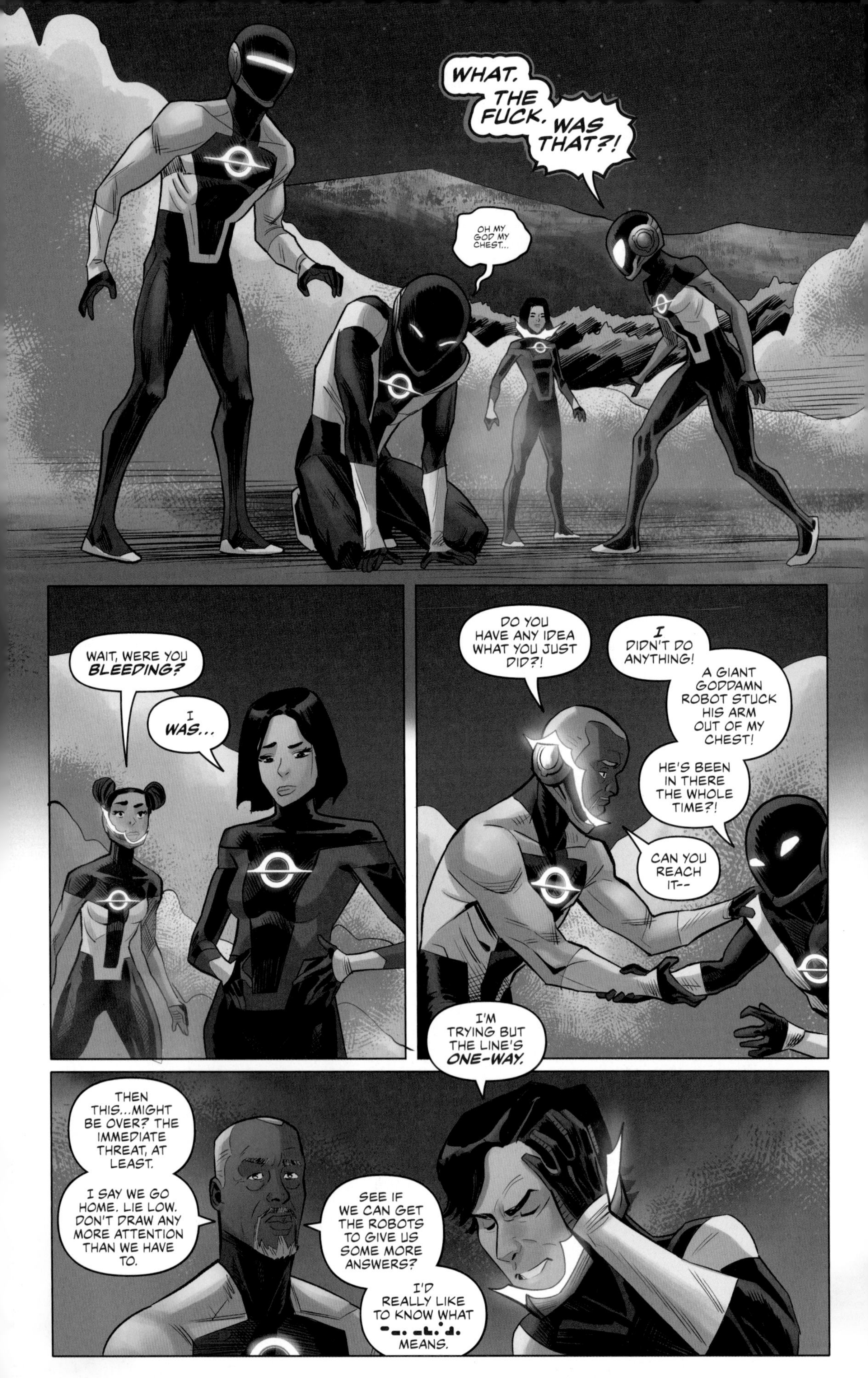
WHAT. THE FUCK. WAS THAT?!
OH MY GOD MY CHEST...
WAIT, WERE YOU BLEEDING?
I WAS...
DO YOU HAVE ANY IDEA WHAT YOU JUST DID?!
I DIDN'T DO ANYTHING!
A GIANT GODDAMN ROBOT STUCK HIS ARM OUT OF MY CHEST!
HE'S BEEN IN THERE THE WHOLE TIME?!
CAN YOU REACH IT--
I'M TRYING BUT THE LINE'S ONE-WAY.
THEN THIS...MIGHT BE OVER? THE IMMEDIATE THREAT, AT LEAST.
I SAY WE GO HOME. LIE LOW. DON'T DRAW ANY MORE ATTENTION THAN WE HAVE TO.
SEE IF WE CAN GET THE ROBOTS TO GIVE US SOME MORE ANSWERS?
I'D REALLY LIKE TO KNOW WHAT
MEANS.

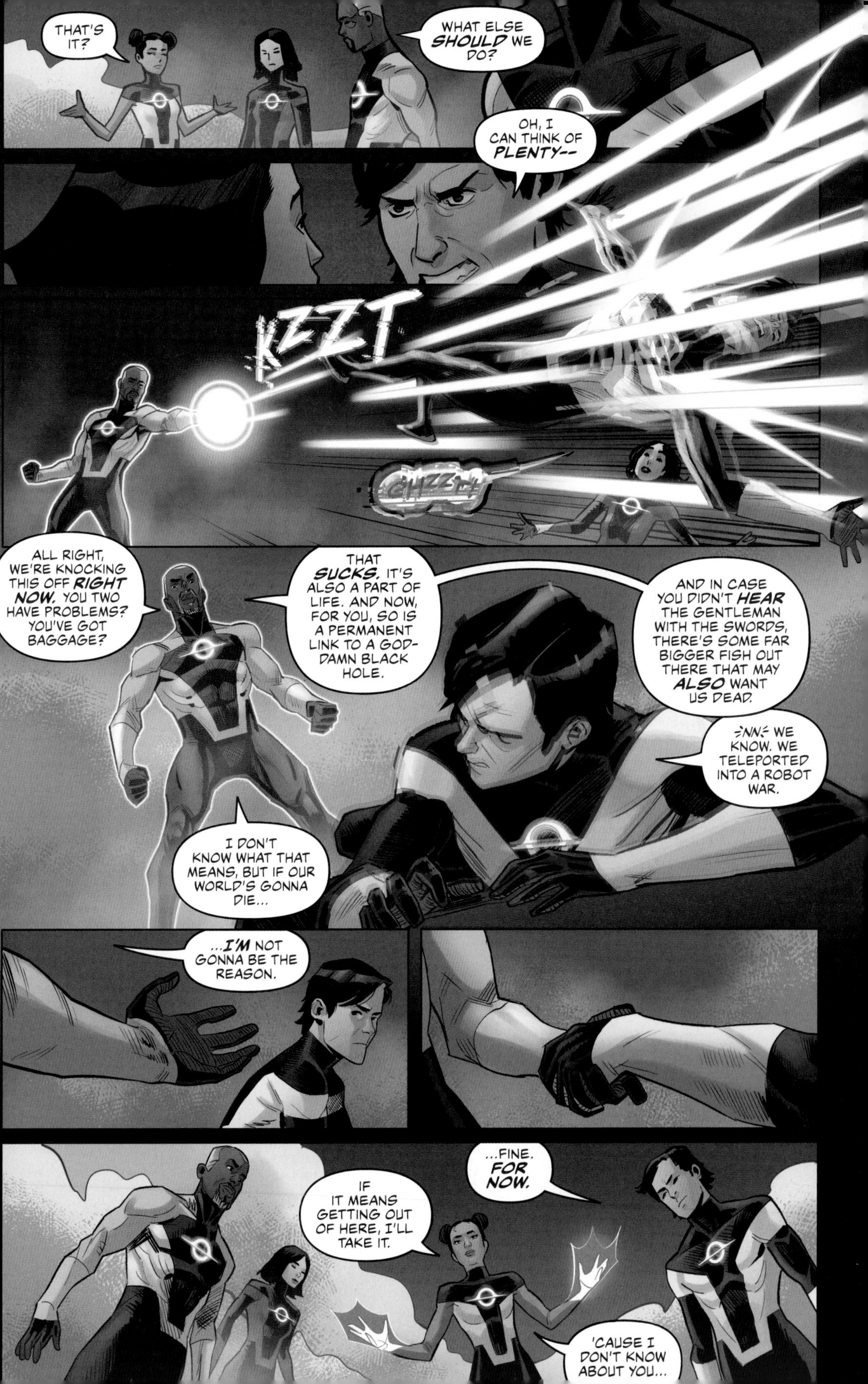

THAT'S IT?
WHAT ELSE SHOULD WE DO?
OH, I CAN THINK OF PLENTY--
KZZT
ALL RIGHT, WE'RE KNOCKING THIS OFF RIGHT NOW. YOU TWO HAVE PROBLEMS? YOU'VE GOT BAGGAGE?
THAT SUCKS. IT'S ALSO A PART OF LIFE. AND NOW, FOR YOU, SO IS A PERMANENT LINK TO A GOD-DAMN BLACK HOLE.
AND IN CASE YOU DIDN'T HEAR THE GENTLEMAN WITH THE SWORDS, THERE'S SOME FAR BIGGER FISH OUT THERE THAT MAY ALSO WANT US DEAD.
=NN= WE KNOW. WE TELEPORTED INTO A ROBOT WAR.
I DON'T KNOW WHAT THAT MEANS, BUT IF OUR WORLD'S GONNA DIE...
...I'M NOT GONNA BE THE REASON.
...FINE. FOR NOW.
IF IT MEANS GETTING OUT OF HERE, I'LL TAKE IT.
'CAUSE I DON'T KNOW ABOUT YOU...

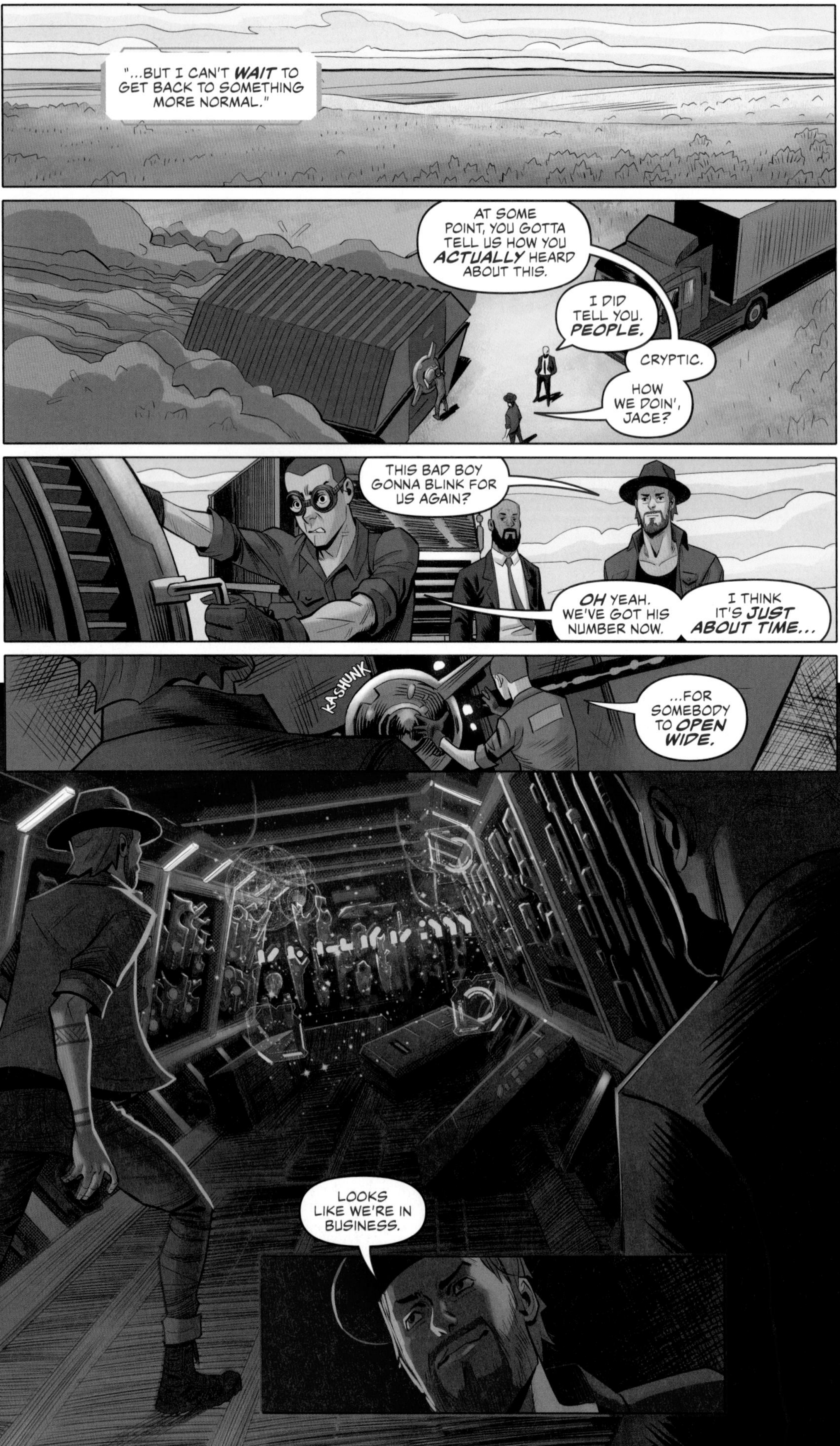
"...BUT I CAN'T WAIT TO GET BACK TO SOMETHING MORE NORMAL."
AT SOME POINT, YOU GOTTA TELL US HOW YOU ACTUALLY HEARD ABOUT THIS.
I DID TELL YOU. PEOPLE.
CRYPTIC.
HOW WE DOIN', JACE?
THIS BAD BOY GONNA BLINK FOR US AGAIN?
OH YEAH. WE'VE GOT HIS NUMBER NOW.
I THINK IT'S JUST ABOUT TIME...
KA-SHUNK
...FOR SOMEBODY TO OPEN WIDE.
LOOKS LIKE WE'RE IN BUSINESS.

CHAPTER NINE

TITLE   Life and Times

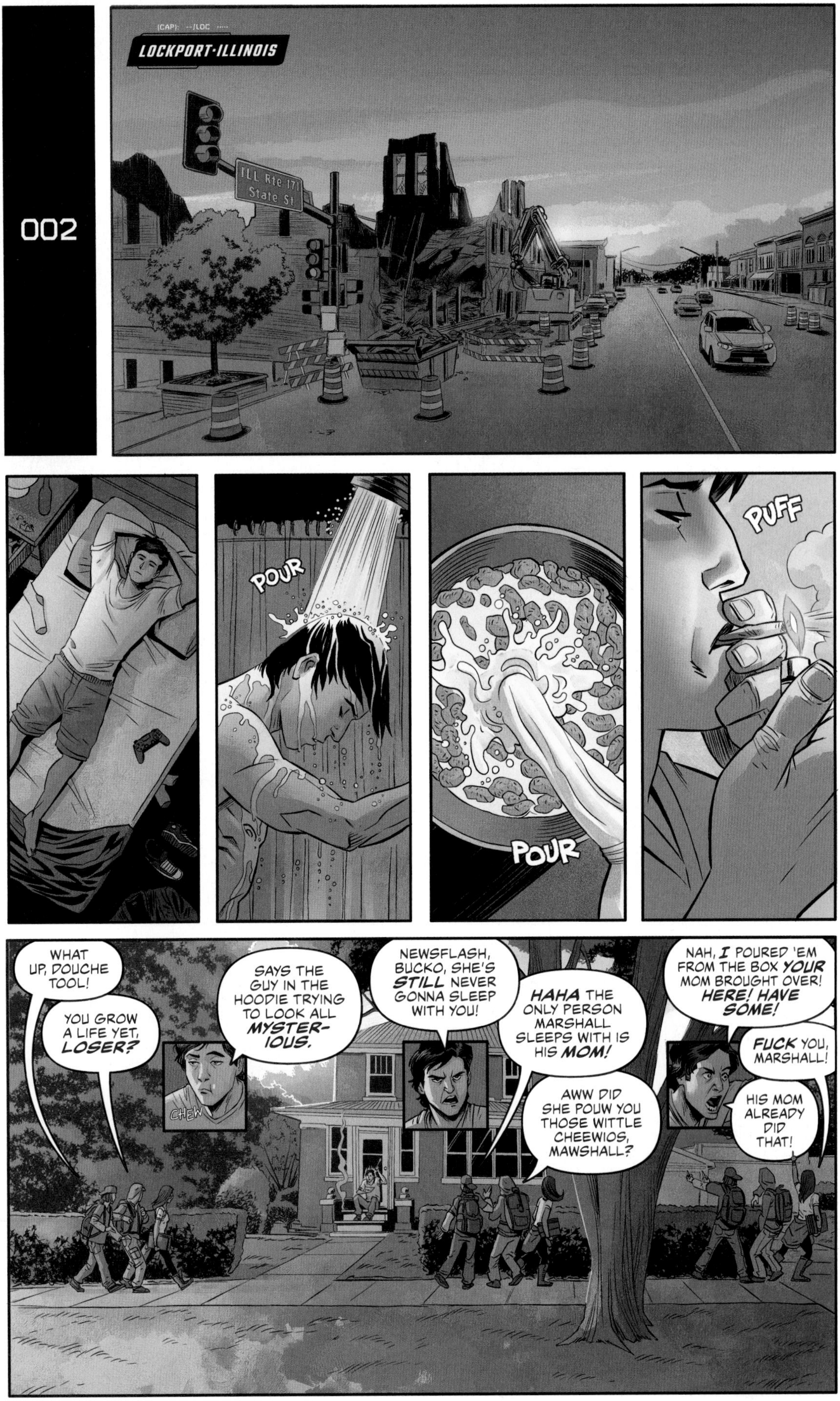
002
(CAP): --/LOC
LOCKPORT·ILLINOIS
ILL Rte 171
State St
POUR
POUR
PUFF
WHAT UP, DOUCHE TOOL!
YOU GROW A LIFE YET, LOSER?
SAYS THE GUY IN THE HOODIE TRYING TO LOOK ALL MYSTER-IOUS.
CHEW
NEWSFLASH, BUCKO, SHE'S STILL NEVER GONNA SLEEP WITH YOU!
HAHA THE ONLY PERSON MARSHALL SLEEPS WITH IS HIS MOM!
AWW DID SHE POUW YOU THOSE WITTLE CHEEWIOS, MAWSHALL?
NAH, I POURED 'EM FROM THE BOX YOUR MOM BROUGHT OVER! HERE! HAVE SOME!
FUCK YOU, MARSHALL!
HIS MOM ALREADY DID THAT!

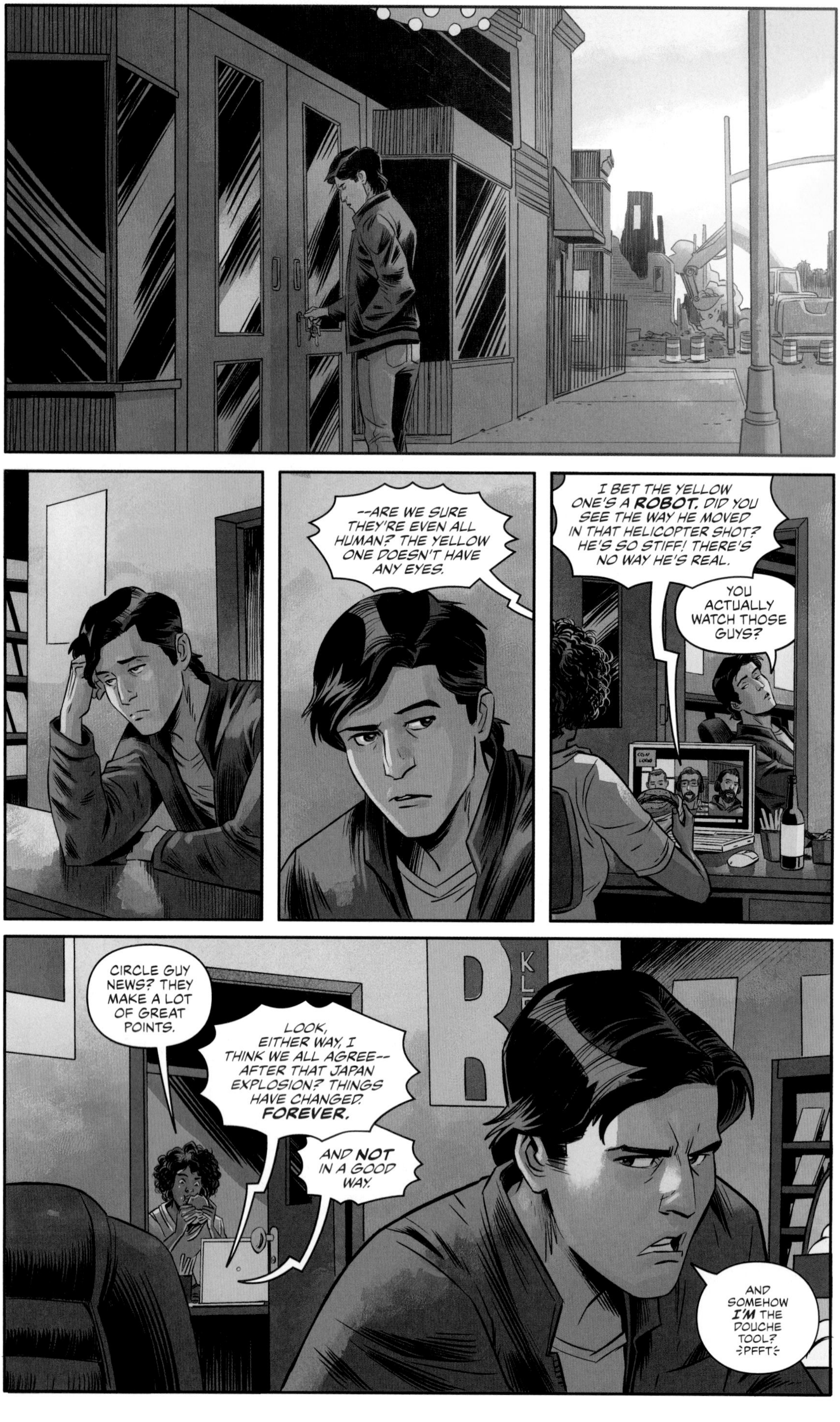
--ARE WE SURE THEY'RE EVEN ALL HUMAN? THE YELLOW ONE DOESN'T HAVE ANY EYES.
I BET THE YELLOW ONE'S A ROBOT. DID YOU SEE THE WAY HE MOVED IN THAT HELICOPTER SHOT? HE'S SO STIFF! THERE'S NO WAY HE'S REAL.
YOU ACTUALLY WATCH THOSE GUYS?
CIRCLE GUY NEWS? THEY MAKE A LOT OF GREAT POINTS.
LOOK, EITHER WAY, I THINK WE ALL AGREE-- AFTER THAT JAPAN EXPLOSION? THINGS HAVE CHANGED. FOREVER.
AND NOT IN A GOOD WAY.
AND SOMEHOW I'M THE DOUCHE TOOL? PFFT

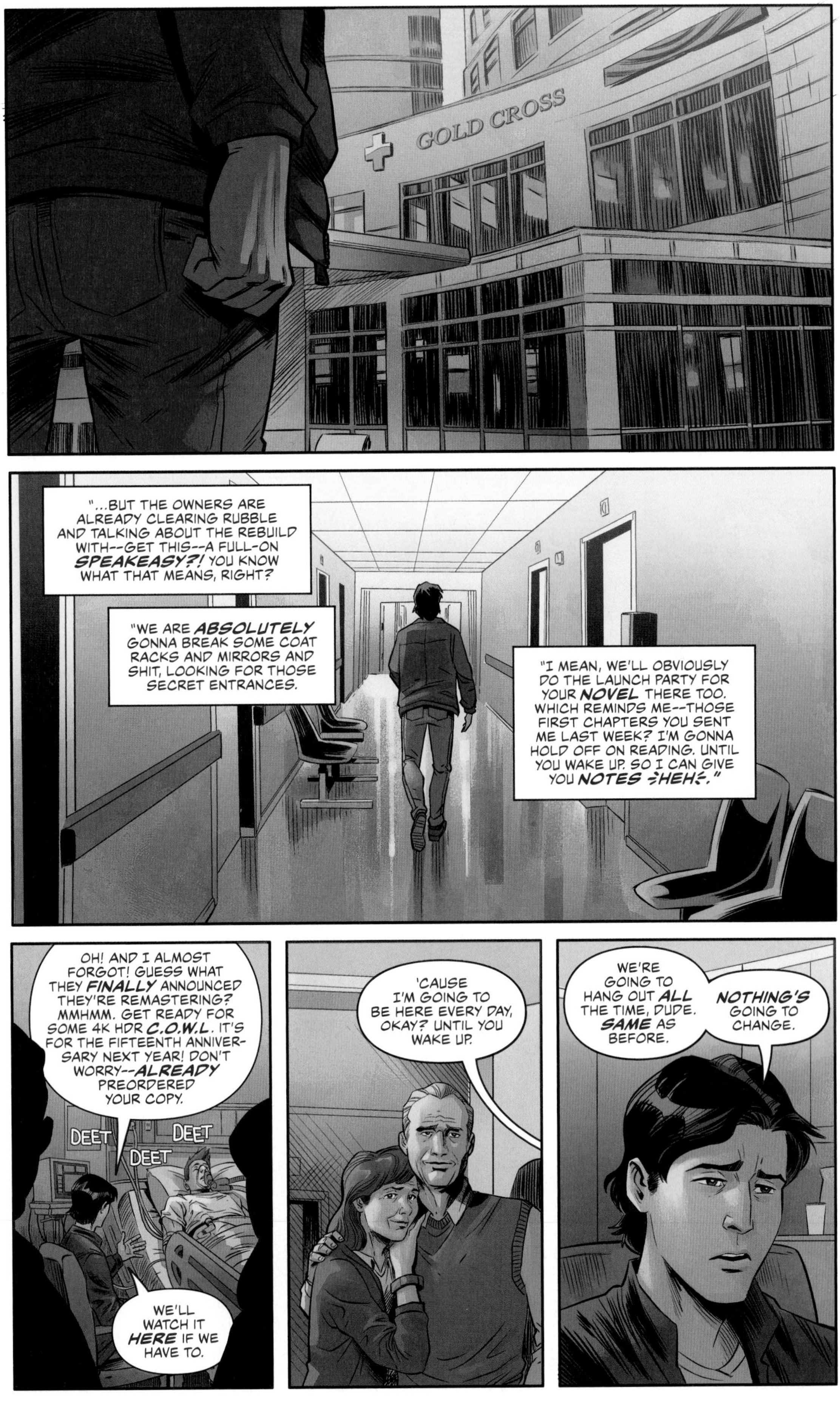
GOLD CROSS
"...BUT THE OWNERS ARE ALREADY CLEARING RUBBLE AND TALKING ABOUT THE REBUILD WITH--GET THIS--A FULL-ON SPEAKEASY?! YOU KNOW WHAT THAT MEANS, RIGHT?
"WE ARE ABSOLUTELY GONNA BREAK SOME COAT RACKS AND MIRRORS AND SHIT, LOOKING FOR THOSE SECRET ENTRANCES.
"I MEAN, WE'LL OBVIOUSLY DO THE LAUNCH PARTY FOR YOUR NOVEL THERE TOO. WHICH REMINDS ME--THOSE FIRST CHAPTERS YOU SENT ME LAST WEEK? I'M GONNA HOLD OFF ON READING. UNTIL YOU WAKE UP. SO I CAN GIVE YOU NOTES <HEH>."
OH! AND I ALMOST FORGOT! GUESS WHAT THEY FINALLY ANNOUNCED THEY'RE REMASTERING? MMHMM. GET READY FOR SOME 4K HDR C.O.W.L. IT'S FOR THE FIFTEENTH ANNIVERSARY NEXT YEAR! DON'T WORRY--ALREADY PREORDERED YOUR COPY.
DEET
DEET
DEET
WE'LL WATCH IT HERE IF WE HAVE TO.
'CAUSE I'M GOING TO BE HERE EVERY DAY, OKAY? UNTIL YOU WAKE UP.
WE'RE GOING TO HANG OUT ALL THE TIME, DUDE. SAME AS BEFORE.
NOTHING'S GOING TO CHANGE.

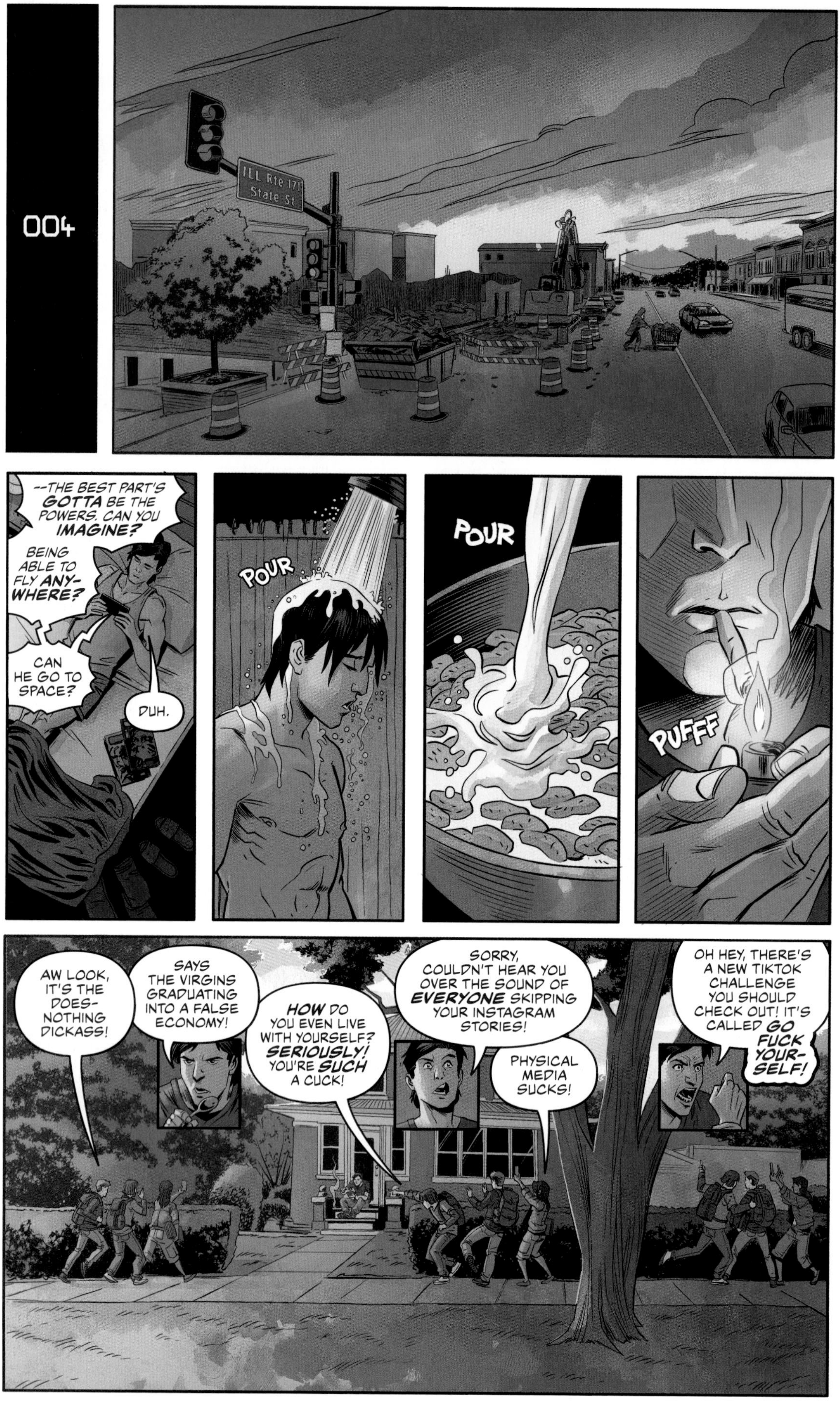
004
ILL Rte 171
State St
--THE BEST PART'S **GOTTA** BE THE POWERS. CAN YOU **IMAGINE?**
BEING ABLE TO FLY **ANY-WHERE?**
CAN HE GO TO SPACE?
DUH.
POUR
POUR
PUFFF
AW LOOK, IT'S THE DOES-NOTHING DICKASS!
SAYS THE VIRGINS GRADUATING INTO A FALSE ECONOMY!
HOW DO YOU EVEN LIVE WITH YOURSELF? **SERIOUSLY!** YOU'RE **SUCH** A CUCK!
SORRY, COULDN'T HEAR YOU OVER THE SOUND OF **EVERYONE** SKIPPING YOUR INSTAGRAM STORIES!
PHYSICAL MEDIA SUCKS!
OH HEY, THERE'S A NEW TIKTOK CHALLENGE YOU SHOULD CHECK OUT! IT'S CALLED **GO FUCK YOUR-SELF!**

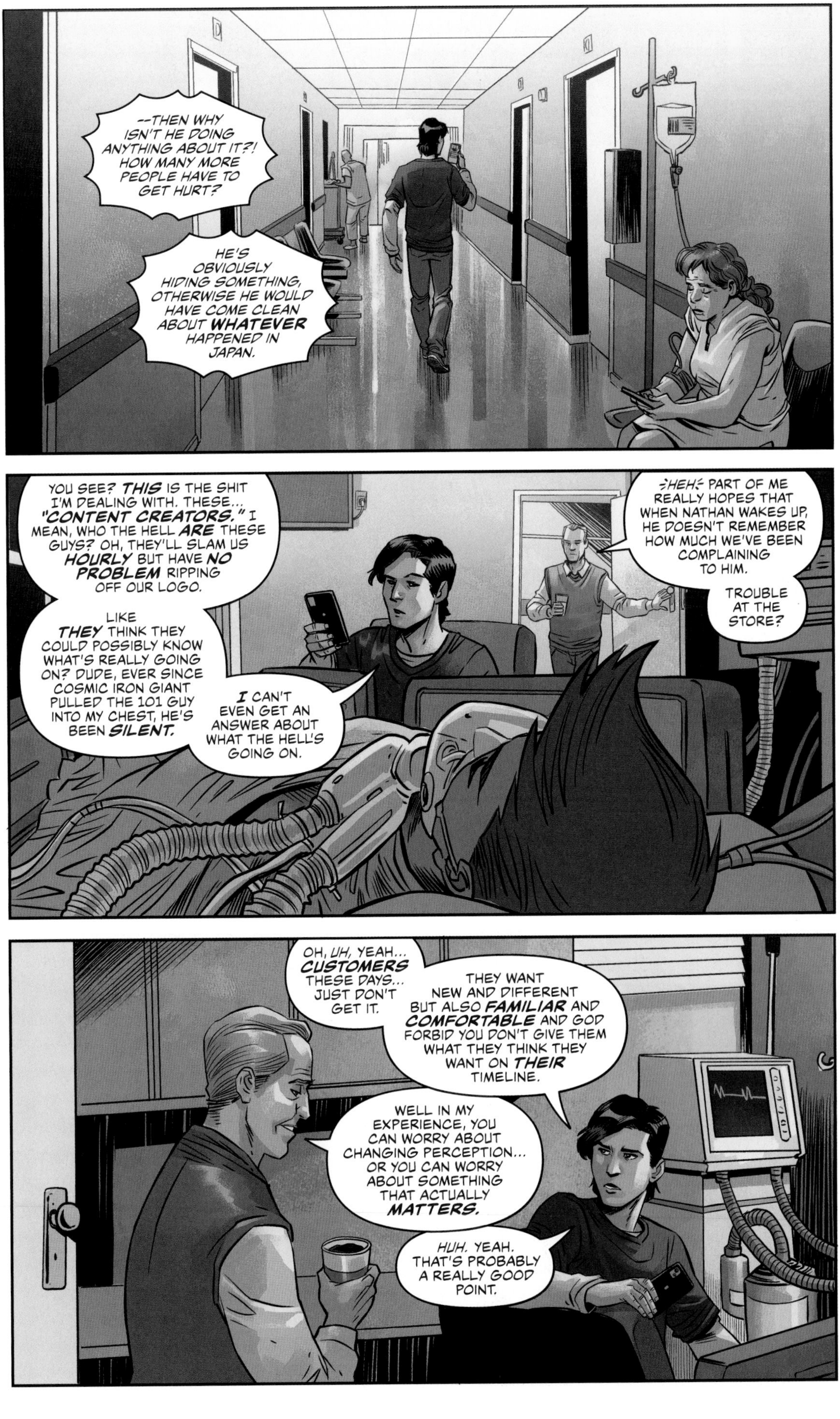
--THEN WHY ISN'T HE DOING ANYTHING ABOUT IT?! HOW MANY MORE PEOPLE HAVE TO GET HURT?
HE'S OBVIOUSLY HIDING SOMETHING, OTHERWISE HE WOULD HAVE COME CLEAN ABOUT WHATEVER HAPPENED IN JAPAN.
YOU SEE? THIS IS THE SHIT I'M DEALING WITH. THESE... "CONTENT CREATORS." I MEAN, WHO THE HELL ARE THESE GUYS? OH, THEY'LL SLAM US HOURLY BUT HAVE NO PROBLEM RIPPING OFF OUR LOGO.
LIKE THEY THINK THEY COULD POSSIBLY KNOW WHAT'S REALLY GOING ON? DUDE, EVER SINCE COSMIC IRON GIANT PULLED THE 101 GUY INTO MY CHEST, HE'S BEEN SILENT.
I CAN'T EVEN GET AN ANSWER ABOUT WHAT THE HELL'S GOING ON.
HEH PART OF ME REALLY HOPES THAT WHEN NATHAN WAKES UP, HE DOESN'T REMEMBER HOW MUCH WE'VE BEEN COMPLAINING TO HIM.
TROUBLE AT THE STORE?
OH, UH, YEAH... CUSTOMERS THESE DAYS... JUST DON'T GET IT.
THEY WANT NEW AND DIFFERENT BUT ALSO FAMILIAR AND COMFORTABLE AND GOD FORBID YOU DON'T GIVE THEM WHAT THEY THINK THEY WANT ON THEIR TIMELINE.
WELL IN MY EXPERIENCE, YOU CAN WORRY ABOUT CHANGING PERCEPTION... OR YOU CAN WORRY ABOUT SOMETHING THAT ACTUALLY MATTERS.
HUH. YEAH. THAT'S PROBABLY A REALLY GOOD POINT.

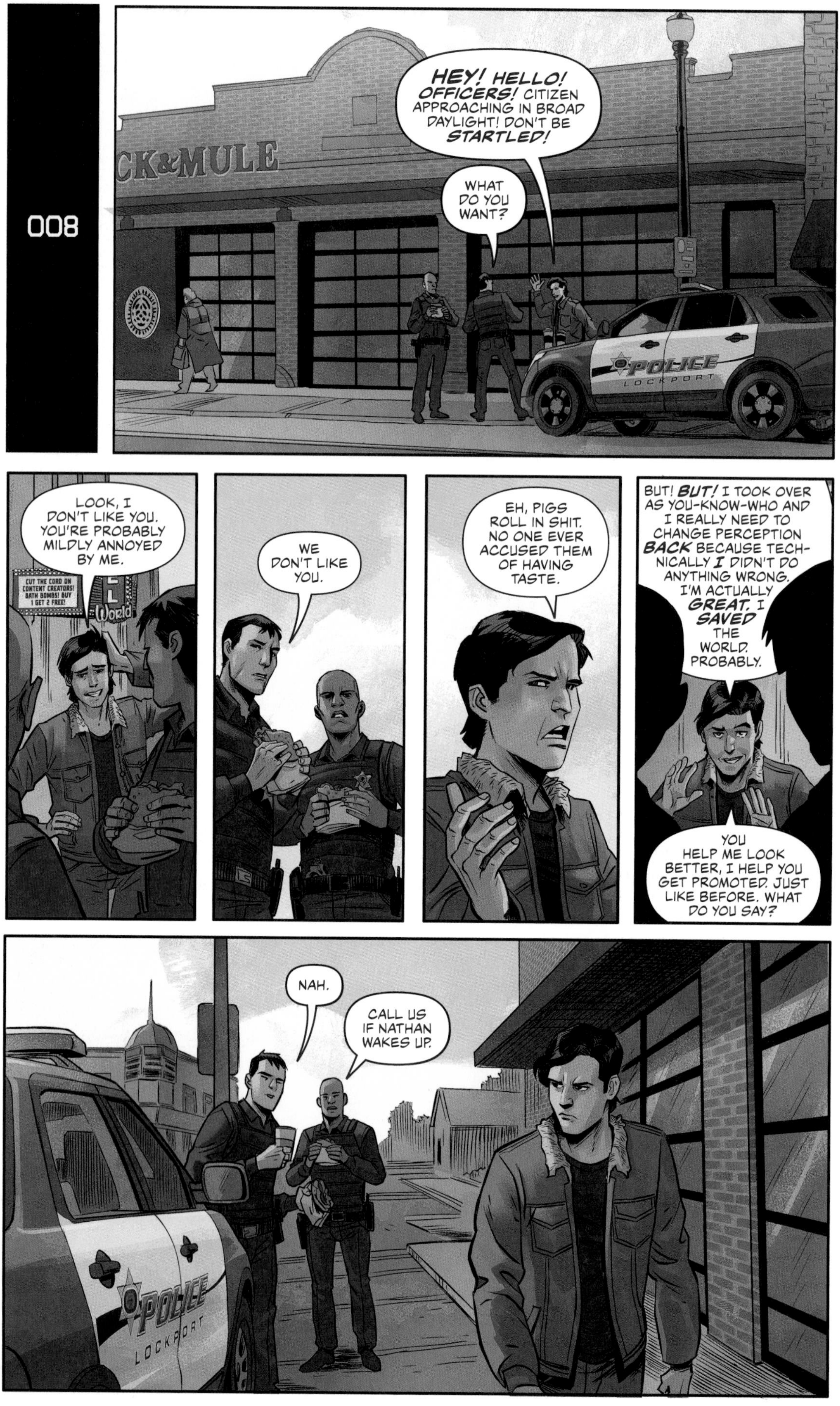
008
CK&MULE
HEY! HELLO! OFFICERS! CITIZEN APPROACHING IN BROAD DAYLIGHT! DON'T BE STARTLED!
WHAT DO YOU WANT?
POLICE
LOCKPORT
LOOK, I DON'T LIKE YOU. YOU'RE PROBABLY MILDLY ANNOYED BY ME.
CUT THE CORD ON CONTENT CREATORS! BATH BOMBS! BUY 1 GET 2 FREE!
World
WE DON'T LIKE YOU.
EH, PIGS ROLL IN SHIT. NO ONE EVER ACCUSED THEM OF HAVING TASTE.
BUT! BUT! I TOOK OVER AS YOU-KNOW-WHO AND I REALLY NEED TO CHANGE PERCEPTION BACK BECAUSE TECH-NICALLY I DIDN'T DO ANYTHING WRONG. I'M ACTUALLY GREAT. I SAVED THE WORLD. PROBABLY.
YOU HELP ME LOOK BETTER, I HELP YOU GET PROMOTED. JUST LIKE BEFORE. WHAT DO YOU SAY?
NAH.
CALL US IF NATHAN WAKES UP.
POLICE
LOCKPORT

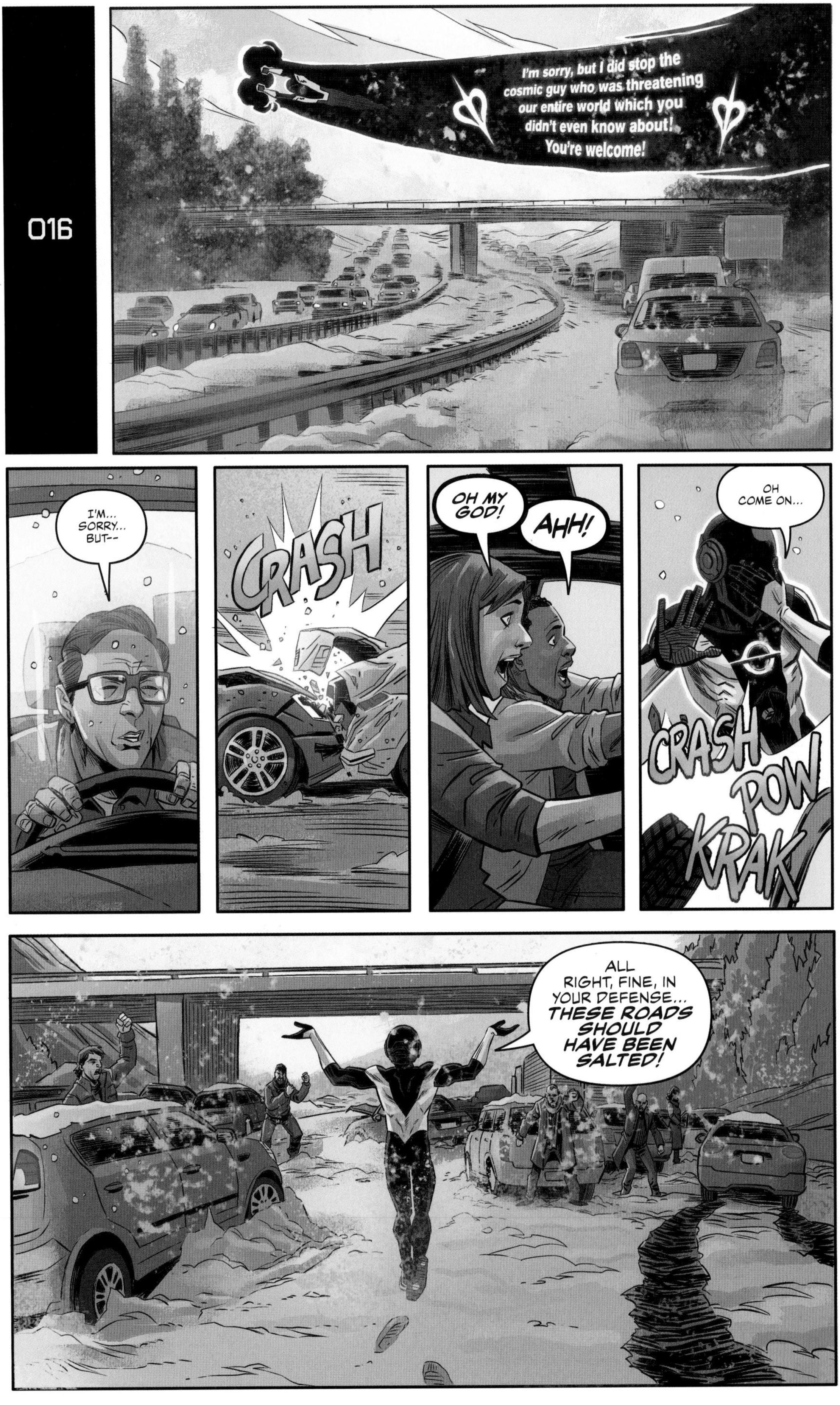
I'm sorry, but I did stop the cosmic guy who was threatening our entire world which you didn't even know about! You're welcome!
I'M... SORRY... BUT--
CRASH
OH MY GOD!
AHH!
OH COME ON...
CRASH
POW
KRAK
ALL RIGHT, FINE, IN YOUR DEFENSE... THESE ROADS SHOULD HAVE BEEN SALTED!

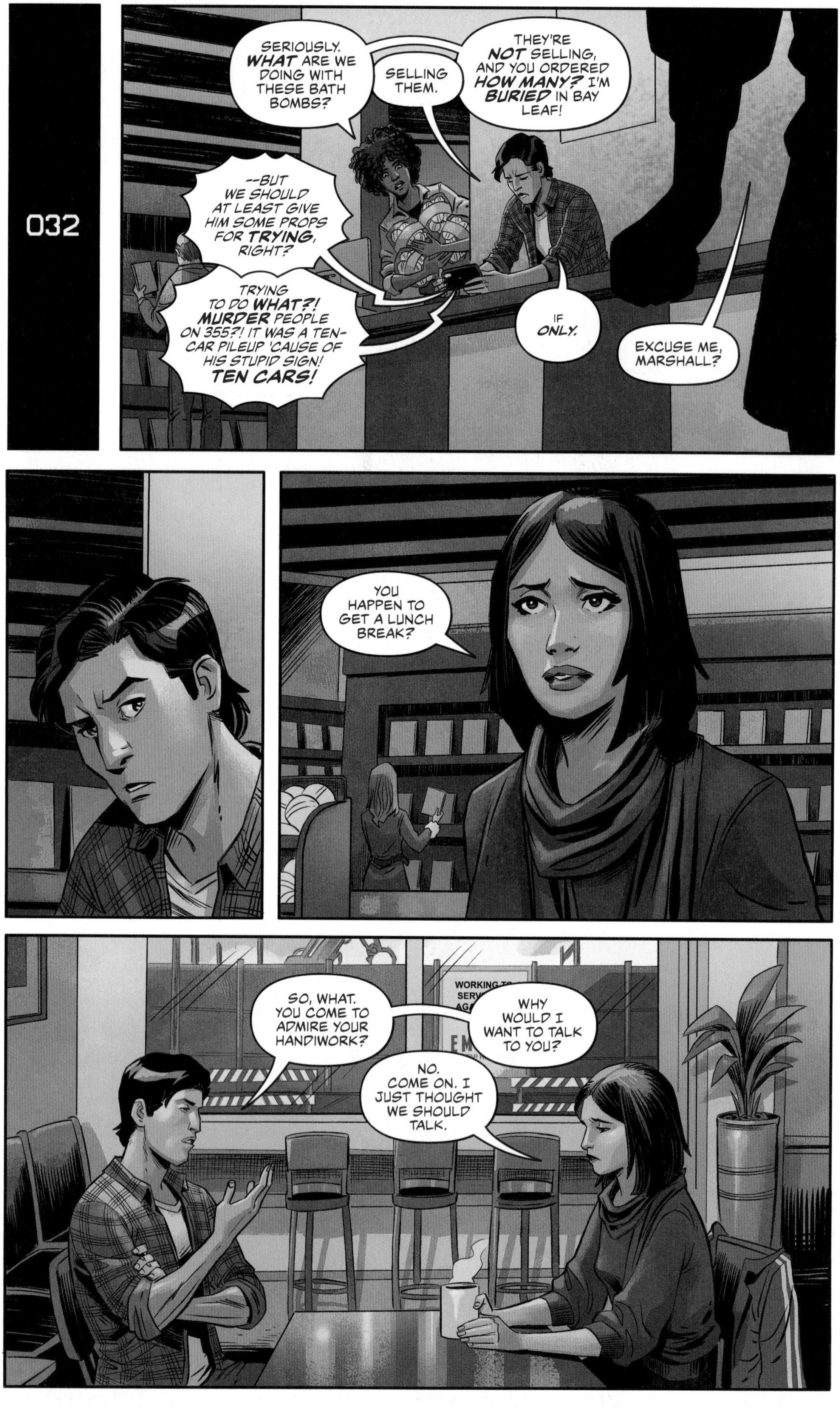
032
SERIOUSLY. WHAT ARE WE DOING WITH THESE BATH BOMBS?
SELLING THEM.
THEY'RE NOT SELLING, AND YOU ORDERED HOW MANY? I'M BURIED IN BAY LEAF!
--BUT WE SHOULD AT LEAST GIVE HIM SOME PROPS FOR TRYING, RIGHT?
TRYING TO DO WHAT?! MURDER PEOPLE ON 355?! IT WAS A TEN-CAR PILEUP 'CAUSE OF HIS STUPID SIGN! TEN CARS!
IF ONLY.
EXCUSE ME, MARSHALL?
YOU HAPPEN TO GET A LUNCH BREAK?
SO, WHAT. YOU COME TO ADMIRE YOUR HANDIWORK?
WHY WOULD I WANT TO TALK TO YOU?
NO. COME ON. I JUST THOUGHT WE SHOULD TALK.

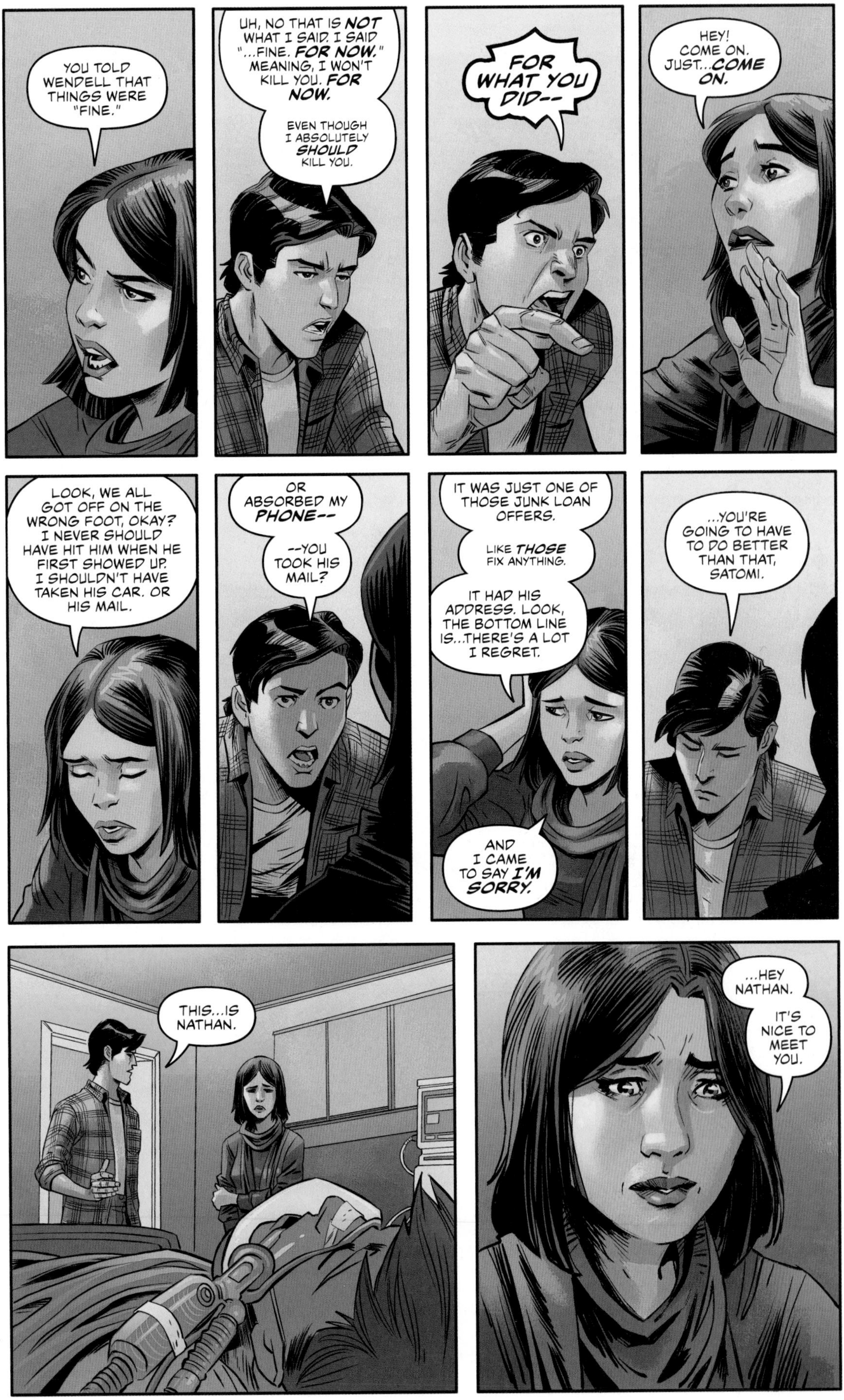

YOU TOLD WENDELL THAT THINGS WERE "FINE."
UH, NO THAT IS NOT WHAT I SAID. I SAID "...FINE. FOR NOW." MEANING, I WON'T KILL YOU. FOR NOW.
EVEN THOUGH I ABSOLUTELY SHOULD KILL YOU.
FOR WHAT YOU DID--
HEY! COME ON. JUST...COME ON.
LOOK, WE ALL GOT OFF ON THE WRONG FOOT, OKAY? I NEVER SHOULD HAVE HIT HIM WHEN HE FIRST SHOWED UP. I SHOULDN'T HAVE TAKEN HIS CAR. OR HIS MAIL.
OR ABSORBED MY PHONE--
--YOU TOOK HIS MAIL?
IT WAS JUST ONE OF THOSE JUNK LOAN OFFERS.
LIKE THOSE FIX ANYTHING.
IT HAD HIS ADDRESS. LOOK, THE BOTTOM LINE IS...THERE'S A LOT I REGRET.
AND I CAME TO SAY I'M SORRY.
...YOU'RE GOING TO HAVE TO DO BETTER THAN THAT, SATOMI.
THIS...IS NATHAN.
...HEY NATHAN.
IT'S NICE TO MEET YOU.

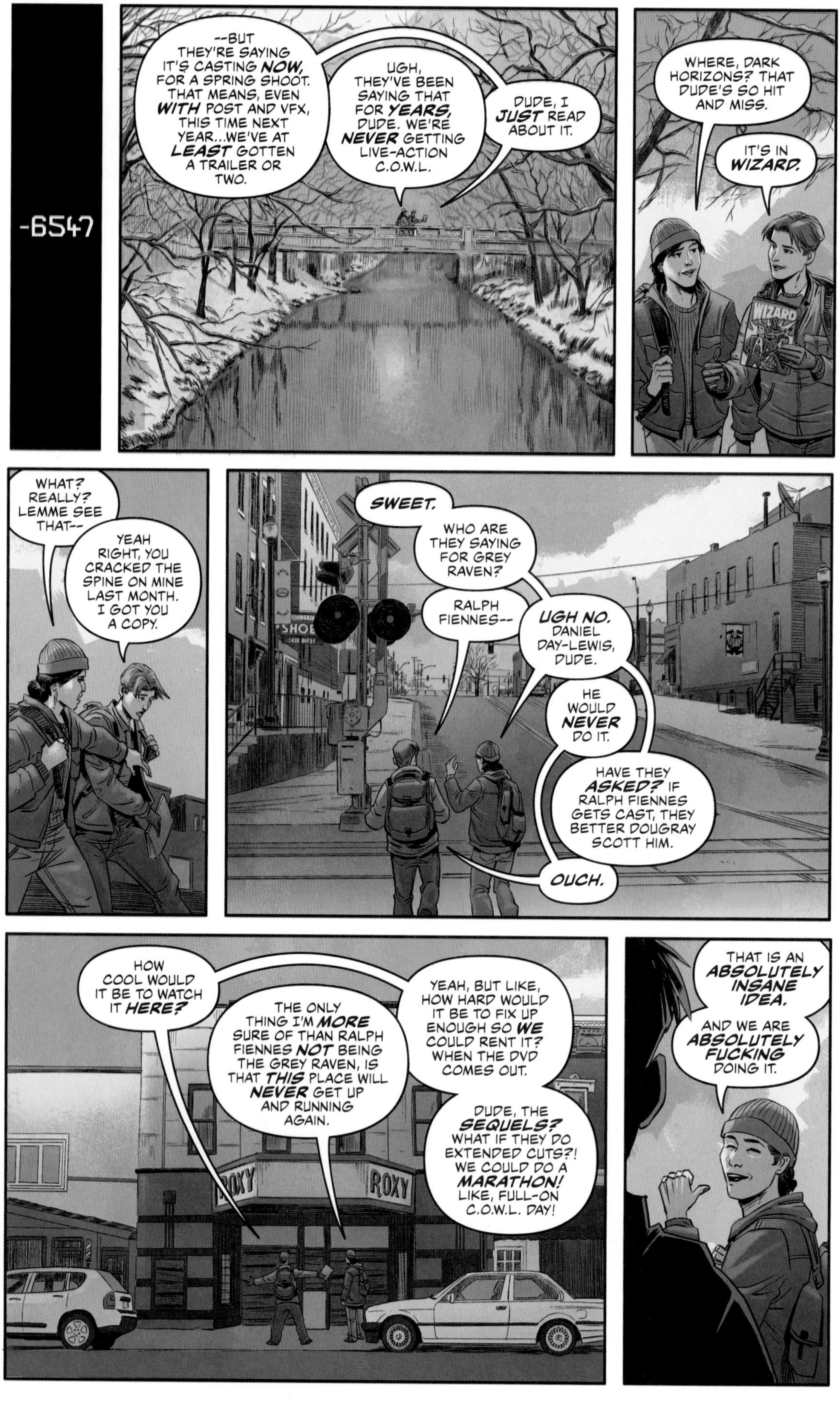

-6547
--BUT THEY'RE SAYING IT'S CASTING NOW, FOR A SPRING SHOOT. THAT MEANS, EVEN WITH POST AND VFX, THIS TIME NEXT YEAR...WE'VE AT LEAST GOTTEN A TRAILER OR TWO.
UGH, THEY'VE BEEN SAYING THAT FOR YEARS, DUDE. WE'RE NEVER GETTING LIVE-ACTION C.O.W.L.
DUDE, I JUST READ ABOUT IT.
WHERE, DARK HORIZONS? THAT DUDE'S SO HIT AND MISS.
IT'S IN WIZARD.
WIZARD
WHAT? REALLY? LEMME SEE THAT--
YEAH RIGHT, YOU CRACKED THE SPINE ON MINE LAST MONTH. I GOT YOU A COPY.
SWEET.
WHO ARE THEY SAYING FOR GREY RAVEN?
RALPH FIENNES--
UGH NO. DANIEL DAY-LEWIS, DUDE.
HE WOULD NEVER DO IT.
HAVE THEY ASKED? IF RALPH FIENNES GETS CAST, THEY BETTER DOUGRAY SCOTT HIM.
OUCH.
HOW COOL WOULD IT BE TO WATCH IT HERE?
THE ONLY THING I'M MORE SURE OF THAN RALPH FIENNES NOT BEING THE GREY RAVEN, IS THAT THIS PLACE WILL NEVER GET UP AND RUNNING AGAIN.
YEAH, BUT LIKE, HOW HARD WOULD IT BE TO FIX UP ENOUGH SO WE COULD RENT IT? WHEN THE DVD COMES OUT.
DUDE, THE SEQUELS? WHAT IF THEY DO EXTENDED CUTS?! WE COULD DO A MARATHON! LIKE, FULL-ON C.O.W.L. DAY!
ROXY
ROXY
THAT IS AN ABSOLUTELY INSANE IDEA.
AND WE ARE ABSOLUTELY FUCKING DOING IT.

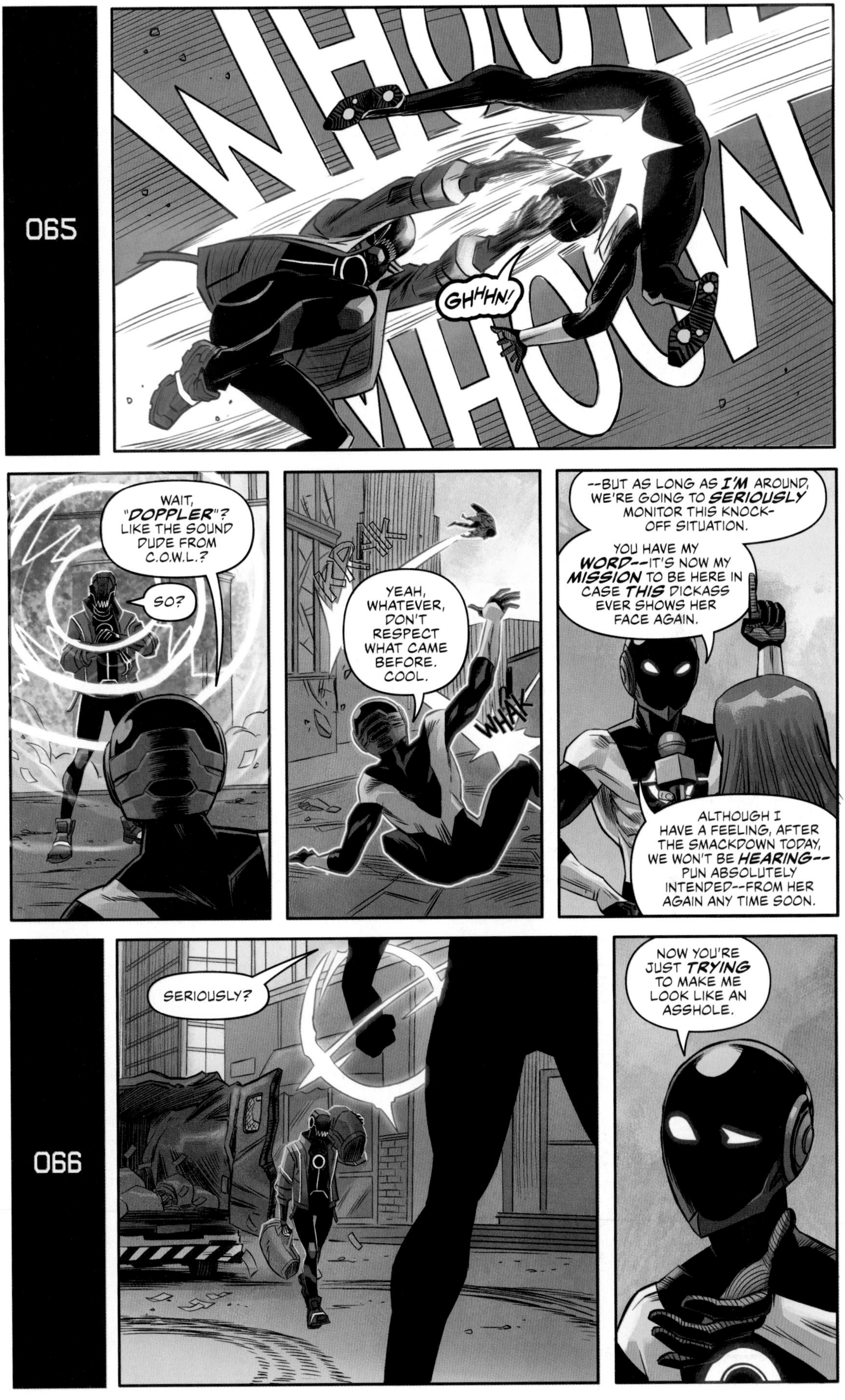
065
GHHHN!
WAIT, "DOPPLER"? LIKE THE SOUND DUDE FROM C.O.W.L.?
SO?
KRAK
YEAH, WHATEVER, DON'T RESPECT WHAT CAME BEFORE. COOL.
WHAK
--BUT AS LONG AS I'M AROUND, WE'RE GOING TO SERIOUSLY MONITOR THIS KNOCK-OFF SITUATION.
YOU HAVE MY WORD--IT'S NOW MY MISSION TO BE HERE IN CASE THIS DICKASS EVER SHOWS HER FACE AGAIN.
ALTHOUGH I HAVE A FEELING, AFTER THE SMACKDOWN TODAY, WE WON'T BE HEARING--PUN ABSOLUTELY INTENDED--FROM HER AGAIN ANY TIME SOON.
066
SERIOUSLY?
NOW YOU'RE JUST TRYING TO MAKE ME LOOK LIKE AN ASSHOLE.

090

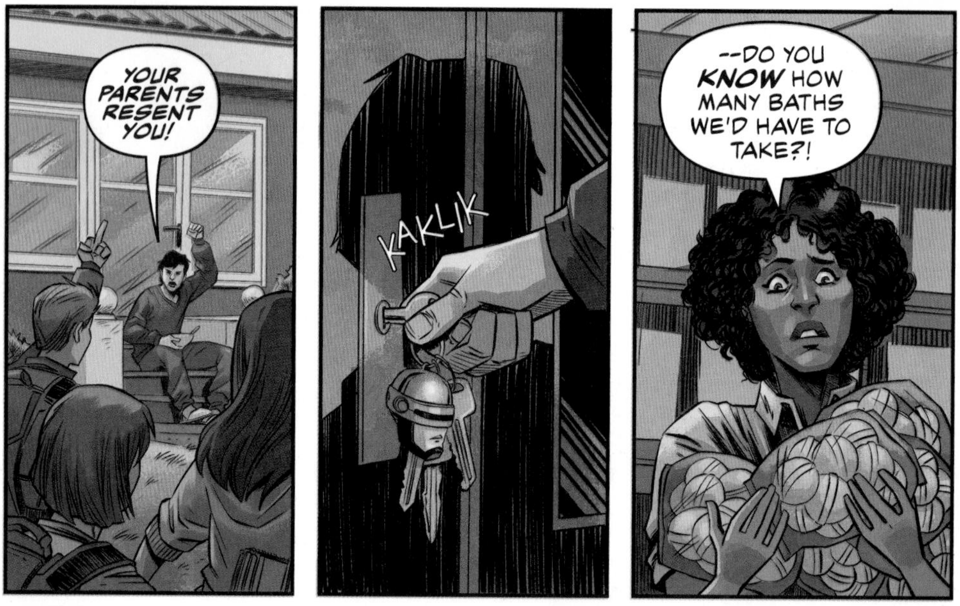

YOUR PARENTS RESENT YOU!
KAKLIK
--DO YOU KNOW HOW MANY BATHS WE'D HAVE TO TAKE?!

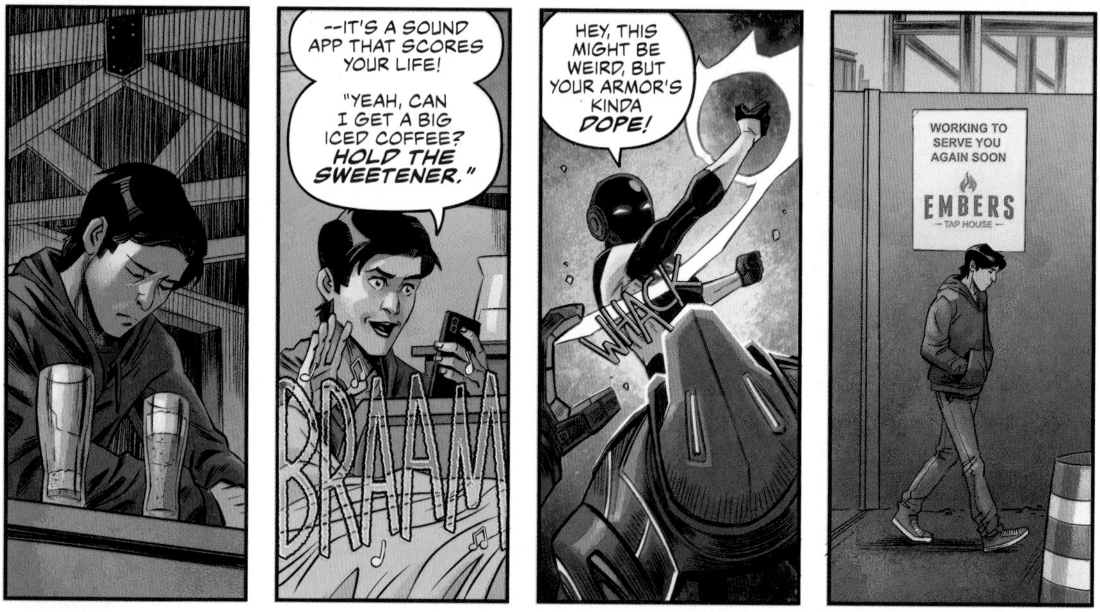

--IT'S A SOUND APP THAT SCORES YOUR LIFE!
"YEAH, CAN I GET A BIG ICED COFFEE? HOLD THE SWEETENER."
BRAAM
HEY, THIS MIGHT BE WEIRD, BUT YOUR ARMOR'S KINDA DOPE!
WHACK
WORKING TO SERVE YOU AGAIN SOON
EMBERS
TAP HOUSE

152

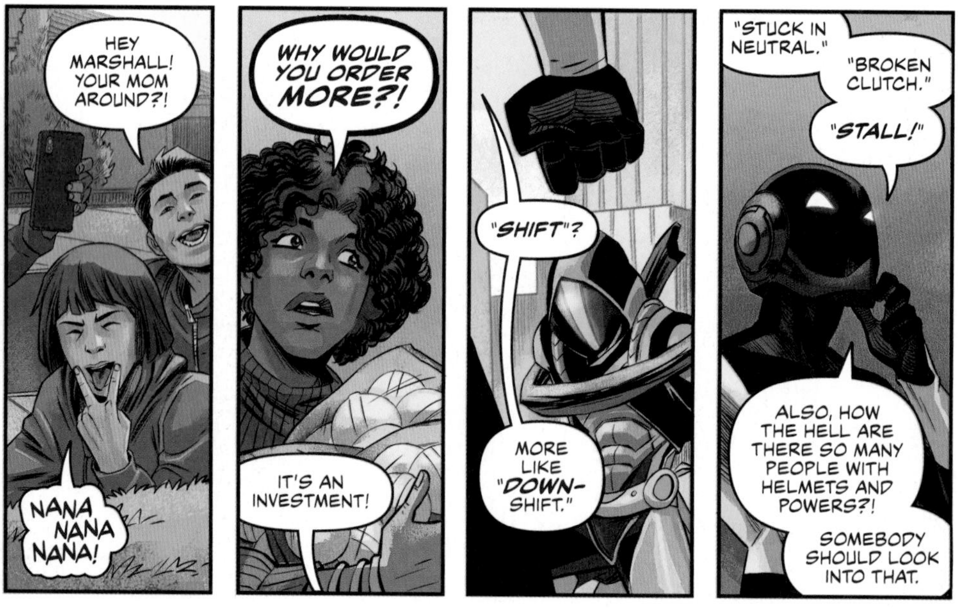

HEY MARSHALL! YOUR MOM AROUND?!
NANA NANA NANA!
WHY WOULD YOU ORDER MORE?!
IT'S AN INVESTMENT!
"SHIFT"?
MORE LIKE "DOWN-SHIFT."
"STUCK IN NEUTRAL."
"BROKEN CLUTCH."
"STALL!"
ALSO, HOW THE HELL ARE THERE SO MANY PEOPLE WITH HELMETS AND POWERS?!
SOMEBODY SHOULD LOOK INTO THAT.

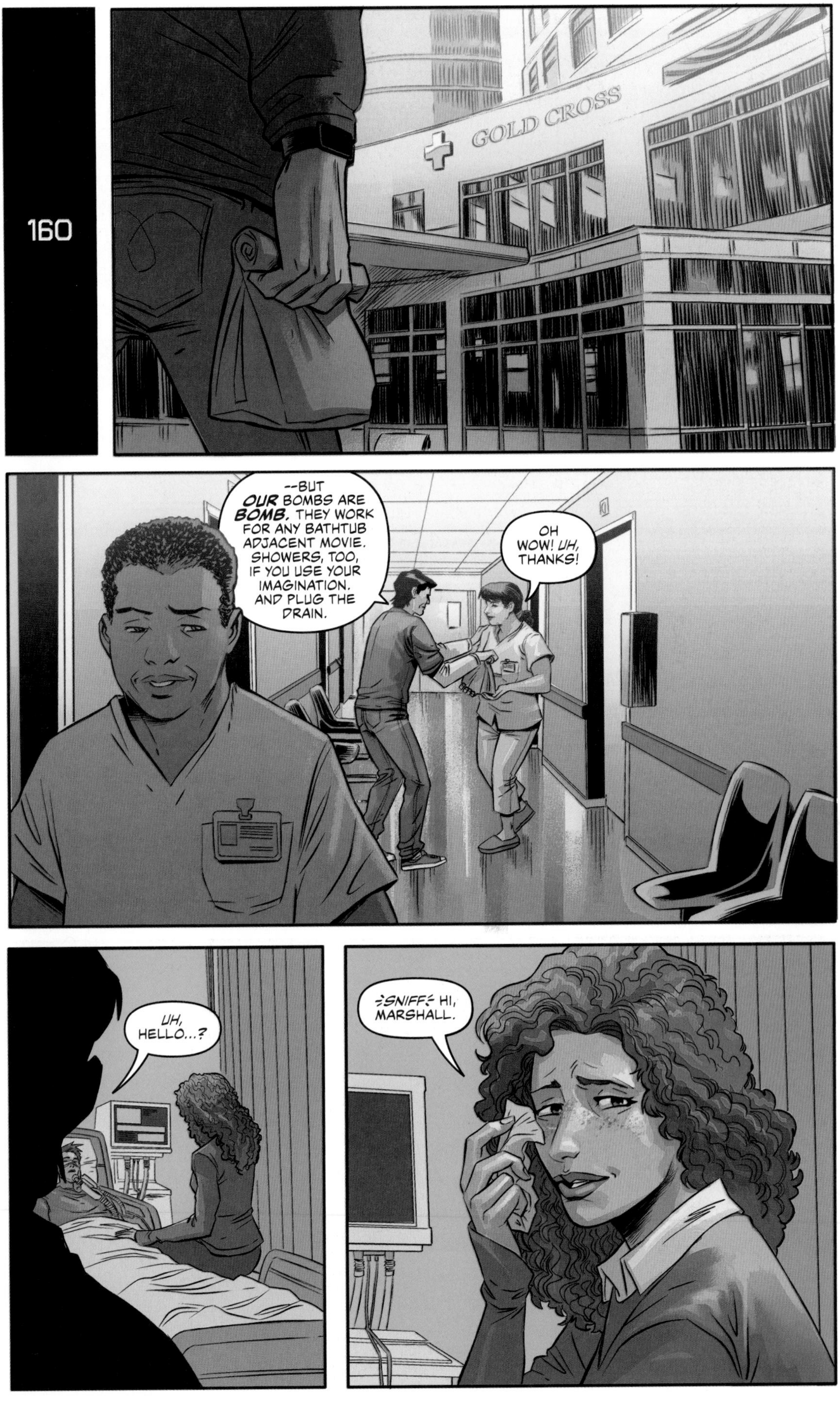
GOLD CROSS
--BUT OUR BOMBS ARE BOMB. THEY WORK FOR ANY BATHTUB ADJACENT MOVIE. SHOWERS, TOO, IF YOU USE YOUR IMAGINATION. AND PLUG THE DRAIN.
OH WOW! UH, THANKS!
UH, HELLO...?
SNIFF HI, MARSHALL.

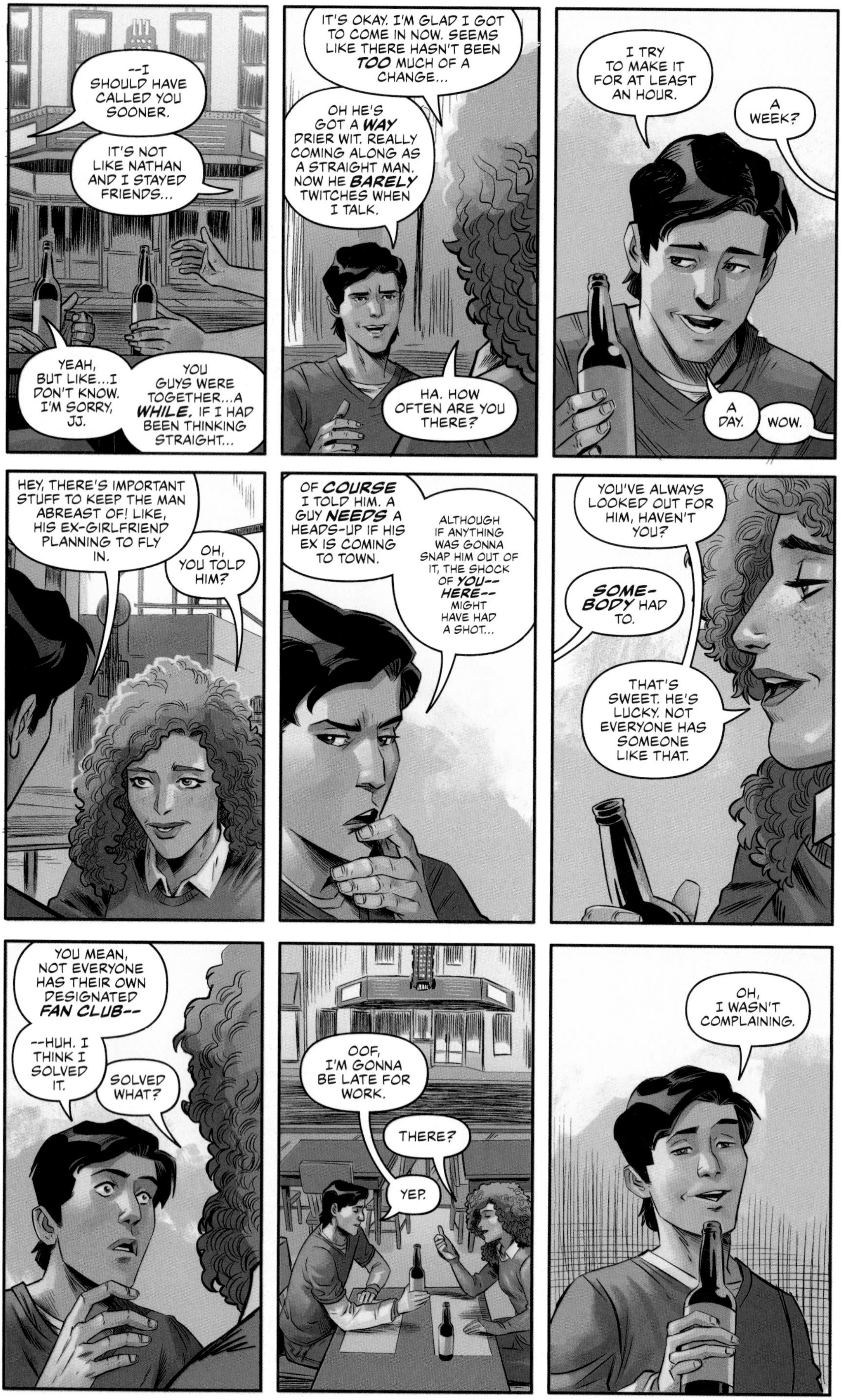
--I SHOULD HAVE CALLED YOU SOONER.
IT'S NOT LIKE NATHAN AND I STAYED FRIENDS...
YEAH, BUT LIKE...I DON'T KNOW. I'M SORRY, JJ.
YOU GUYS WERE TOGETHER...A WHILE. IF I HAD BEEN THINKING STRAIGHT...
IT'S OKAY. I'M GLAD I GOT TO COME IN NOW. SEEMS LIKE THERE HASN'T BEEN TOO MUCH OF A CHANGE...
OH HE'S GOT A WAY DRIER WIT. REALLY COMING ALONG AS A STRAIGHT MAN. NOW HE BARELY TWITCHES WHEN I TALK.
HA. HOW OFTEN ARE YOU THERE?
I TRY TO MAKE IT FOR AT LEAST AN HOUR.
A WEEK?
A DAY.
WOW.
HEY, THERE'S IMPORTANT STUFF TO KEEP THE MAN ABREAST OF! LIKE, HIS EX-GIRLFRIEND PLANNING TO FLY IN.
OH, YOU TOLD HIM?
OF COURSE I TOLD HIM. A GUY NEEDS A HEADS-UP IF HIS EX IS COMING TO TOWN.
ALTHOUGH IF ANYTHING WAS GONNA SNAP HIM OUT OF IT, THE SHOCK OF YOU--HERE--MIGHT HAVE HAD A SHOT...
YOU'VE ALWAYS LOOKED OUT FOR HIM, HAVEN'T YOU?
SOME-BODY HAD TO.
THAT'S SWEET. HE'S LUCKY. NOT EVERYONE HAS SOMEONE LIKE THAT.
YOU MEAN, NOT EVERYONE HAS THEIR OWN DESIGNATED FAN CLUB--
--HUH. I THINK I SOLVED IT.
SOLVED WHAT?
OOF, I'M GONNA BE LATE FOR WORK.
THERE?
YEP.
OH, I WASN'T COMPLAINING.

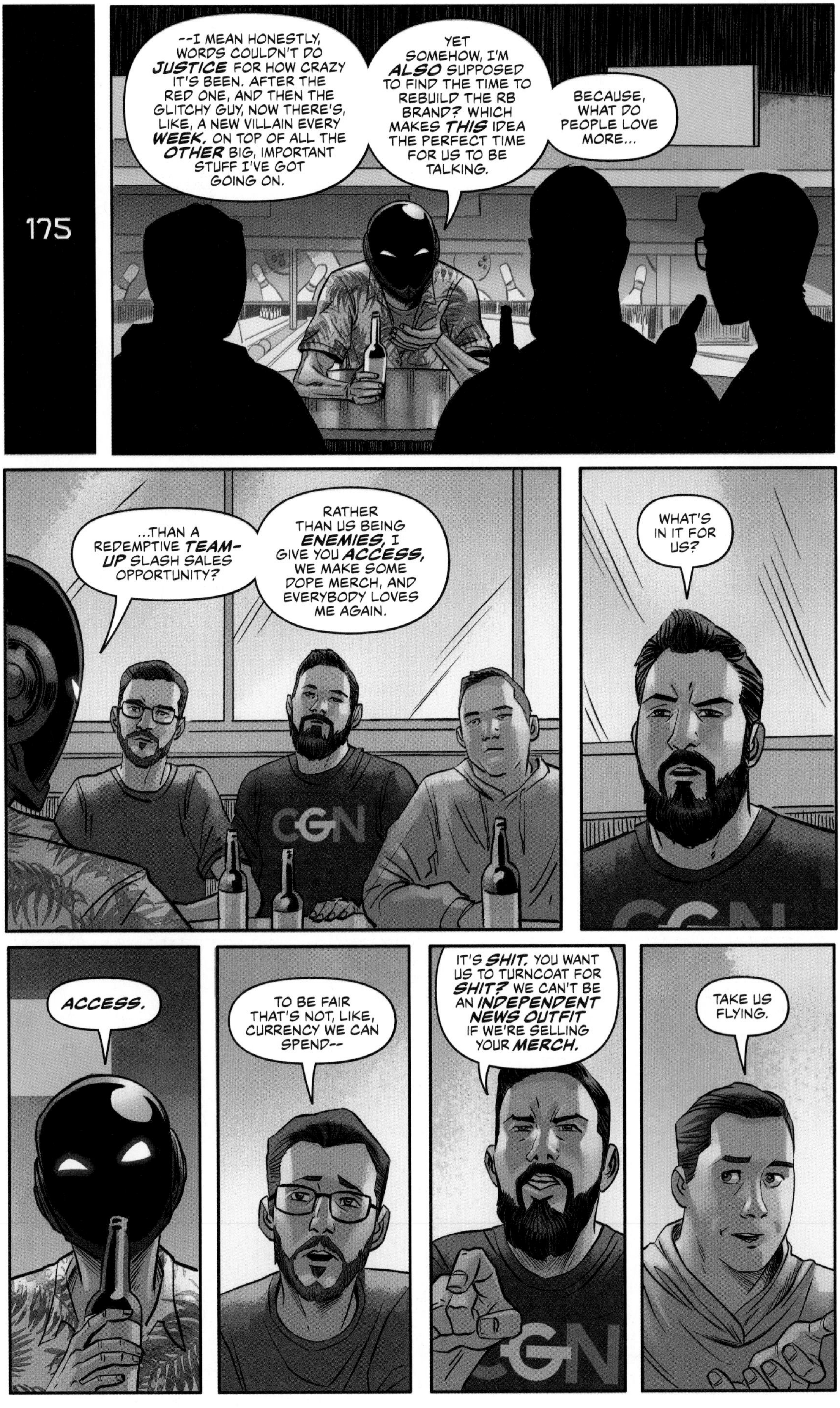
175
--I MEAN HONESTLY, WORDS COULDN'T DO JUSTICE FOR HOW CRAZY IT'S BEEN. AFTER THE RED ONE, AND THEN THE GLITCHY GUY, NOW THERE'S, LIKE, A NEW VILLAIN EVERY WEEK. ON TOP OF ALL THE OTHER BIG, IMPORTANT STUFF I'VE GOT GOING ON.
YET SOMEHOW, I'M ALSO SUPPOSED TO FIND THE TIME TO REBUILD THE RB BRAND? WHICH MAKES THIS IDEA THE PERFECT TIME FOR US TO BE TALKING.
BECAUSE, WHAT DO PEOPLE LOVE MORE...
...THAN A REDEMPTIVE TEAM-UP SLASH SALES OPPORTUNITY?
RATHER THAN US BEING ENEMIES, I GIVE YOU ACCESS, WE MAKE SOME DOPE MERCH, AND EVERYBODY LOVES ME AGAIN.
WHAT'S IN IT FOR US?
ACCESS.
TO BE FAIR THAT'S NOT, LIKE, CURRENCY WE CAN SPEND--
IT'S SHIT. YOU WANT US TO TURNCOAT FOR SHIT? WE CAN'T BE AN INDEPENDENT NEWS OUTFIT IF WE'RE SELLING YOUR MERCH.
TAKE US FLYING.

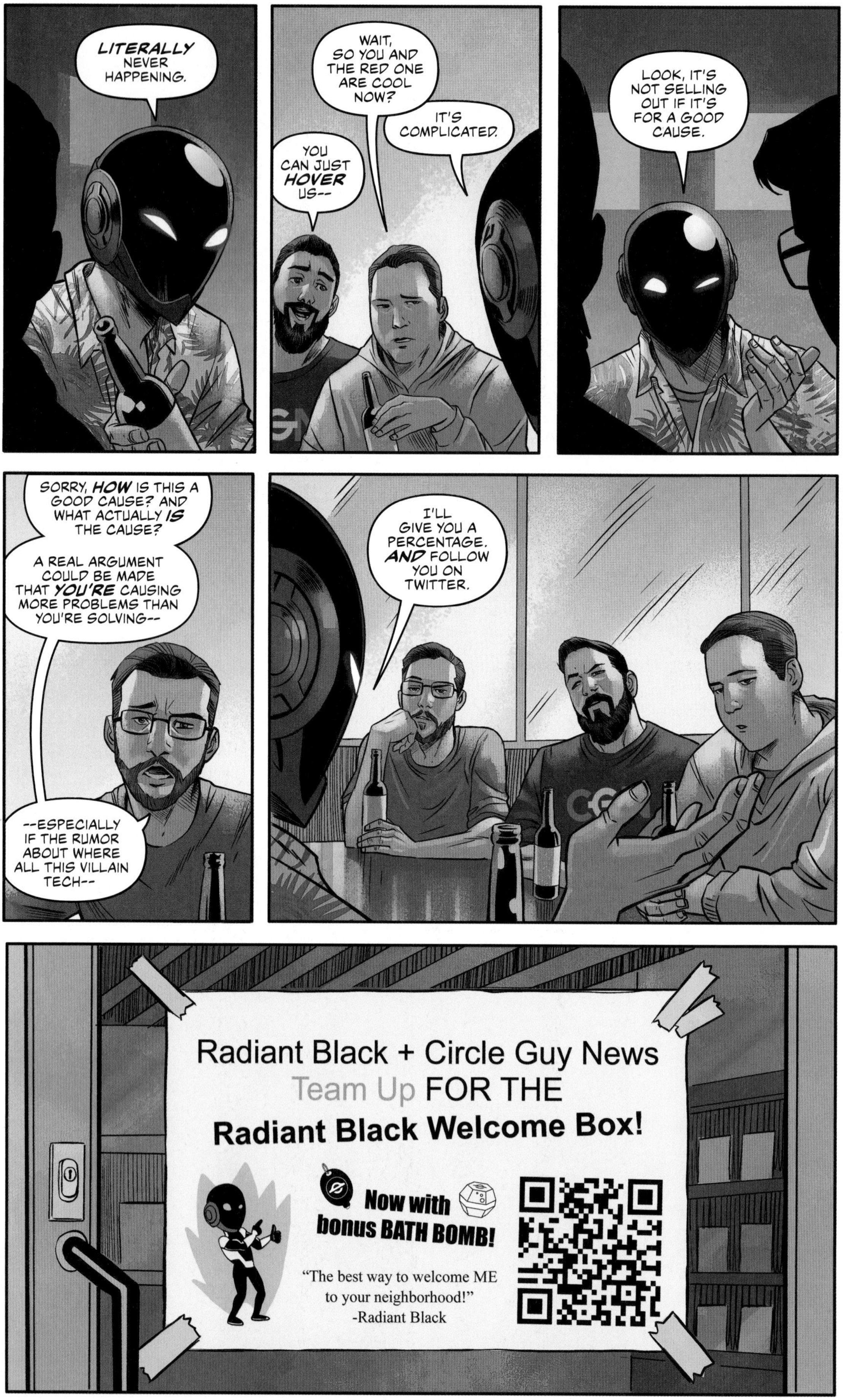
LITERALLY NEVER HAPPENING.
WAIT, SO YOU AND THE RED ONE ARE COOL NOW?
YOU CAN JUST HOVER US--
IT'S COMPLICATED.
LOOK, IT'S NOT SELLING OUT IF IT'S FOR A GOOD CAUSE.
SORRY, HOW IS THIS A GOOD CAUSE? AND WHAT ACTUALLY IS THE CAUSE?
A REAL ARGUMENT COULD BE MADE THAT YOU'RE CAUSING MORE PROBLEMS THAN YOU'RE SOLVING--
--ESPECIALLY IF THE RUMOR ABOUT WHERE ALL THIS VILLAIN TECH--
I'LL GIVE YOU A PERCENTAGE. AND FOLLOW YOU ON TWITTER.
Radiant Black + Circle Guy News
Team Up FOR THE
Radiant Black Welcome Box!
Now with bonus BATH BOMB!
"The best way to welcome ME to your neighborhood!"
-Radiant Black

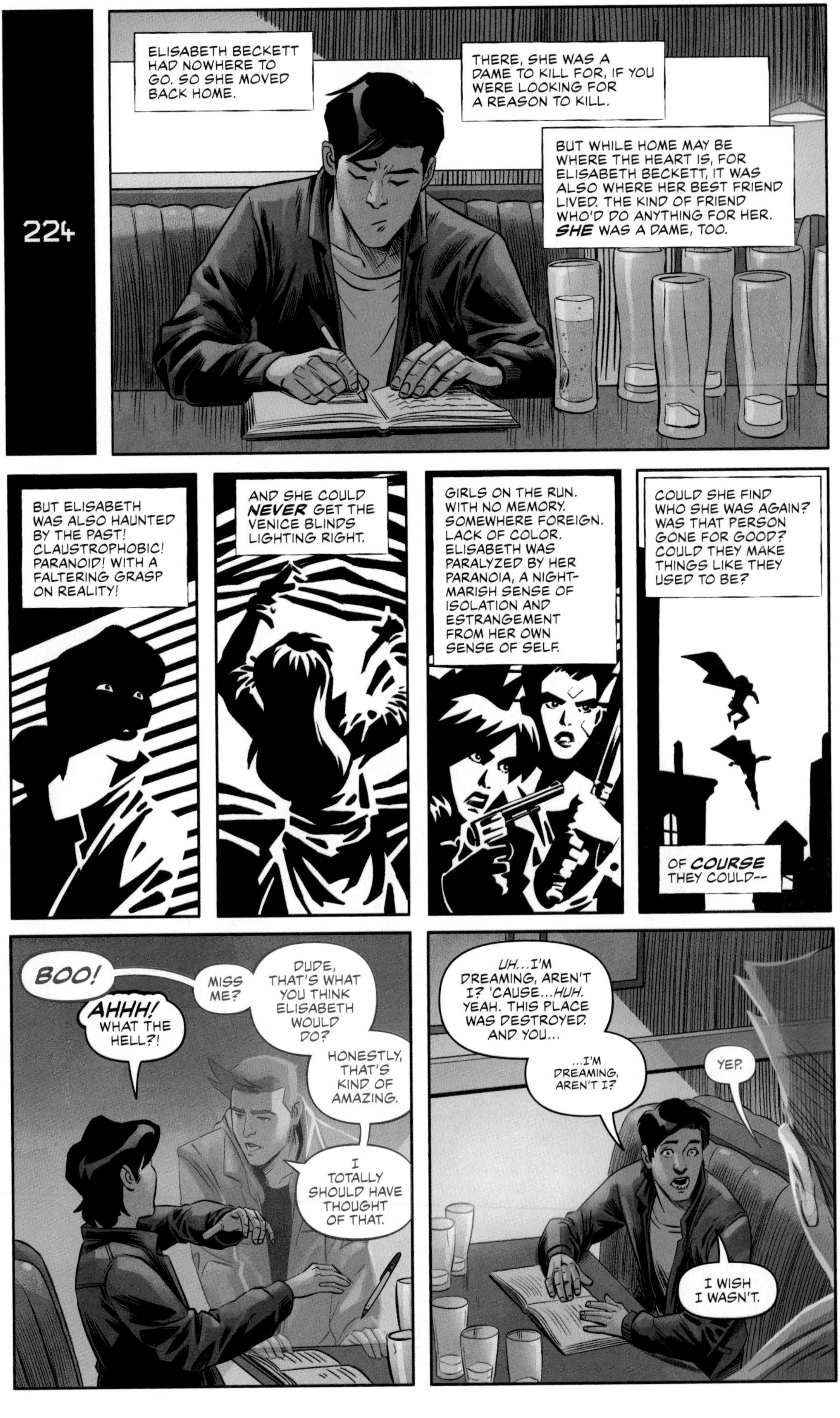
ELISABETH BECKETT HAD NOWHERE TO GO. SO SHE MOVED BACK HOME.
THERE, SHE WAS A DAME TO KILL FOR, IF YOU WERE LOOKING FOR A REASON TO KILL.
BUT WHILE HOME MAY BE WHERE THE HEART IS, FOR ELISABETH BECKETT, IT WAS ALSO WHERE HER BEST FRIEND LIVED. THE KIND OF FRIEND WHO'D DO ANYTHING FOR HER. SHE WAS A DAME, TOO.
BUT ELISABETH WAS ALSO HAUNTED BY THE PAST! CLAUSTROPHOBIC! PARANOID! WITH A FALTERING GRASP ON REALITY!
AND SHE COULD NEVER GET THE VENICE BLINDS LIGHTING RIGHT.
GIRLS ON THE RUN. WITH NO MEMORY. SOMEWHERE FOREIGN. LACK OF COLOR. ELISABETH WAS PARALYZED BY HER PARANOIA, A NIGHT-MARISH SENSE OF ISOLATION AND ESTRANGEMENT FROM HER OWN SENSE OF SELF.
COULD SHE FIND WHO SHE WAS AGAIN? WAS THAT PERSON GONE FOR GOOD? COULD THEY MAKE THINGS LIKE THEY USED TO BE?
OF COURSE THEY COULD--
BOO!
MISS ME?
AHHH! WHAT THE HELL?!
DUDE, THAT'S WHAT YOU THINK ELISABETH WOULD DO?
HONESTLY, THAT'S KIND OF AMAZING.
I TOTALLY SHOULD HAVE THOUGHT OF THAT.
UH...I'M DREAMING, AREN'T I? 'CAUSE...HUH. YEAH. THIS PLACE WAS DESTROYED. AND YOU...
...I'M DREAMING, AREN'T I?
YEP.
I WISH I WASN'T.

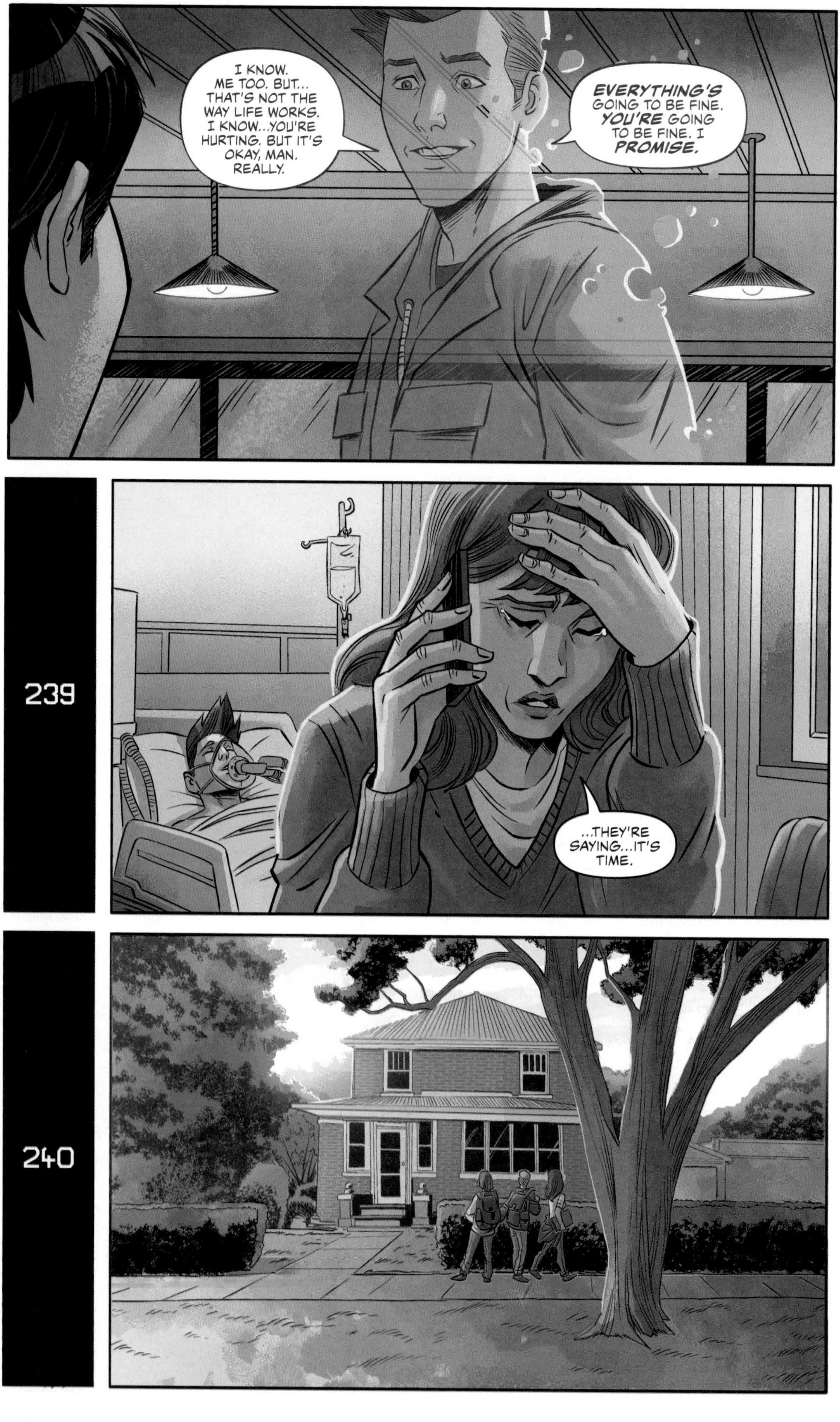
I KNOW. ME TOO. BUT... THAT'S NOT THE WAY LIFE WORKS. I KNOW...YOU'RE HURTING. BUT IT'S OKAY, MAN. REALLY.
EVERYTHING'S GOING TO BE FINE. YOU'RE GOING TO BE FINE. I PROMISE.
239
...THEY'RE SAYING...IT'S TIME.
240

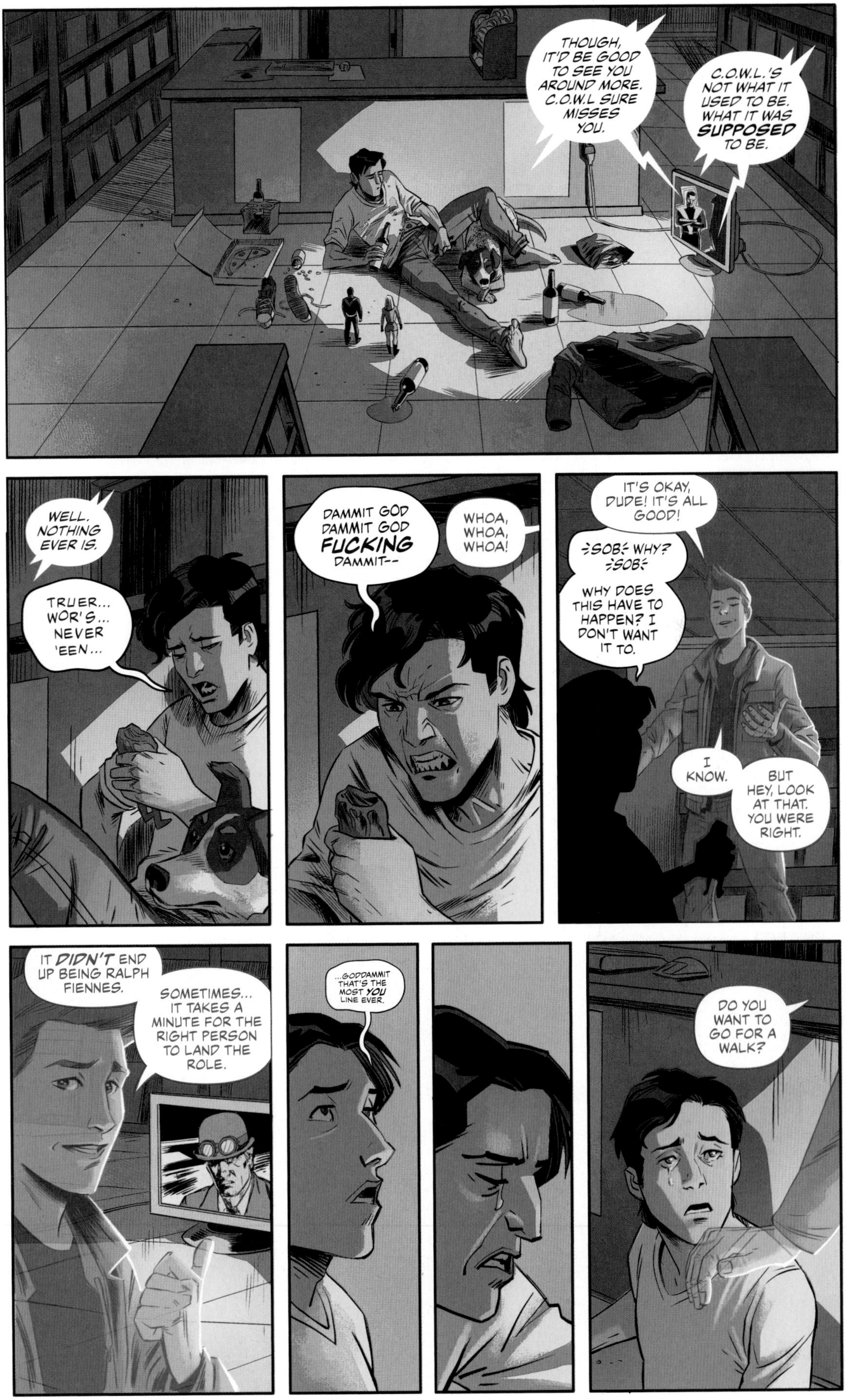
THOUGH, IT'D BE GOOD TO SEE YOU AROUND MORE. C.O.W.L SURE MISSES YOU.
C.O.W.L.'S NOT WHAT IT USED TO BE. WHAT IT WAS SUPPOSED TO BE.
WELL. NOTHING EVER IS.
TRUER... WOR'S... NEVER 'EEN...
DAMMIT GOD DAMMIT GOD FUCKING DAMMIT--
WHOA, WHOA, WHOA!
IT'S OKAY, DUDE! IT'S ALL GOOD!
SOB WHY? *SOB*
WHY DOES THIS HAVE TO HAPPEN? I DON'T WANT IT TO.
I KNOW.
BUT HEY, LOOK AT THAT. YOU WERE RIGHT.
IT DIDN'T END UP BEING RALPH FIENNES.
SOMETIMES... IT TAKES A MINUTE FOR THE RIGHT PERSON TO LAND THE ROLE.
...GODDAMMIT THAT'S THE MOST YOU LINE EVER.
DO YOU WANT TO GO FOR A WALK?

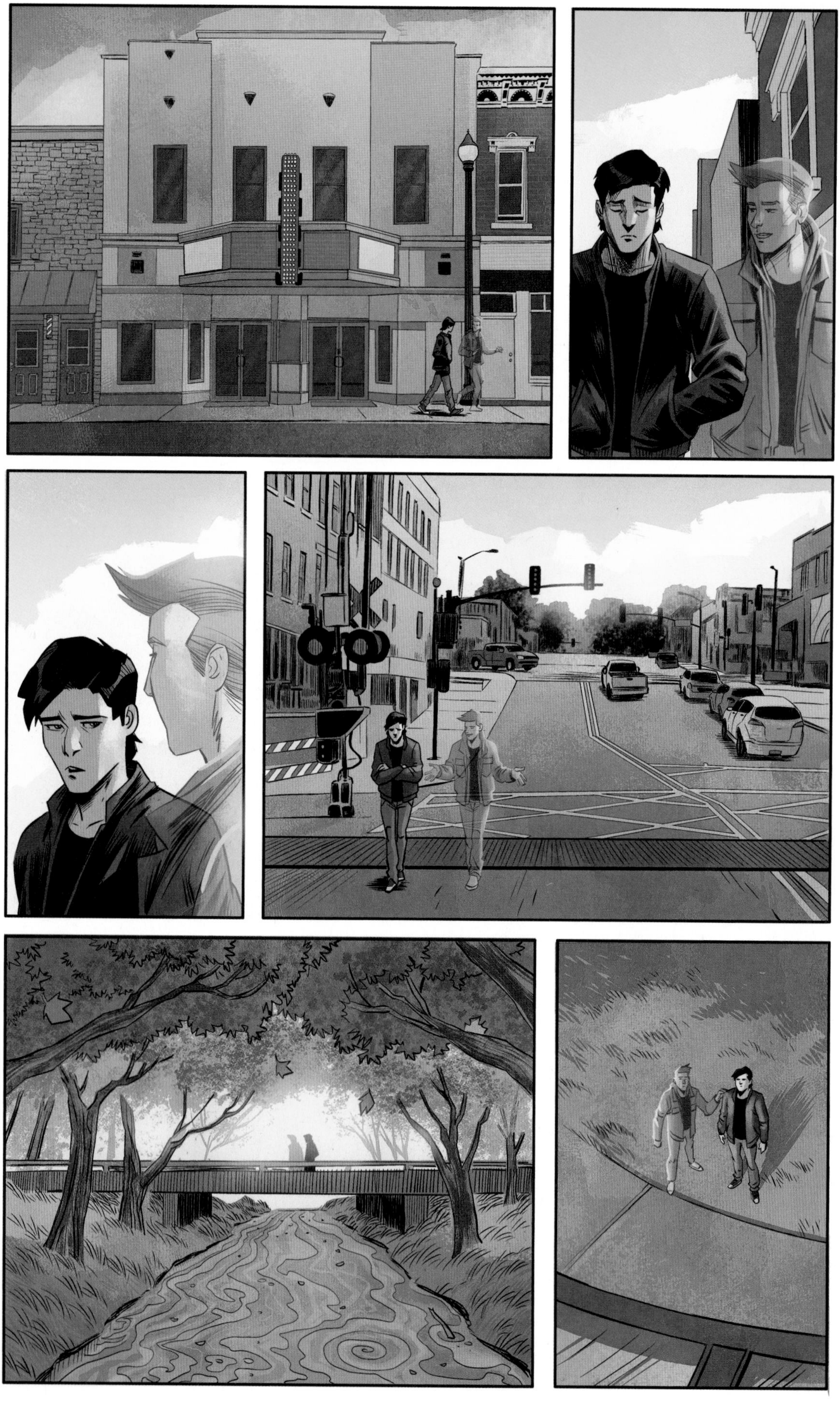

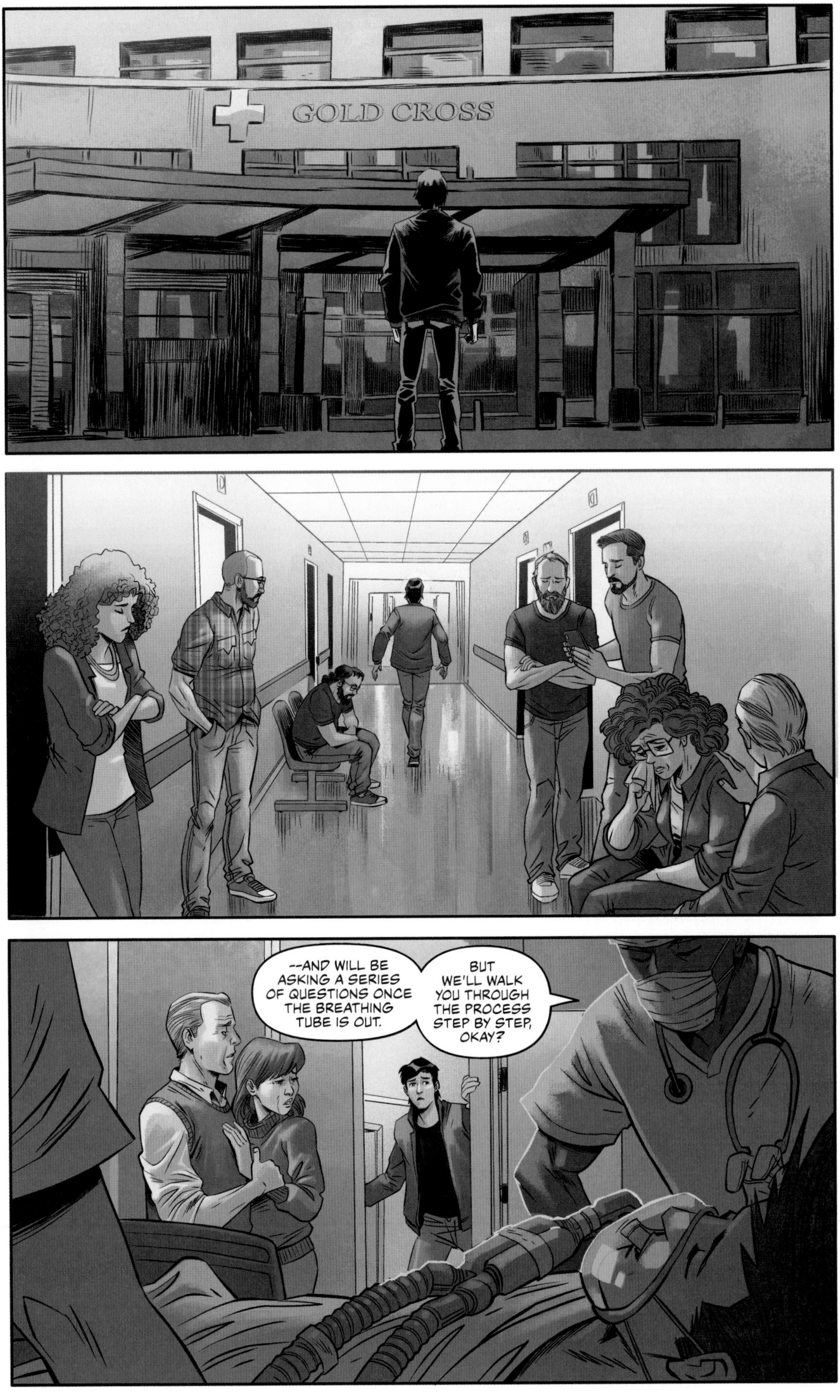
GOLD CROSS
--AND WILL BE ASKING A SERIES OF QUESTIONS ONCE THE BREATHING TUBE IS OUT.
BUT WE'LL WALK YOU THROUGH THE PROCESS STEP BY STEP, OKAY?

OKAY...

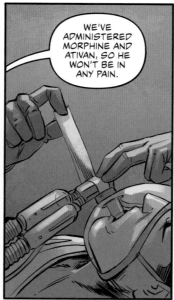

WE'VE ADMINISTERED MORPHINE AND ATIVAN, SO HE WON'T BE IN ANY PAIN.

ALL RIGHT, WE'RE GOING TO GO AHEAD AND START REMOVING THE TUBE...

ELISABETH, CAN YOU HAND ME THE SCISSORS?

WAIT...

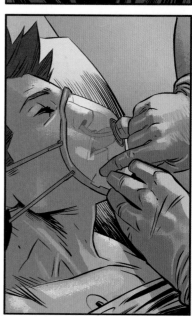

WAIT, HOLD ON, I KNOW I HAVE IT...

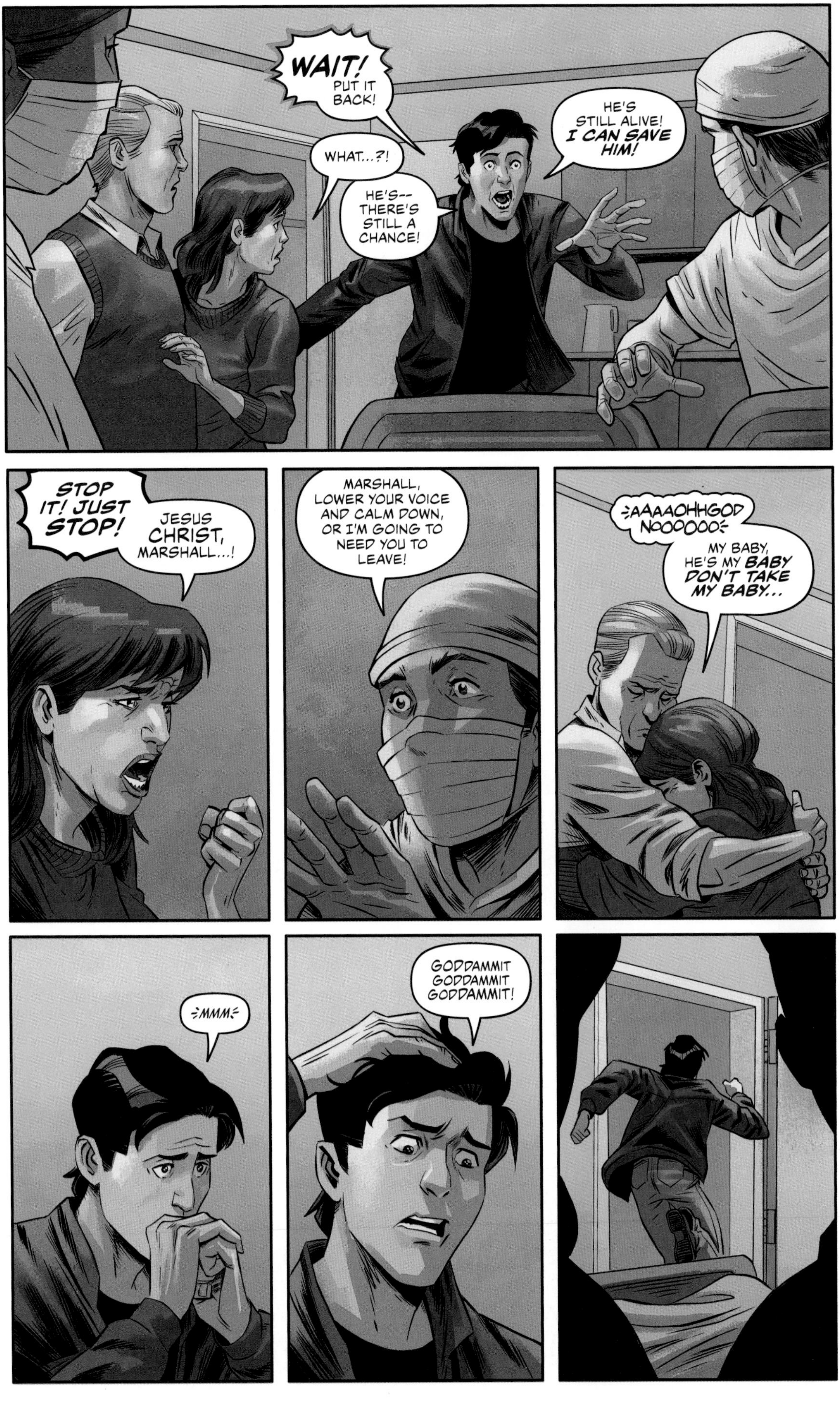
WAIT! PUT IT BACK!
WHAT...?!
HE'S-- THERE'S STILL A CHANCE!
HE'S STILL ALIVE! I CAN SAVE HIM!
STOP IT! JUST STOP!
JESUS CHRIST, MARSHALL...!
MARSHALL, LOWER YOUR VOICE AND CALM DOWN, OR I'M GOING TO NEED YOU TO LEAVE!
AAAAOHHGOD NOOOOOO
MY BABY, HE'S MY BABY DON'T TAKE MY BABY...
MMM
GODDAMMIT GODDAMMIT GODDAMMIT!

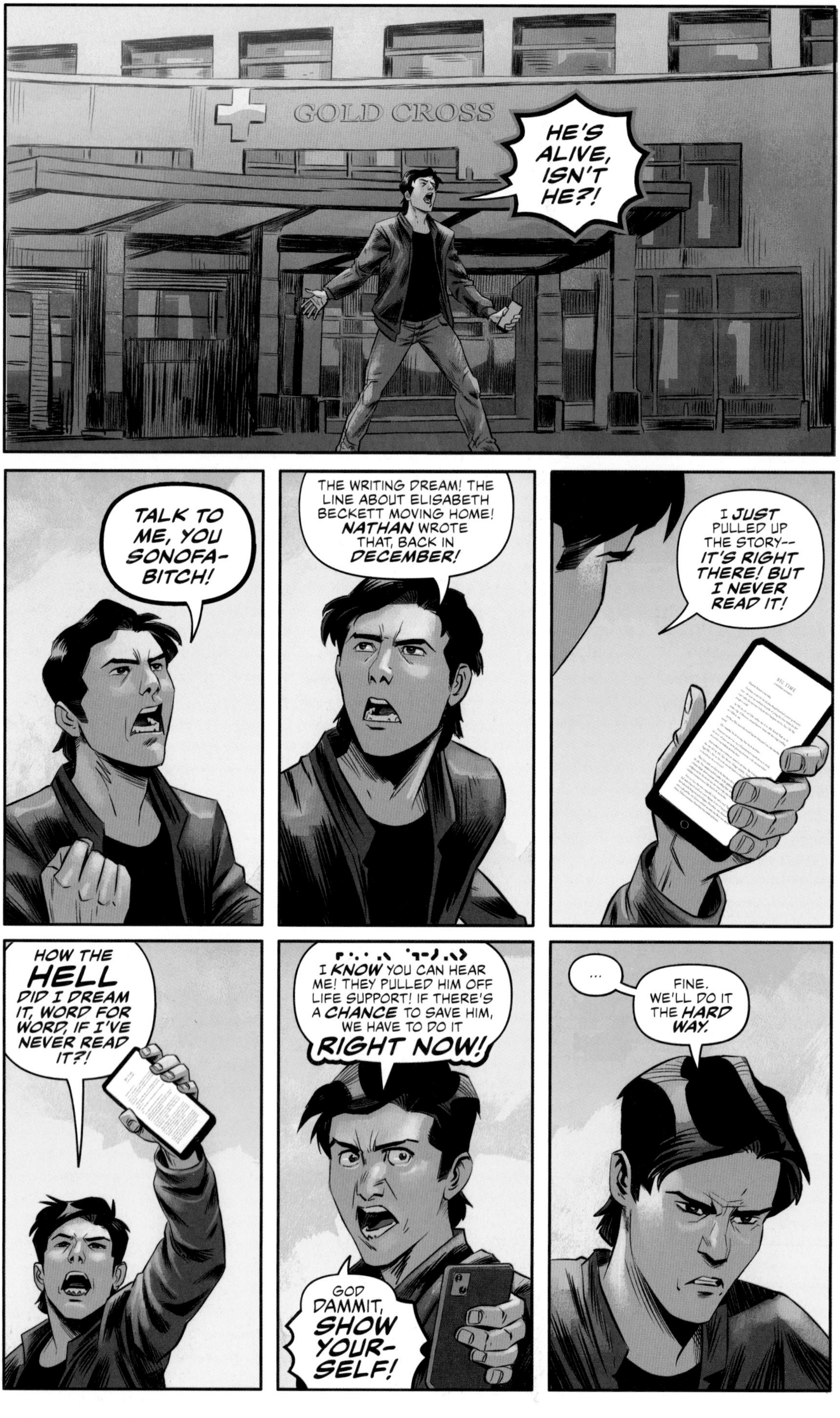
GOLD CROSS
HE'S ALIVE, ISN'T HE?!
TALK TO ME, YOU SONOFA-BITCH!
THE WRITING DREAM! THE LINE ABOUT ELISABETH BECKETT MOVING HOME! NATHAN WROTE THAT, BACK IN DECEMBER!
I JUST PULLED UP THE STORY-- IT'S RIGHT THERE! BUT I NEVER READ IT!
HOW THE HELL DID I DREAM IT, WORD FOR WORD, IF I'VE NEVER READ IT?!
I KNOW YOU CAN HEAR ME! THEY PULLED HIM OFF LIFE SUPPORT! IF THERE'S A CHANCE TO SAVE HIM, WE HAVE TO DO IT RIGHT NOW!
GOD DAMMIT, SHOW YOUR-SELF!
...
FINE. WE'LL DO IT THE HARD WAY.

YOU DON'T WANT TO *TALK?* COOL.

WHOOO

BUT I'M NOT GETTING OFF THESE TRACKS UNTIL WE *DO.*

WHOOO WHOOO

GOD DAMMIT IF I DIE, IT *ABSOLUTELY* AFFECTS YOU!

HOO

MAYBE SOMEBODY *WORSE* THAN ME BONDS WITH THIS GODDAMN THING--

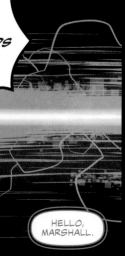

HELLO, MARSHALL.

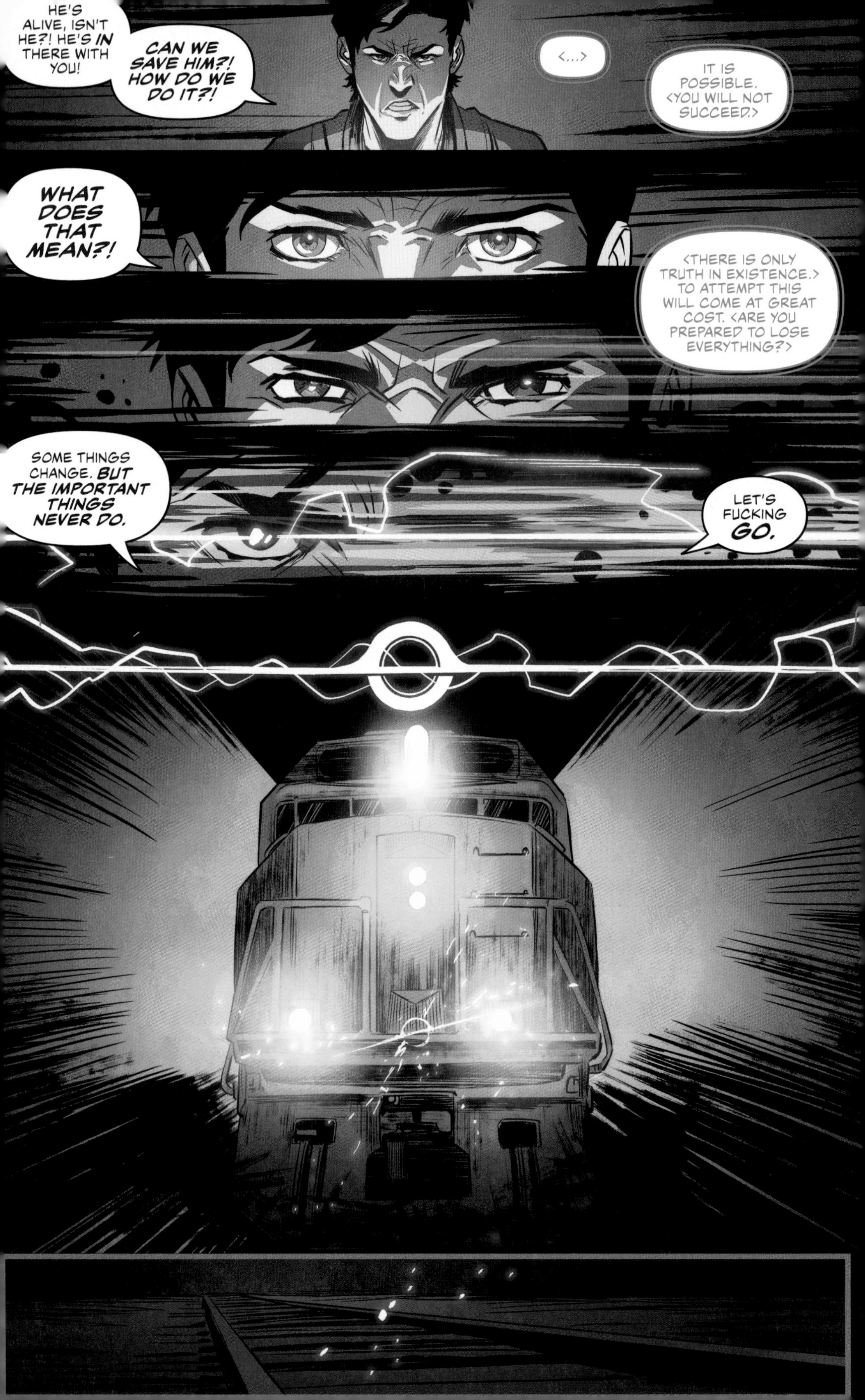

HE'S ALIVE, ISN'T HE?! HE'S IN THERE WITH YOU!
CAN WE SAVE HIM?! HOW DO WE DO IT?!
<...>
IT IS POSSIBLE. <YOU WILL NOT SUCCEED.>
WHAT DOES THAT MEAN?!
<THERE IS ONLY TRUTH IN EXISTENCE.> TO ATTEMPT THIS WILL COME AT GREAT COST. <ARE YOU PREPARED TO LOSE EVERYTHING?>
SOME THINGS CHANGE. BUT THE IMPORTANT THINGS NEVER DO.
LET'S FUCKING GO.

CHAPTER TEN

TITLE

Existence

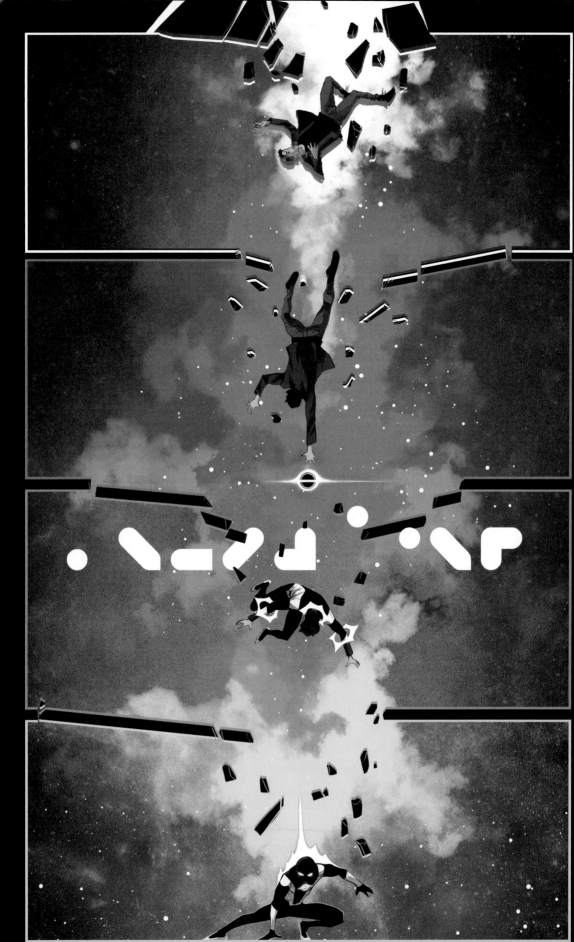

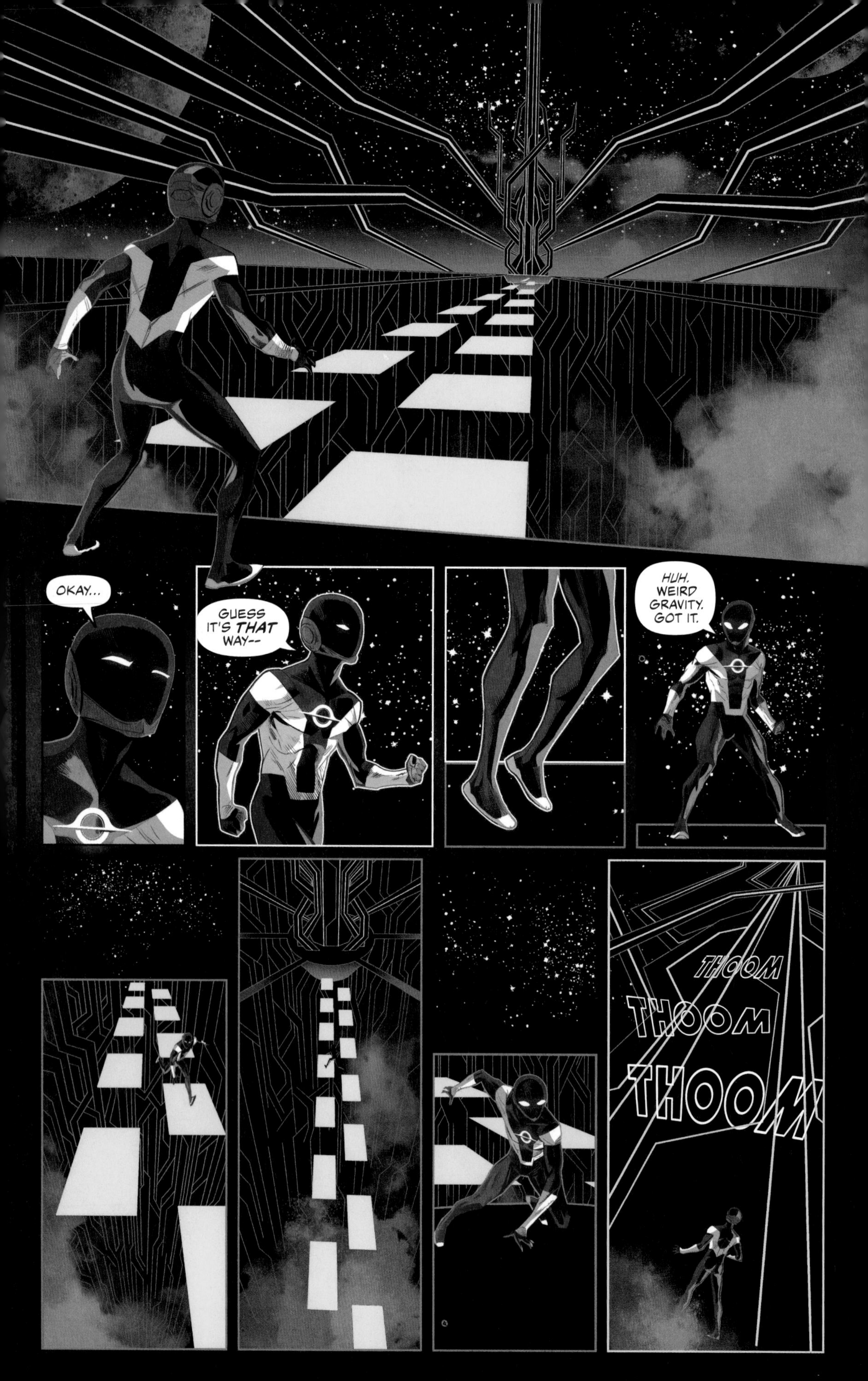
OKAY...
GUESS IT'S THAT WAY--
HUH. WEIRD GRAVITY. GOT IT.
THOOM
THOOM
THOOM

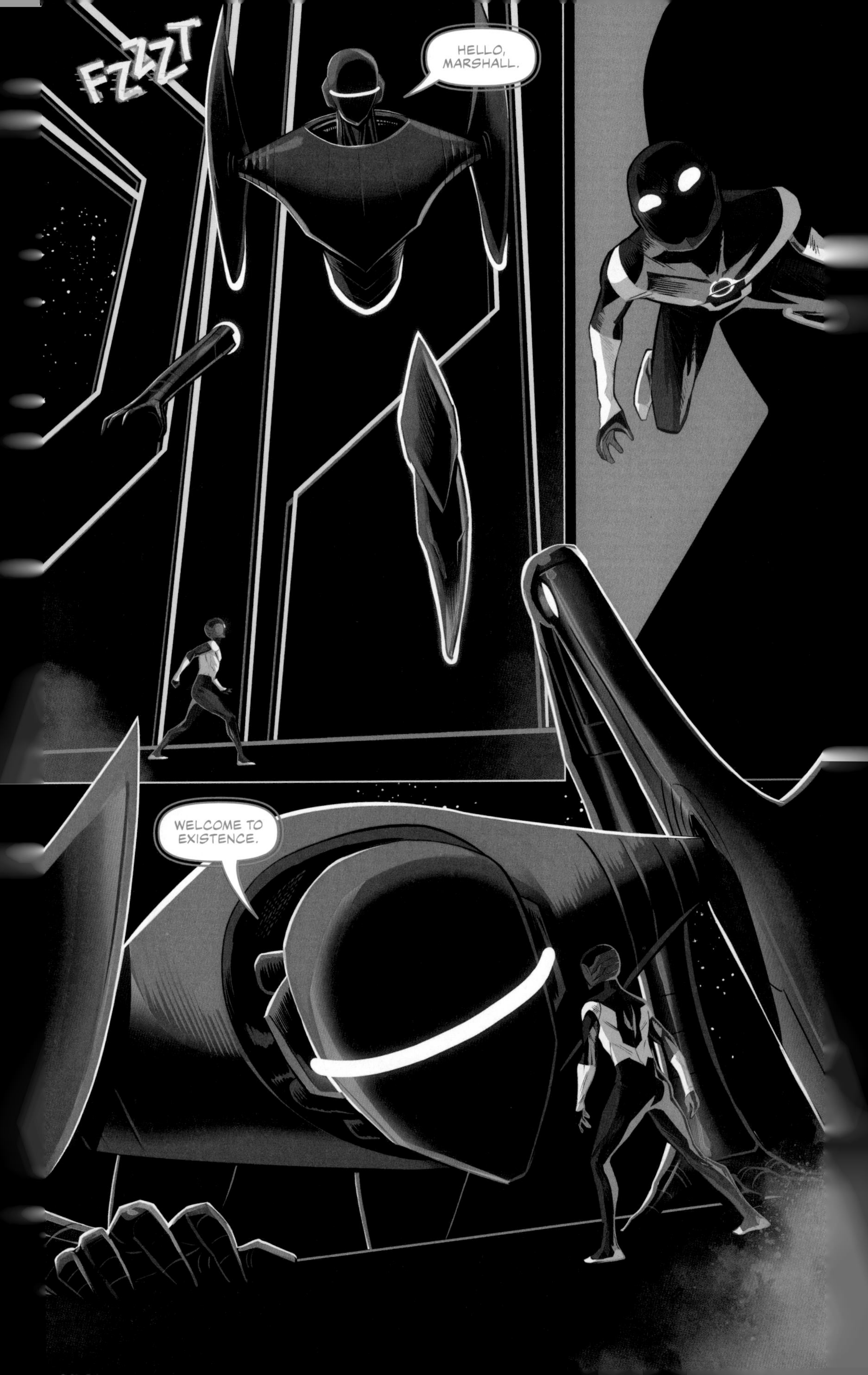
FZZZT
HELLO, MARSHALL.
WELCOME TO EXISTENCE.

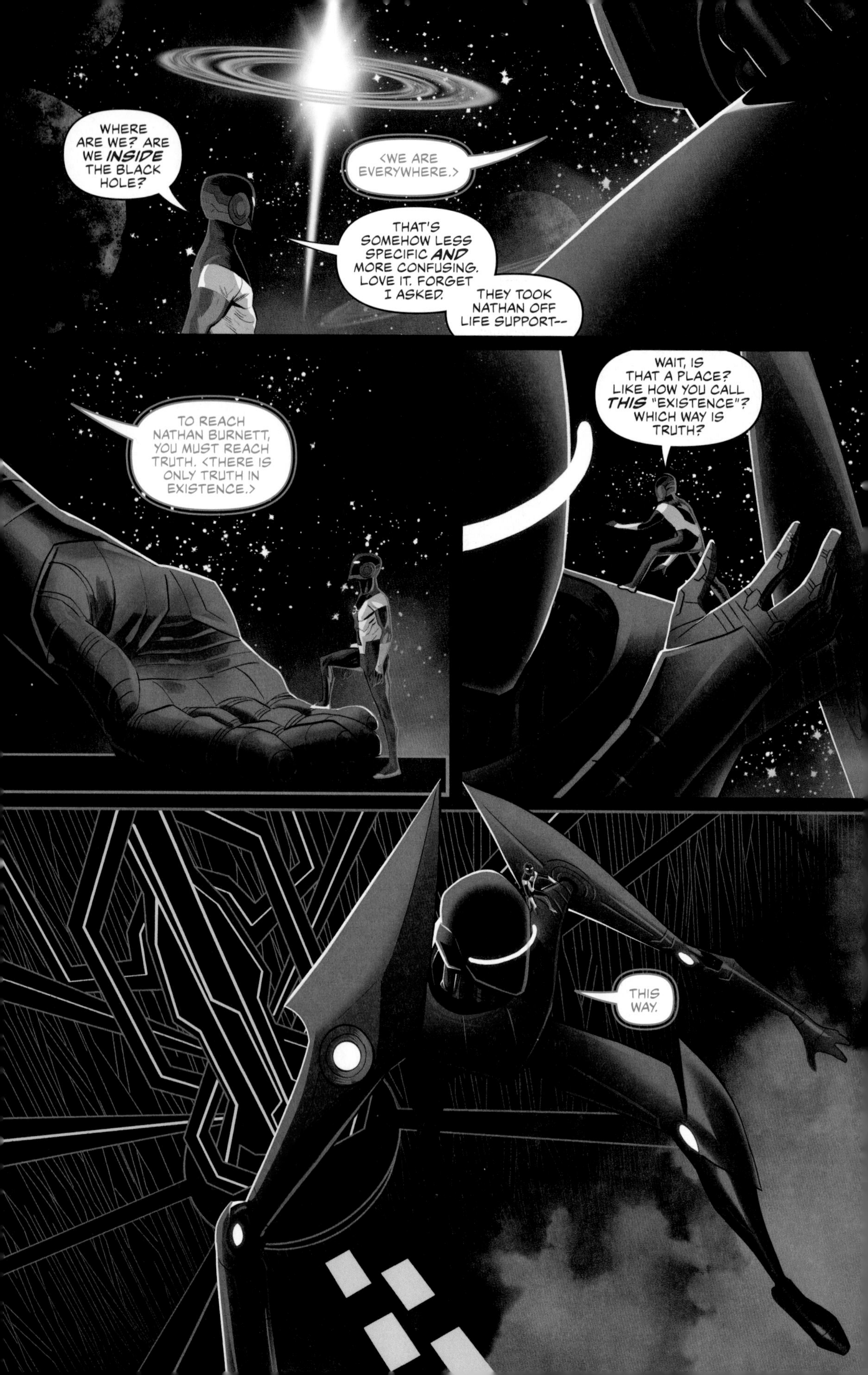
WHERE ARE WE? ARE WE *INSIDE* THE BLACK HOLE?
<WE ARE EVERYWHERE.>
THAT'S SOMEHOW LESS SPECIFIC *AND* MORE CONFUSING. LOVE IT. FORGET I ASKED.
THEY TOOK NATHAN OFF LIFE SUPPORT--
TO REACH NATHAN BURNETT, YOU MUST REACH TRUTH. <THERE IS ONLY TRUTH IN EXISTENCE.>
WAIT, IS THAT A PLACE? LIKE HOW YOU CALL *THIS* "EXISTENCE"? WHICH WAY IS TRUTH?
THIS WAY.

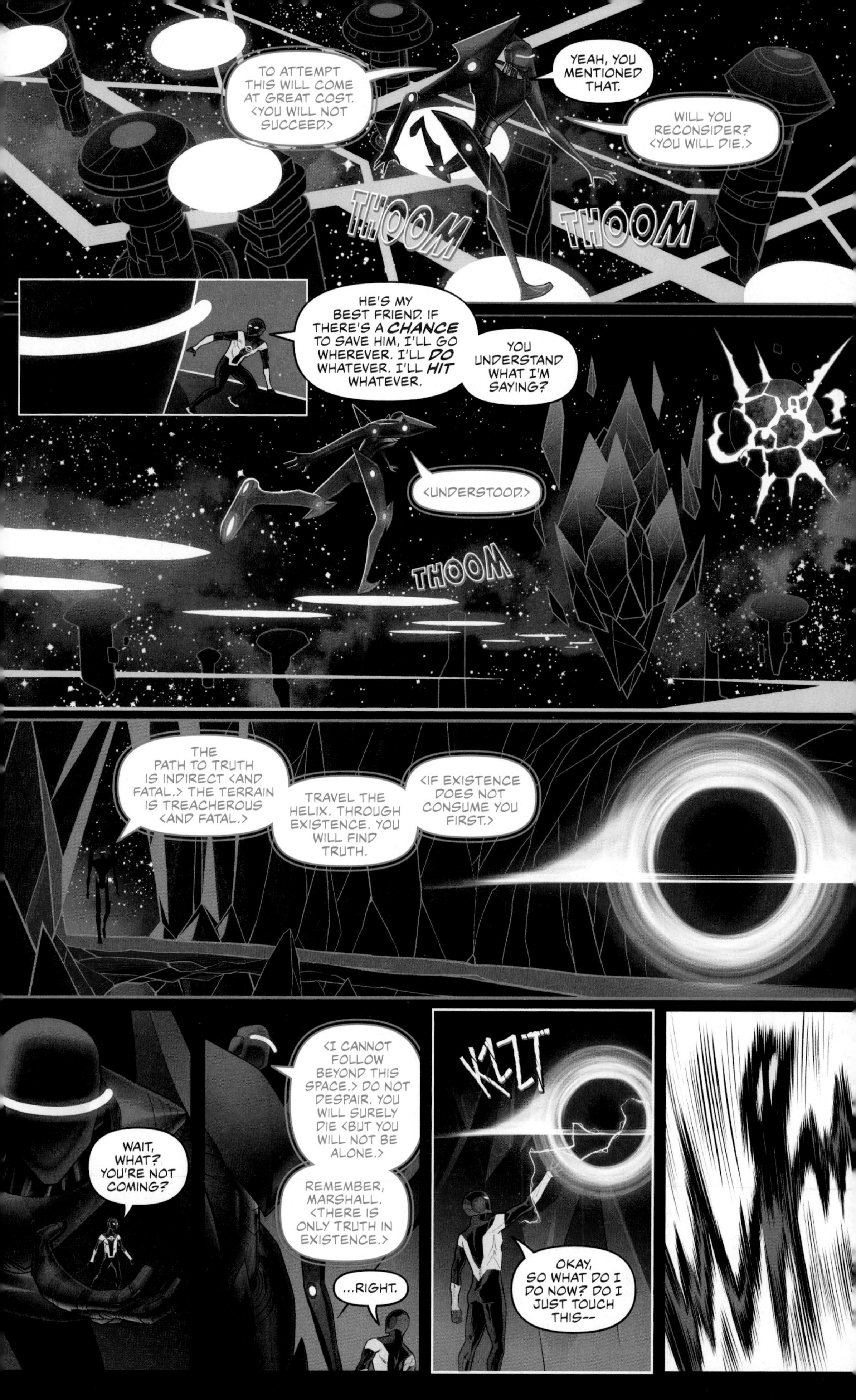
TO ATTEMPT THIS WILL COME AT GREAT COST. <YOU WILL NOT SUCCEED.>
YEAH, YOU MENTIONED THAT.
WILL YOU RECONSIDER? <YOU WILL DIE.>
THOOM
THOOM
HE'S MY BEST FRIEND. IF THERE'S A CHANCE TO SAVE HIM, I'LL GO WHEREVER. I'LL DO WHATEVER. I'LL HIT WHATEVER.
YOU UNDERSTAND WHAT I'M SAYING?
<UNDERSTOOD.>
THOOM
THE PATH TO TRUTH IS INDIRECT <AND FATAL.> THE TERRAIN IS TREACHEROUS <AND FATAL.>
TRAVEL THE HELIX. THROUGH EXISTENCE. YOU WILL FIND TRUTH.
<IF EXISTENCE DOES NOT CONSUME YOU FIRST.>
WAIT, WHAT? YOU'RE NOT COMING?
<I CANNOT FOLLOW BEYOND THIS SPACE.> DO NOT DESPAIR. YOU WILL SURELY DIE <BUT YOU WILL NOT BE ALONE.>
REMEMBER, MARSHALL. <THERE IS ONLY TRUTH IN EXISTENCE.>
...RIGHT.
KZZT
OKAY, SO WHAT DO I DO NOW? DO I JUST TOUCH THIS--

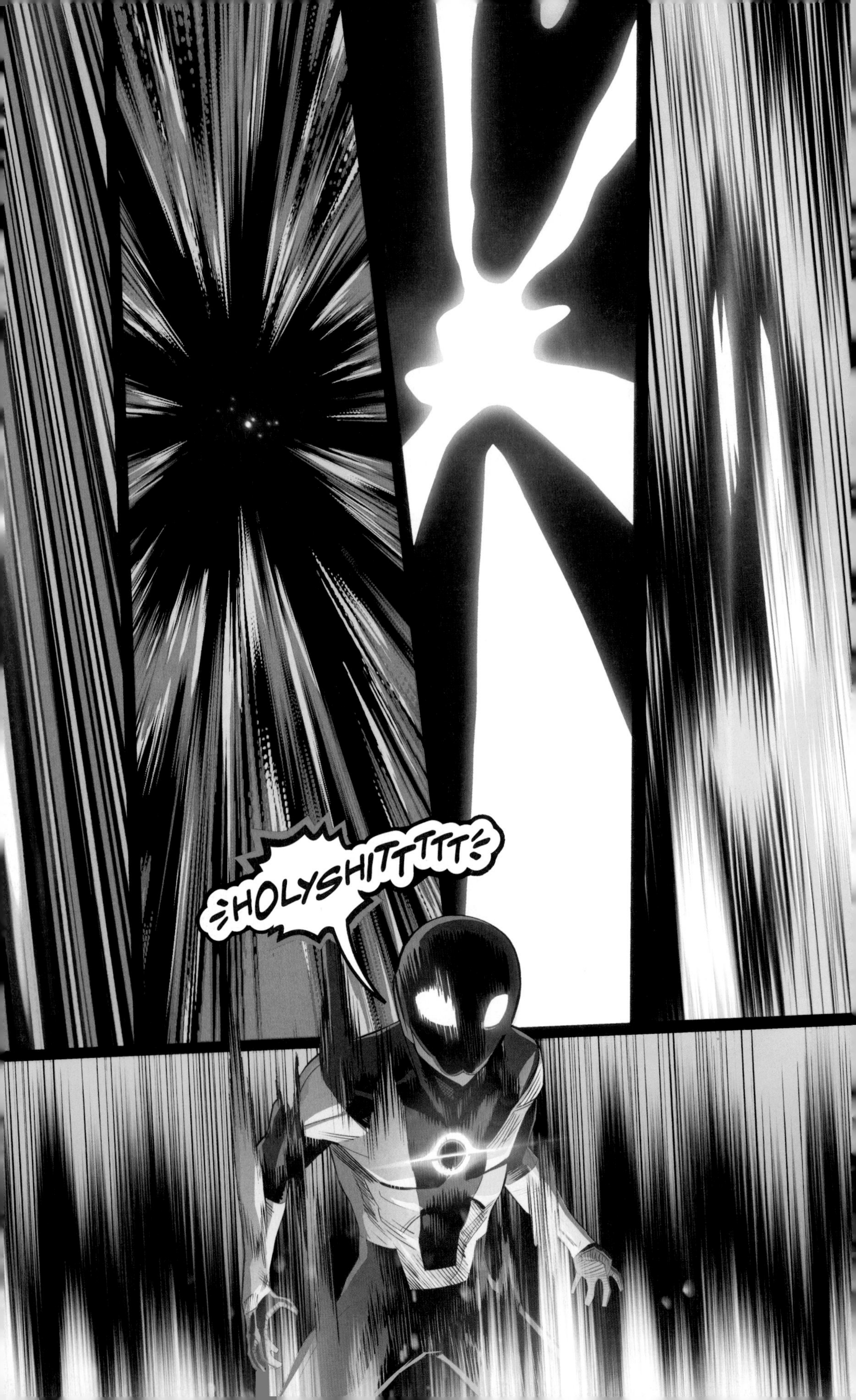
HOLYSHITTTTTT

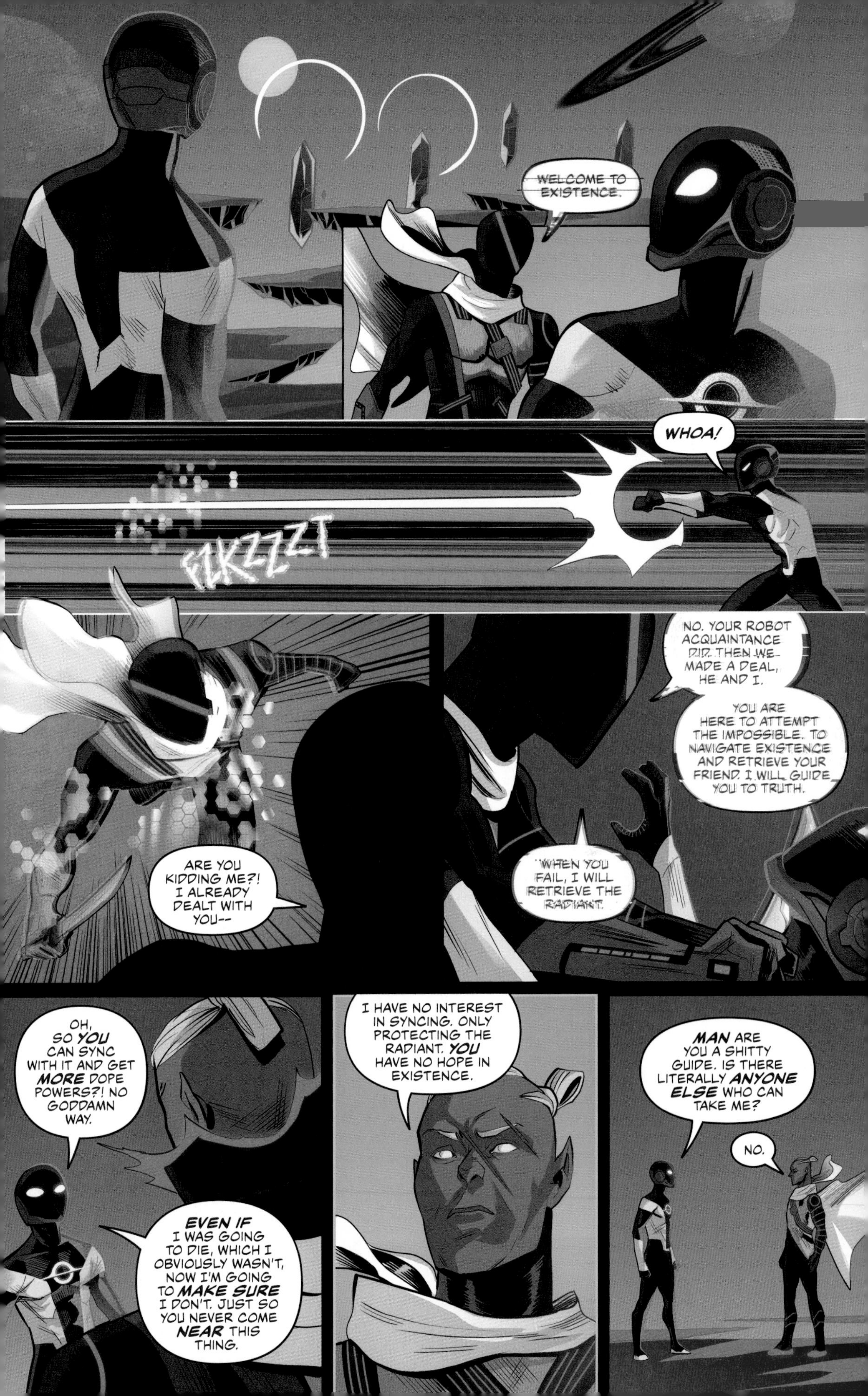

WELCOME TO EXISTENCE.
WHOA!
FZKZZZT
NO. YOUR ROBOT ACQUAINTANCE DID. THEN WE MADE A DEAL, HE AND I.
YOU ARE HERE TO ATTEMPT THE IMPOSSIBLE. TO NAVIGATE EXISTENCE AND RETRIEVE YOUR FRIEND. I WILL GUIDE YOU TO TRUTH.
ARE YOU KIDDING ME?! I ALREADY DEALT WITH YOU--
WHEN YOU FAIL, I WILL RETRIEVE THE RADIANT.
OH, SO YOU CAN SYNC WITH IT AND GET MORE DOPE POWERS?! NO GODDAMN WAY.
EVEN IF I WAS GOING TO DIE, WHICH I OBVIOUSLY WASN'T, NOW I'M GOING TO MAKE SURE I DON'T. JUST SO YOU NEVER COME NEAR THIS THING.
I HAVE NO INTEREST IN SYNCING. ONLY PROTECTING THE RADIANT. YOU HAVE NO HOPE IN EXISTENCE.
MAN ARE YOU A SHITTY GUIDE. IS THERE LITERALLY ANYONE ELSE WHO CAN TAKE ME?
NO.

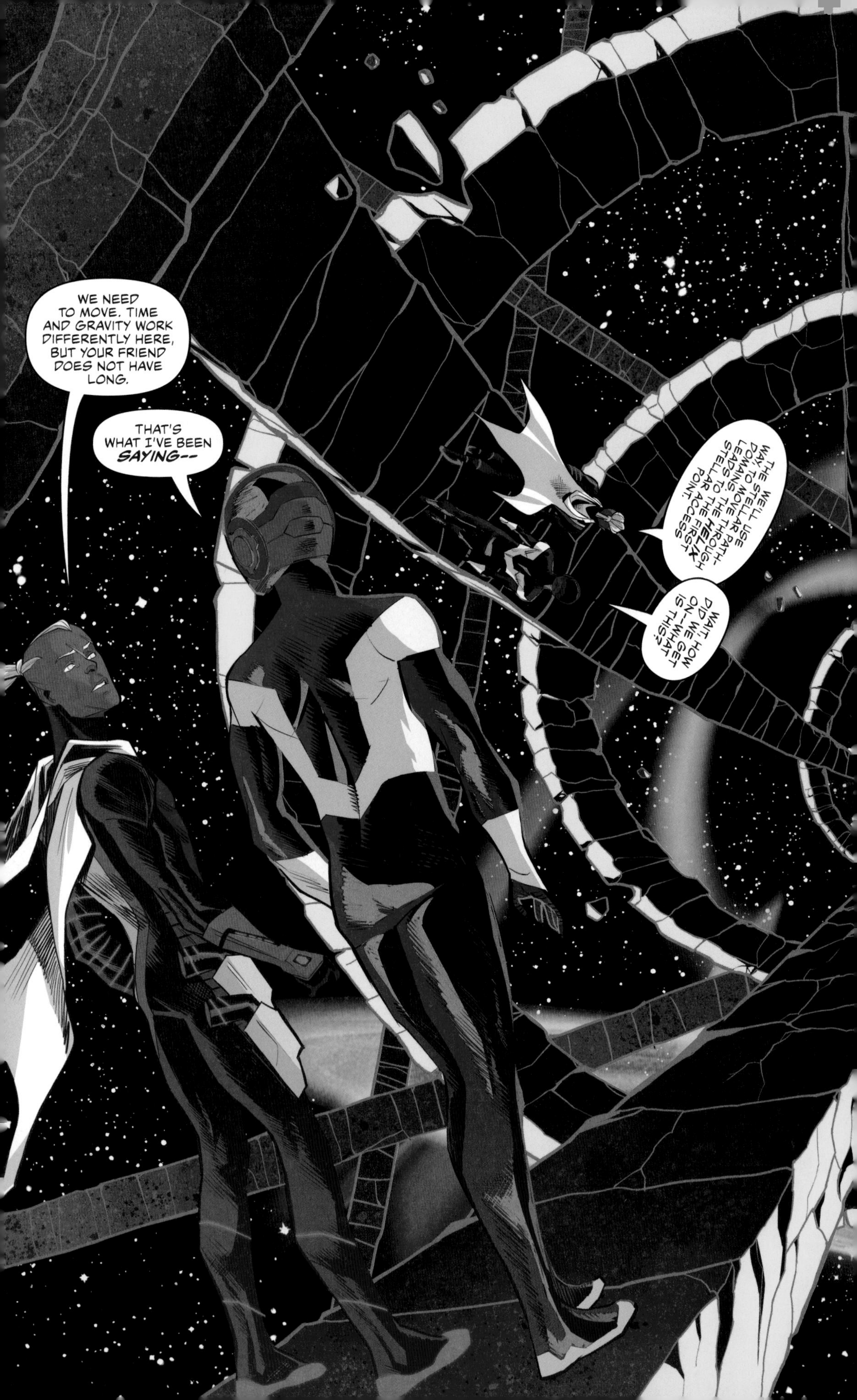
WE NEED TO MOVE. TIME AND GRAVITY WORK DIFFERENTLY HERE, BUT YOUR FRIEND DOES NOT HAVE LONG.
THAT'S WHAT I'VE BEEN *SAYING--*
WE'LL USE THE STELLAR PATH-WAY, TO MOVE THROUGH DOMAINS. THE *HELIX* LEADS TO THE FIRST STELLAR ACCESS POINT.
WAIT, HOW DID WE GET ON--WHAT IS THIS?

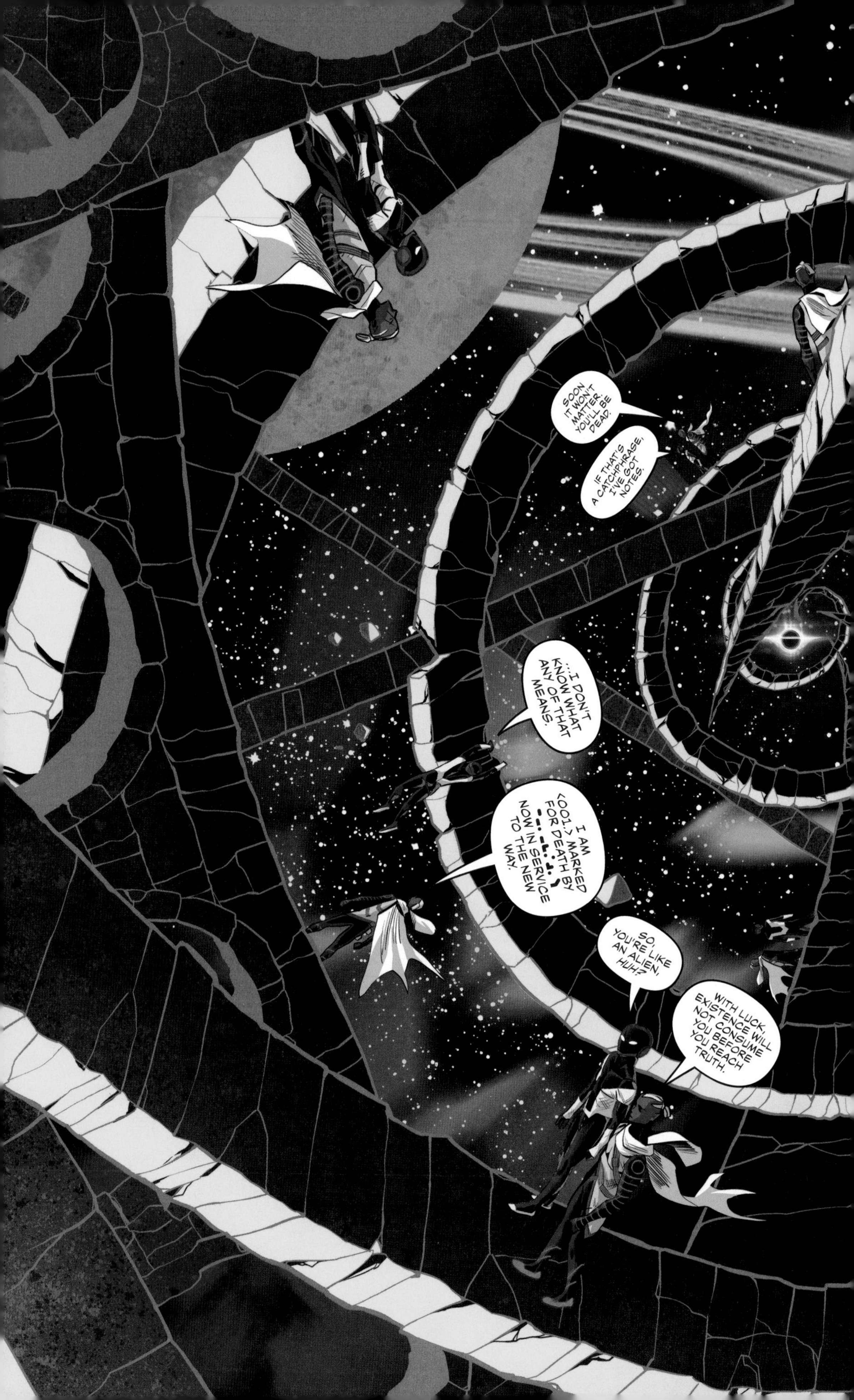
WITH LUCK, EXISTENCE WILL NOT CONSUME YOU BEFORE YOU REACH TRUTH.
SO, YOU'RE LIKE AN ALIEN, HUH?
I AM <001> MARKED FOR DEATH BY NOW IN SERVICE TO THE NEW WAY.
...I DON'T KNOW WHAT ANY OF THAT MEANS.
SOON IT WON'T MATTER. YOU'LL BE DEAD.
IF THAT'S A CATCHPHRASE, I'VE GOT NOTES.

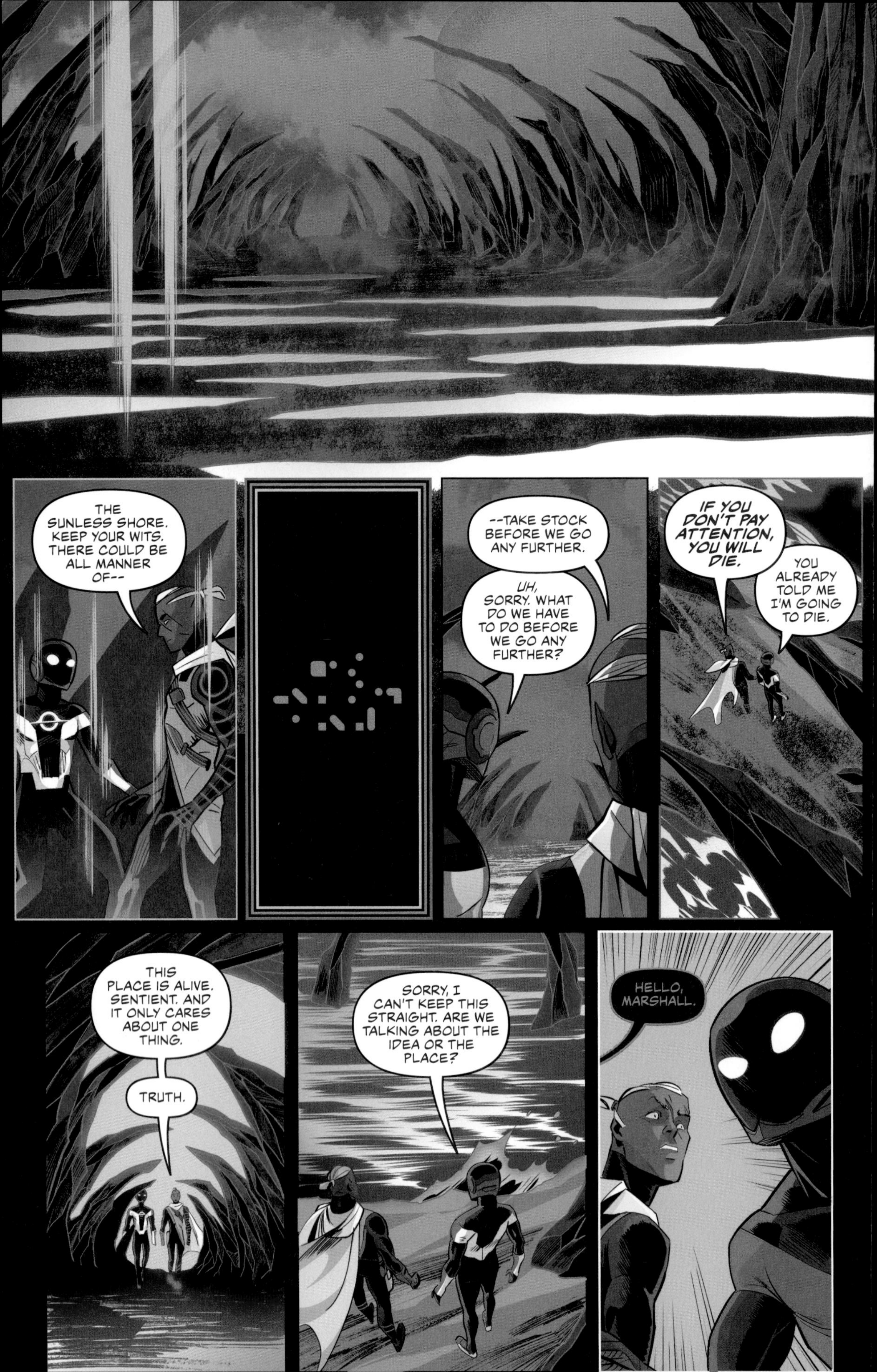
THE SUNLESS SHORE. KEEP YOUR WITS. THERE COULD BE ALL MANNER OF--
--TAKE STOCK BEFORE WE GO ANY FURTHER.
UH, SORRY. WHAT DO WE HAVE TO DO BEFORE WE GO ANY FURTHER?
IF YOU DON'T PAY ATTENTION, YOU WILL DIE.
YOU ALREADY TOLD ME I'M GOING TO DIE.
THIS PLACE IS ALIVE. SENTIENT. AND IT ONLY CARES ABOUT ONE THING.
TRUTH.
SORRY, I CAN'T KEEP THIS STRAIGHT. ARE WE TALKING ABOUT THE IDEA OR THE PLACE?
HELLO, MARSHALL.

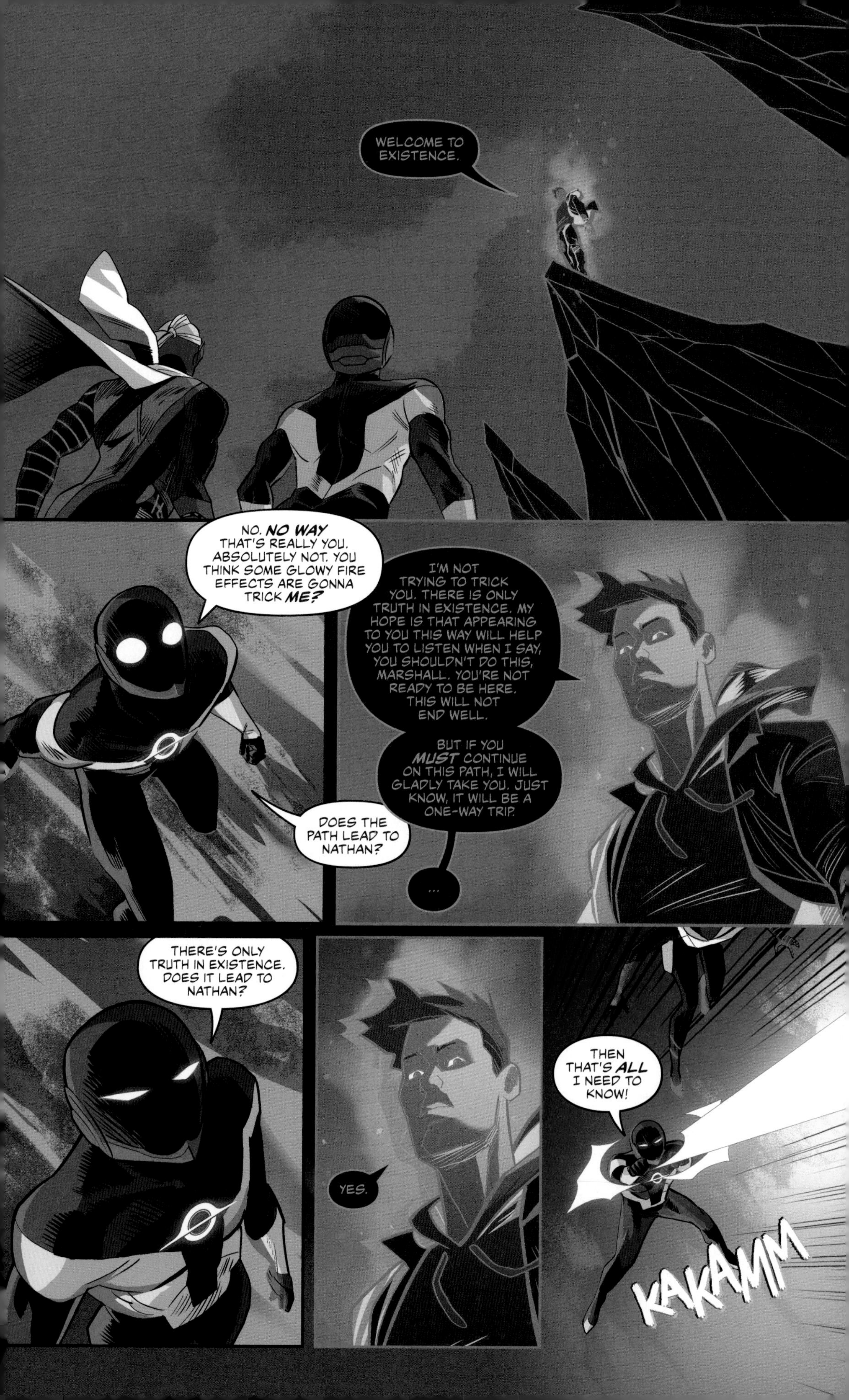
WELCOME TO EXISTENCE.
NO. *NO WAY* THAT'S REALLY YOU. ABSOLUTELY NOT. YOU THINK SOME GLOWY FIRE EFFECTS ARE GONNA TRICK *ME?*
I'M NOT TRYING TO TRICK YOU. THERE IS ONLY TRUTH IN EXISTENCE. MY HOPE IS THAT APPEARING TO YOU THIS WAY WILL HELP YOU TO LISTEN WHEN I SAY, YOU SHOULDN'T DO THIS, MARSHALL. YOU'RE NOT READY TO BE HERE. THIS WILL NOT END WELL.
BUT IF YOU *MUST* CONTINUE ON THIS PATH, I WILL GLADLY TAKE YOU. JUST KNOW, IT WILL BE A ONE-WAY TRIP.
DOES THE PATH LEAD TO NATHAN?
...
THERE'S ONLY TRUTH IN EXISTENCE. DOES IT LEAD TO NATHAN?
YES.
THEN THAT'S *ALL* I NEED TO KNOW!
KAKAMM

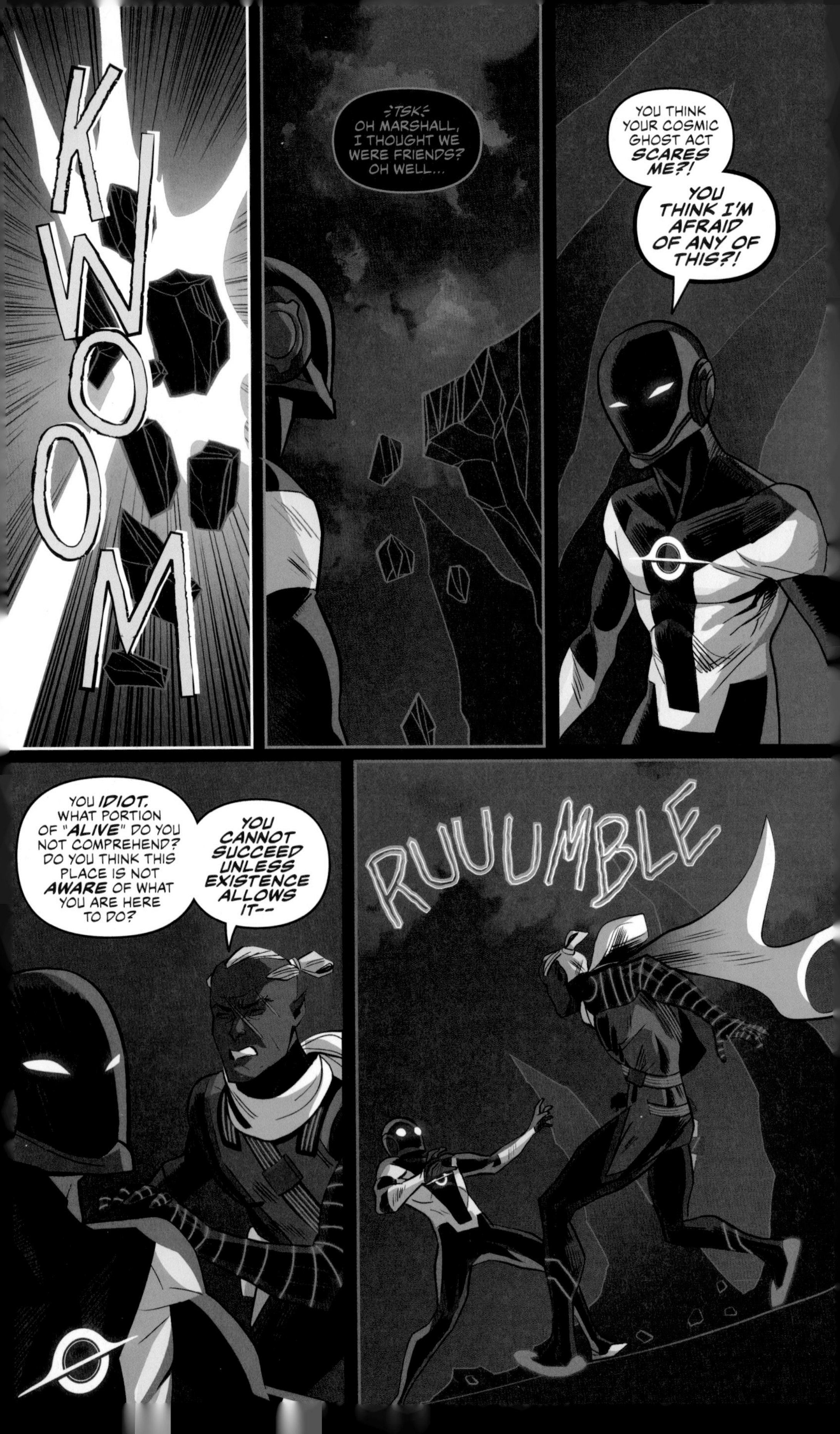
KWOOM
⇌TSK⇋ OH MARSHALL, I THOUGHT WE WERE FRIENDS? OH WELL...
YOU THINK YOUR COSMIC GHOST ACT SCARES ME?!
YOU THINK I'M AFRAID OF ANY OF THIS?!
YOU IDIOT. WHAT PORTION OF "ALIVE" DO YOU NOT COMPREHEND? DO YOU THINK THIS PLACE IS NOT AWARE OF WHAT YOU ARE HERE TO DO?
YOU CANNOT SUCCEED UNLESS EXISTENCE ALLOWS IT--
RUUUMBLE

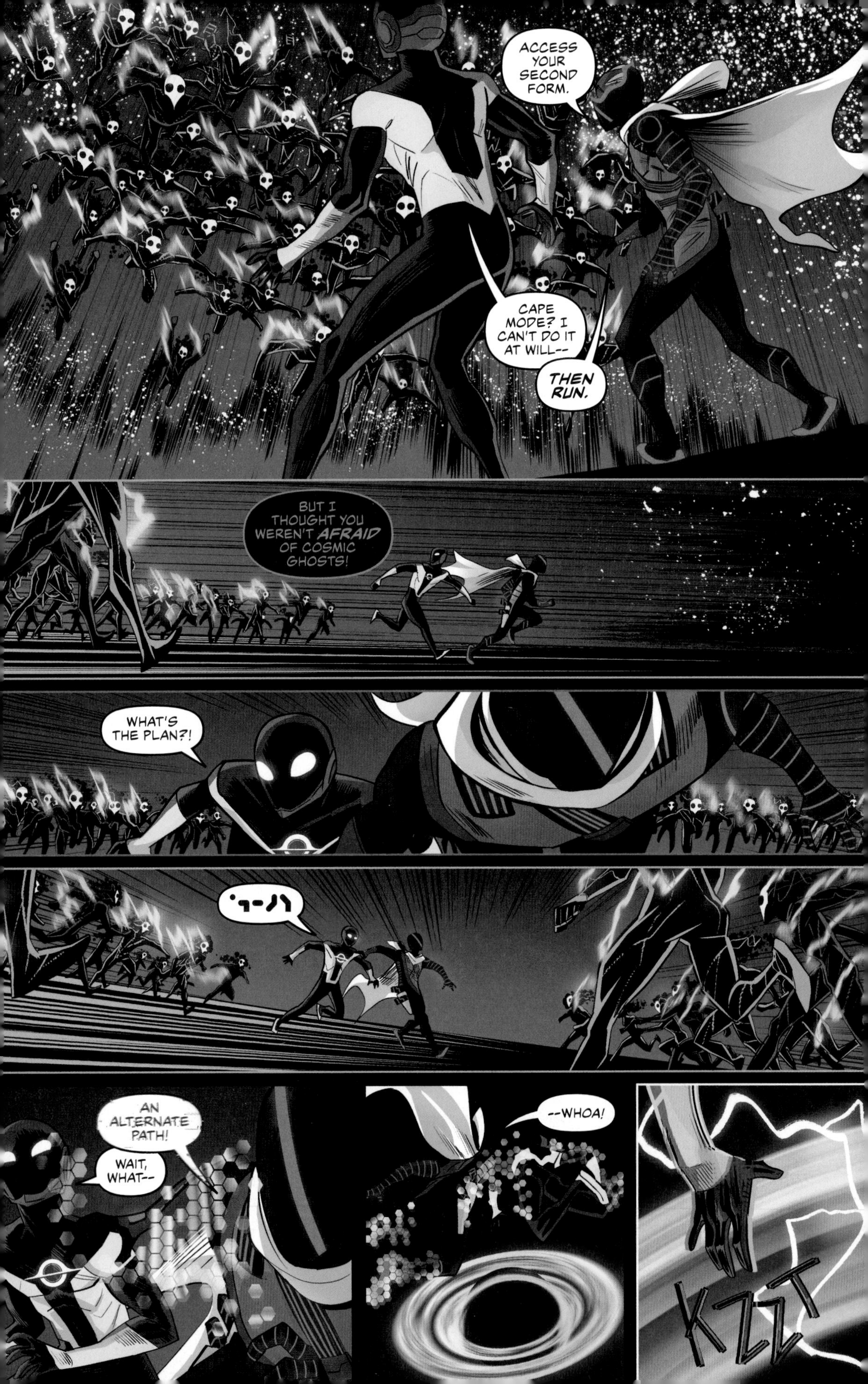
ACCESS YOUR SECOND FORM.
CAPE MODE? I CAN'T DO IT AT WILL--
THEN RUN.
BUT I THOUGHT YOU WEREN'T AFRAID OF COSMIC GHOSTS!
WHAT'S THE PLAN?!
AN ALTERNATE PATH!
WAIT, WHAT--
--WHOA!
KZZT

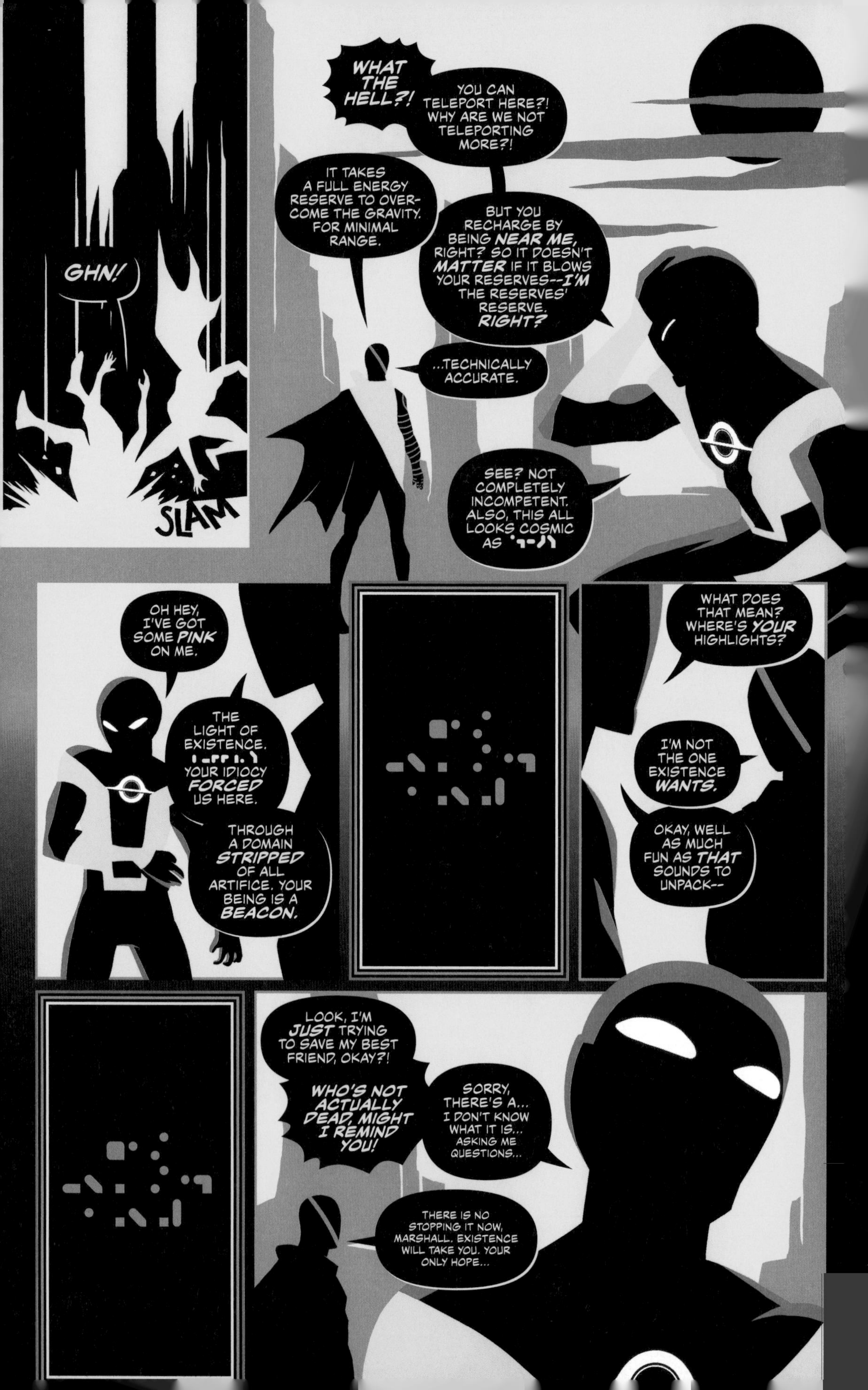
GHN!
SLAM
WHAT THE HELL?!
YOU CAN TELEPORT HERE?! WHY ARE WE NOT TELEPORTING MORE?!
IT TAKES A FULL ENERGY RESERVE TO OVER-COME THE GRAVITY. FOR MINIMAL RANGE.
BUT YOU RECHARGE BY BEING NEAR ME, RIGHT? SO IT DOESN'T MATTER IF IT BLOWS YOUR RESERVES--I'M THE RESERVES' RESERVE. RIGHT?
...TECHNICALLY ACCURATE.
SEE? NOT COMPLETELY INCOMPETENT. ALSO, THIS ALL LOOKS COSMIC AS
OH HEY, I'VE GOT SOME PINK ON ME.
THE LIGHT OF EXISTENCE.
YOUR IDIOCY FORCED US HERE.
THROUGH A DOMAIN STRIPPED OF ALL ARTIFICE. YOUR BEING IS A BEACON.
WHAT DOES THAT MEAN? WHERE'S YOUR HIGHLIGHTS?
I'M NOT THE ONE EXISTENCE WANTS.
OKAY, WELL AS MUCH FUN AS THAT SOUNDS TO UNPACK--
LOOK, I'M JUST TRYING TO SAVE MY BEST FRIEND, OKAY?!
WHO'S NOT ACTUALLY DEAD, MIGHT I REMIND YOU!
SORRY, THERE'S A... I DON'T KNOW WHAT IT IS... ASKING ME QUESTIONS...
THERE IS NO STOPPING IT NOW, MARSHALL. EXISTENCE WILL TAKE YOU. YOUR ONLY HOPE...

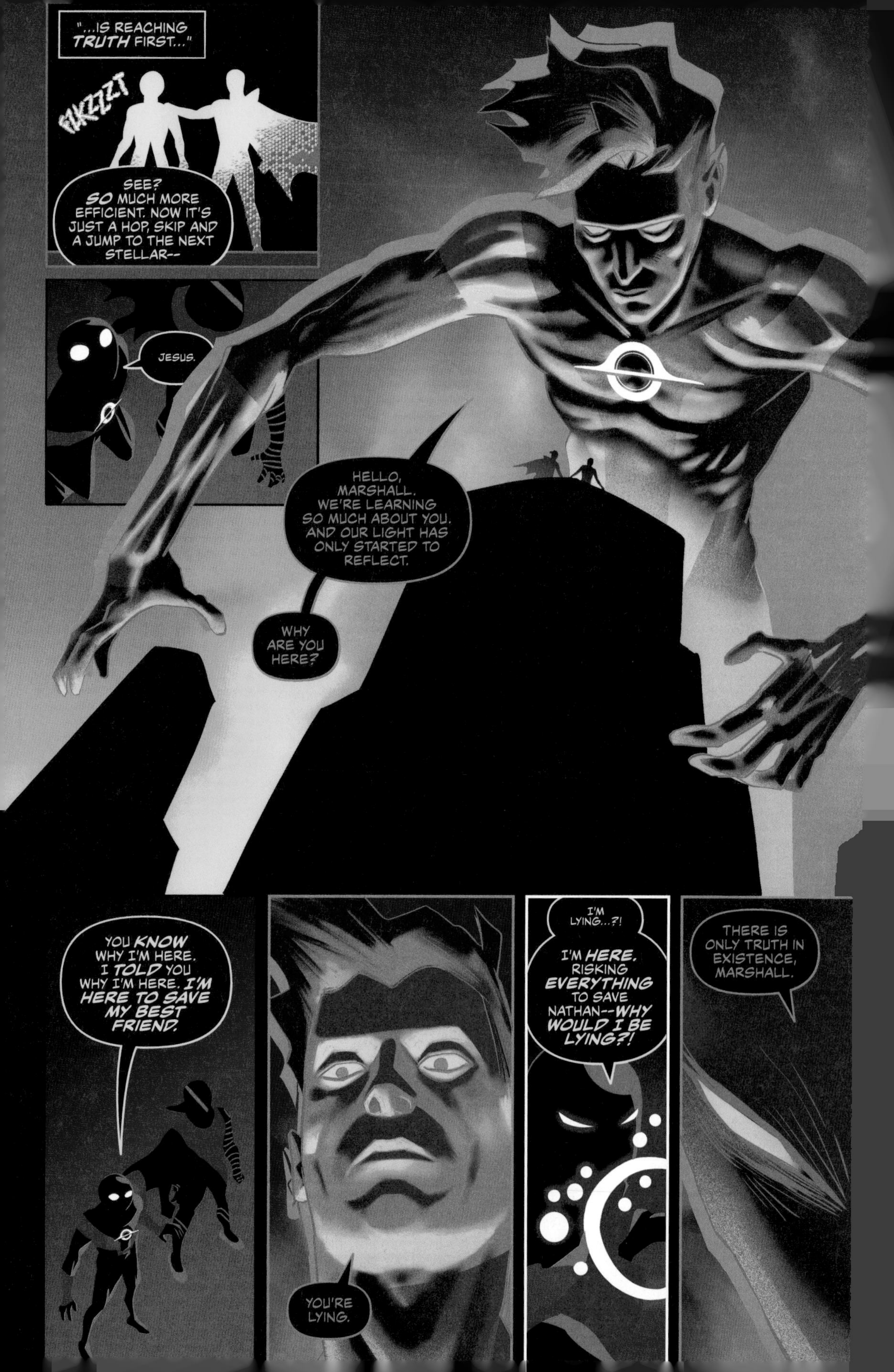
"...IS REACHING TRUTH FIRST..."
FZKZZZT
SEE? SO MUCH MORE EFFICIENT. NOW IT'S JUST A HOP, SKIP AND A JUMP TO THE NEXT STELLAR--
JESUS.
HELLO, MARSHALL. WE'RE LEARNING SO MUCH ABOUT YOU. AND OUR LIGHT HAS ONLY STARTED TO REFLECT.
WHY ARE YOU HERE?
YOU KNOW WHY I'M HERE. I TOLD YOU WHY I'M HERE. I'M HERE TO SAVE MY BEST FRIEND.
YOU'RE LYING.
I'M LYING...?!
I'M HERE. RISKING EVERYTHING TO SAVE NATHAN--WHY WOULD I BE LYING?!
THERE IS ONLY TRUTH IN EXISTENCE, MARSHALL.

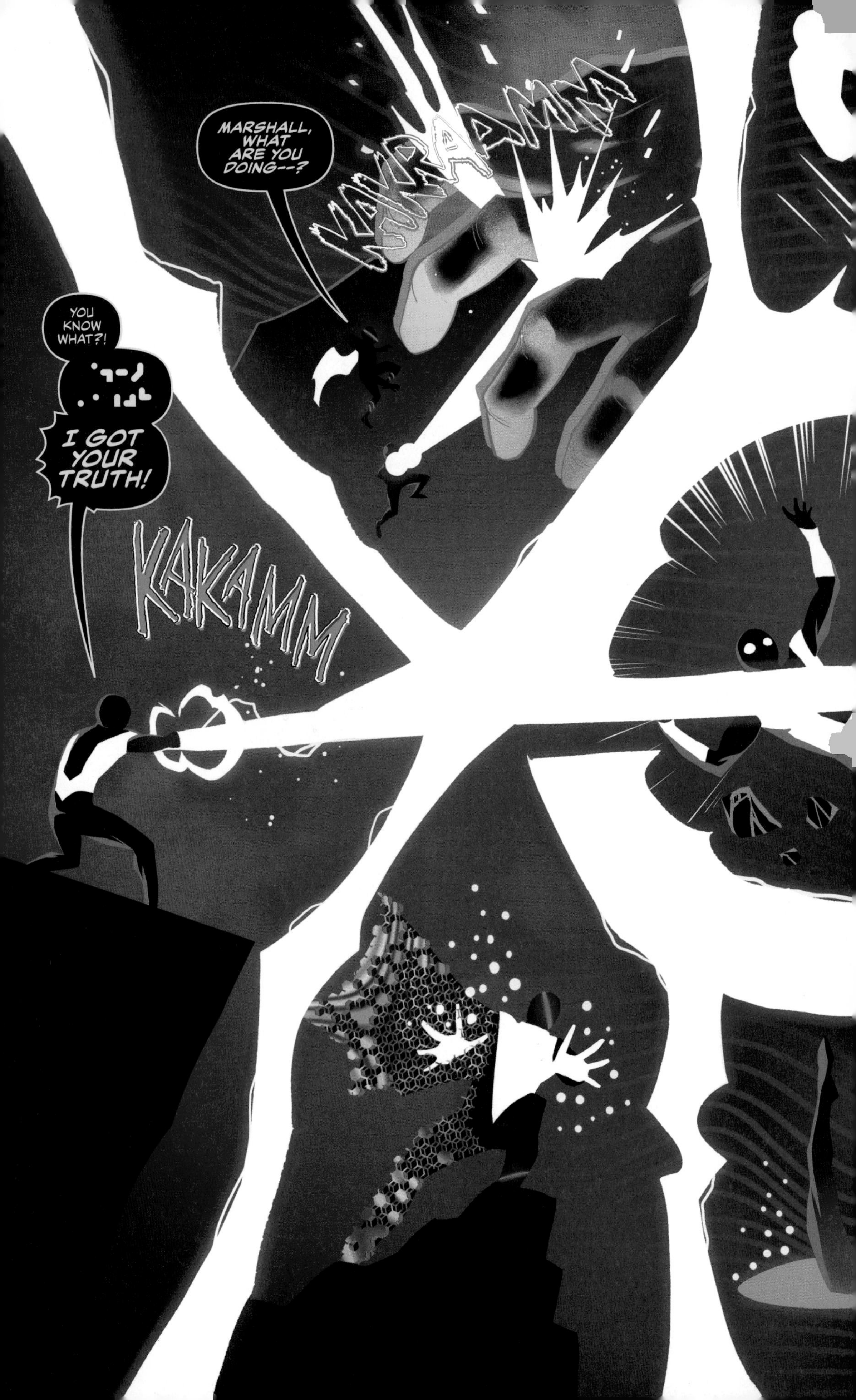
MARSHALL, WHAT ARE YOU DOING--?
KVRAMM
YOU KNOW WHAT?!
I GOT YOUR TRUTH!
KAKAMM

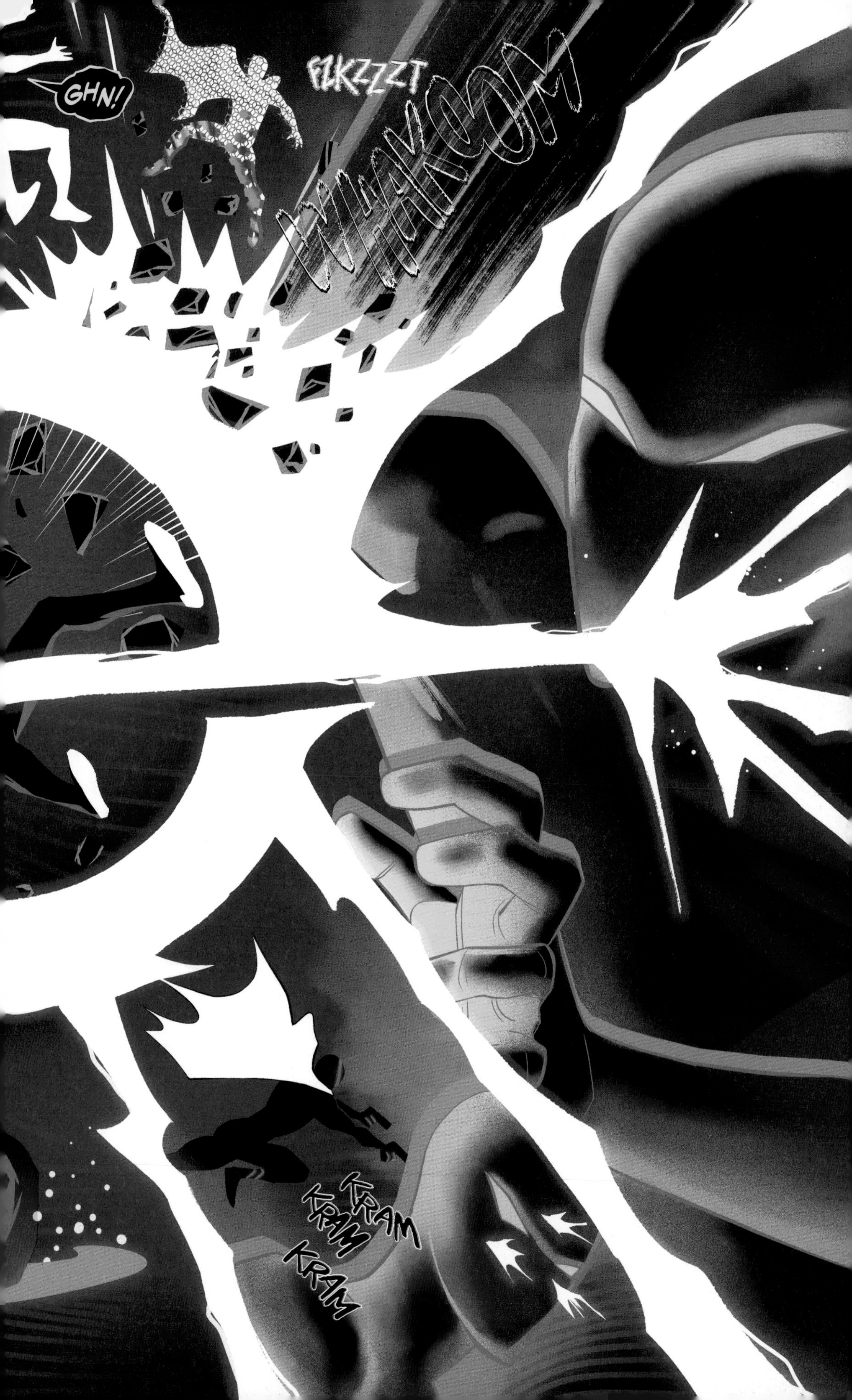
GHN!
FZKZZZT
WHAKOOM
KRAM
KRAM
KRAM

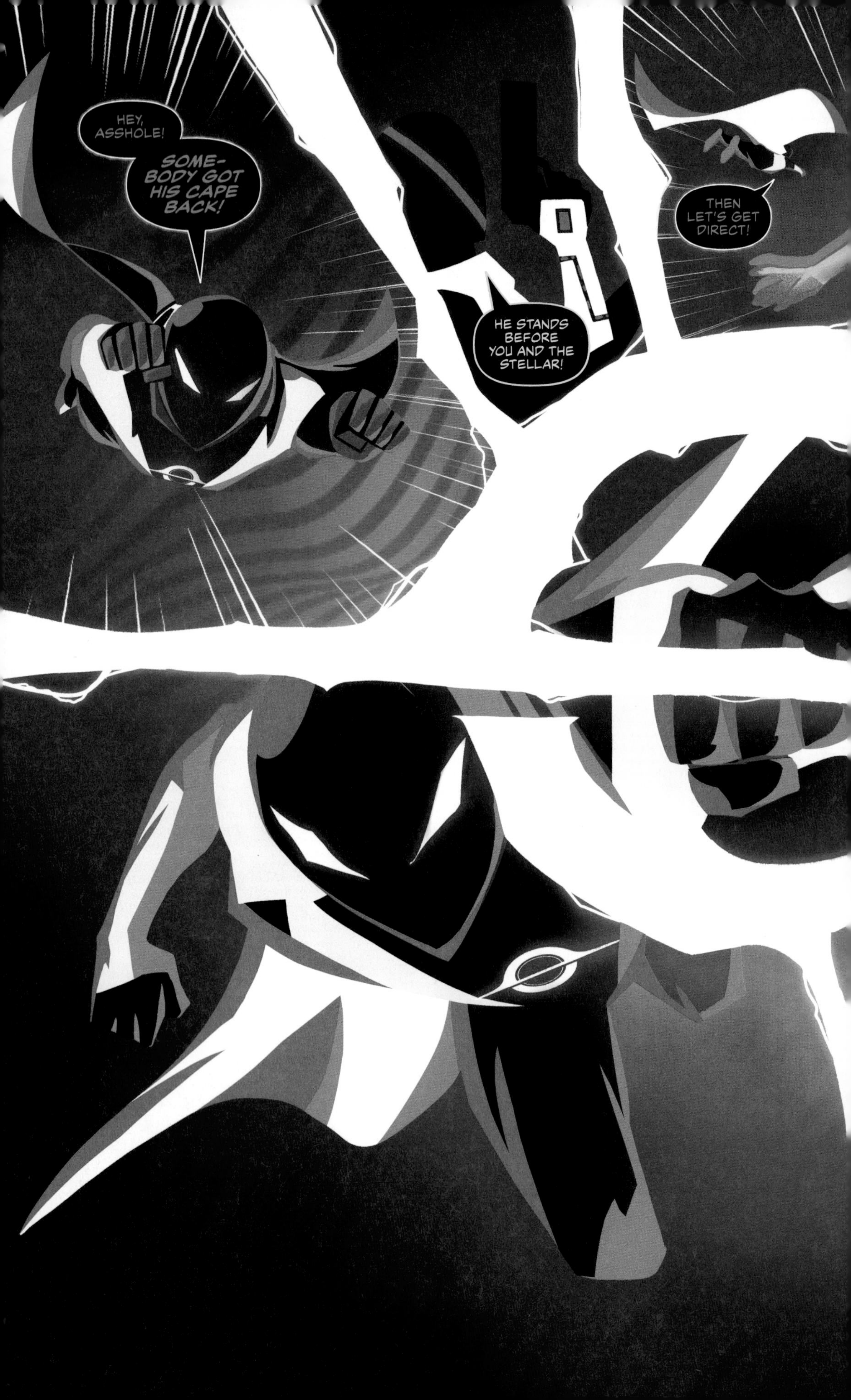
HEY, ASSHOLE!
SOME-BODY GOT HIS CAPE BACK!
HE STANDS BEFORE YOU AND THE STELLAR!
THEN LET'S GET DIRECT!

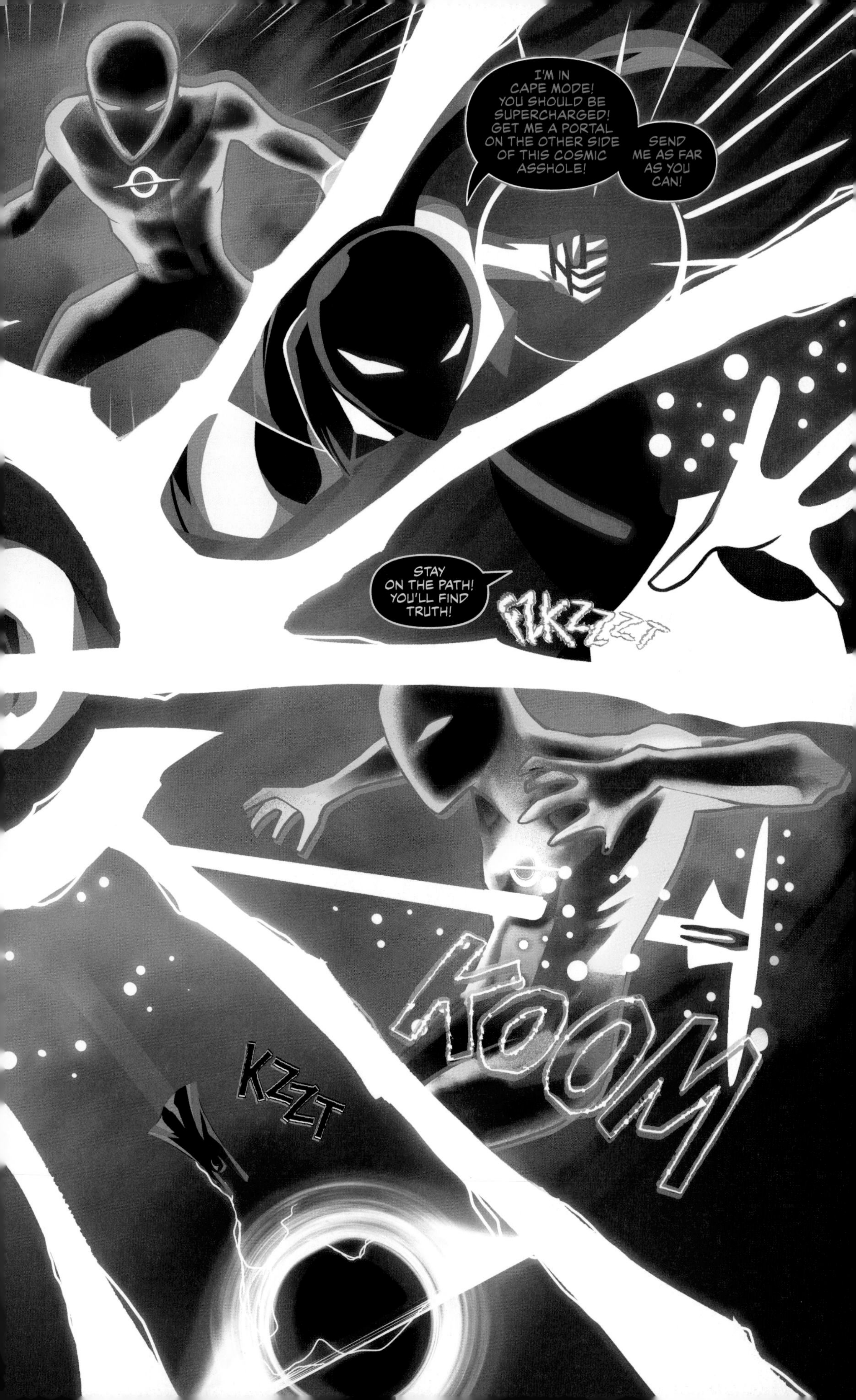
I'M IN CAPE MODE! YOU SHOULD BE SUPERCHARGED! GET ME A PORTAL ON THE OTHER SIDE OF THIS COSMIC ASSHOLE!
SEND ME AS FAR AS YOU CAN!
STAY ON THE PATH! YOU'LL FIND TRUTH!
FZKZZZT
KOOM
KZZT

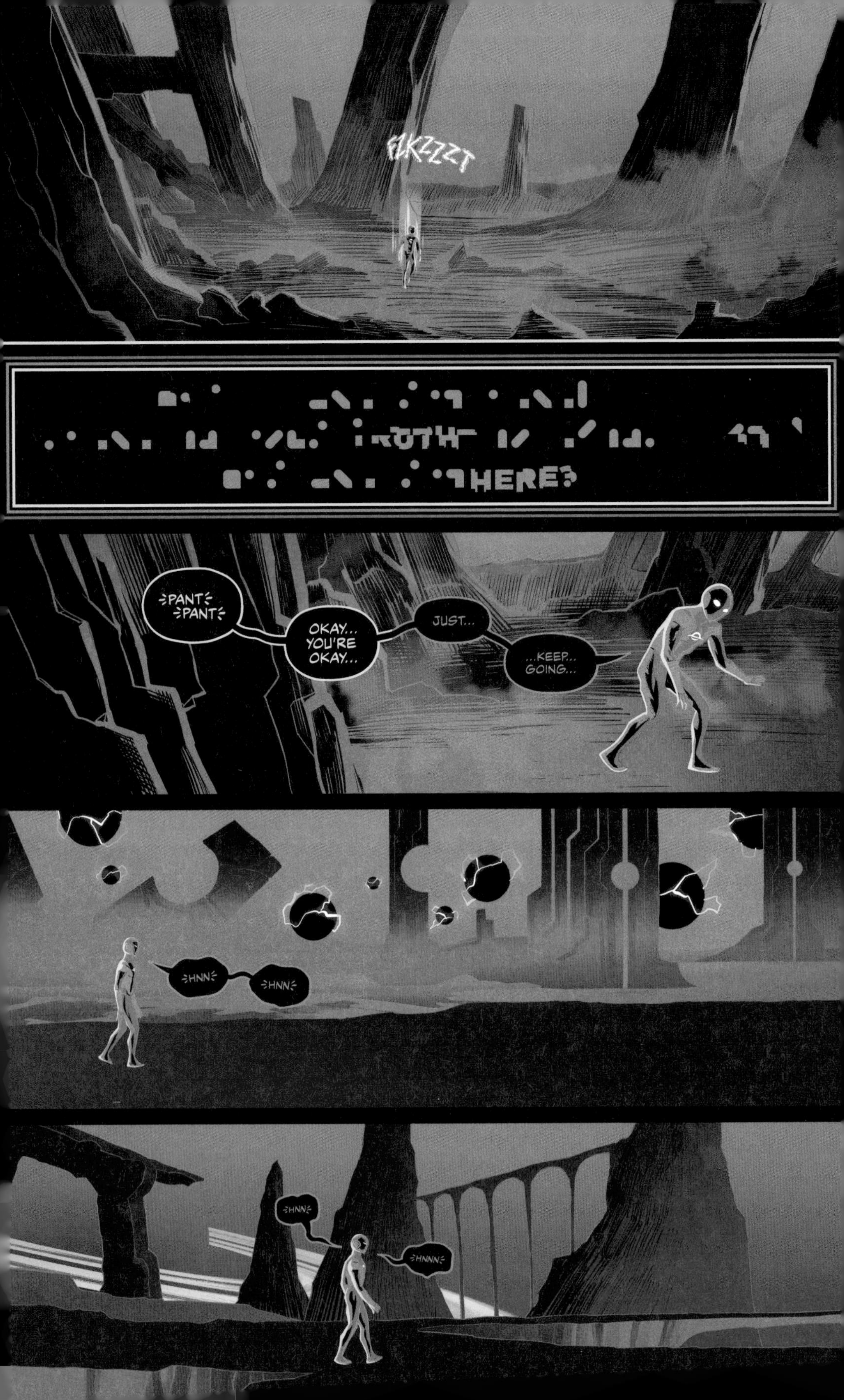
FZKZZZT
TRUTH
THERE?
PANT PANT
OKAY... YOU'RE OKAY...
JUST...
...KEEP... GOING...
HNN
HNN
HNN
HNNN

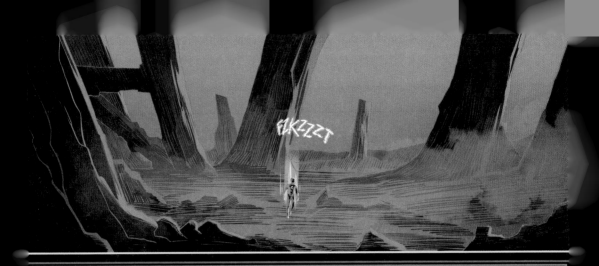

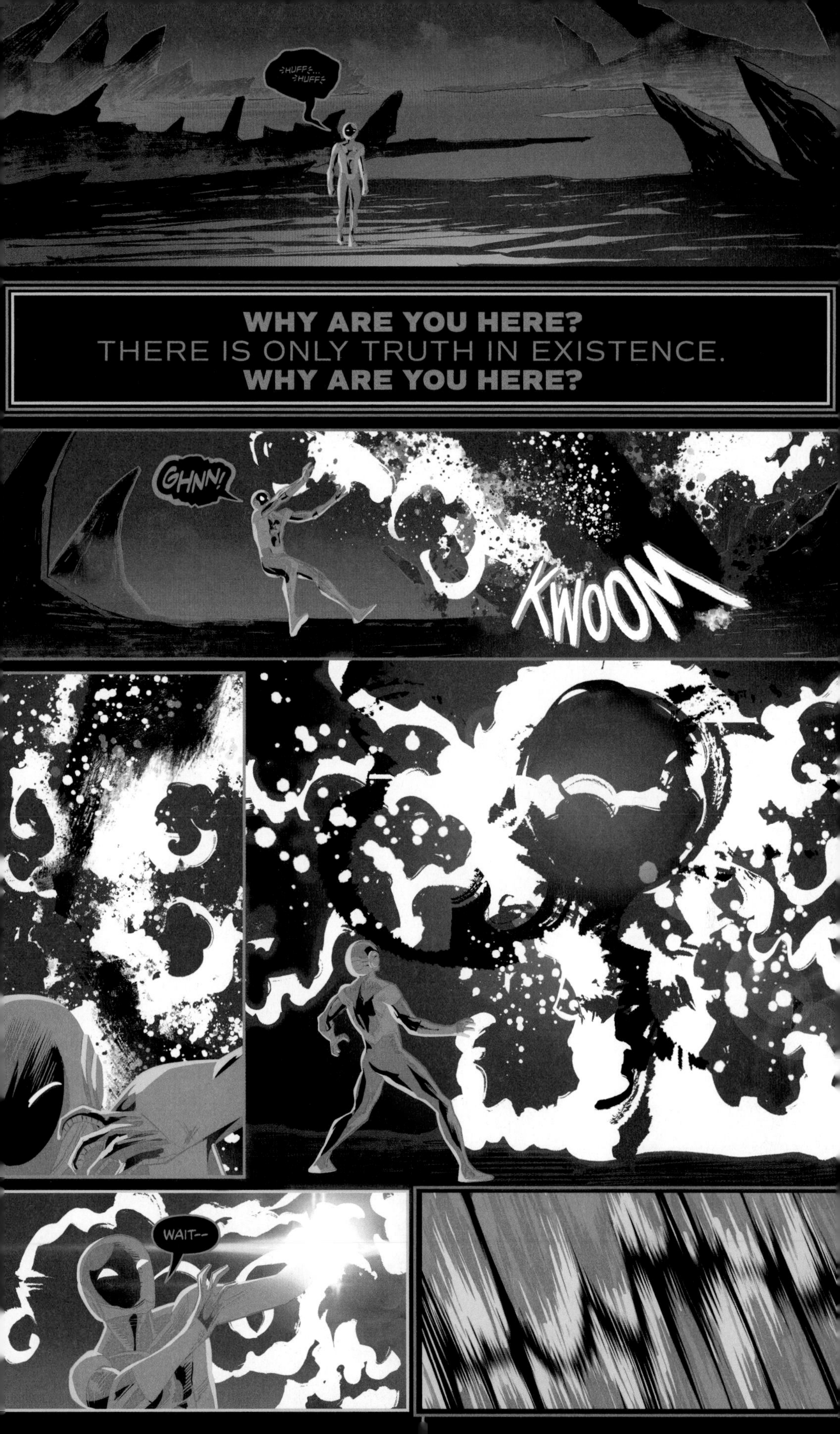
HUFF... HUFF
WHY ARE YOU HERE?
THERE IS ONLY TRUTH IN EXISTENCE.
WHY ARE YOU HERE?
GHNN!
KWOOM
WAIT--

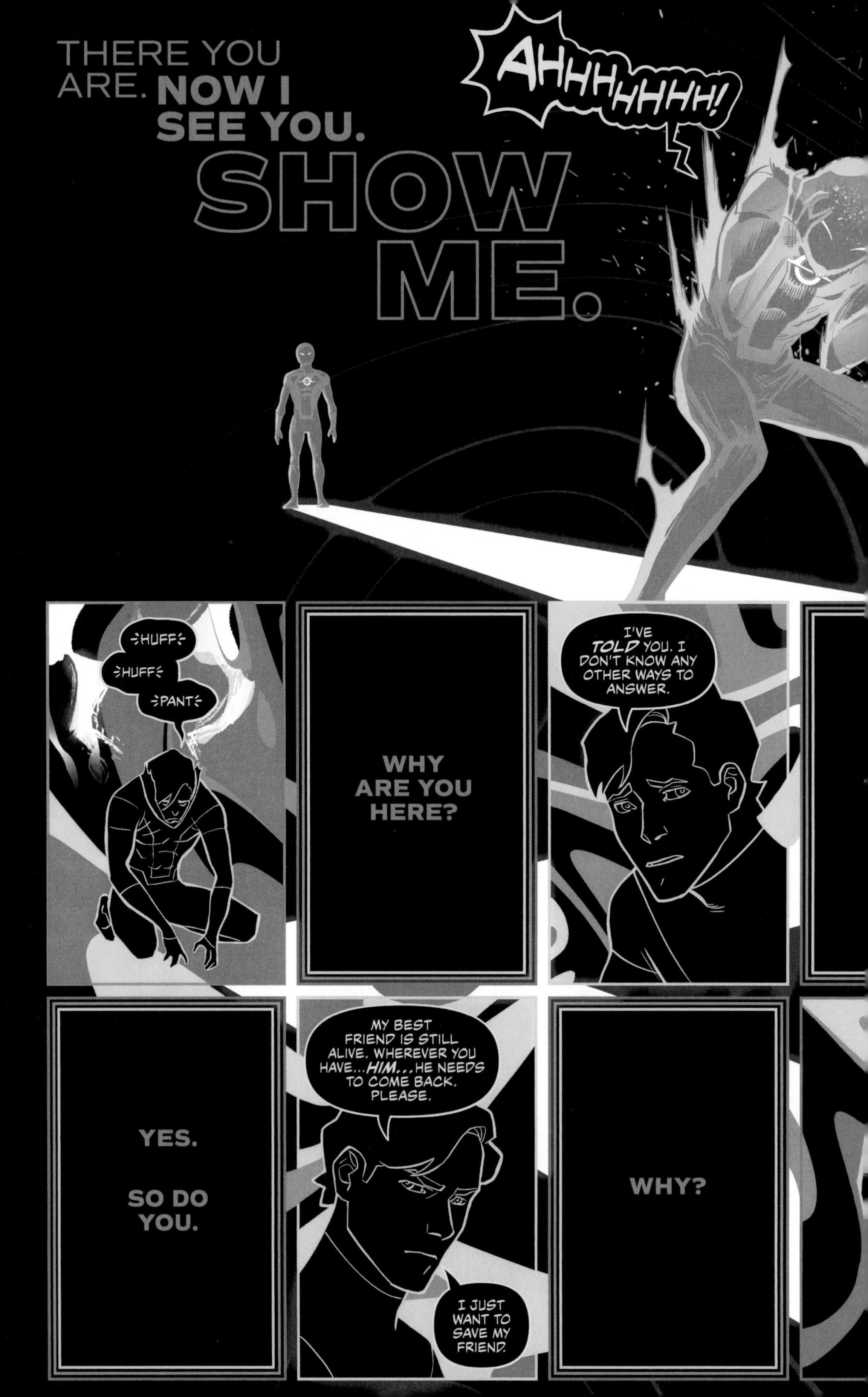
THERE YOU ARE. NOW I SEE YOU.
SHOW ME.
AHHHHHHH!
HUFF
HUFF
PANT
WHY ARE YOU HERE?
I'VE TOLD YOU. I DON'T KNOW ANY OTHER WAYS TO ANSWER.
YES.
SO DO YOU.
MY BEST FRIEND IS STILL ALIVE. WHEREVER YOU HAVE...HIM...HE NEEDS TO COME BACK. PLEASE.
I JUST WANT TO SAVE MY FRIEND.
WHY?

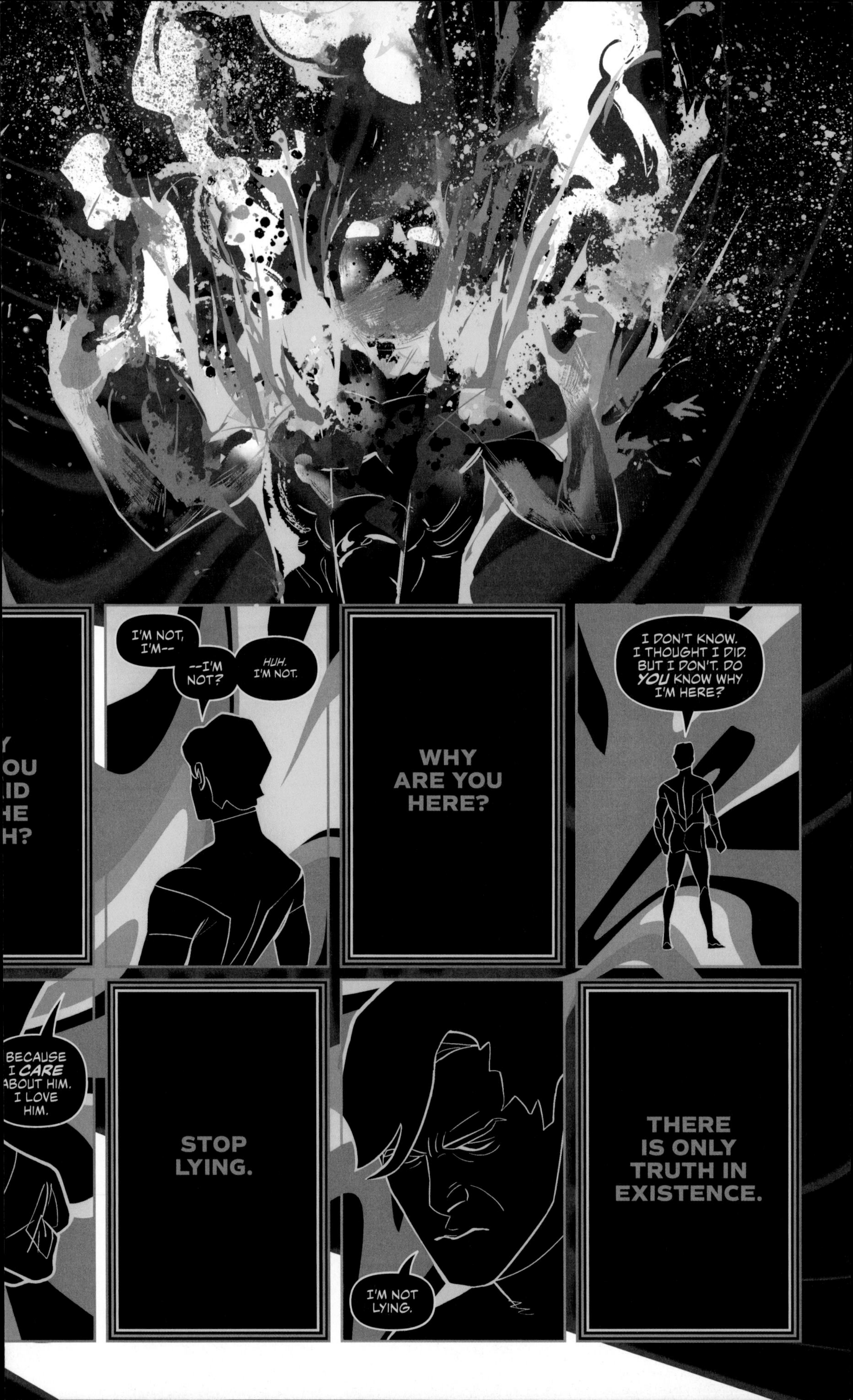
I'M NOT, I'M--
--I'M NOT?
HUH. I'M NOT.
WHY ARE YOU HERE?
I DON'T KNOW. I THOUGHT I DID. BUT I DON'T. DO YOU KNOW WHY I'M HERE?
BECAUSE I CARE ABOUT HIM. I LOVE HIM.
STOP LYING.
I'M NOT LYING.
THERE IS ONLY TRUTH IN EXISTENCE.

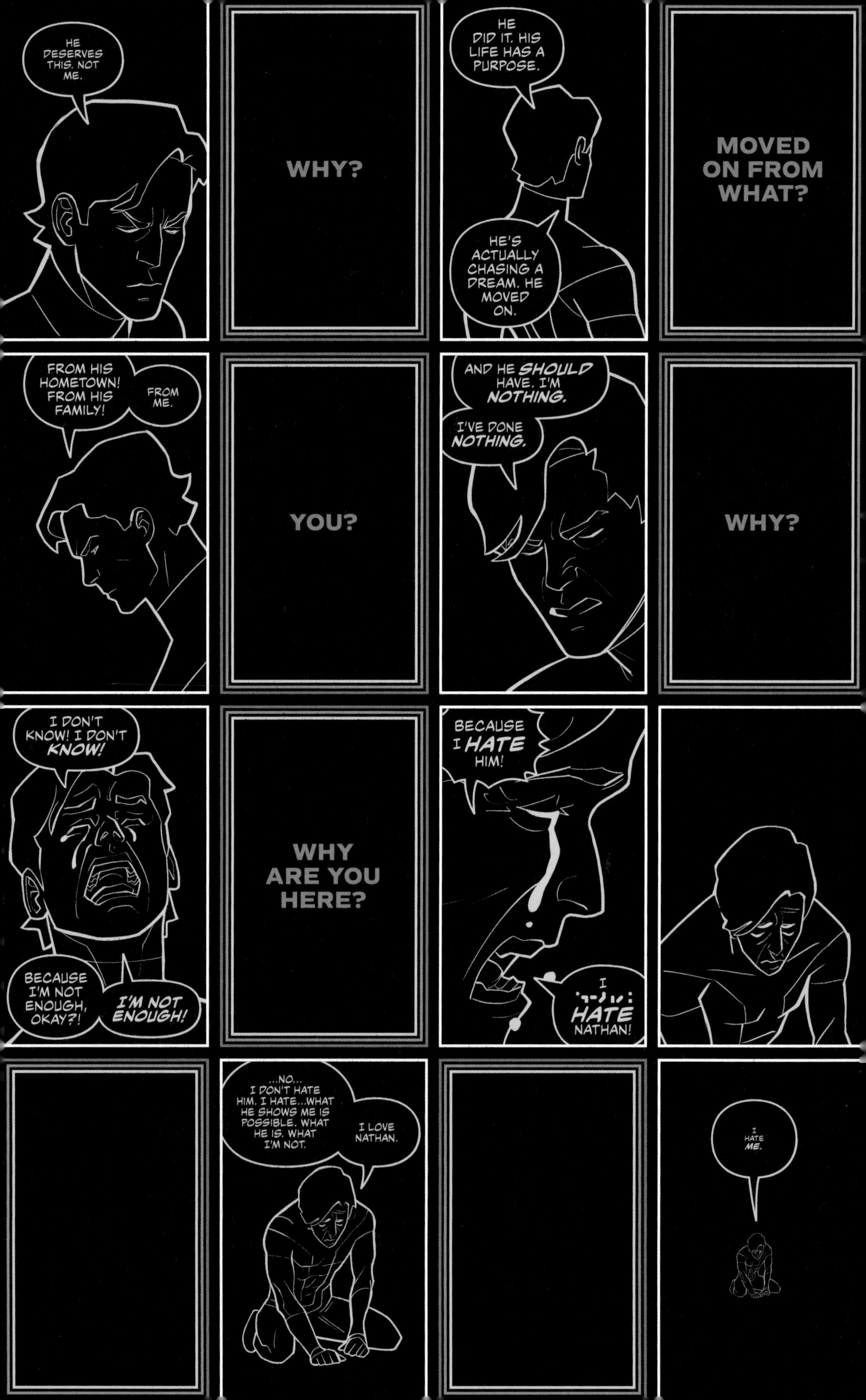

HE DESERVES THIS. NOT ME.
WHY?
HE DID IT. HIS LIFE HAS A PURPOSE.
HE'S ACTUALLY CHASING A DREAM. HE MOVED ON.
MOVED ON FROM WHAT?
FROM HIS HOMETOWN! FROM HIS FAMILY!
FROM ME.
YOU?
AND HE *SHOULD* HAVE. I'M *NOTHING.*
I'VE DONE *NOTHING.*
WHY?
I DON'T KNOW! I DON'T *KNOW!*
BECAUSE I'M NOT ENOUGH, OKAY?!
I'M NOT ENOUGH!
WHY ARE YOU HERE?
BECAUSE I *HATE* HIM!
I
HATE NATHAN!
...NO... I DON'T HATE HIM. I HATE...WHAT HE SHOWS ME IS POSSIBLE. WHAT HE IS. WHAT I'M NOT.
I LOVE NATHAN.
I HATE *ME.*

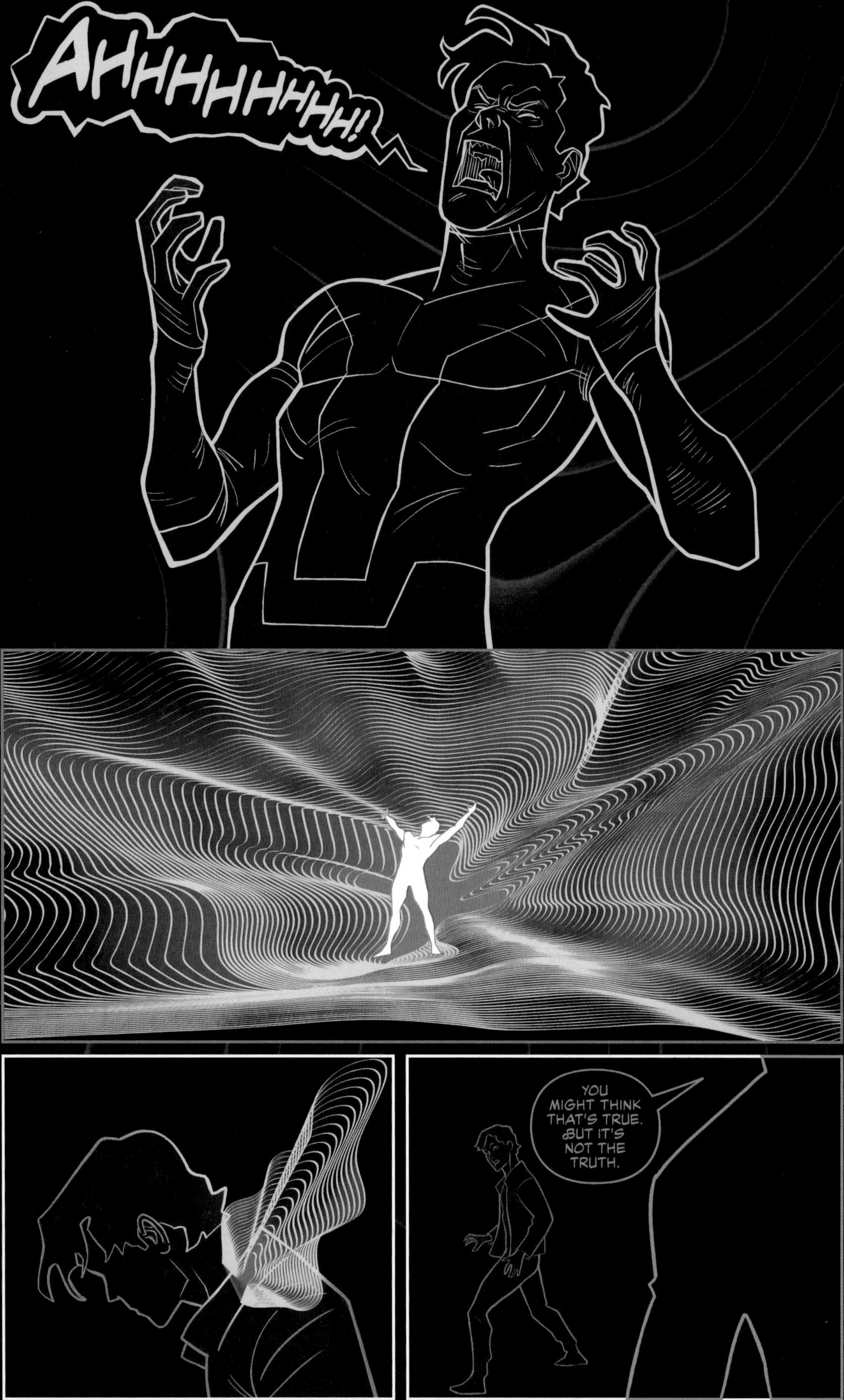
AHHHHHHHHHH!!
YOU MIGHT THINK THAT'S TRUE. BUT IT'S NOT THE TRUTH.

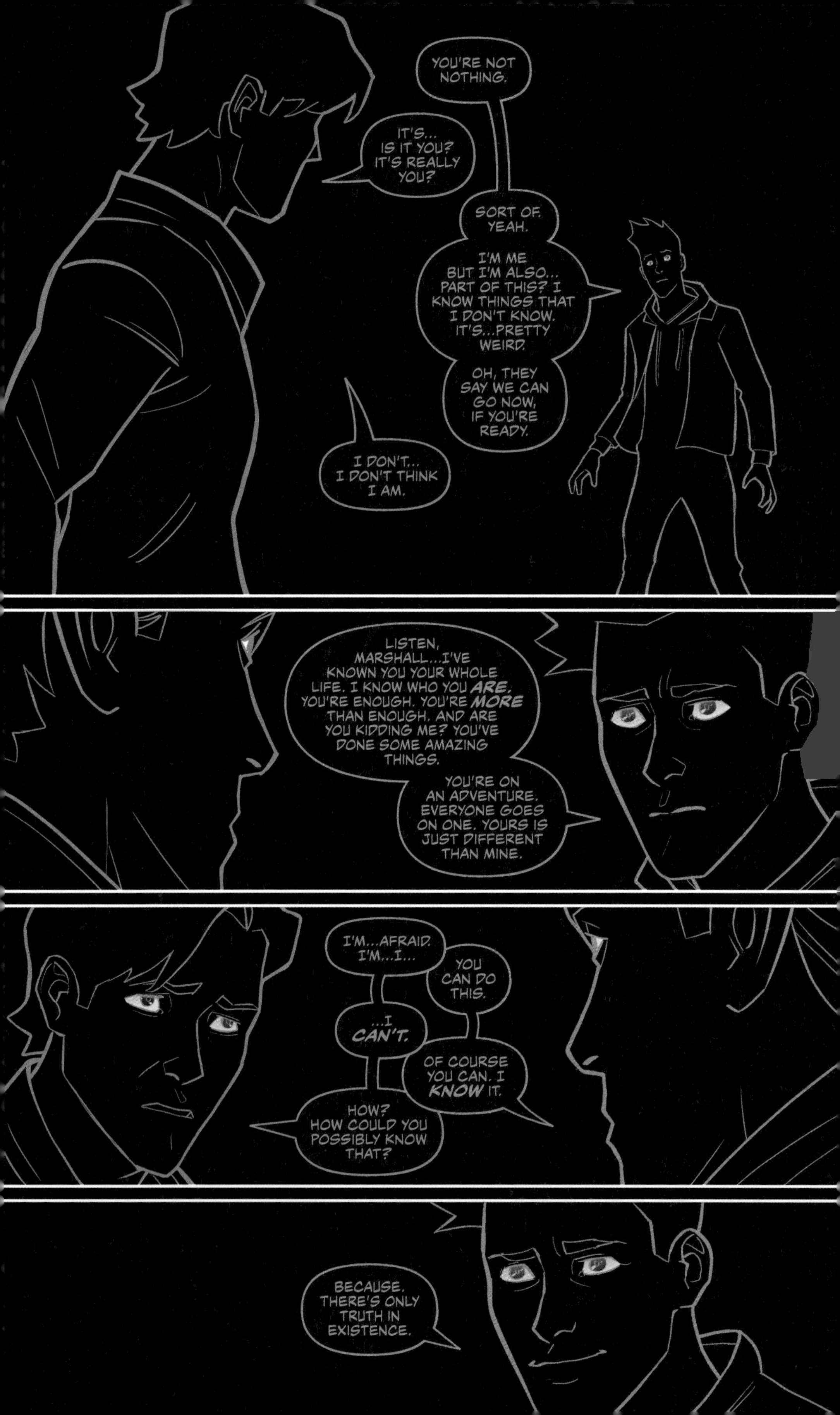

YOU'RE NOT NOTHING.
IT'S... IS IT YOU? IT'S REALLY YOU?
SORT OF. YEAH.
I'M ME BUT I'M ALSO... PART OF THIS? I KNOW THINGS THAT I DON'T KNOW. IT'S...PRETTY WEIRD.
OH, THEY SAY WE CAN GO NOW, IF YOU'RE READY.
I DON'T... I DON'T THINK I AM.
LISTEN, MARSHALL...I'VE KNOWN YOU YOUR WHOLE LIFE. I KNOW WHO YOU ARE. YOU'RE ENOUGH. YOU'RE MORE THAN ENOUGH. AND ARE YOU KIDDING ME? YOU'VE DONE SOME AMAZING THINGS.
YOU'RE ON AN ADVENTURE. EVERYONE GOES ON ONE. YOURS IS JUST DIFFERENT THAN MINE.
I'M...AFRAID. I'M...I...
YOU CAN DO THIS.
...I CAN'T.
OF COURSE YOU CAN. I KNOW IT.
HOW? HOW COULD YOU POSSIBLY KNOW THAT?
BECAUSE. THERE'S ONLY TRUTH IN EXISTENCE.

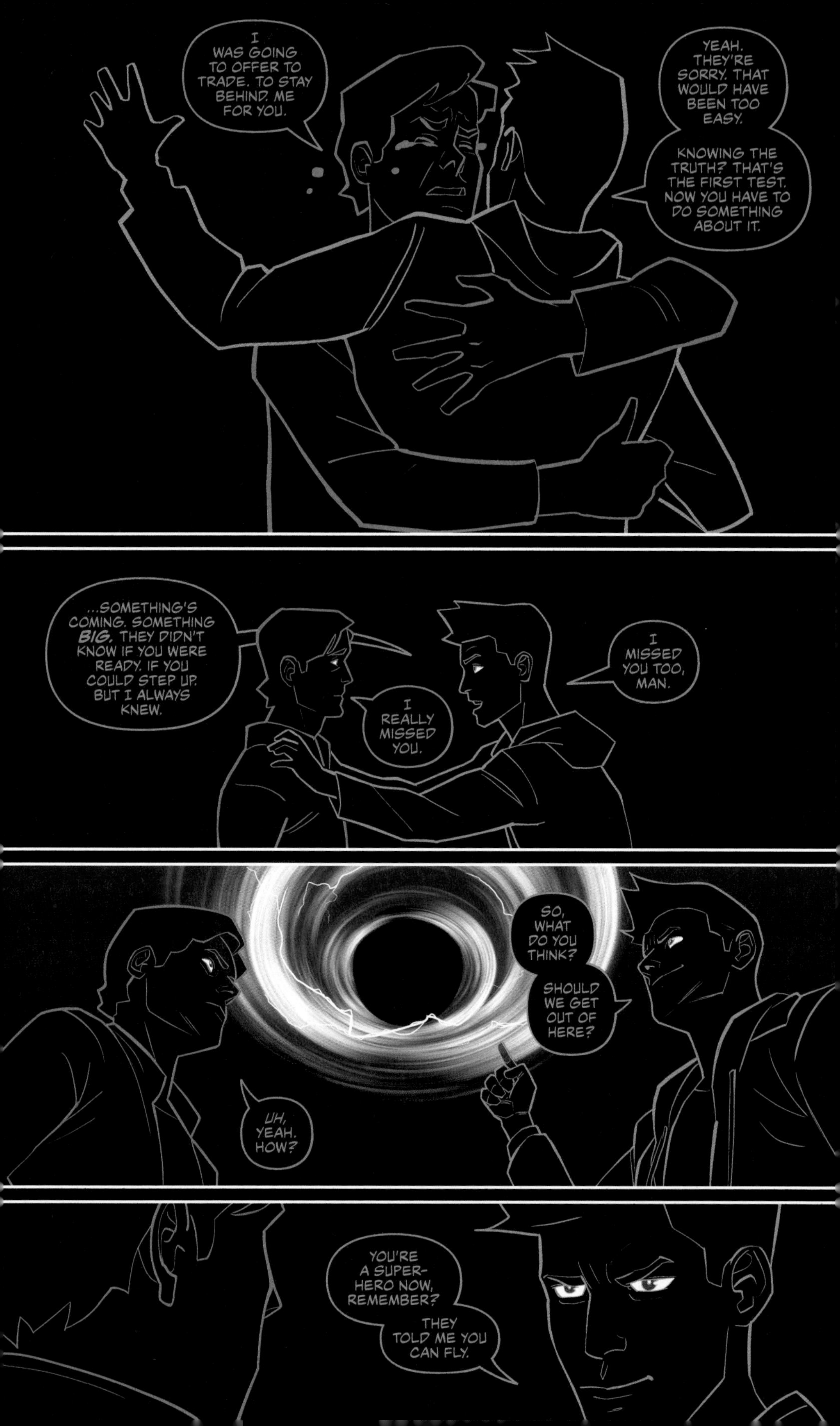
I WAS GOING TO OFFER TO TRADE. TO STAY BEHIND. ME FOR YOU.
YEAH. THEY'RE SORRY. THAT WOULD HAVE BEEN TOO EASY.
KNOWING THE TRUTH? THAT'S THE FIRST TEST. NOW YOU HAVE TO DO SOMETHING ABOUT IT.
...SOMETHING'S COMING. SOMETHING BIG. THEY DIDN'T KNOW IF YOU WERE READY. IF YOU COULD STEP UP. BUT I ALWAYS KNEW.
I REALLY MISSED YOU.
I MISSED YOU TOO, MAN.
SO, WHAT DO YOU THINK?
SHOULD WE GET OUT OF HERE?
UH, YEAH. HOW?
YOU'RE A SUPER-HERO NOW, REMEMBER?
THEY TOLD ME YOU CAN FLY.

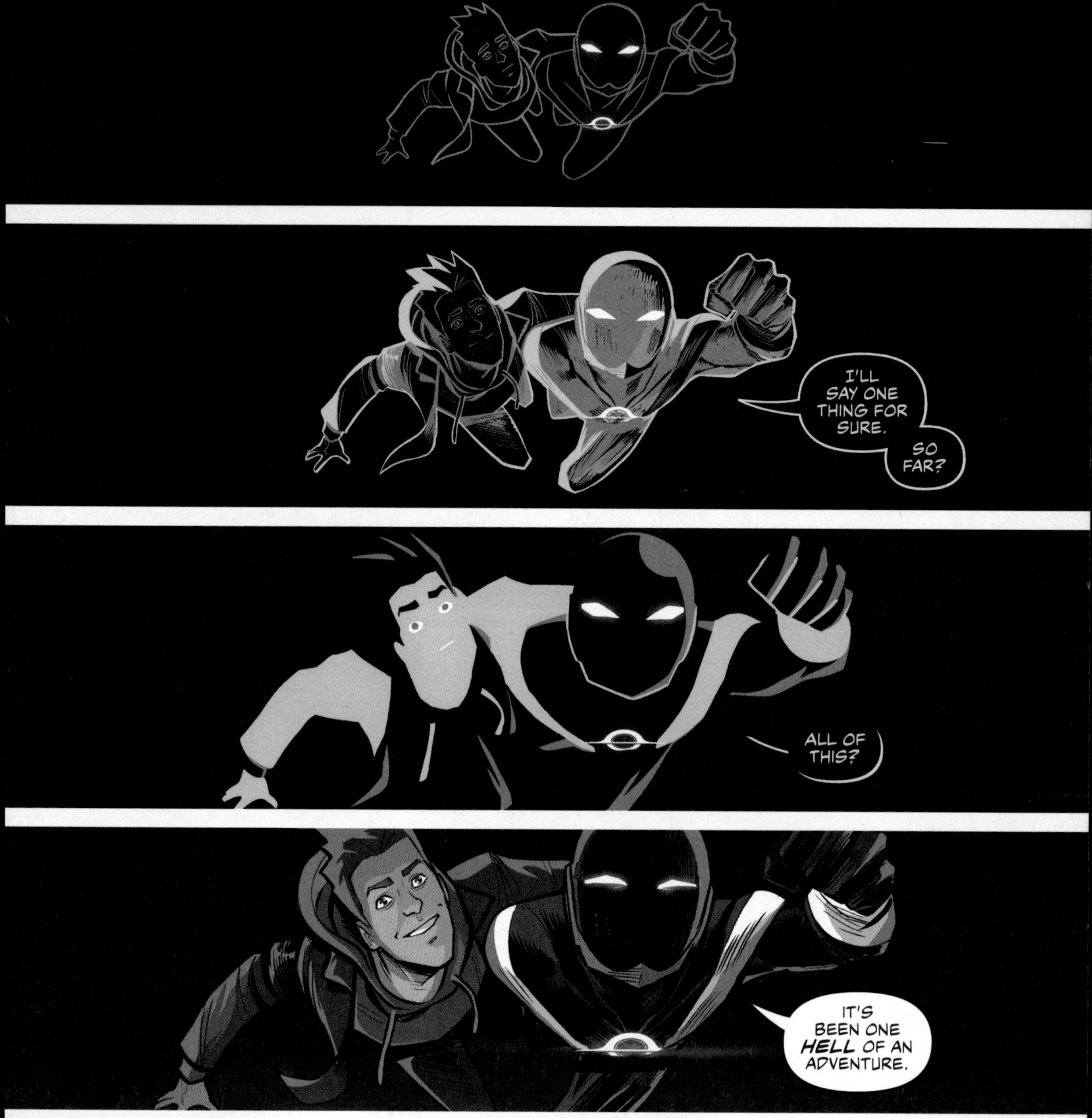
I'LL SAY ONE THING FOR SURE.
SO FAR?
ALL OF THIS?
IT'S BEEN ONE HELL OF AN ADVENTURE.
YOU SAID IT, MAN.

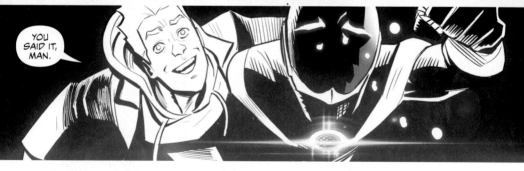

CHAPTER ELEVEN

TITLE   Awake

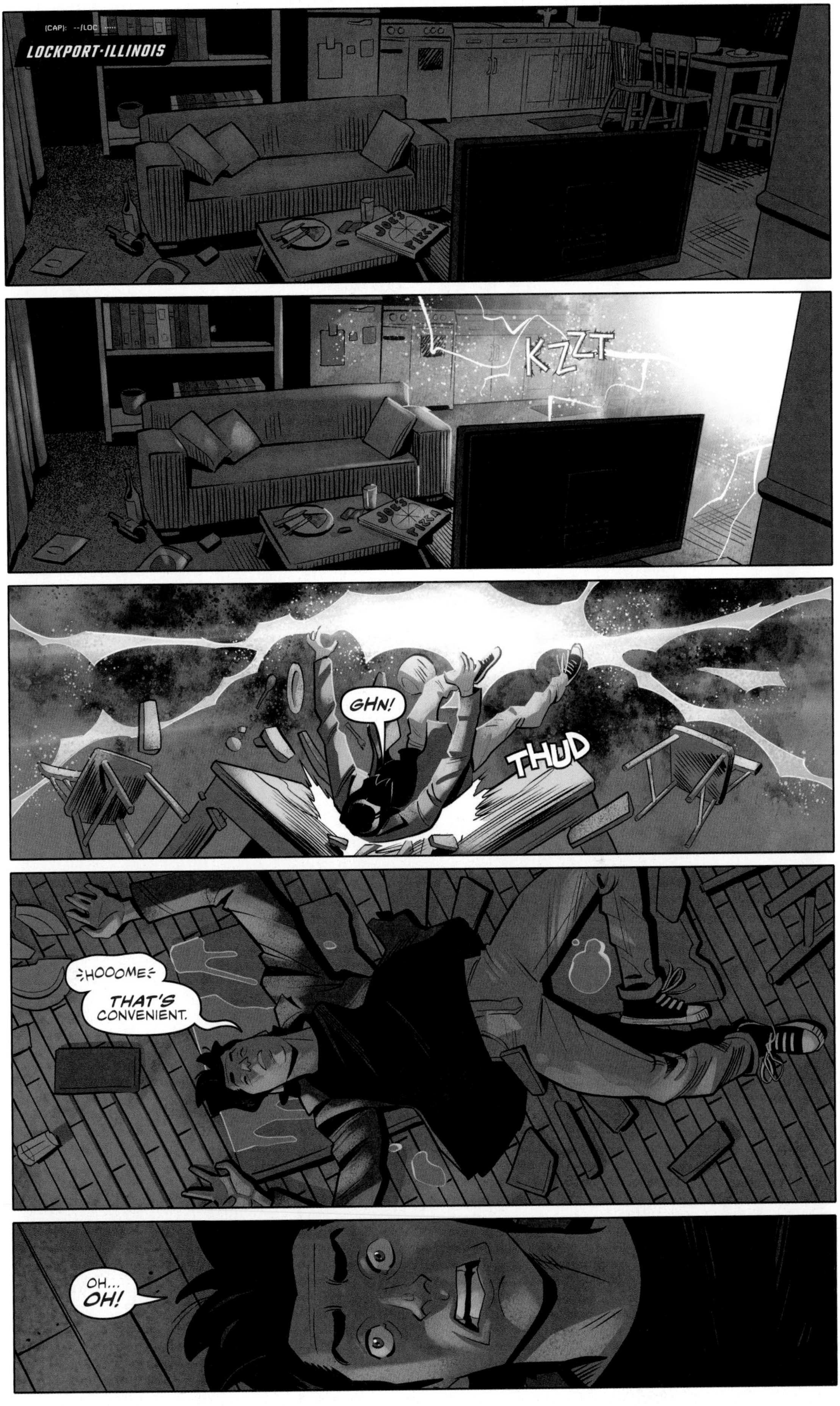

(CAP): --/LOC
LOCKPORT·ILLINOIS
KZZT
GHN!
THUD
HOOOME
THAT'S CONVENIENT.
OH... OH!

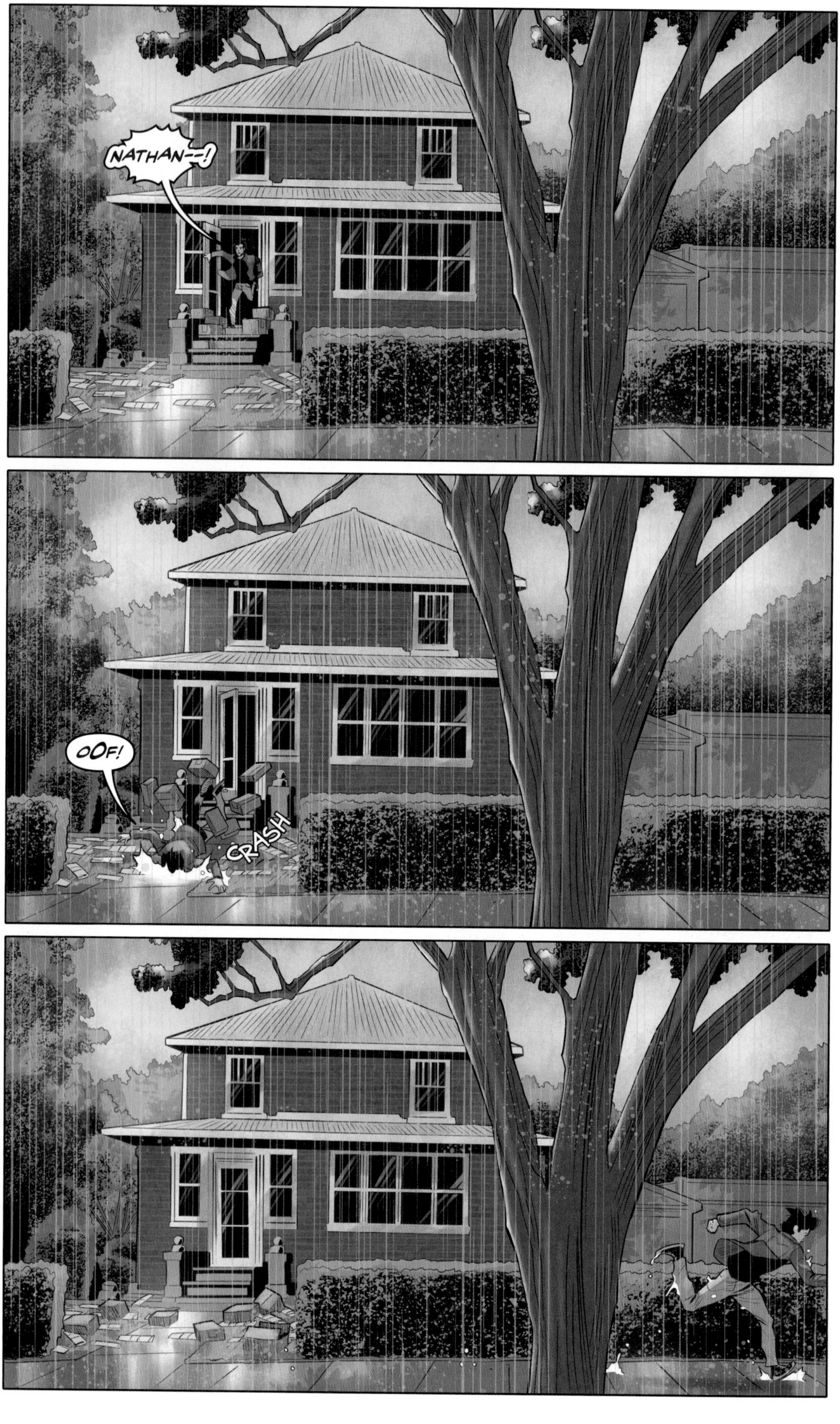
NATHAN--!
OOF!
CRASH

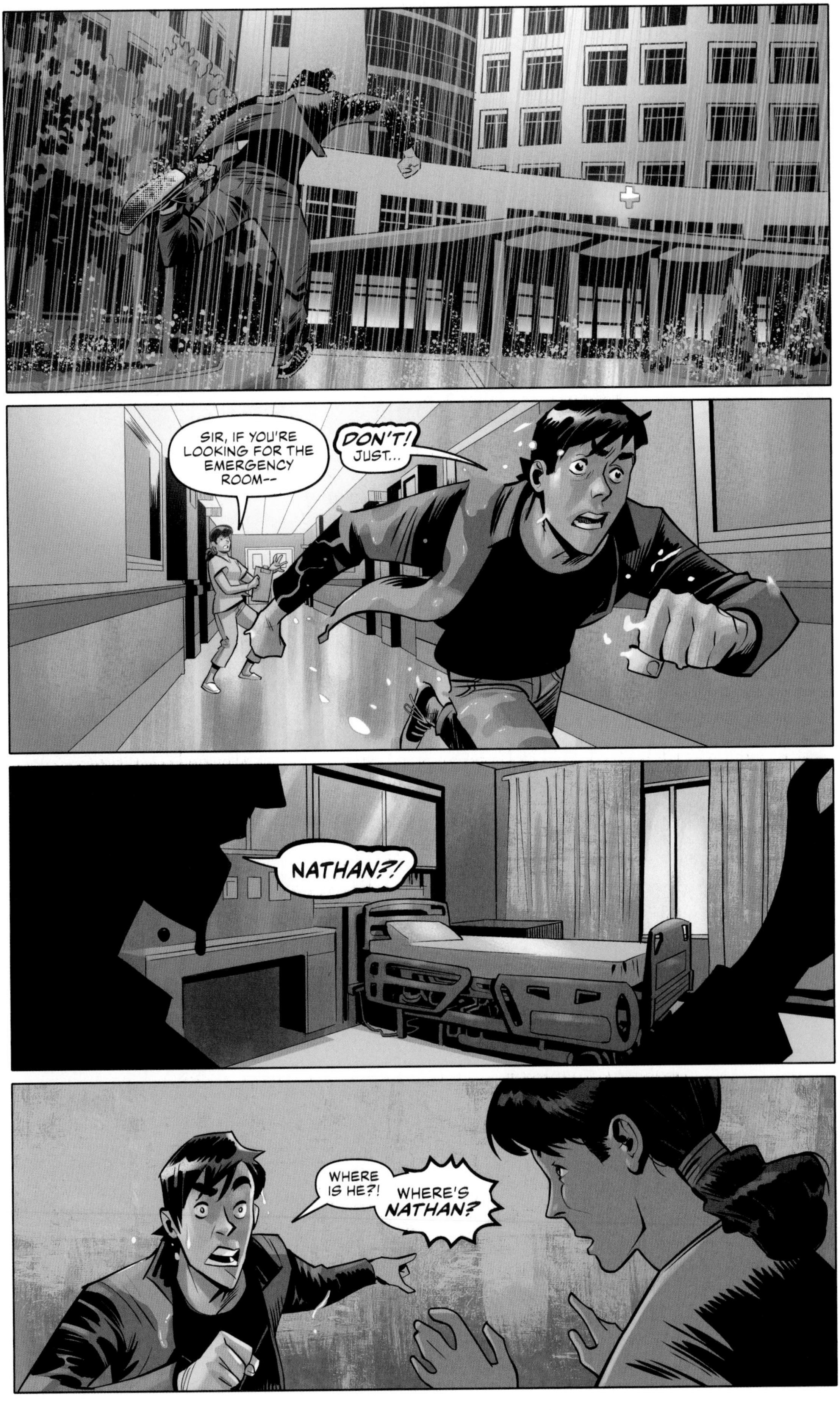
SIR, IF YOU'RE LOOKING FOR THE EMERGENCY ROOM--
DON'T! JUST...
NATHAN?!
WHERE IS HE?!
WHERE'S NATHAN?

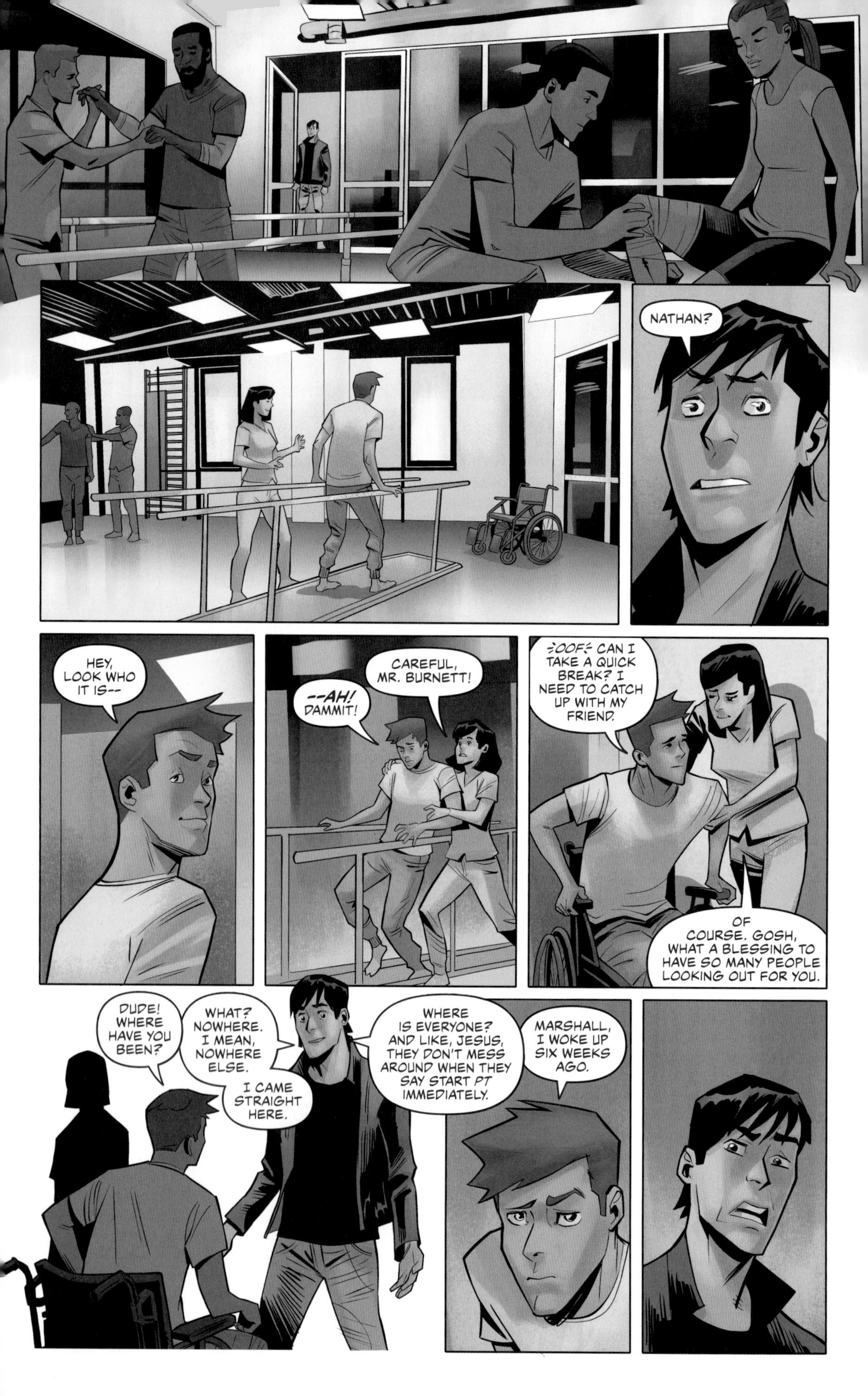
NATHAN?
HEY, LOOK WHO IT IS--
CAREFUL, MR. BURNETT!
--AH! DAMMIT!
OOF CAN I TAKE A QUICK BREAK? I NEED TO CATCH UP WITH MY FRIEND.
OF COURSE. GOSH, WHAT A BLESSING TO HAVE SO MANY PEOPLE LOOKING OUT FOR YOU.
DUDE! WHERE HAVE YOU BEEN?
WHAT? NOWHERE. I MEAN, NOWHERE ELSE.
I CAME STRAIGHT HERE.
WHERE IS EVERYONE? AND LIKE, JESUS, THEY DON'T MESS AROUND WHEN THEY SAY START PT IMMEDIATELY.
MARSHALL, I WOKE UP SIX WEEKS AGO.

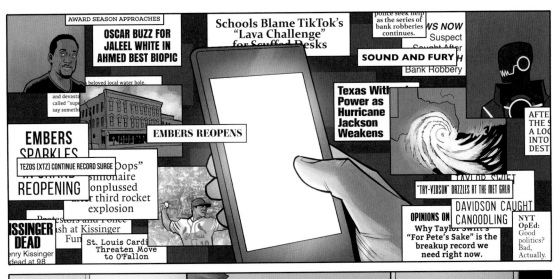

AWARD SEASON APPROACHES

OSCAR BUZZ FOR JALEEL WHITE IN AHMED BEST BIOPIC

Schools Blame TikTok's "Lava Challenge" for Scuffed Desks

police seek help as the series of bank robberies continues.

WS NOW

Suspect Caught After

SOUND AND FURY

Bank Robbery

beloved local water hole,

and devasta called "supe say somethi

EMBERS REOPENS

Texas Without Power as Hurricane Jackson Weakens

AFTE THE S A LOO INTO DEST

EMBERS SPARKLES

TEZOS (XTZ) CONTINUE RECORD SURGE

Oops" sillionaire onplussed r third rocket explosion

REOPENING

TAYLOR SWIFT

"TRY-VIDSON" DAZZLES AT THE MET GALA

DAVIDSON CAUGHT CANOODLING

KISSINGER DEAD

enry Kissinger dead at 98

Protestors and Police sh at Kissinger Fun

St. Louis Cardi Threaten Move to O'Fallon

OPINIONS ON

Why Taylor Swift's "For Pete's Sake" is the breakup record we need right now.

NYT OpEd: Good politics? Bad, Actually.

YOU OKAY?

THE ROBOT DID SAY TIME WORKED DIFFERENTLY...

...YOU TALKED TO THE ROBOT?

YEAAAAH. THERE'S SO MUCH WE GOTTA CATCH UP ON. LIKE, DO YOU EVEN **KNOW** ABOUT THE GLITCHY GUY OR THE OTHER ONES?

RED'S MAYBE NOT AS AWFUL AS WE THOUGHT. PINK IS COOL. YELLOW SUCKS.

...RIGHT.

SORRY. WE DON'T, YOU KNOW, HAVE TO TALK ABOUT ALL THAT. IF YOU DON'T WANT. IF IT'S... WEIRD.

NAH MAN, IT'S COOL. I'M HAPPY FOR YOU. I'M JUST TIRED AND--

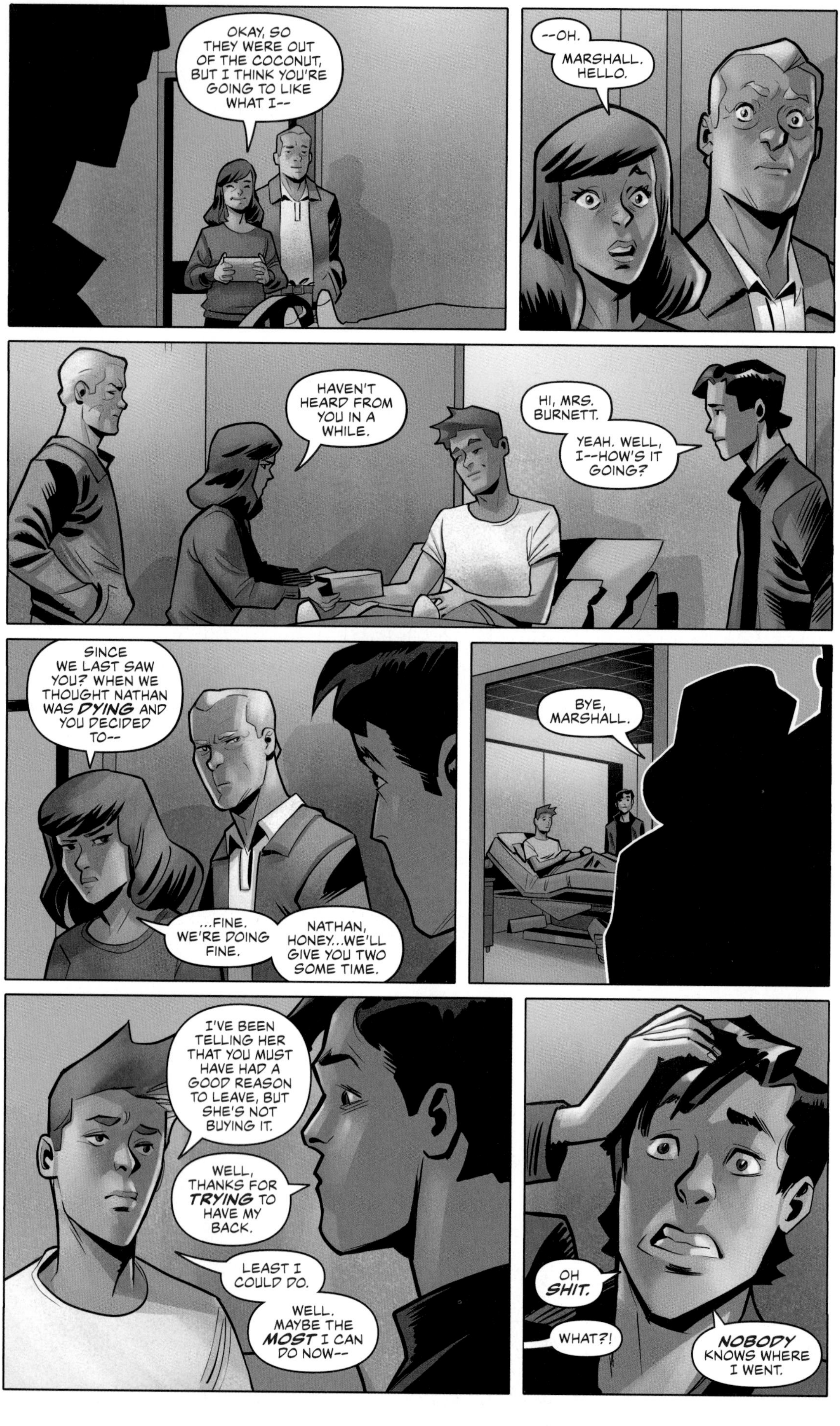
OKAY, SO THEY WERE OUT OF THE COCONUT, BUT I THINK YOU'RE GOING TO LIKE WHAT I--
--OH.
MARSHALL. HELLO.
HAVEN'T HEARD FROM YOU IN A WHILE.
HI, MRS. BURNETT.
YEAH. WELL, I--HOW'S IT GOING?
SINCE WE LAST SAW YOU? WHEN WE THOUGHT NATHAN WAS DYING AND YOU DECIDED TO--
...FINE. WE'RE DOING FINE.
NATHAN, HONEY...WE'LL GIVE YOU TWO SOME TIME.
BYE, MARSHALL.
I'VE BEEN TELLING HER THAT YOU MUST HAVE HAD A GOOD REASON TO LEAVE, BUT SHE'S NOT BUYING IT.
WELL, THANKS FOR TRYING TO HAVE MY BACK.
LEAST I COULD DO.
WELL. MAYBE THE MOST I CAN DO NOW--
OH SHIT.
WHAT?!
NOBODY KNOWS WHERE I WENT.

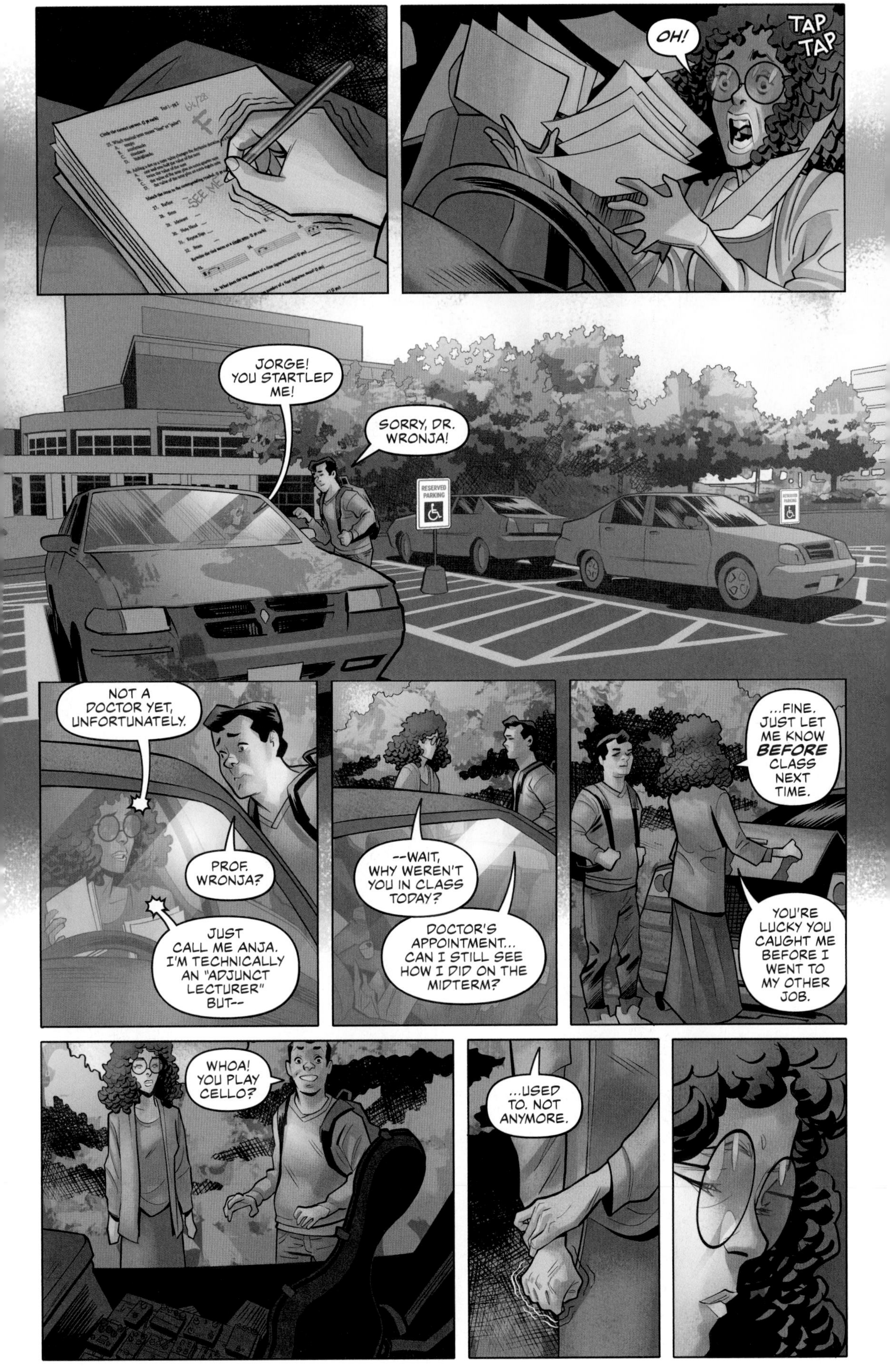
SEE ME
TAP TAP
OH!
JORGE! YOU STARTLED ME!
SORRY, DR. WRONJA!
RESERVED PARKING
RESERVED PARKING
NOT A DOCTOR YET, UNFORTUNATELY.
PROF. WRONJA?
JUST CALL ME ANJA. I'M TECHNICALLY AN "ADJUNCT LECTURER" BUT--
--WAIT, WHY WEREN'T YOU IN CLASS TODAY?
DOCTOR'S APPOINTMENT... CAN I STILL SEE HOW I DID ON THE MIDTERM?
...FINE. JUST LET ME KNOW ***BEFORE*** CLASS NEXT TIME.
YOU'RE LUCKY YOU CAUGHT ME BEFORE I WENT TO MY OTHER JOB.
WHOA! YOU PLAY CELLO?
...USED TO. NOT ANYMORE.

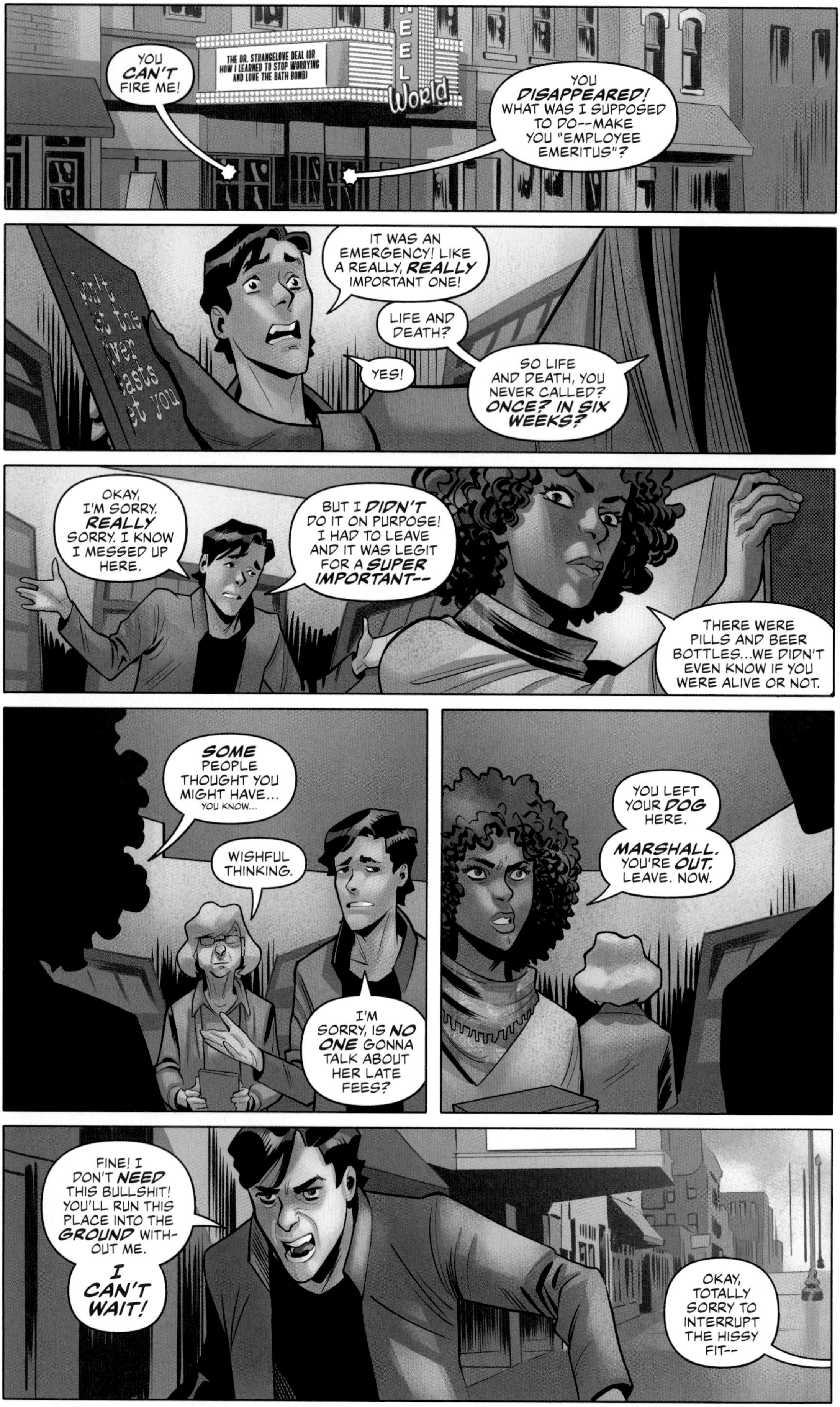
THE DR. STRANGELOVE DEAL (OR HOW I LEARNED TO STOP WORRYING AND LOVE THE BATH BOMB)
World
YOU CAN'T FIRE ME!
YOU DISAPPEARED! WHAT WAS I SUPPOSED TO DO--MAKE YOU "EMPLOYEE EMERITUS"?
IT WAS AN EMERGENCY! LIKE A REALLY, REALLY IMPORTANT ONE!
LIFE AND DEATH?
YES!
SO LIFE AND DEATH, YOU NEVER CALLED? ONCE? IN SIX WEEKS?
OKAY, I'M SORRY. REALLY SORRY. I KNOW I MESSED UP HERE.
BUT I DIDN'T DO IT ON PURPOSE! I HAD TO LEAVE AND IT WAS LEGIT FOR A SUPER IMPORTANT--
THERE WERE PILLS AND BEER BOTTLES...WE DIDN'T EVEN KNOW IF YOU WERE ALIVE OR NOT.
SOME PEOPLE THOUGHT YOU MIGHT HAVE... YOU KNOW...
WISHFUL THINKING.
I'M SORRY, IS NO ONE GONNA TALK ABOUT HER LATE FEES?
YOU LEFT YOUR DOG HERE.
MARSHALL, YOU'RE OUT. LEAVE. NOW.
FINE! I DON'T NEED THIS BULLSHIT! YOU'LL RUN THIS PLACE INTO THE GROUND WITHOUT ME.
I CAN'T WAIT!
OKAY, TOTALLY SORRY TO INTERRUPT THE HISSY FIT--

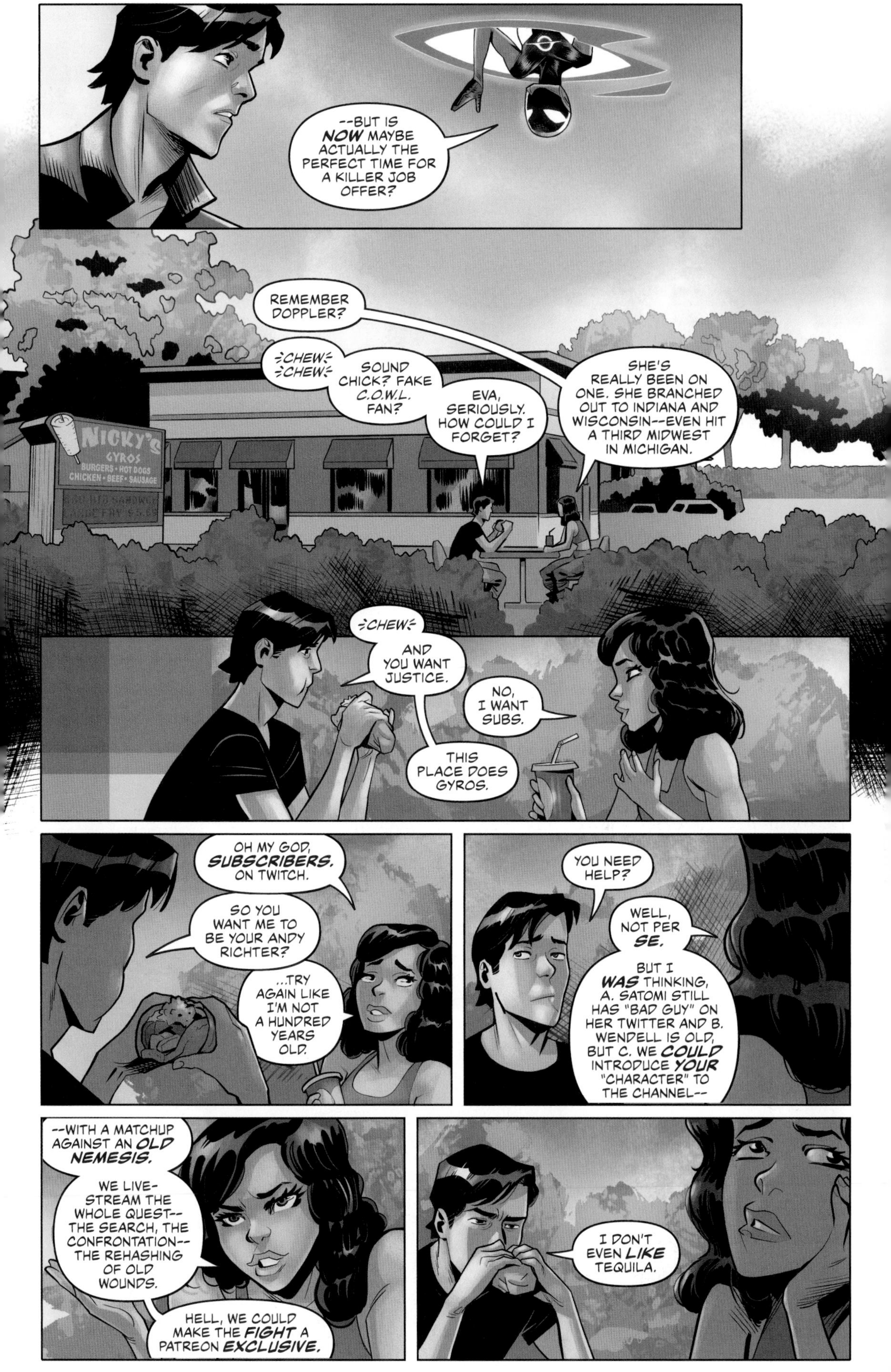
--BUT IS NOW MAYBE ACTUALLY THE PERFECT TIME FOR A KILLER JOB OFFER?
REMEMBER DOPPLER?
CHEW CHEW
SOUND CHICK? FAKE C.O.W.L. FAN?
EVA, SERIOUSLY. HOW COULD I FORGET?
SHE'S REALLY BEEN ON ONE. SHE BRANCHED OUT TO INDIANA AND WISCONSIN--EVEN HIT A THIRD MIDWEST IN MICHIGAN.
NICKY'S
GYROS
BURGERS • HOT DOGS
CHICKEN • BEEF • SAUSAGE
CHEW
AND YOU WANT JUSTICE.
NO, I WANT SUBS.
THIS PLACE DOES GYROS.
OH MY GOD, SUBSCRIBERS. ON TWITCH.
SO YOU WANT ME TO BE YOUR ANDY RICHTER?
...TRY AGAIN LIKE I'M NOT A HUNDRED YEARS OLD.
YOU NEED HELP?
WELL, NOT PER SE.
BUT I WAS THINKING, A. SATOMI STILL HAS "BAD GUY" ON HER TWITTER AND B. WENDELL IS OLD, BUT C. WE COULD INTRODUCE YOUR "CHARACTER" TO THE CHANNEL--
--WITH A MATCHUP AGAINST AN OLD NEMESIS.
WE LIVE-STREAM THE WHOLE QUEST--THE SEARCH, THE CONFRONTATION--THE REHASHING OF OLD WOUNDS.
HELL, WE COULD MAKE THE FIGHT A PATREON EXCLUSIVE.
I DON'T EVEN LIKE TEQUILA.

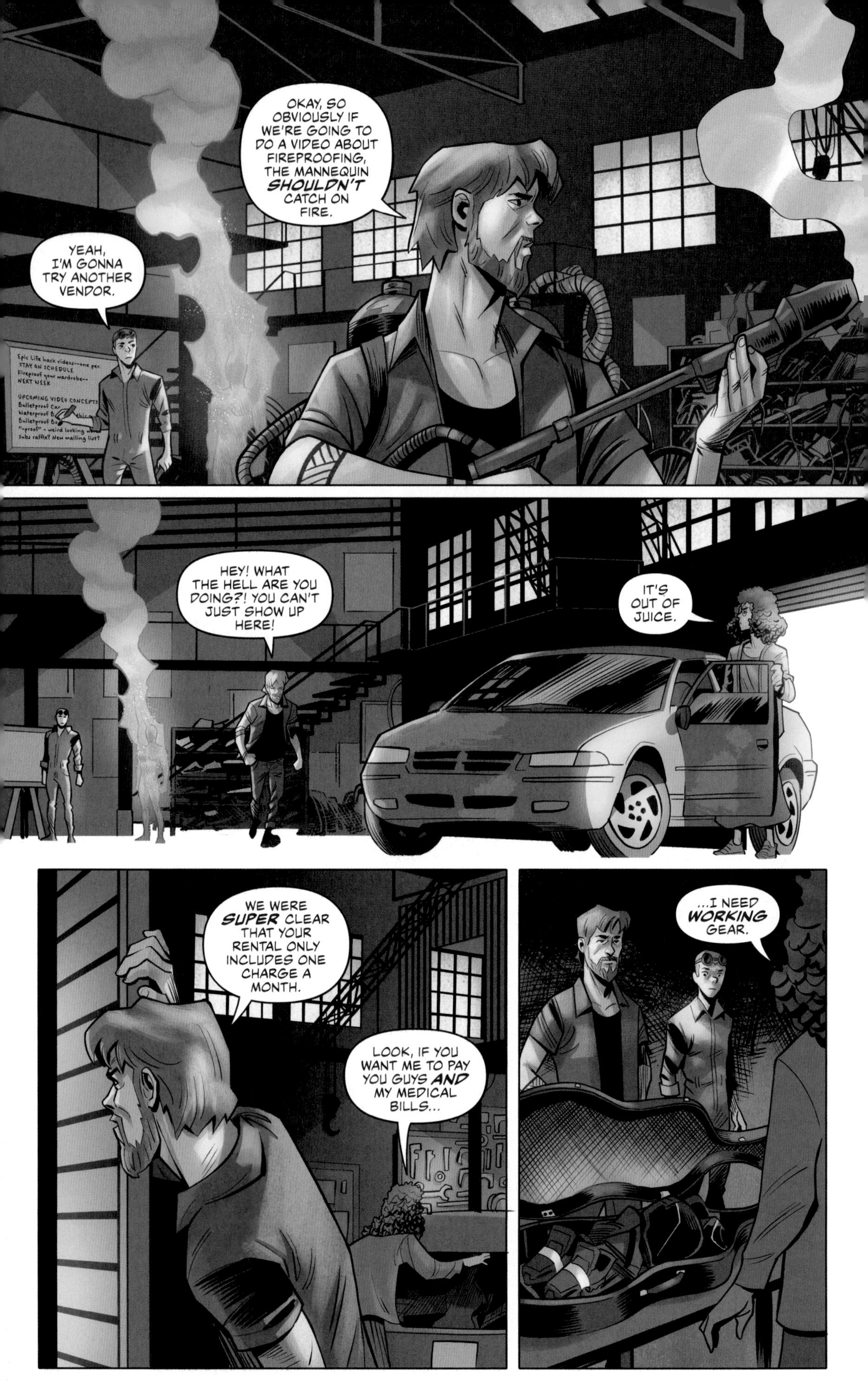

OKAY, SO OBVIOUSLY IF WE'RE GOING TO DO A VIDEO ABOUT FIREPROOFING, THE MANNEQUIN *SHOULDN'T* CATCH ON FIRE.
YEAH, I'M GONNA TRY ANOTHER VENDOR.
Epic Life hack videos--one per.
STAY ON SCHEDULE
Fireproof your wardrobe--
NEXT WEEK
UPCOMING VIDEO CONCEPTS
Bulletproof Car
Waterproof B
Bulletproof Bo
"-proof" - weird looking
Subs raffle? New mailing list?
HEY! WHAT THE HELL ARE YOU DOING?! YOU CAN'T JUST SHOW UP HERE!
IT'S OUT OF JUICE.
WE WERE *SUPER* CLEAR THAT YOUR RENTAL ONLY INCLUDES ONE CHARGE A MONTH.
LOOK, IF YOU WANT ME TO PAY YOU GUYS *AND* MY MEDICAL BILLS...
...I NEED *WORKING* GEAR.

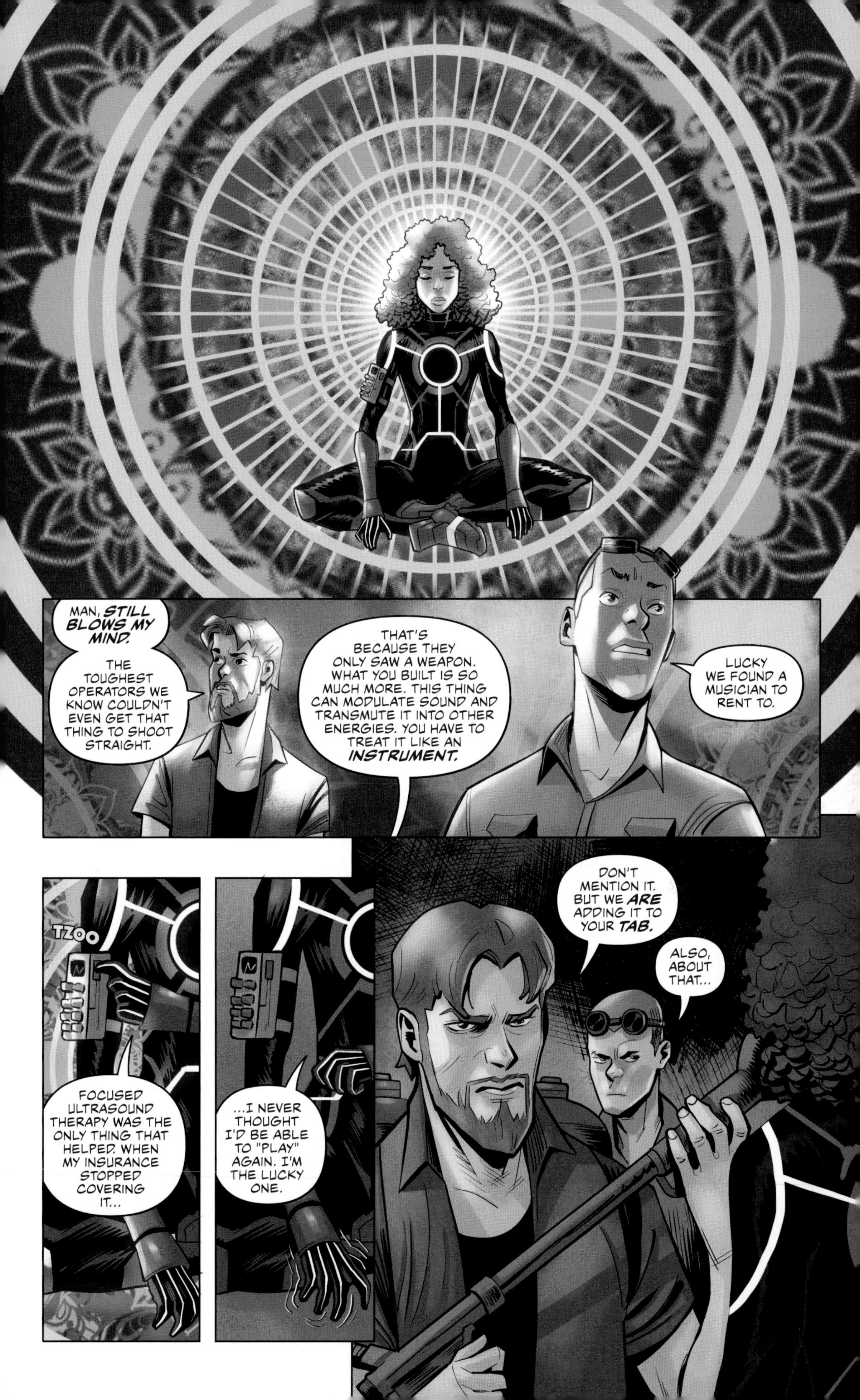
MAN, STILL BLOWS MY MIND.
THE TOUGHEST OPERATORS WE KNOW COULDN'T EVEN GET THAT THING TO SHOOT STRAIGHT.
THAT'S BECAUSE THEY ONLY SAW A WEAPON. WHAT YOU BUILT IS SO MUCH MORE. THIS THING CAN MODULATE SOUND AND TRANSMUTE IT INTO OTHER ENERGIES. YOU HAVE TO TREAT IT LIKE AN INSTRUMENT.
LUCKY WE FOUND A MUSICIAN TO RENT TO.
TZOO
FOCUSED ULTRASOUND THERAPY WAS THE ONLY THING THAT HELPED. WHEN MY INSURANCE STOPPED COVERING IT...
...I NEVER THOUGHT I'D BE ABLE TO "PLAY" AGAIN. I'M THE LUCKY ONE.
DON'T MENTION IT. BUT WE ARE ADDING IT TO YOUR TAB.
ALSO, ABOUT THAT...

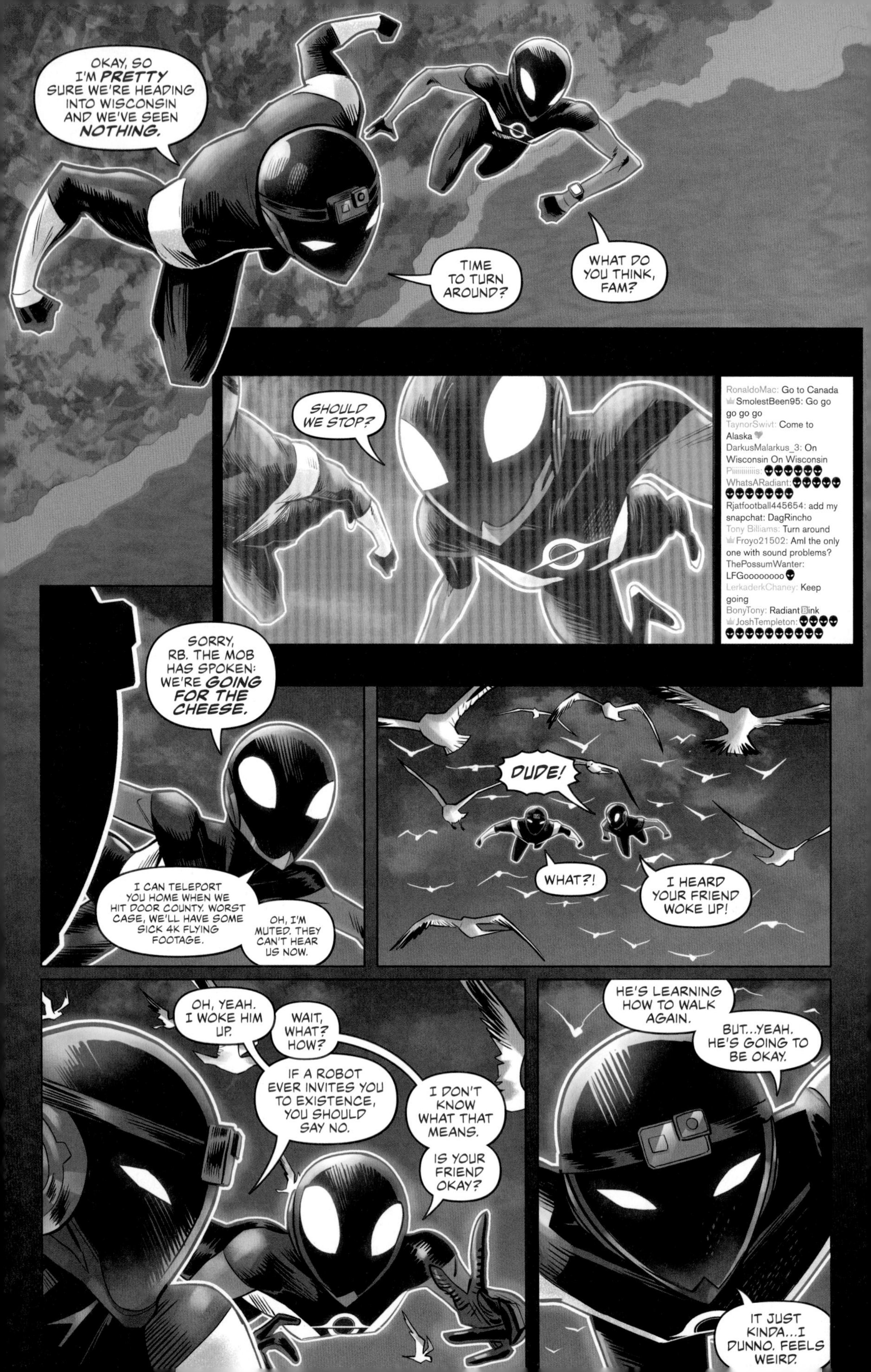

OKAY, SO I'M PRETTY SURE WE'RE HEADING INTO WISCONSIN AND WE'VE SEEN NOTHING.
TIME TO TURN AROUND?
WHAT DO YOU THINK, FAM?
SHOULD WE STOP?
RonaldoMac: Go to Canada
SmolestBeen95: Go go go go go
TaynorSwivt: Come to Alaska
DarkusMalarkus_3: On Wisconsin On Wisconsin
Piiiiiiiiiiis:
WhatsARadiant:
Rjatfootball445654: add my snapchat: DagRincho
Tony Billiams: Turn around
Froyo21502: AmI the only one with sound problems?
ThePossumWanter: LFGoooooooo
LerkaderkChaney: Keep going
BonyTony: Radiant Bink
JoshTempleton:
SORRY, RB. THE MOB HAS SPOKEN: WE'RE GOING FOR THE CHEESE.
I CAN TELEPORT YOU HOME WHEN WE HIT DOOR COUNTY. WORST CASE, WE'LL HAVE SOME SICK 4K FLYING FOOTAGE.
OH, I'M MUTED. THEY CAN'T HEAR US NOW.
DUDE!
WHAT?!
I HEARD YOUR FRIEND WOKE UP!
OH, YEAH. I WOKE HIM UP.
WAIT, WHAT? HOW?
IF A ROBOT EVER INVITES YOU TO EXISTENCE, YOU SHOULD SAY NO.
I DON'T KNOW WHAT THAT MEANS.
IS YOUR FRIEND OKAY?
HE'S LEARNING HOW TO WALK AGAIN.
BUT...YEAH. HE'S GOING TO BE OKAY.
IT JUST KINDA...I DUNNO. FEELS WEIRD.

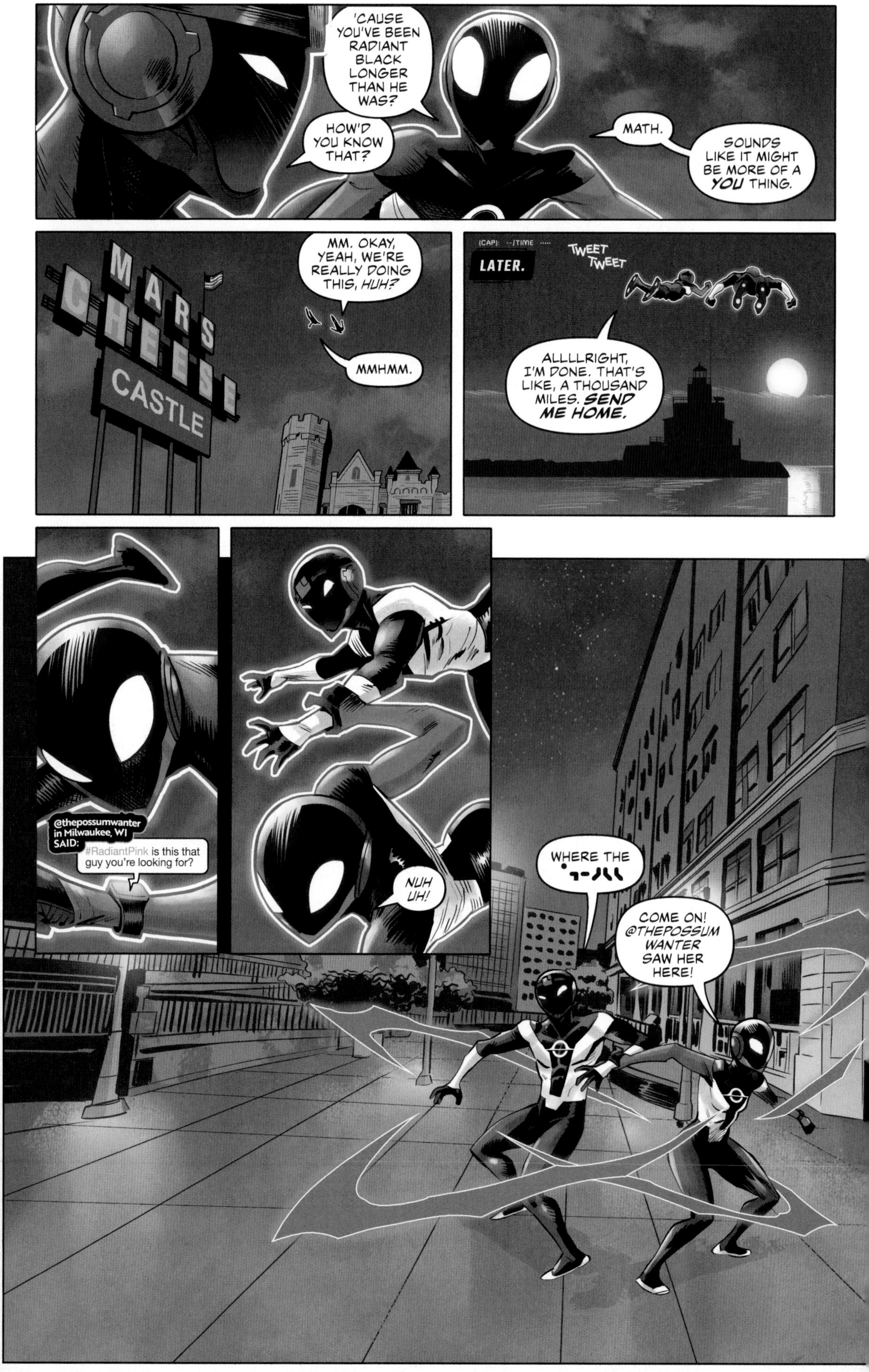
'CAUSE YOU'VE BEEN RADIANT BLACK LONGER THAN HE WAS?
HOW'D YOU KNOW THAT?
MATH.
SOUNDS LIKE IT MIGHT BE MORE OF A *YOU* THING.
MARS CHEESE CASTLE
MM. OKAY, YEAH, WE'RE REALLY DOING THIS, *HUH?*
MMHMM.
LATER.
TWEET TWEET
ALLLLRIGHT, I'M DONE. THAT'S LIKE, A THOUSAND MILES. ***SEND ME HOME.***
@thepossumwanter in Milwaukee, WI SAID:
#RadiantPink is this that guy you're looking for?
NUH UH!
WHERE THE
COME ON! @THEPOSSUMWANTER SAW HER HERE!

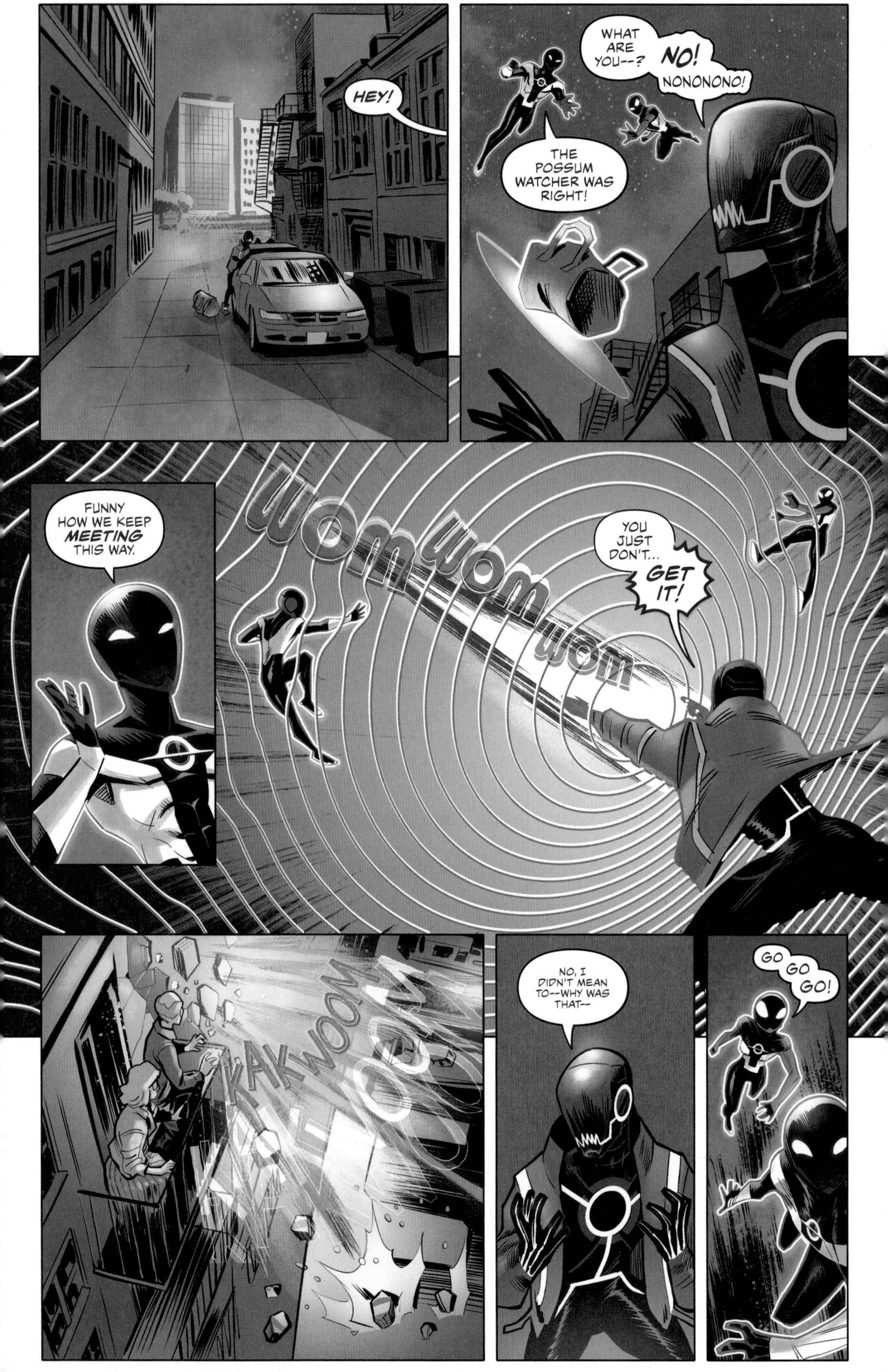
HEY!
WHAT ARE YOU--?
NO! NONONONO!
THE POSSUM WATCHER WAS RIGHT!
FUNNY HOW WE KEEP MEETING THIS WAY.
WOM WOM WOM
YOU JUST DON'T... GET IT!
KAKWOOM
NO, I DIDN'T MEAN TO--WHY WAS THAT--
GO GO GO!

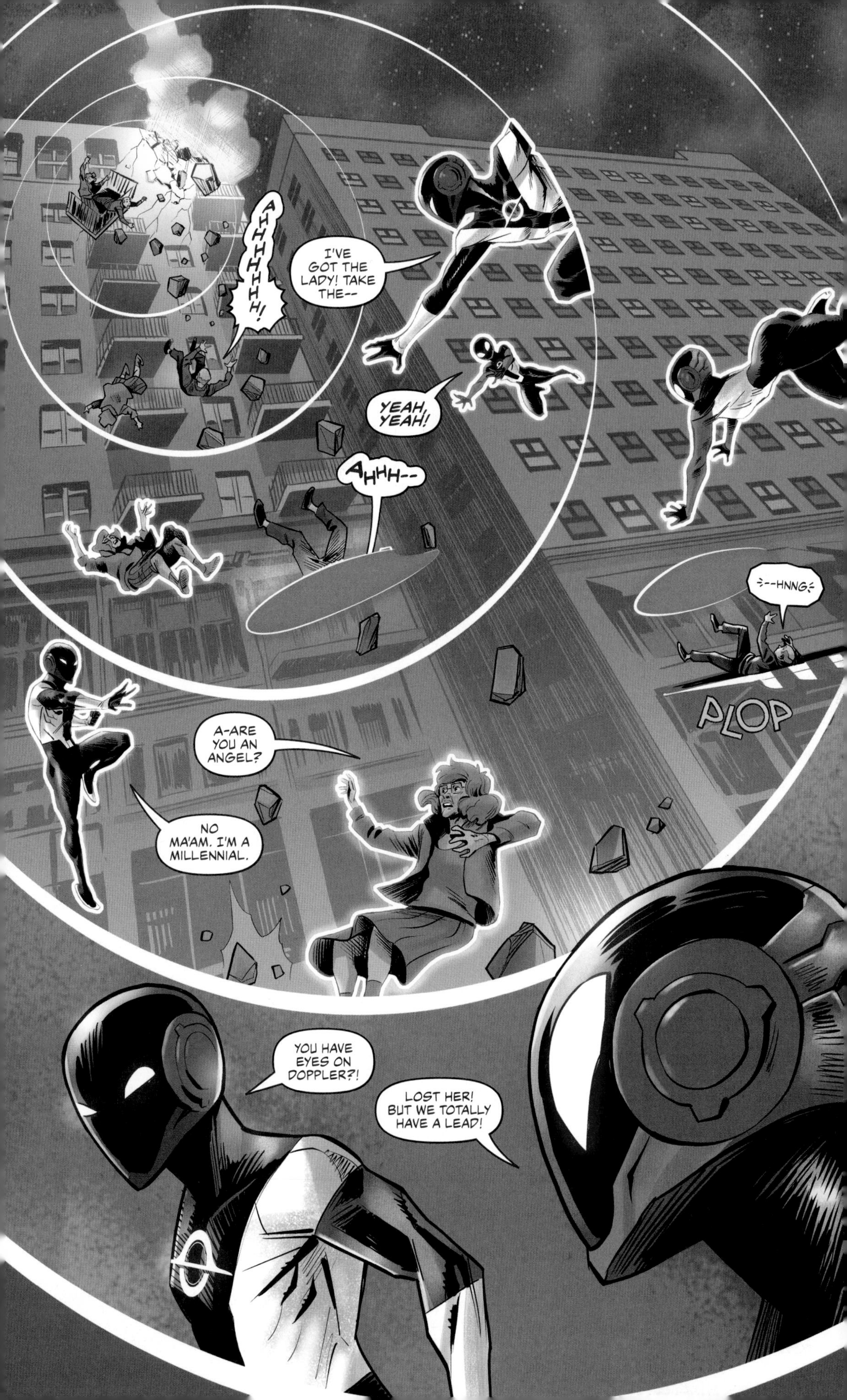
AHHHHHHH!
I'VE GOT THE LADY! TAKE THE--
YEAH, YEAH!
AHHH--
--HNNG
PLOP
A-ARE YOU AN ANGEL?
NO MA'AM. I'M A MILLENNIAL.
YOU HAVE EYES ON DOPPLER?!
LOST HER! BUT WE TOTALLY HAVE A LEAD!

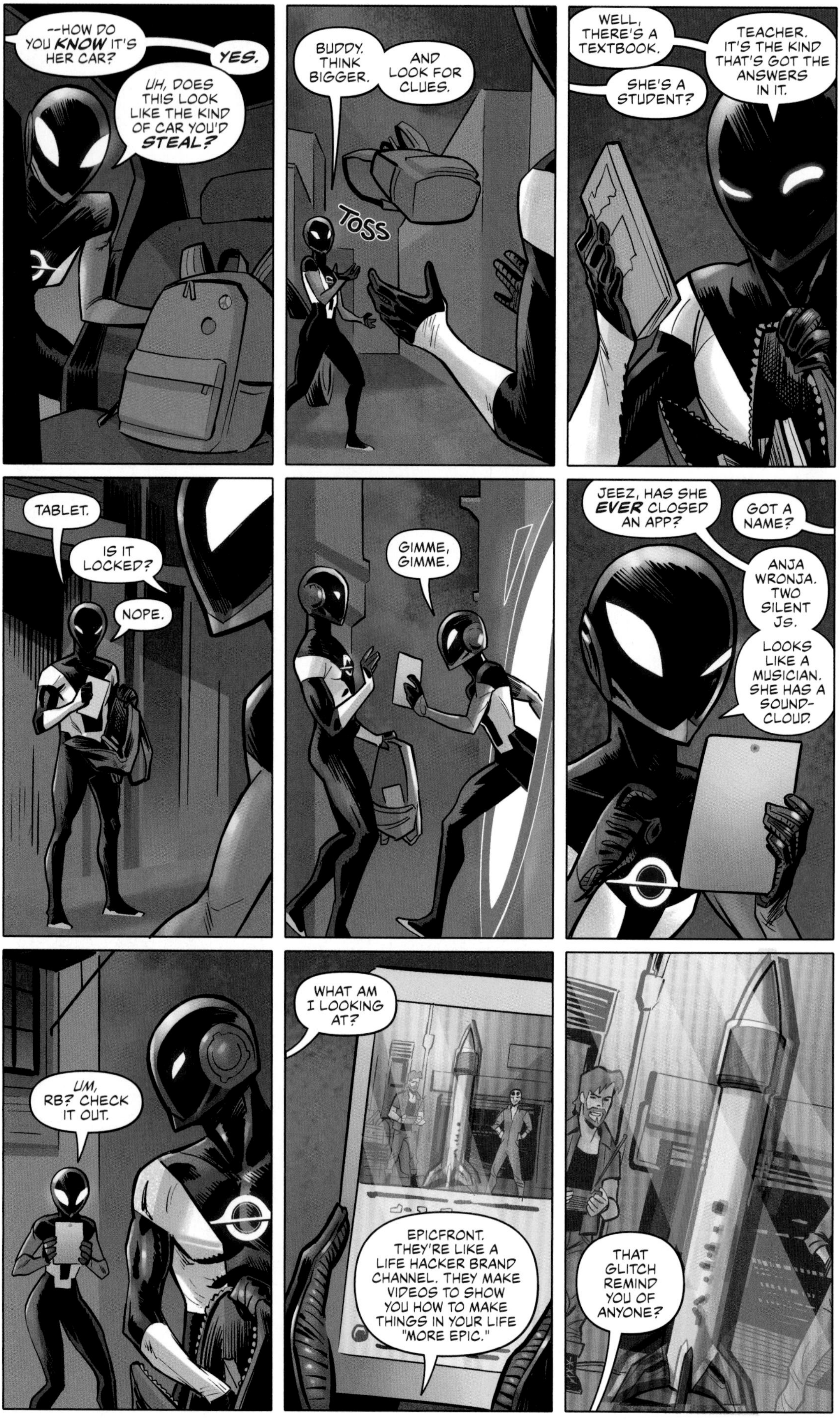

--HOW DO YOU **KNOW** IT'S HER CAR?
YES.
UH, DOES THIS LOOK LIKE THE KIND OF CAR YOU'D ***STEAL?***
BUDDY. THINK BIGGER.
AND LOOK FOR CLUES.
TOSS
WELL, THERE'S A TEXTBOOK.
SHE'S A STUDENT?
TEACHER. IT'S THE KIND THAT'S GOT THE ANSWERS IN IT.
TABLET.
IS IT LOCKED?
NOPE.
GIMME, GIMME.
JEEZ, HAS SHE ***EVER*** CLOSED AN APP?
GOT A NAME?
ANJA WRONJA. TWO SILENT JS.
LOOKS LIKE A MUSICIAN. SHE HAS A SOUND-CLOUD.
UM, RB? CHECK IT OUT.
WHAT AM I LOOKING AT?
EPICFRONT. THEY'RE LIKE A LIFE HACKER BRAND CHANNEL. THEY MAKE VIDEOS TO SHOW YOU HOW TO MAKE THINGS IN YOUR LIFE "MORE EPIC."
THAT GLITCH REMIND YOU OF ANYONE?

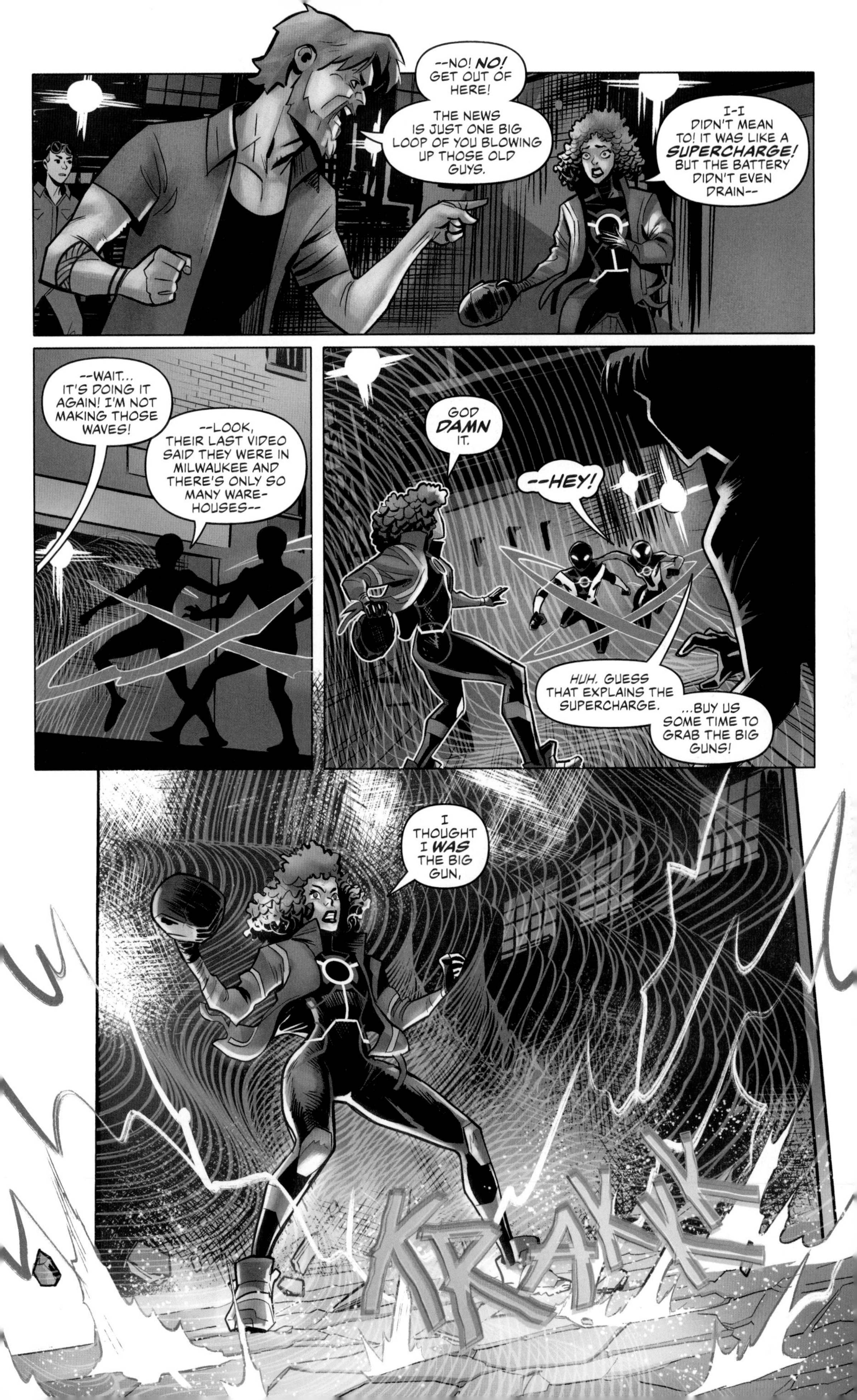
--NO! NO! GET OUT OF HERE!
THE NEWS IS JUST ONE BIG LOOP OF YOU BLOWING UP THOSE OLD GUYS.
I-I DIDN'T MEAN TO! IT WAS LIKE A SUPERCHARGE! BUT THE BATTERY DIDN'T EVEN DRAIN--
--WAIT... IT'S DOING IT AGAIN! I'M NOT MAKING THOSE WAVES!
--LOOK, THEIR LAST VIDEO SAID THEY WERE IN MILWAUKEE AND THERE'S ONLY SO MANY WARE-HOUSES--
GOD DAMN IT.
--HEY!
HUH. GUESS THAT EXPLAINS THE SUPERCHARGE.
...BUY US SOME TIME TO GRAB THE BIG GUNS!
I THOUGHT I WAS THE BIG GUN,
KRAKK

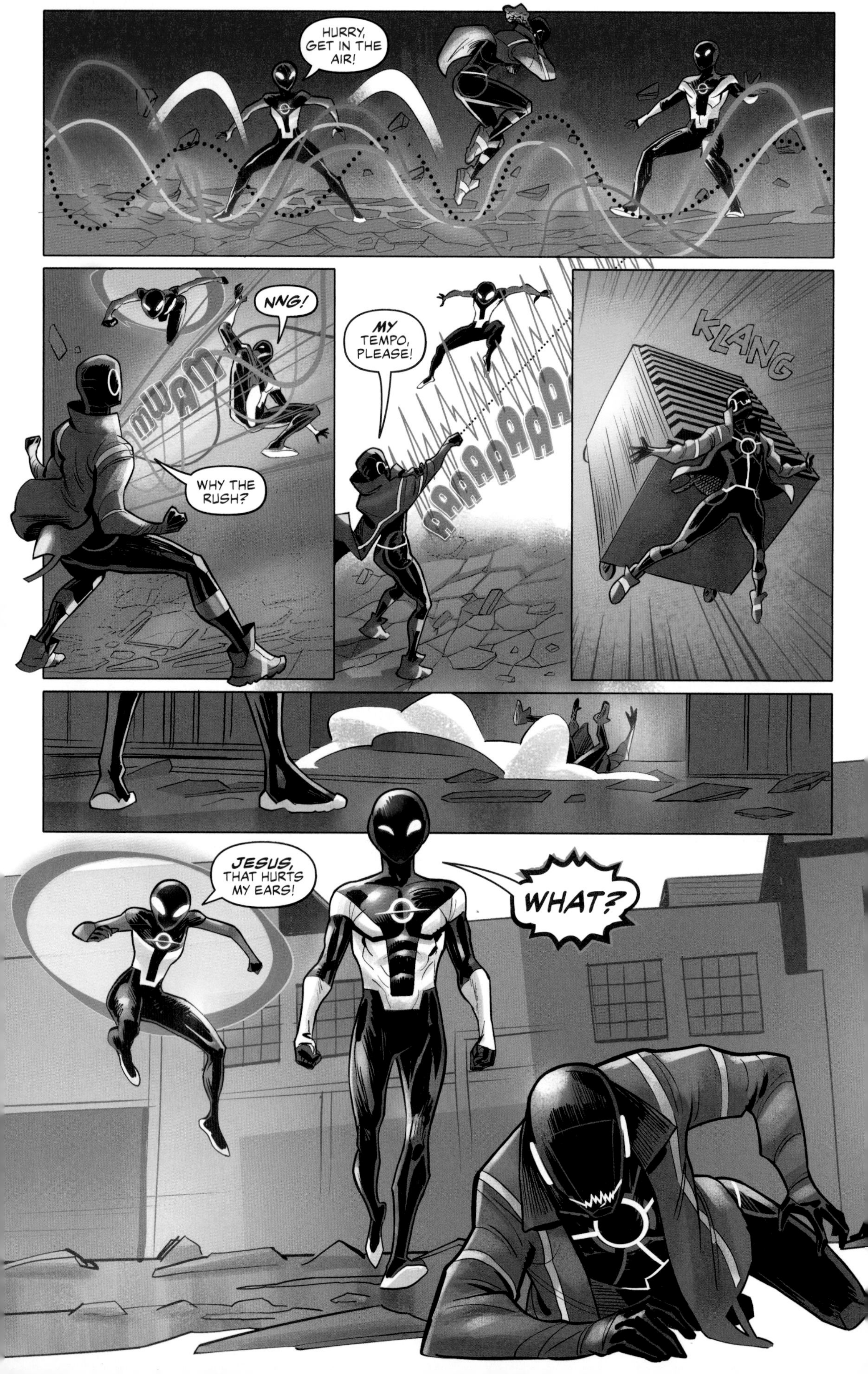
HURRY, GET IN THE AIR!
NNG!
mWAM
WHY THE RUSH?
MY TEMPO, PLEASE!
AAAAAAAAAA
KLANG
JESUS, THAT HURTS MY EARS!
WHAT?

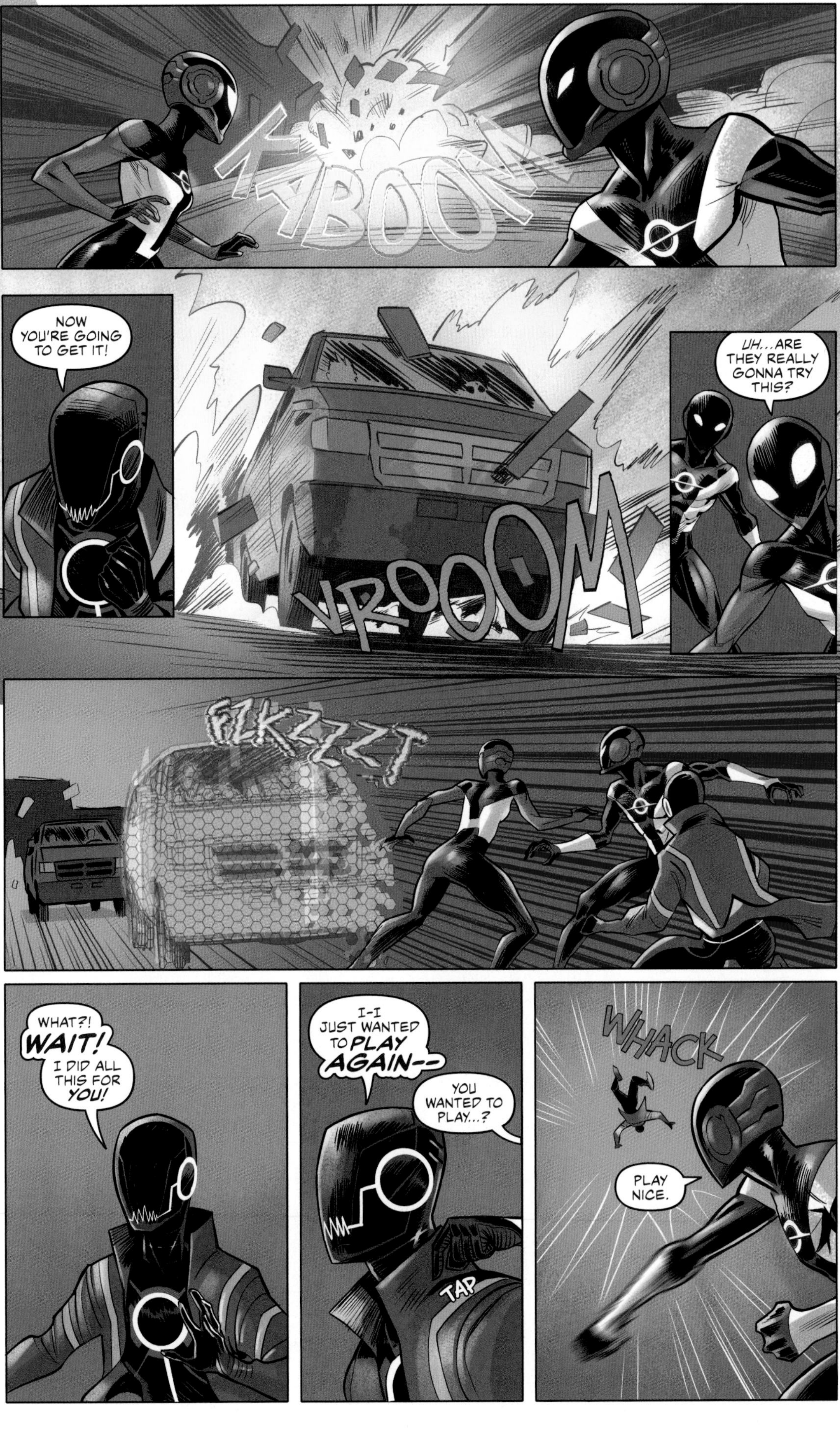
KABOOM
NOW YOU'RE GOING TO GET IT!
UH...ARE THEY REALLY GONNA TRY THIS?
VROOOM
FZKZZZT
WHAT?! WAIT! I DID ALL THIS FOR YOU!
I-I JUST WANTED TO PLAY AGAIN--
YOU WANTED TO PLAY...?
TAP
WHACK
PLAY NICE.

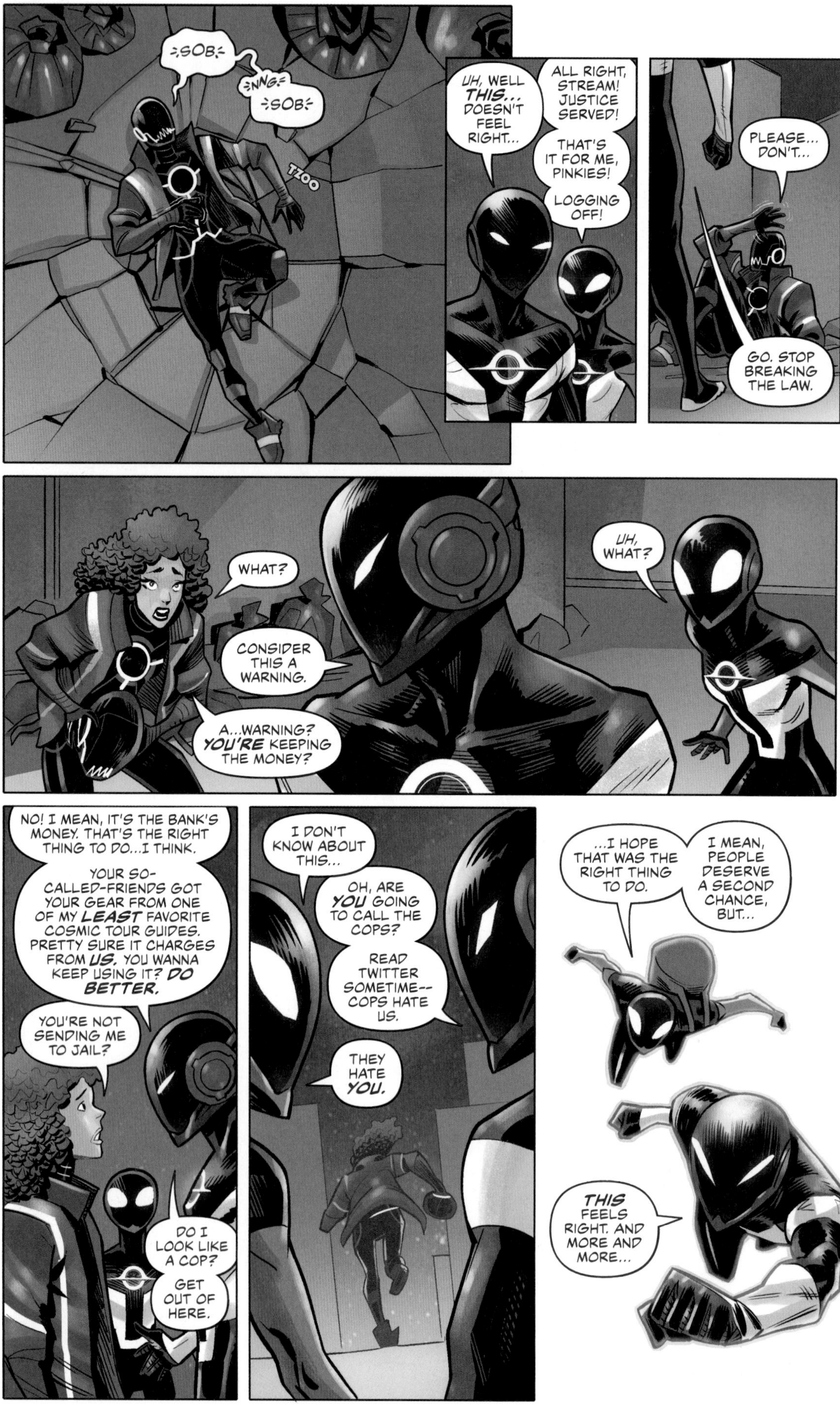

-SOB-
-NNG-
-SOB-
TZOO
UH, WELL THIS... DOESN'T FEEL RIGHT...
ALL RIGHT, STREAM! JUSTICE SERVED!
THAT'S IT FOR ME, PINKIES!
LOGGING OFF!
PLEASE... DON'T...
GO. STOP BREAKING THE LAW.
WHAT?
UH, WHAT?
CONSIDER THIS A WARNING.
A...WARNING? YOU'RE KEEPING THE MONEY?
NO! I MEAN, IT'S THE BANK'S MONEY. THAT'S THE RIGHT THING TO DO...I THINK.
YOUR SO-CALLED-FRIENDS GOT YOUR GEAR FROM ONE OF MY LEAST FAVORITE COSMIC TOUR GUIDES. PRETTY SURE IT CHARGES FROM US. YOU WANNA KEEP USING IT? DO BETTER.
YOU'RE NOT SENDING ME TO JAIL?
DO I LOOK LIKE A COP?
GET OUT OF HERE.
I DON'T KNOW ABOUT THIS...
OH, ARE YOU GOING TO CALL THE COPS?
READ TWITTER SOMETIME--COPS HATE US.
THEY HATE YOU.
...I HOPE THAT WAS THE RIGHT THING TO DO.
I MEAN, PEOPLE DESERVE A SECOND CHANCE, BUT...
THIS FEELS RIGHT. AND MORE AND MORE...

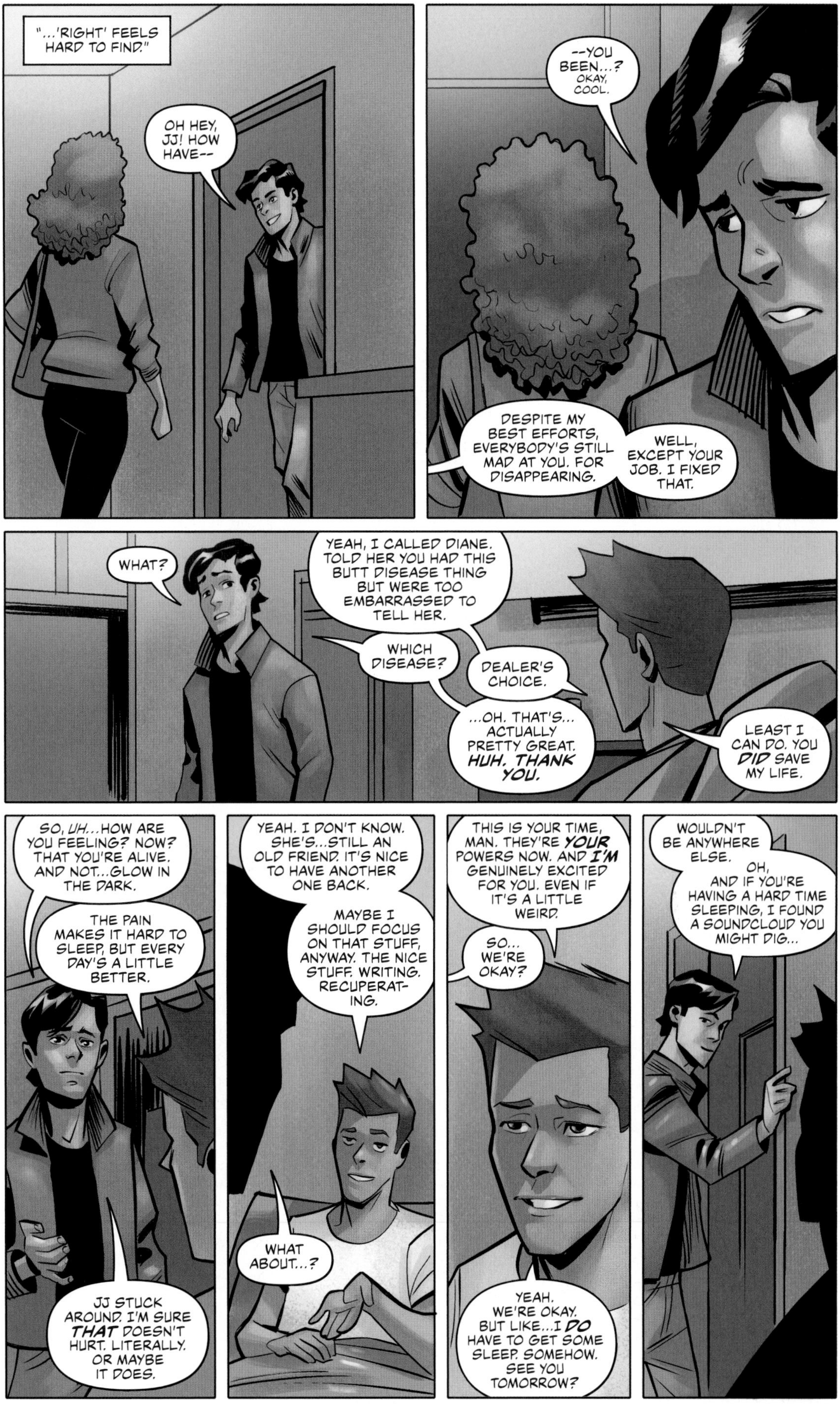
"...'RIGHT' FEELS HARD TO FIND."
OH HEY, JJ! HOW HAVE--
--YOU BEEN...? OKAY, COOL.
DESPITE MY BEST EFFORTS, EVERYBODY'S STILL MAD AT YOU. FOR DISAPPEARING.
WELL, EXCEPT YOUR JOB. I FIXED THAT.
WHAT?
YEAH, I CALLED DIANE. TOLD HER YOU HAD THIS BUTT DISEASE THING BUT WERE TOO EMBARRASSED TO TELL HER.
WHICH DISEASE?
DEALER'S CHOICE.
...OH. THAT'S... ACTUALLY PRETTY GREAT. HUH. THANK YOU.
LEAST I CAN DO. YOU DID SAVE MY LIFE.
SO, UH...HOW ARE YOU FEELING? NOW? THAT YOU'RE ALIVE. AND NOT...GLOW IN THE DARK.
THE PAIN MAKES IT HARD TO SLEEP, BUT EVERY DAY'S A LITTLE BETTER.
JJ STUCK AROUND. I'M SURE THAT DOESN'T HURT. LITERALLY. OR MAYBE IT DOES.
YEAH. I DON'T KNOW. SHE'S...STILL AN OLD FRIEND. IT'S NICE TO HAVE ANOTHER ONE BACK.
MAYBE I SHOULD FOCUS ON THAT STUFF, ANYWAY. THE NICE STUFF. WRITING. RECUPERAT-ING.
WHAT ABOUT...?
THIS IS YOUR TIME, MAN. THEY'RE YOUR POWERS NOW. AND I'M GENUINELY EXCITED FOR YOU. EVEN IF IT'S A LITTLE WEIRD.
SO... WE'RE OKAY?
YEAH. WE'RE OKAY. BUT LIKE...I DO HAVE TO GET SOME SLEEP. SOMEHOW. SEE YOU TOMORROW?
WOULDN'T BE ANYWHERE ELSE.
OH, AND IF YOU'RE HAVING A HARD TIME SLEEPING, I FOUND A SOUNDCLOUD YOU MIGHT DIG...

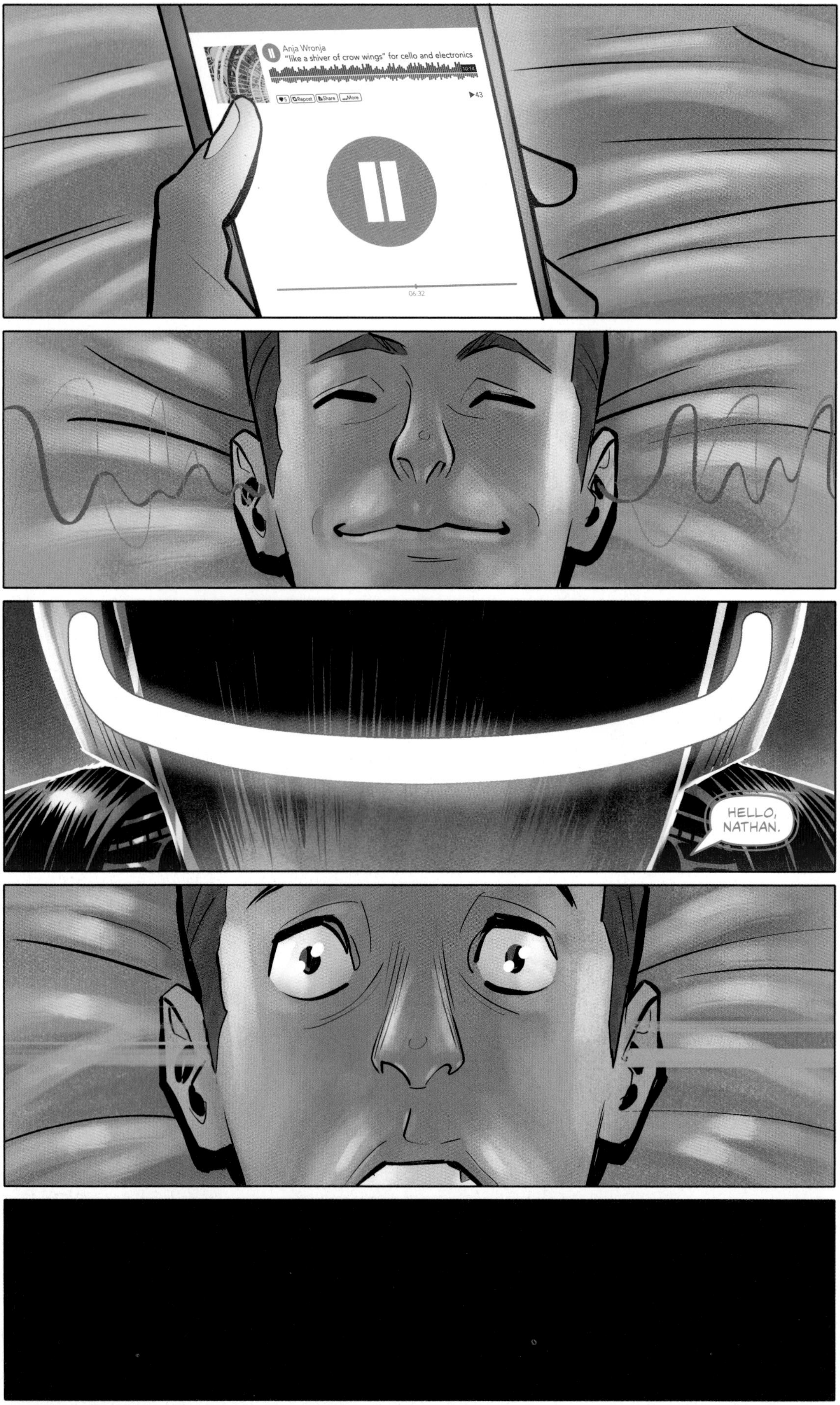
Anja Wronja
"like a shiver of crow wings" for cello and electronics
10:14
5
Repost
Share
...More
▶43
06:32
HELLO, NATHAN.

CHAPTER
TWELVE

TITLE

Pink

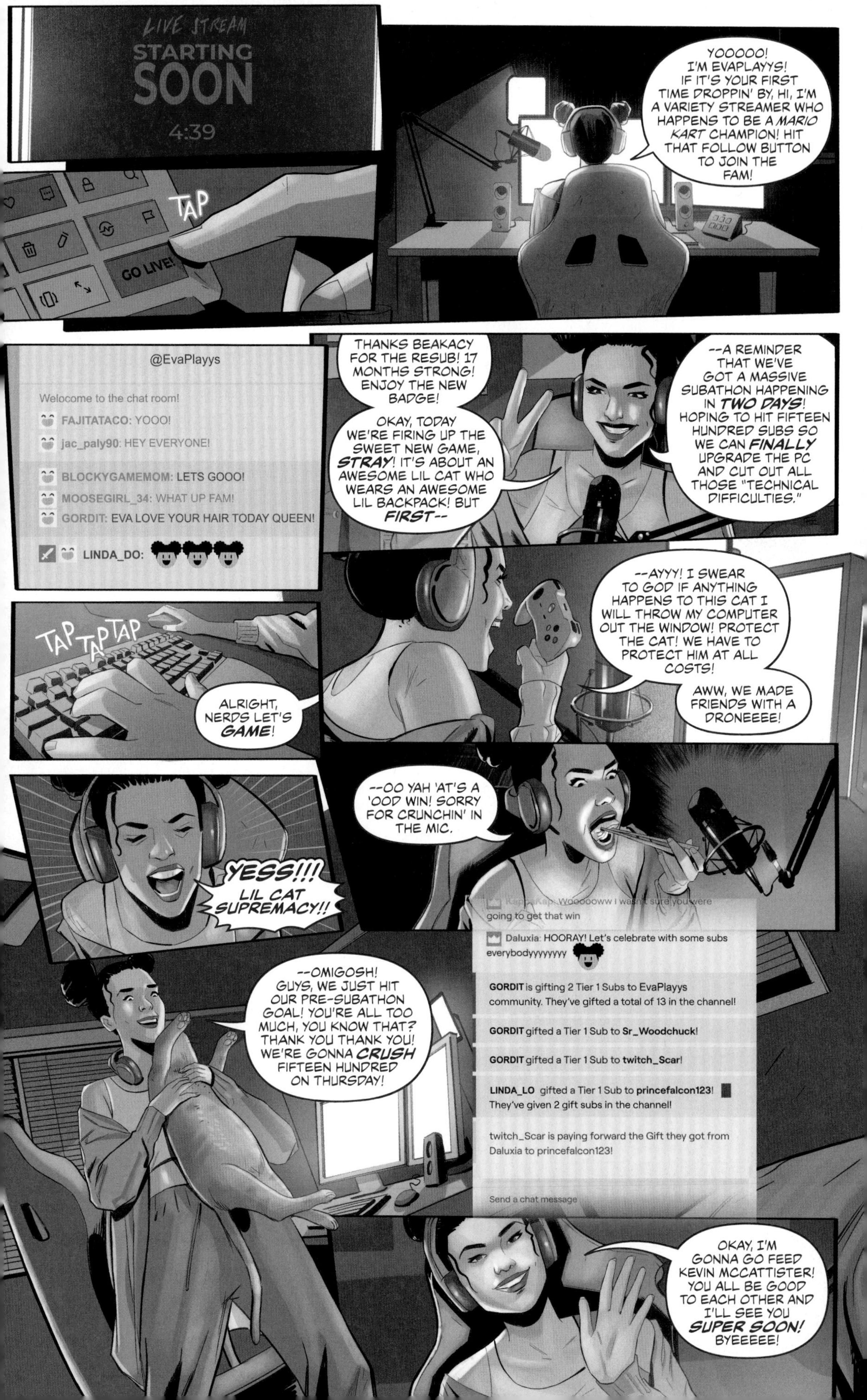
LIVE STREAM
STARTING SOON
4:39
GO LIVE!
TAP
YOOOOO! I'M EVAPLAYYS! IF IT'S YOUR FIRST TIME DROPPIN' BY, HI, I'M A VARIETY STREAMER WHO HAPPENS TO BE A MARIO KART CHAMPION! HIT THAT FOLLOW BUTTON TO JOIN THE FAM!
@EvaPlayys
Welcome to the chat room!
FAJITATACO: YOOO!
jac_paly90: HEY EVERYONE!
BLOCKYGAMEMOM: LETS GOOO!
MOOSEGIRL_34: WHAT UP FAM!
GORDIT: EVA LOVE YOUR HAIR TODAY QUEEN!
LINDA_DO:
THANKS BEAKACY FOR THE RESUB! 17 MONTHS STRONG! ENJOY THE NEW BADGE!
OKAY, TODAY WE'RE FIRING UP THE SWEET NEW GAME, STRAY! IT'S ABOUT AN AWESOME LIL CAT WHO WEARS AN AWESOME LIL BACKPACK! BUT FIRST--
--A REMINDER THAT WE'VE GOT A MASSIVE SUBATHON HAPPENING IN TWO DAYS! HOPING TO HIT FIFTEEN HUNDRED SUBS SO WE CAN FINALLY UPGRADE THE PC AND CUT OUT ALL THOSE "TECHNICAL DIFFICULTIES."
TAP TAP TAP
ALRIGHT, NERDS LET'S GAME!
--AYYY! I SWEAR TO GOD IF ANYTHING HAPPENS TO THIS CAT I WILL THROW MY COMPUTER OUT THE WINDOW! PROTECT THE CAT! WE HAVE TO PROTECT HIM AT ALL COSTS!
AWW, WE MADE FRIENDS WITH A DRONEEEE!
YESS!!! LIL CAT SUPREMACY!!
--OO YAH 'AT'S A 'OOD WIN! SORRY FOR CRUNCHIN' IN THE MIC.
Wooooooww I wasn't sure you were going to get that win
Daluxia: HOORAY! Let's celebrate with some subs everybodyyyyyyy
GORDIT is gifting 2 Tier 1 Subs to EvaPlayys community. They've gifted a total of 13 in the channel!
GORDIT gifted a Tier 1 Sub to Sr_Woodchuck!
GORDIT gifted a Tier 1 Sub to twitch_Scar!
LINDA_LO gifted a Tier 1 Sub to princefalcon123! They've given 2 gift subs in the channel!
twitch_Scar is paying forward the Gift they got from Daluxia to princefalcon123!
Send a chat message
--OMIGOSH! GUYS, WE JUST HIT OUR PRE-SUBATHON GOAL! YOU'RE ALL TOO MUCH, YOU KNOW THAT? THANK YOU THANK YOU! WE'RE GONNA CRUSH FIFTEEN HUNDRED ON THURSDAY!
OKAY, I'M GONNA GO FEED KEVIN MCCATTISTER! YOU ALL BE GOOD TO EACH OTHER AND I'LL SEE YOU SUPER SOON! BYEEEEE!

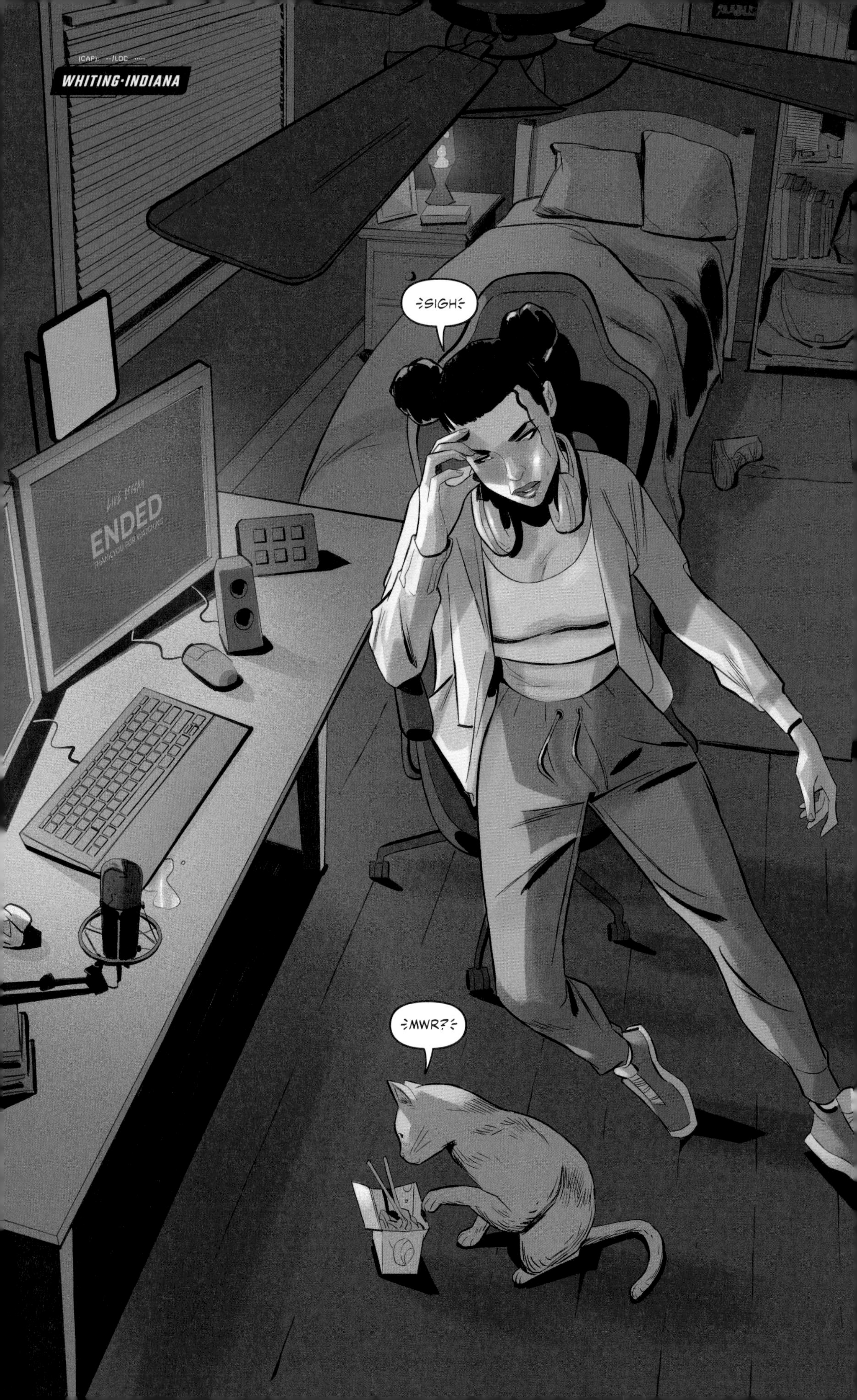
(CAP): --/LOC
WHITING·INDIANA
ENDED
THANKYOU FOR WATCHING
SIGH
MWR?

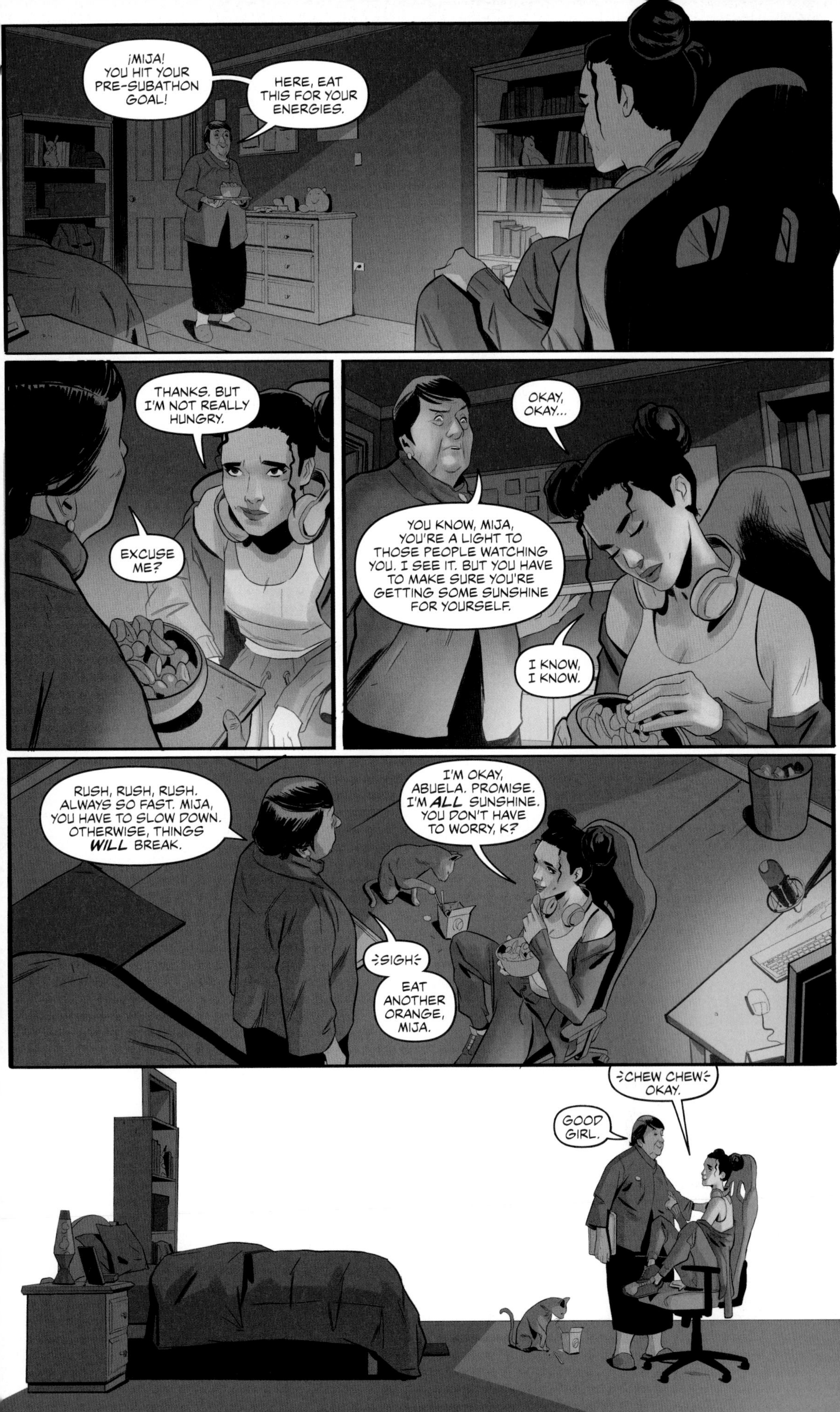
¡MIJA! YOU HIT YOUR PRE-SUBATHON GOAL!
HERE, EAT THIS FOR YOUR ENERGIES.
THANKS. BUT I'M NOT REALLY HUNGRY.
EXCUSE ME?
OKAY, OKAY...
YOU KNOW, MIJA, YOU'RE A LIGHT TO THOSE PEOPLE WATCHING YOU. I SEE IT. BUT YOU HAVE TO MAKE SURE YOU'RE GETTING SOME SUNSHINE FOR YOURSELF.
I KNOW, I KNOW.
RUSH, RUSH, RUSH. ALWAYS SO FAST. MIJA, YOU HAVE TO SLOW DOWN. OTHERWISE, THINGS WILL BREAK.
I'M OKAY, ABUELA. PROMISE. I'M ALL SUNSHINE. YOU DON'T HAVE TO WORRY, K?
SIGH
EAT ANOTHER ORANGE, MIJA.
CHEW CHEW OKAY.
GOOD GIRL.

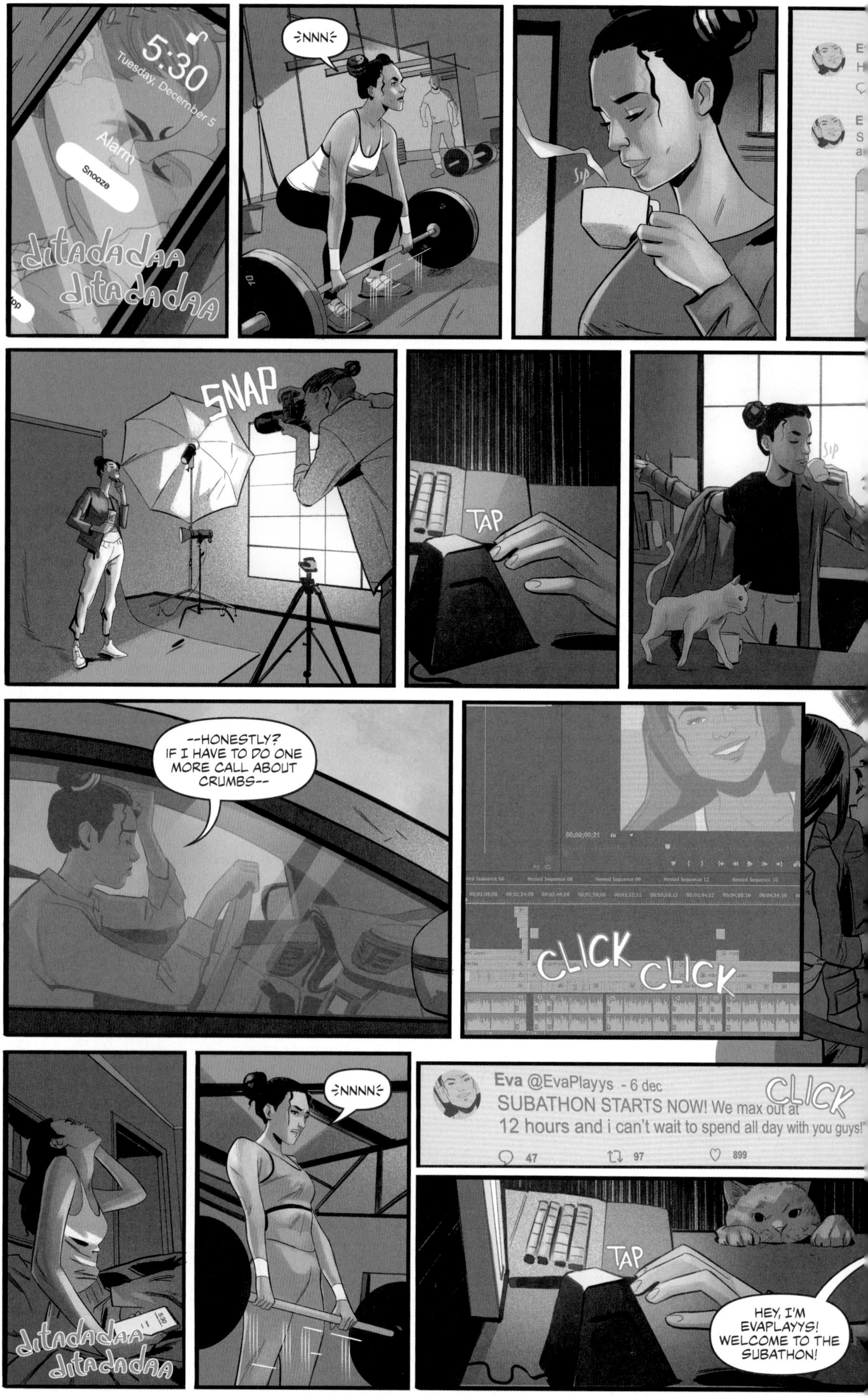
5:30
Tuesday, December 5
Alarm
Snooze
ditadadaa
ditadadaa
NNN
sip
SNAP
TAP
sip
--HONESTLY? IF I HAVE TO DO ONE MORE CALL ABOUT CRUMBS--
CLICK
CLICK
ditadadaa
ditadadaa
NNNN
Eva @EvaPlayys - 6 dec
SUBATHON STARTS NOW! We max out at 12 hours and i can't wait to spend all day with you guys!"
47
97
899
CLICK
TAP
HEY, I'M EVAPLAYYS! WELCOME TO THE SUBATHON!

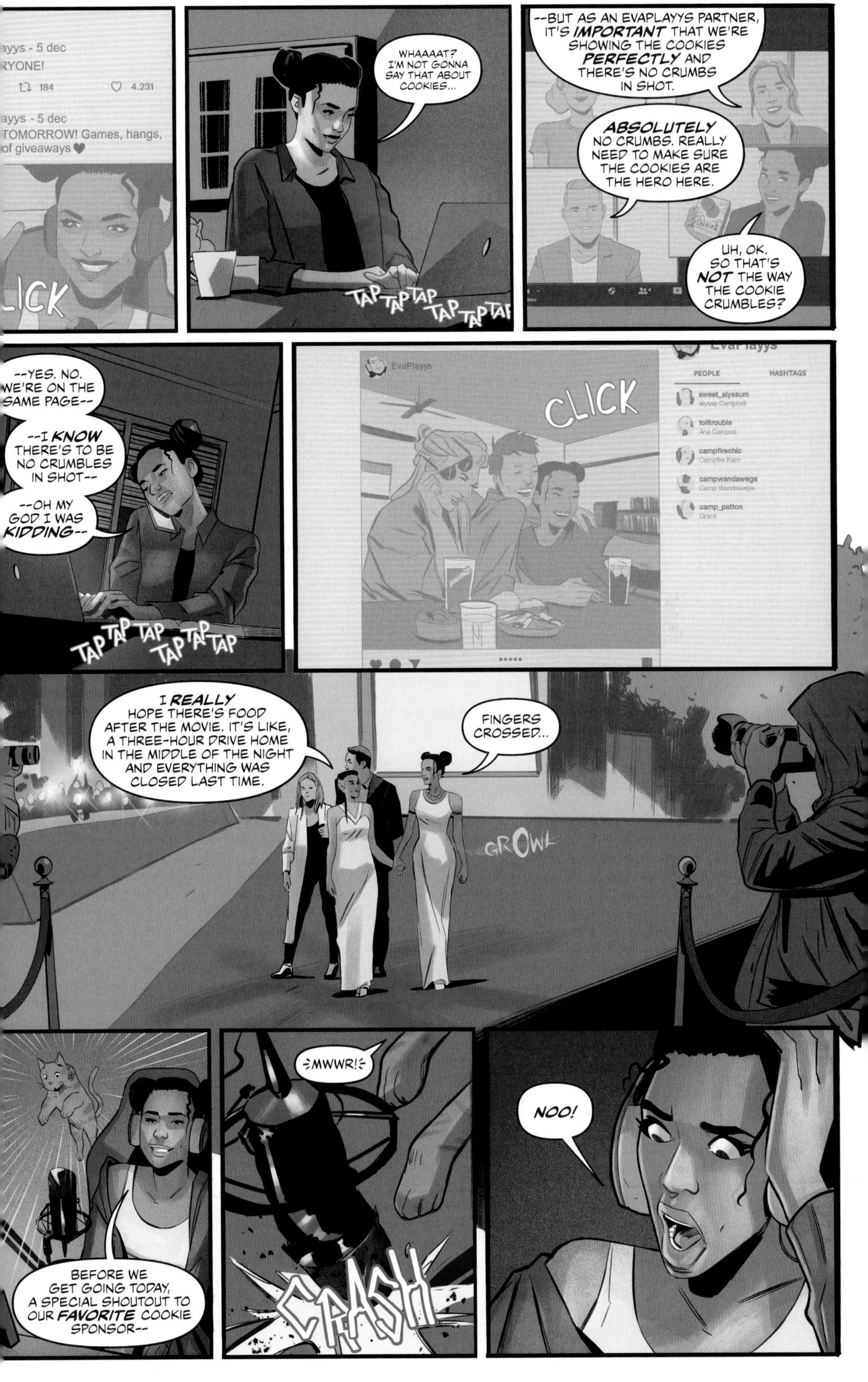
ayys - 5 dec
RYONE!
184
4,231
ayys - 5 dec
TOMORROW! Games, hangs,
of giveaways
LICK
WHAAAAT? I'M NOT GONNA SAY THAT ABOUT COOKIES...
TAP TAP TAP TAP TAP TAP
--BUT AS AN EVAPLAYYS PARTNER, IT'S IMPORTANT THAT WE'RE SHOWING THE COOKIES PERFECTLY AND THERE'S NO CRUMBS IN SHOT.
ABSOLUTELY NO CRUMBS. REALLY NEED TO MAKE SURE THE COOKIES ARE THE HERO HERE.
UH, OK. SO THAT'S NOT THE WAY THE COOKIE CRUMBLES?
--YES. NO. WE'RE ON THE SAME PAGE--
--I KNOW THERE'S TO BE NO CRUMBLES IN SHOT--
--OH MY GOD I WAS KIDDING--
TAP TAP TAP TAP TAP TAP
EvaPlayys
CLICK
PEOPLE
HASHTAGS
sweet_alyssum
Alyssa Campbell
toiltrouble
Ana Campos
campfirechic
Campfire Kam
campwandawega
Camp Wandawega
camp_patton
Grace
I REALLY HOPE THERE'S FOOD AFTER THE MOVIE. IT'S LIKE, A THREE-HOUR DRIVE HOME IN THE MIDDLE OF THE NIGHT AND EVERYTHING WAS CLOSED LAST TIME.
FINGERS CROSSED...
GROWL
BEFORE WE GET GOING TODAY, A SPECIAL SHOUTOUT TO OUR FAVORITE COOKIE SPONSOR--
MWWR!
CRASH
NOO!

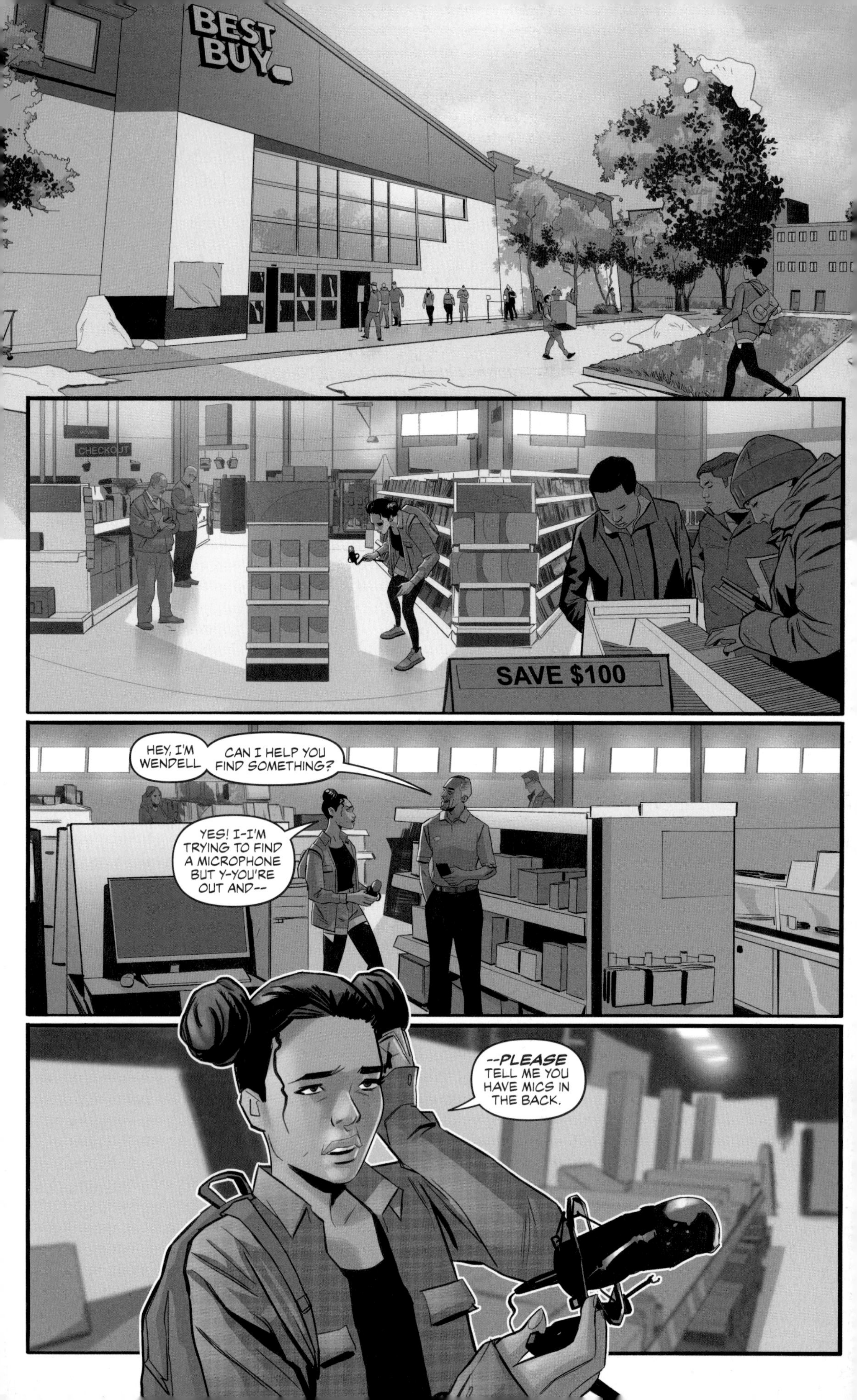
BEST BUY
MOVIES
CHECKOUT
SAVE $100
HEY, I'M WENDELL
CAN I HELP YOU FIND SOMETHING?
YES! I-I'M TRYING TO FIND A MICROPHONE BUT Y-YOU'RE OUT AND--
--PLEASE TELL ME YOU HAVE MICS IN THE BACK.

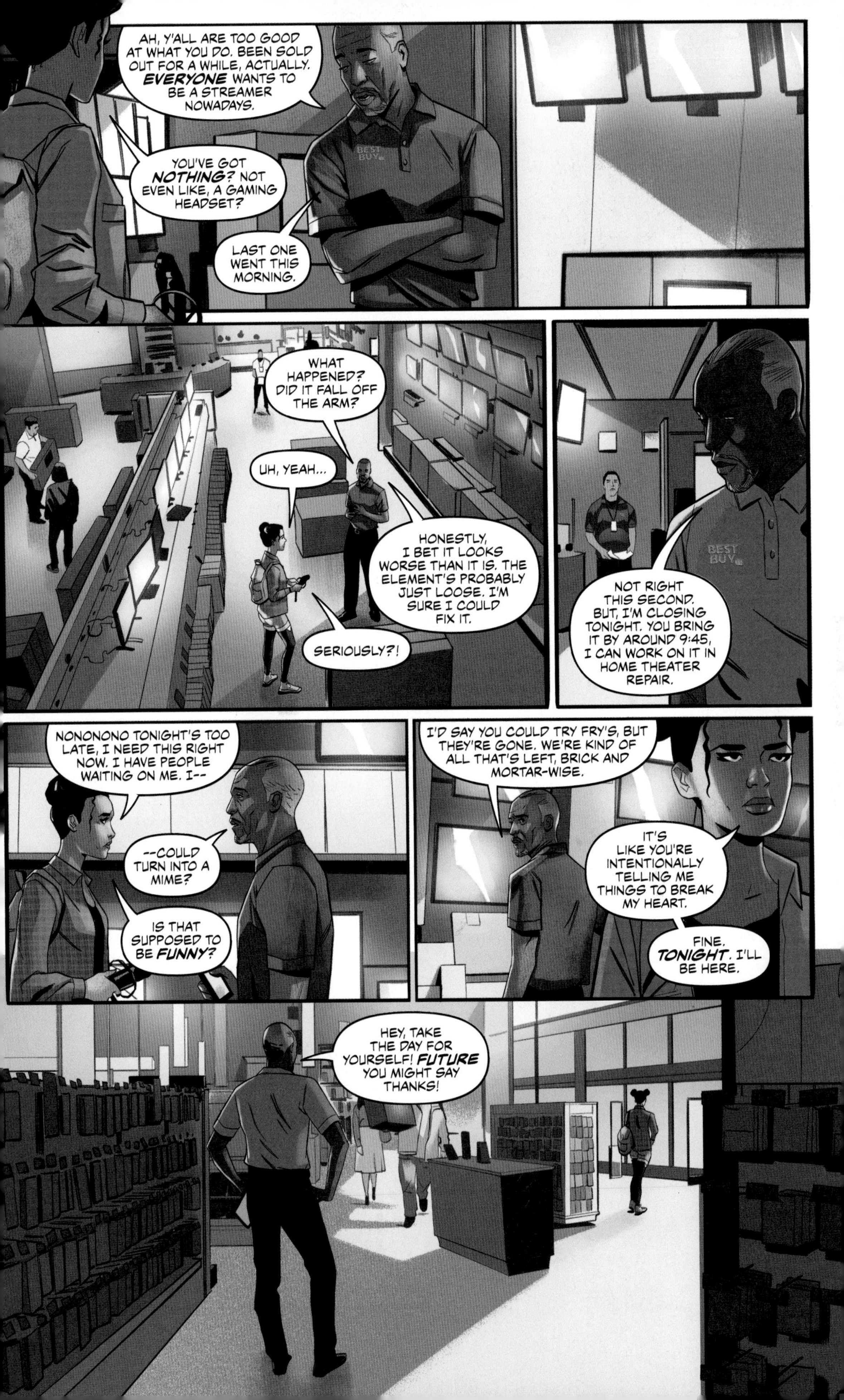
AH, Y'ALL ARE TOO GOOD AT WHAT YOU DO. BEEN SOLD OUT FOR A WHILE, ACTUALLY. EVERYONE WANTS TO BE A STREAMER NOWADAYS.
YOU'VE GOT NOTHING? NOT EVEN LIKE, A GAMING HEADSET?
LAST ONE WENT THIS MORNING.
BEST BUY
WHAT HAPPENED? DID IT FALL OFF THE ARM?
UH, YEAH...
HONESTLY, I BET IT LOOKS WORSE THAN IT IS. THE ELEMENT'S PROBABLY JUST LOOSE. I'M SURE I COULD FIX IT.
SERIOUSLY?!
BEST BUY
NOT RIGHT THIS SECOND. BUT, I'M CLOSING TONIGHT. YOU BRING IT BY AROUND 9:45, I CAN WORK ON IT IN HOME THEATER REPAIR.
NONONONO TONIGHT'S TOO LATE, I NEED THIS RIGHT NOW. I HAVE PEOPLE WAITING ON ME. I--
--COULD TURN INTO A MIME?
IS THAT SUPPOSED TO BE FUNNY?
I'D SAY YOU COULD TRY FRY'S, BUT THEY'RE GONE. WE'RE KIND OF ALL THAT'S LEFT, BRICK AND MORTAR-WISE.
IT'S LIKE YOU'RE INTENTIONALLY TELLING ME THINGS TO BREAK MY HEART.
FINE. TONIGHT. I'LL BE HERE.
HEY, TAKE THE DAY FOR YOURSELF! FUTURE YOU MIGHT SAY THANKS!

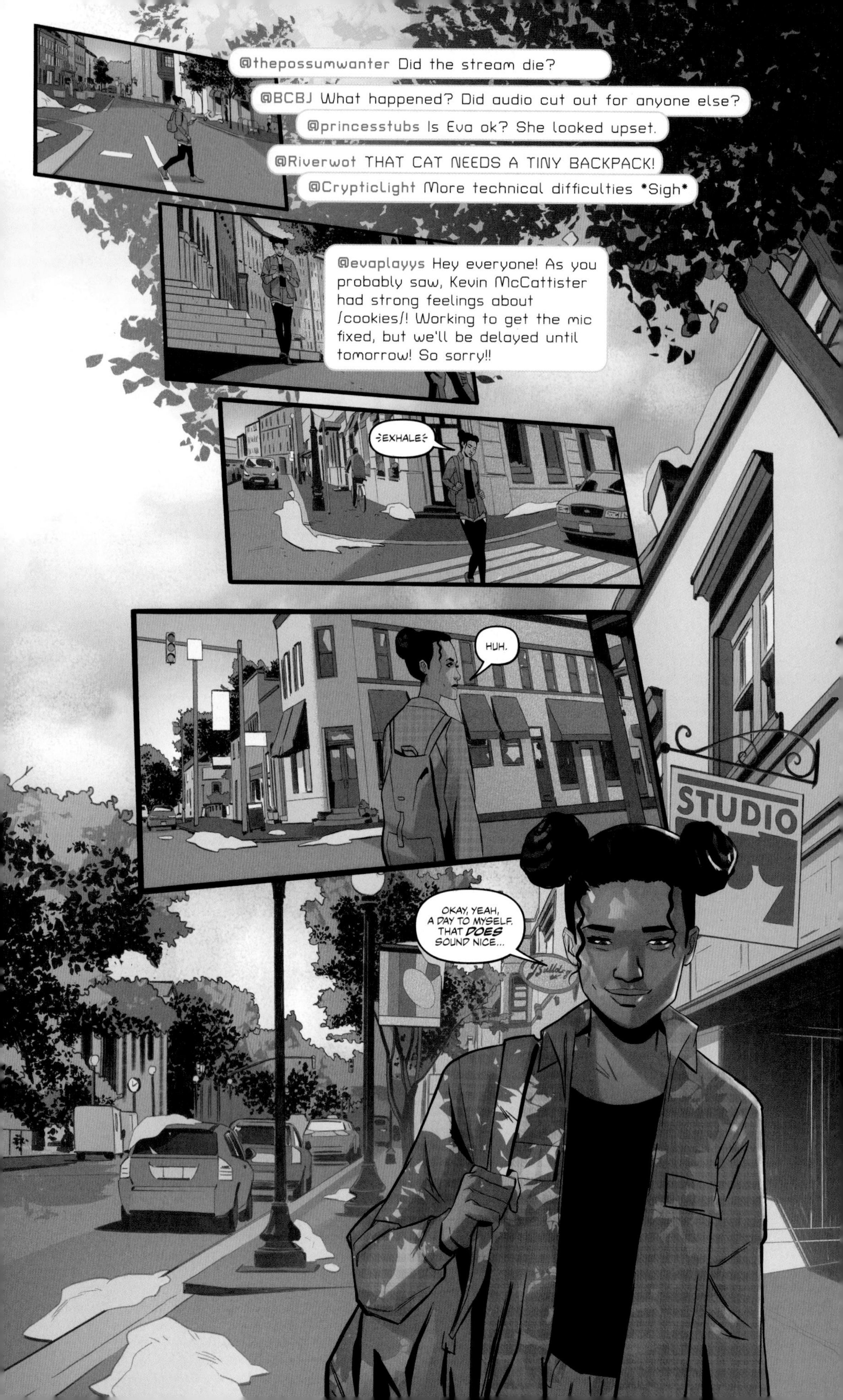
@thepossumwanter Did the stream die?
@BCBJ What happened? Did audio cut out for anyone else?
@princesstubs Is Eva ok? She looked upset.
@Riverwot THAT CAT NEEDS A TINY BACKPACK!
@Crypticlight More technical difficulties *Sigh*
@evaplayys Hey everyone! As you probably saw, Kevin McCattister had strong feelings about /cookies/! Working to get the mic fixed, but we'll be delayed until tomorrow! So sorry!!
EXHALE
HUH.
STUDIO
OKAY, YEAH, A DAY TO MYSELF. THAT DOES SOUND NICE...

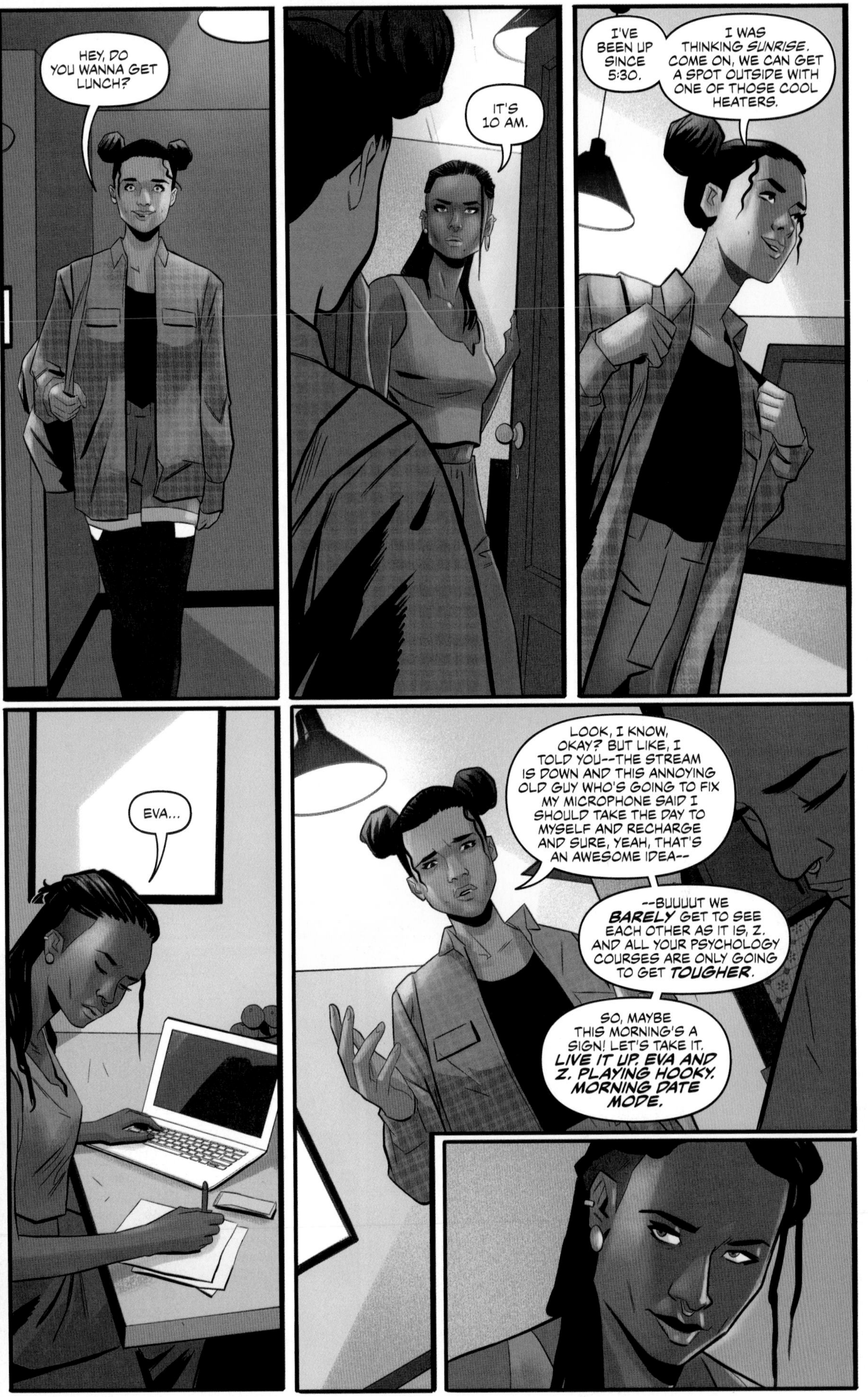
HEY, DO YOU WANNA GET LUNCH?
IT'S 10 AM.
I'VE BEEN UP SINCE 5:30.
I WAS THINKING *SUNRISE*. COME ON, WE CAN GET A SPOT OUTSIDE WITH ONE OF THOSE COOL HEATERS.
EVA...
LOOK, I KNOW, OKAY? BUT LIKE, I TOLD YOU--THE STREAM IS DOWN AND THIS ANNOYING OLD GUY WHO'S GOING TO FIX MY MICROPHONE SAID I SHOULD TAKE THE DAY TO MYSELF AND RECHARGE AND SURE, YEAH, THAT'S AN AWESOME IDEA--
--BUUUUT WE ***BARELY*** GET TO SEE EACH OTHER AS IT IS, Z. AND ALL YOUR PSYCHOLOGY COURSES ARE ONLY GOING TO GET ***TOUGHER***.
SO, MAYBE THIS MORNING'S A SIGN! LET'S TAKE IT. ***LIVE IT UP. EVA AND Z. PLAYING HOOKY. MORNING DATE MODE.***

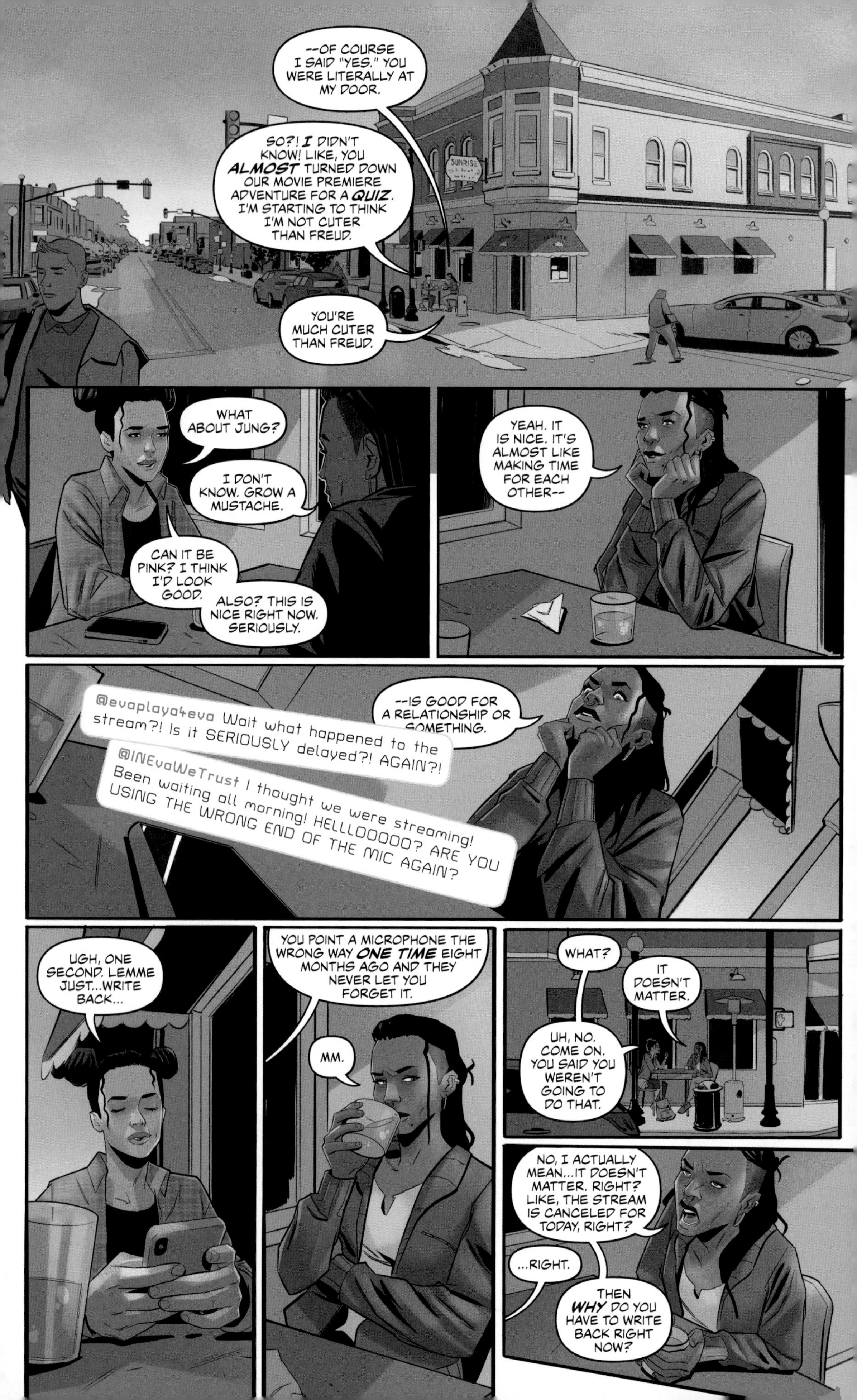
--OF COURSE I SAID "YES." YOU WERE LITERALLY AT MY DOOR.
SO?! I DIDN'T KNOW! LIKE, YOU ALMOST TURNED DOWN OUR MOVIE PREMIERE ADVENTURE FOR A QUIZ. I'M STARTING TO THINK I'M NOT CUTER THAN FREUD.
YOU'RE MUCH CUTER THAN FREUD.
SUNRISE
WHAT ABOUT JUNG?
I DON'T KNOW. GROW A MUSTACHE.
CAN IT BE PINK? I THINK I'D LOOK GOOD.
ALSO? THIS IS NICE RIGHT NOW. SERIOUSLY.
YEAH. IT IS NICE. IT'S ALMOST LIKE MAKING TIME FOR EACH OTHER--
--IS GOOD FOR A RELATIONSHIP OR SOMETHING.
@evaplaya4eva Wait what happened to the stream?! Is it SERIOUSLY delayed?! AGAIN?!
@INEvaWeTrust I thought we were streaming! Been waiting all morning! HELLLOOOOO? ARE YOU USING THE WRONG END OF THE MIC AGAIN?
UGH, ONE SECOND. LEMME JUST...WRITE BACK...
YOU POINT A MICROPHONE THE WRONG WAY ONE TIME EIGHT MONTHS AGO AND THEY NEVER LET YOU FORGET IT.
MM.
WHAT?
IT DOESN'T MATTER.
UH, NO. COME ON. YOU SAID YOU WEREN'T GOING TO DO THAT.
NO, I ACTUALLY MEAN...IT DOESN'T MATTER. RIGHT? LIKE, THE STREAM IS CANCELED FOR TODAY, RIGHT?
...RIGHT.
THEN WHY DO YOU HAVE TO WRITE BACK RIGHT NOW?

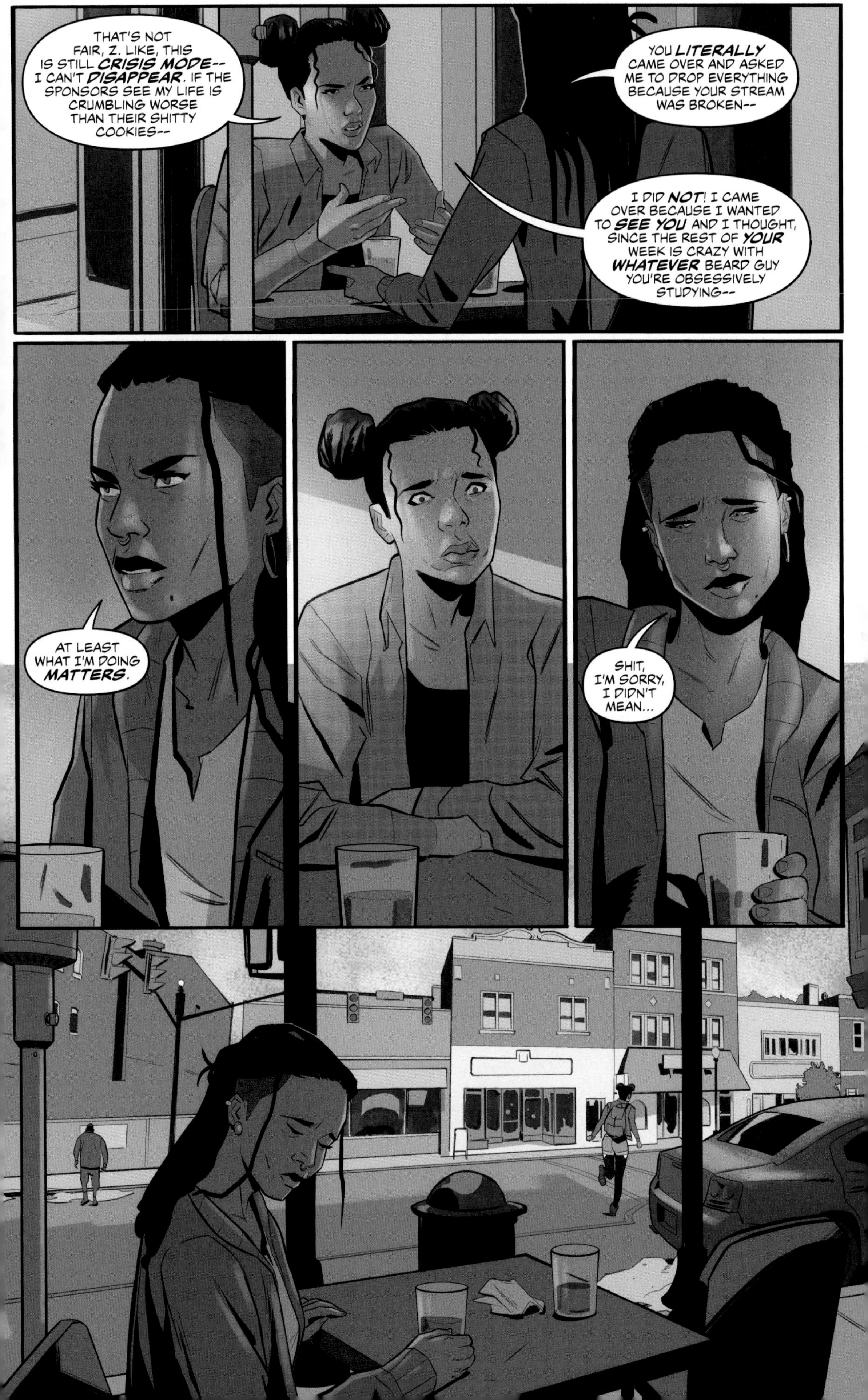
THAT'S NOT FAIR, Z. LIKE, THIS IS STILL CRISIS MODE-- I CAN'T DISAPPEAR. IF THE SPONSORS SEE MY LIFE IS CRUMBLING WORSE THAN THEIR SHITTY COOKIES--
YOU LITERALLY CAME OVER AND ASKED ME TO DROP EVERYTHING BECAUSE YOUR STREAM WAS BROKEN--
I DID NOT! I CAME OVER BECAUSE I WANTED TO SEE YOU AND I THOUGHT, SINCE THE REST OF YOUR WEEK IS CRAZY WITH WHATEVER BEARD GUY YOU'RE OBSESSIVELY STUDYING--
AT LEAST WHAT I'M DOING MATTERS.
SHIT, I'M SORRY, I DIDN'T MEAN...

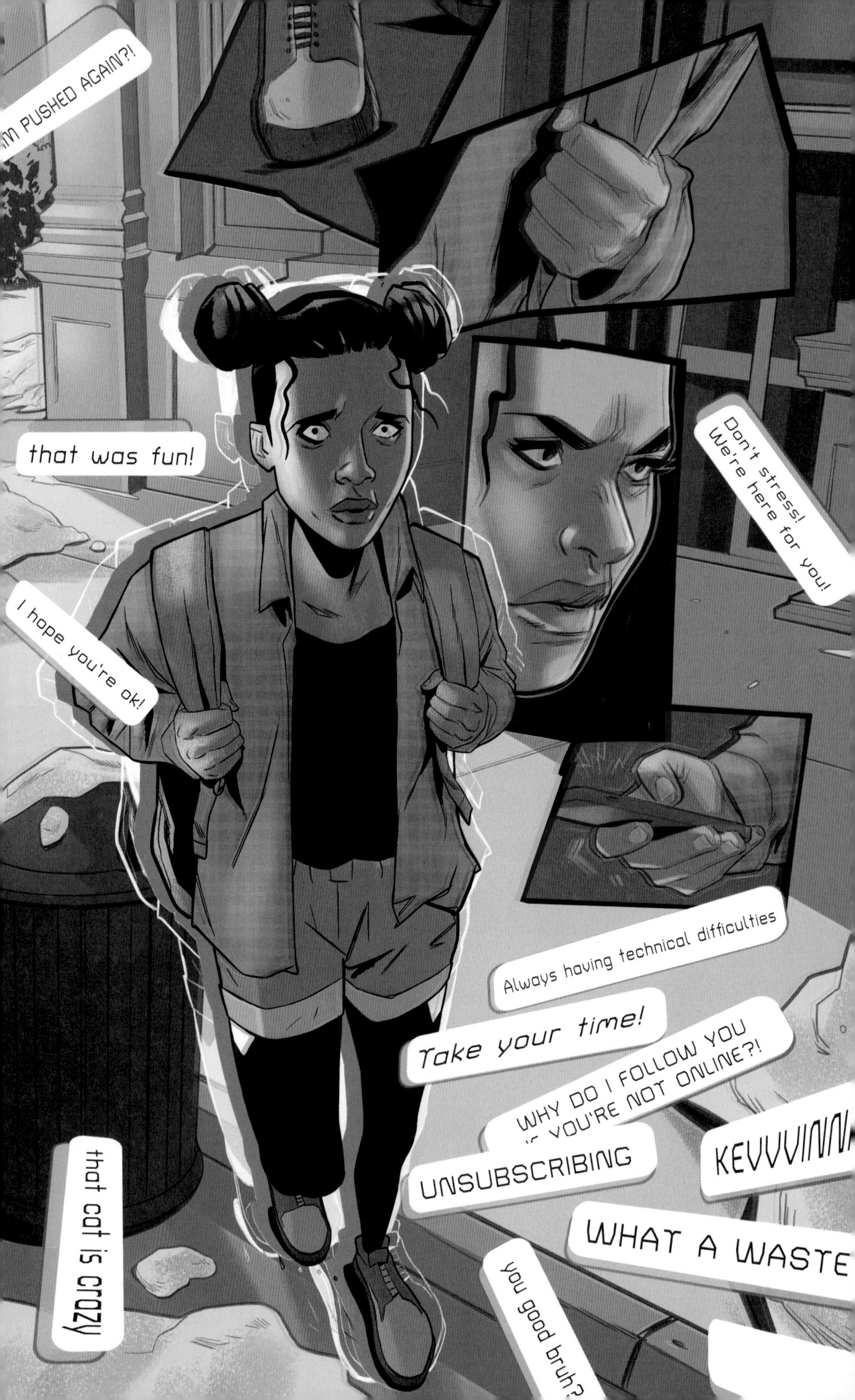

...M PUSHED AGAIN?!
that was fun!
Don't stress! We're here for you!
I hope you're ok!
Always having technical difficulties
Take your time!
WHY DO I FOLLOW YOU IF YOU'RE NOT ONLINE?!
UNSUBSCRIBING
KEVVVINN
that cat is crazy
WHAT A WASTE
you good bruh?

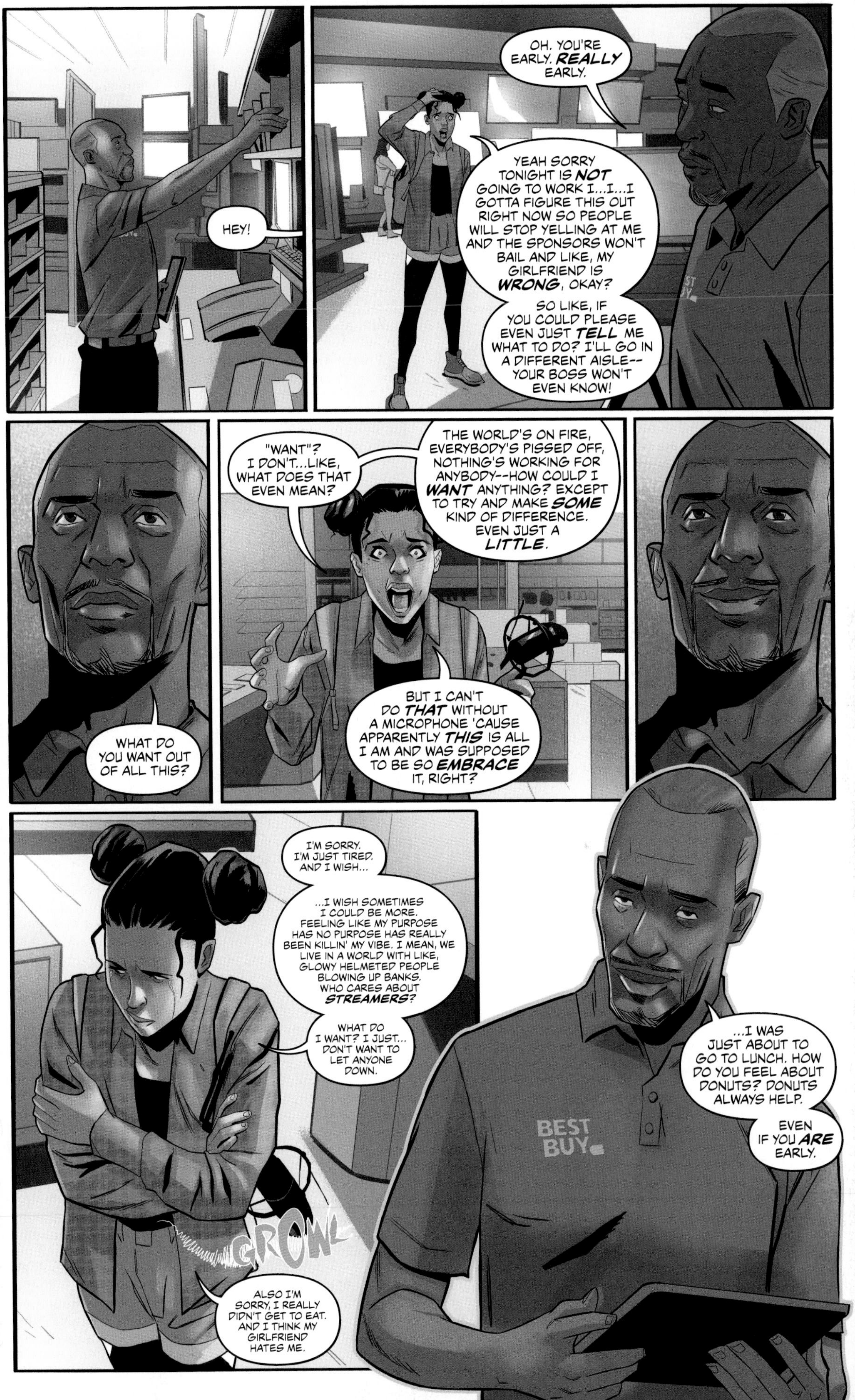
HEY!
OH. YOU'RE EARLY. REALLY EARLY.
YEAH SORRY TONIGHT IS NOT GOING TO WORK I...I...I GOTTA FIGURE THIS OUT RIGHT NOW SO PEOPLE WILL STOP YELLING AT ME AND THE SPONSORS WON'T BAIL AND LIKE, MY GIRLFRIEND IS WRONG, OKAY?
SO LIKE, IF YOU COULD PLEASE EVEN JUST TELL ME WHAT TO DO? I'LL GO IN A DIFFERENT AISLE-- YOUR BOSS WON'T EVEN KNOW!
WHAT DO YOU WANT OUT OF ALL THIS?
"WANT"? I DON'T...LIKE, WHAT DOES THAT EVEN MEAN?
THE WORLD'S ON FIRE, EVERYBODY'S PISSED OFF, NOTHING'S WORKING FOR ANYBODY--HOW COULD I WANT ANYTHING? EXCEPT TO TRY AND MAKE SOME KIND OF DIFFERENCE. EVEN JUST A LITTLE.
BUT I CAN'T DO THAT WITHOUT A MICROPHONE 'CAUSE APPARENTLY THIS IS ALL I AM AND WAS SUPPOSED TO BE SO EMBRACE IT, RIGHT?
I'M SORRY. I'M JUST TIRED. AND I WISH...
...I WISH SOMETIMES I COULD BE MORE. FEELING LIKE MY PURPOSE HAS NO PURPOSE HAS REALLY BEEN KILLIN' MY VIBE. I MEAN, WE LIVE IN A WORLD WITH LIKE, GLOWY HELMETED PEOPLE BLOWING UP BANKS. WHO CARES ABOUT STREAMERS?
WHAT DO I WANT? I JUST... DON'T WANT TO LET ANYONE DOWN.
GROWL
ALSO I'M SORRY, I REALLY DIDN'T GET TO EAT. AND I THINK MY GIRLFRIEND HATES ME.
...I WAS JUST ABOUT TO GO TO LUNCH. HOW DO YOU FEEL ABOUT DONUTS? DONUTS ALWAYS HELP.
EVEN IF YOU ARE EARLY.
BEST BUY

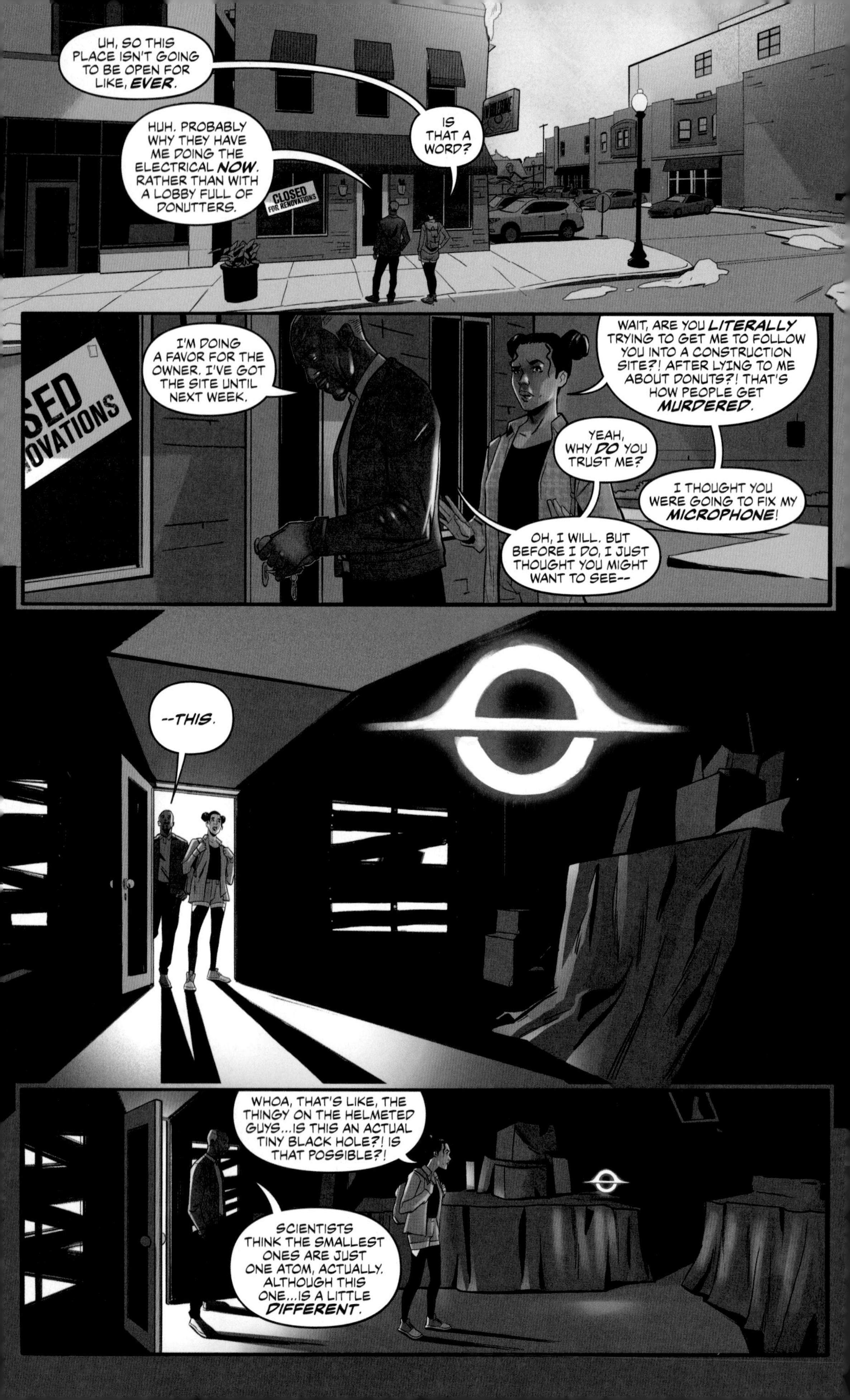
UH, SO THIS PLACE ISN'T GOING TO BE OPEN FOR LIKE, EVER.
HUH. PROBABLY WHY THEY HAVE ME DOING THE ELECTRICAL NOW. RATHER THAN WITH A LOBBY FULL OF DONUTTERS.
IS THAT A WORD?
CLOSED FOR RENOVATIONS
I'M DOING A FAVOR FOR THE OWNER. I'VE GOT THE SITE UNTIL NEXT WEEK.
WAIT, ARE YOU LITERALLY TRYING TO GET ME TO FOLLOW YOU INTO A CONSTRUCTION SITE?! AFTER LYING TO ME ABOUT DONUTS?! THAT'S HOW PEOPLE GET MURDERED.
I THOUGHT YOU WERE GOING TO FIX MY MICROPHONE!
YEAH, WHY DO YOU TRUST ME?
OH, I WILL. BUT BEFORE I DO, I JUST THOUGHT YOU MIGHT WANT TO SEE--
--THIS.
WHOA, THAT'S LIKE, THE THINGY ON THE HELMETED GUYS...IS THIS AN ACTUAL TINY BLACK HOLE?! IS THAT POSSIBLE?!
SCIENTISTS THINK THE SMALLEST ONES ARE JUST ONE ATOM, ACTUALLY. ALTHOUGH THIS ONE...IS A LITTLE DIFFERENT.

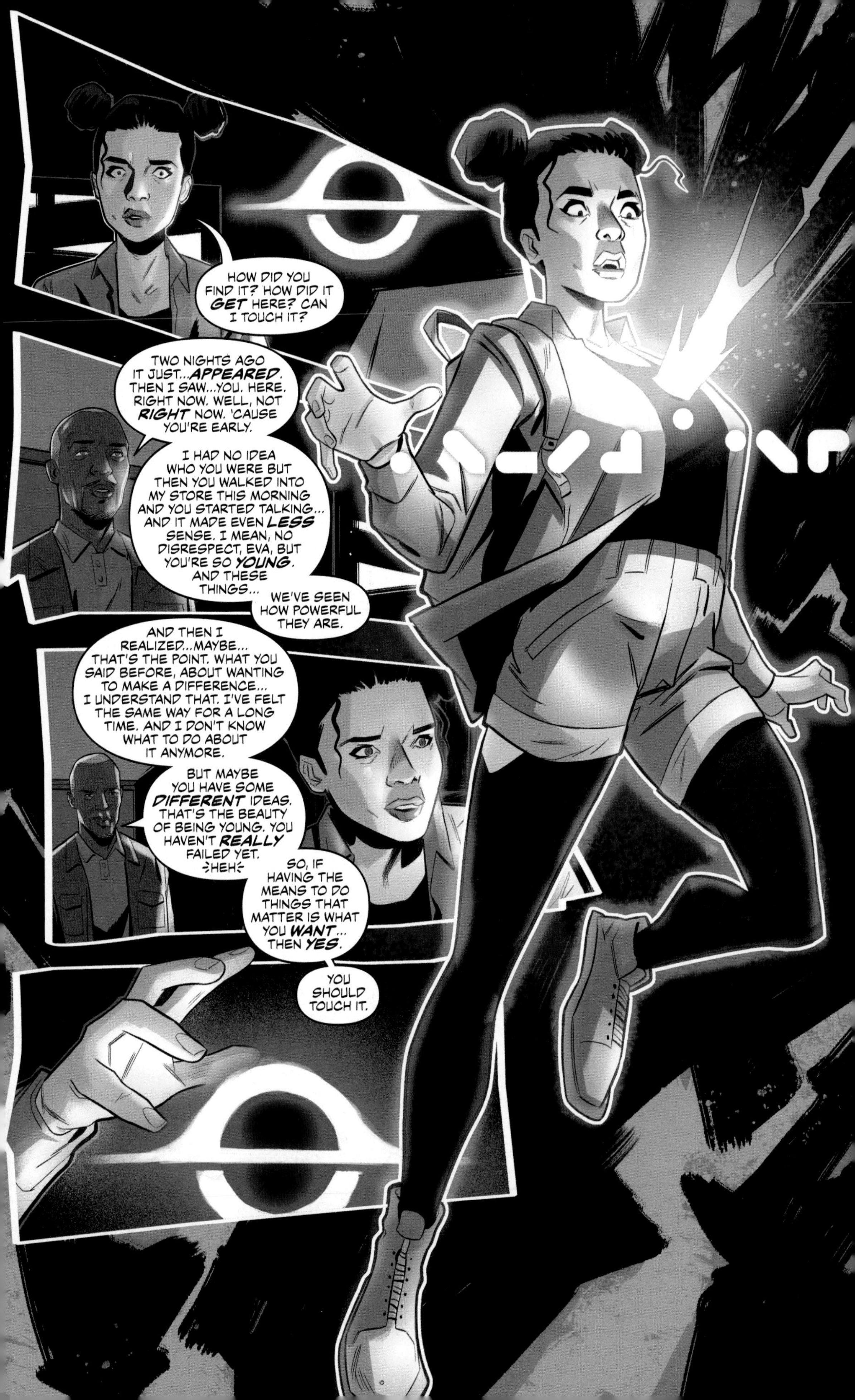
HOW DID YOU FIND IT? HOW DID IT GET HERE? CAN I TOUCH IT?
TWO NIGHTS AGO IT JUST...APPEARED. THEN I SAW...YOU. HERE. RIGHT NOW. WELL, NOT RIGHT NOW. 'CAUSE YOU'RE EARLY.
I HAD NO IDEA WHO YOU WERE BUT THEN YOU WALKED INTO MY STORE THIS MORNING AND YOU STARTED TALKING... AND IT MADE EVEN LESS SENSE. I MEAN, NO DISRESPECT, EVA, BUT YOU'RE SO YOUNG. AND THESE THINGS...
WE'VE SEEN HOW POWERFUL THEY ARE.
AND THEN I REALIZED...MAYBE... THAT'S THE POINT. WHAT YOU SAID BEFORE, ABOUT WANTING TO MAKE A DIFFERENCE... I UNDERSTAND THAT. I'VE FELT THE SAME WAY FOR A LONG TIME. AND I DON'T KNOW WHAT TO DO ABOUT IT ANYMORE.
BUT MAYBE YOU HAVE SOME DIFFERENT IDEAS. THAT'S THE BEAUTY OF BEING YOUNG. YOU HAVEN'T REALLY FAILED YET. HEH
SO, IF HAVING THE MEANS TO DO THINGS THAT MATTER IS WHAT YOU WANT... THEN YES.
YOU SHOULD TOUCH IT.

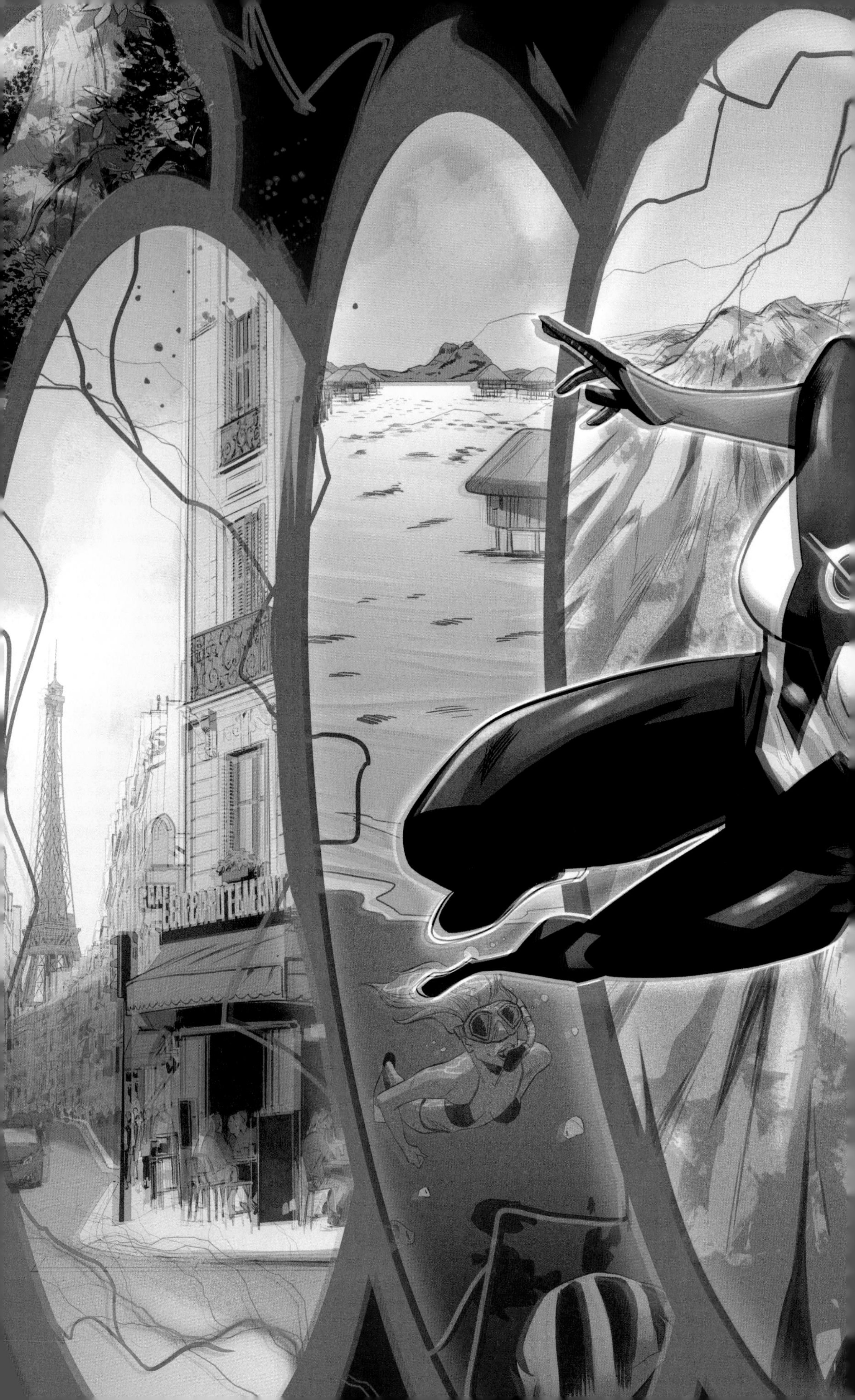

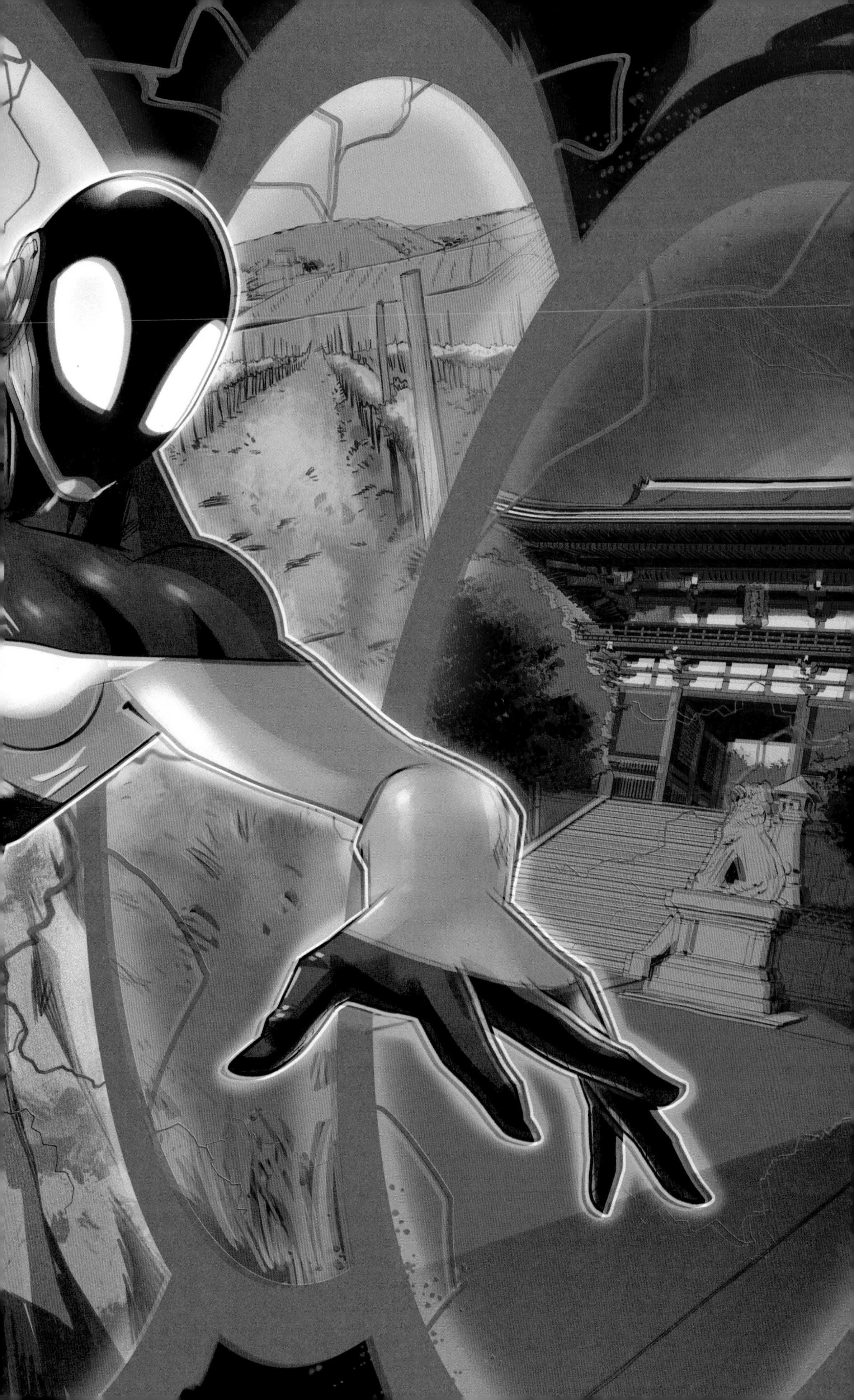

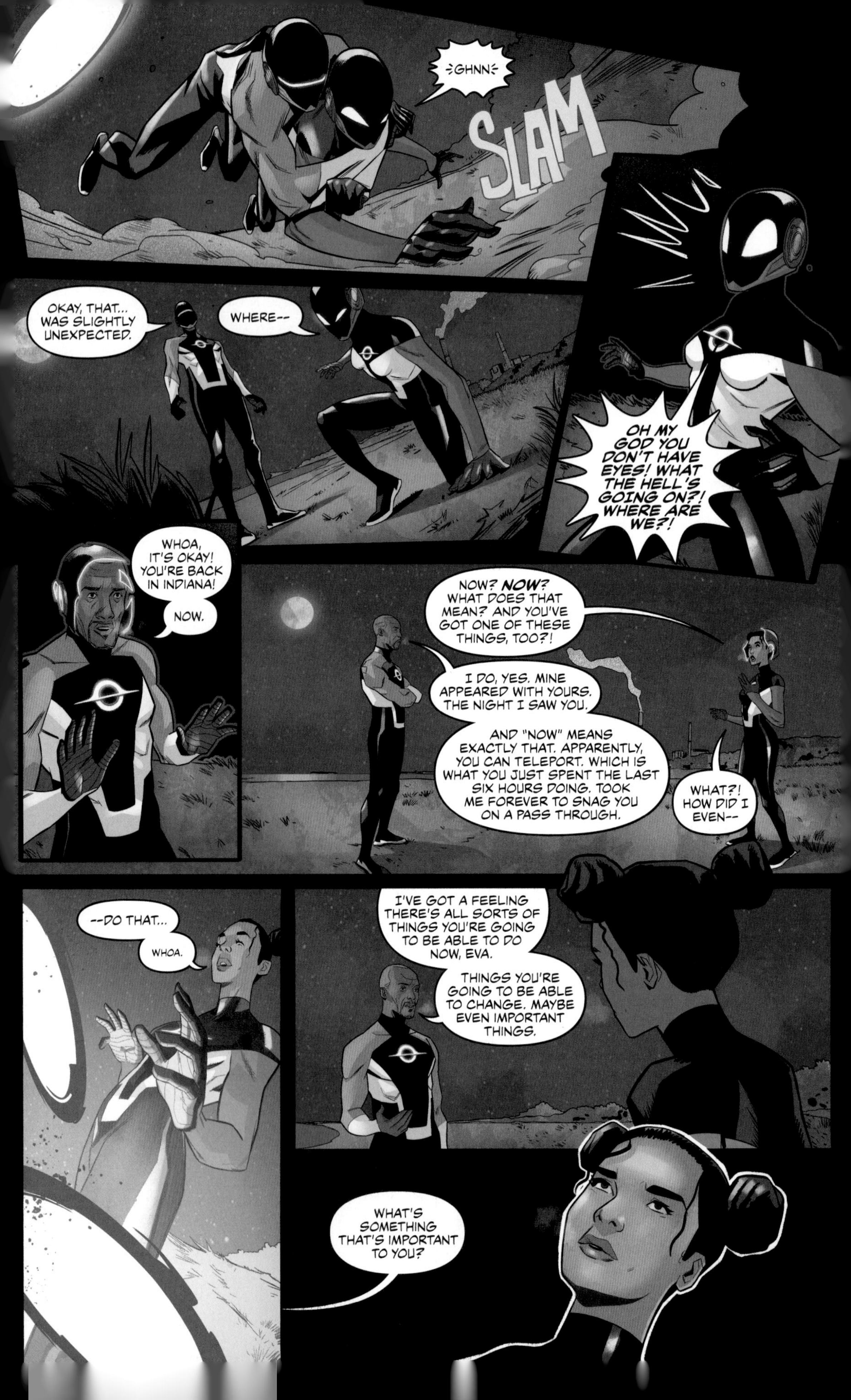

GHNN
SLAM
OKAY, THAT... WAS SLIGHTLY UNEXPECTED.
WHERE--
OH MY GOD YOU DON'T HAVE EYES! WHAT THE HELL'S GOING ON?! WHERE ARE WE?!
WHOA, IT'S OKAY! YOU'RE BACK IN INDIANA!
NOW.
NOW? NOW? WHAT DOES THAT MEAN? AND YOU'VE GOT ONE OF THESE THINGS, TOO?!
I DO, YES. MINE APPEARED WITH YOURS. THE NIGHT I SAW YOU.
AND "NOW" MEANS EXACTLY THAT. APPARENTLY, YOU CAN TELEPORT. WHICH IS WHAT YOU JUST SPENT THE LAST SIX HOURS DOING. TOOK ME FOREVER TO SNAG YOU ON A PASS THROUGH.
WHAT?! HOW DID I EVEN--
--DO THAT...
WHOA.
I'VE GOT A FEELING THERE'S ALL SORTS OF THINGS YOU'RE GOING TO BE ABLE TO DO NOW, EVA.
THINGS YOU'RE GOING TO BE ABLE TO CHANGE. MAYBE EVEN IMPORTANT THINGS.
WHAT'S SOMETHING THAT'S IMPORTANT TO YOU?

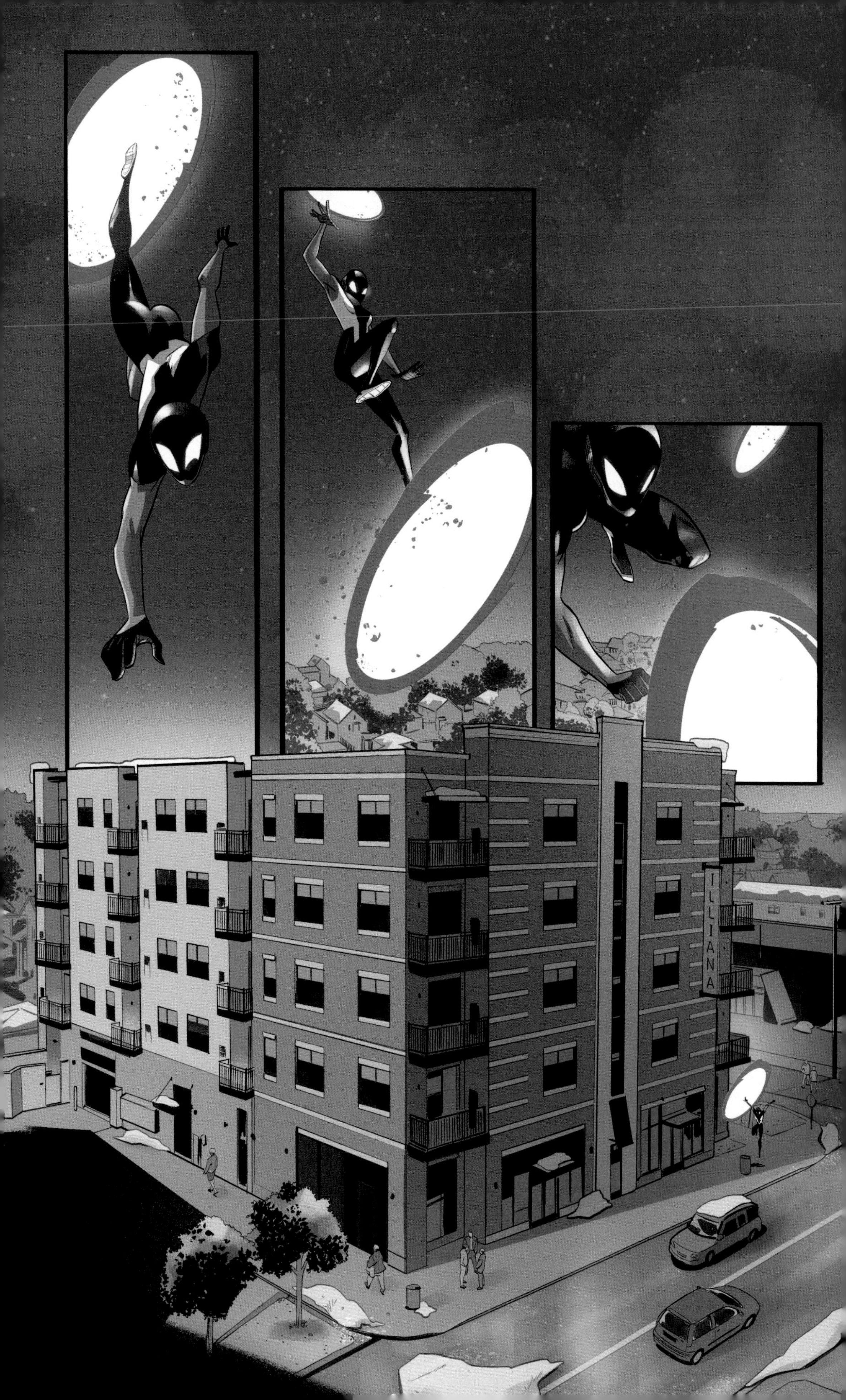
ILLIANA

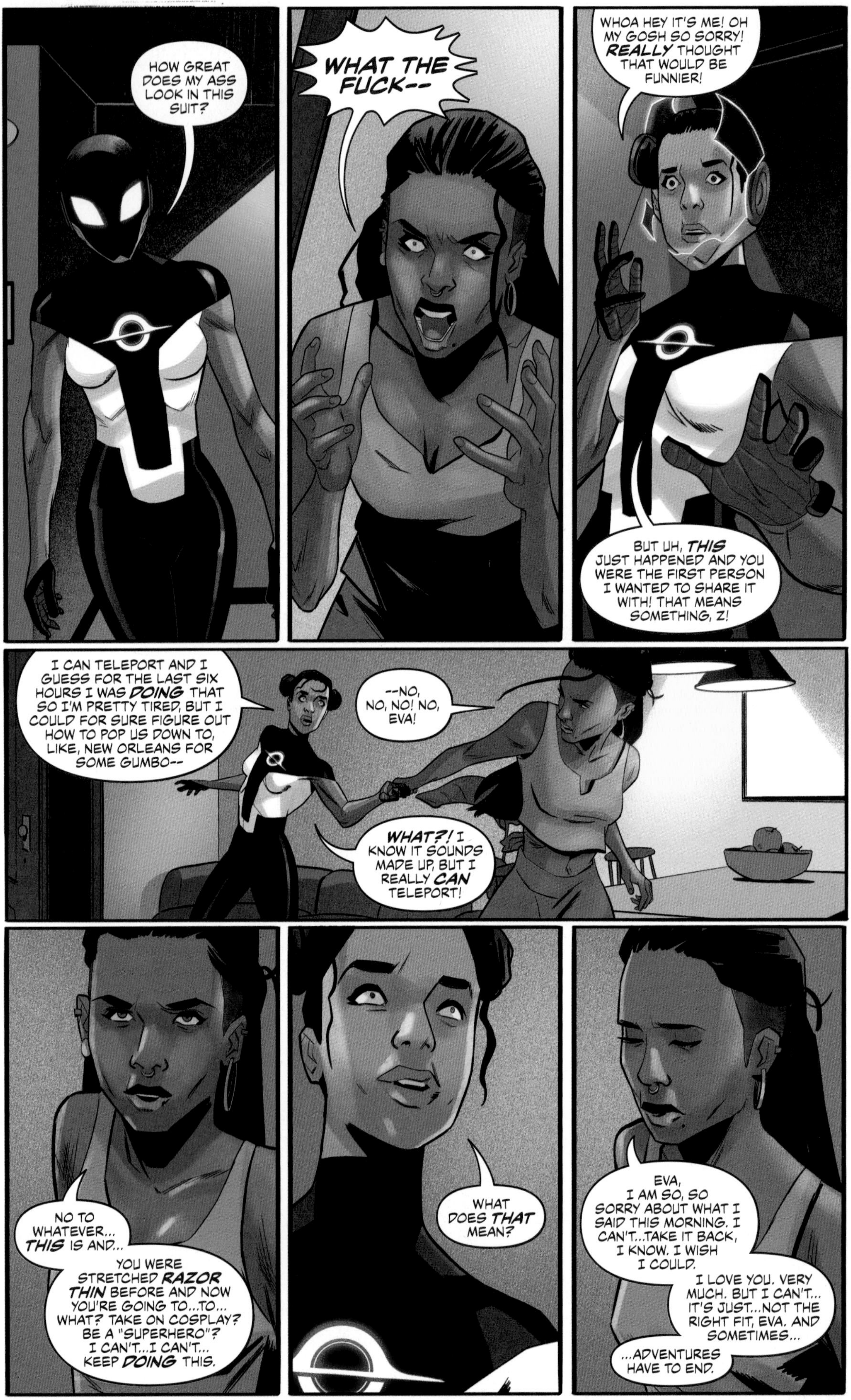
HOW GREAT DOES MY ASS LOOK IN THIS SUIT?
WHAT THE FUCK--
WHOA HEY IT'S ME! OH MY GOSH SO SORRY! REALLY THOUGHT THAT WOULD BE FUNNIER!
BUT UH, THIS JUST HAPPENED AND YOU WERE THE FIRST PERSON I WANTED TO SHARE IT WITH! THAT MEANS SOMETHING, Z!
I CAN TELEPORT AND I GUESS FOR THE LAST SIX HOURS I WAS DOING THAT SO I'M PRETTY TIRED, BUT I COULD FOR SURE FIGURE OUT HOW TO POP US DOWN TO, LIKE, NEW ORLEANS FOR SOME GUMBO--
--NO, NO, NO! NO, EVA!
WHAT?! I KNOW IT SOUNDS MADE UP, BUT I REALLY CAN TELEPORT!
NO TO WHATEVER... THIS IS AND...
YOU WERE STRETCHED RAZOR THIN BEFORE AND NOW YOU'RE GOING TO...TO... WHAT? TAKE ON COSPLAY? BE A "SUPERHERO"? I CAN'T...I CAN'T... KEEP DOING THIS.
WHAT DOES THAT MEAN?
EVA, I AM SO, SO SORRY ABOUT WHAT I SAID THIS MORNING. I CAN'T...TAKE IT BACK, I KNOW. I WISH I COULD.
I LOVE YOU. VERY MUCH. BUT I CAN'T... IT'S JUST...NOT THE RIGHT FIT, EVA. AND SOMETIMES...
...ADVENTURES HAVE TO END.

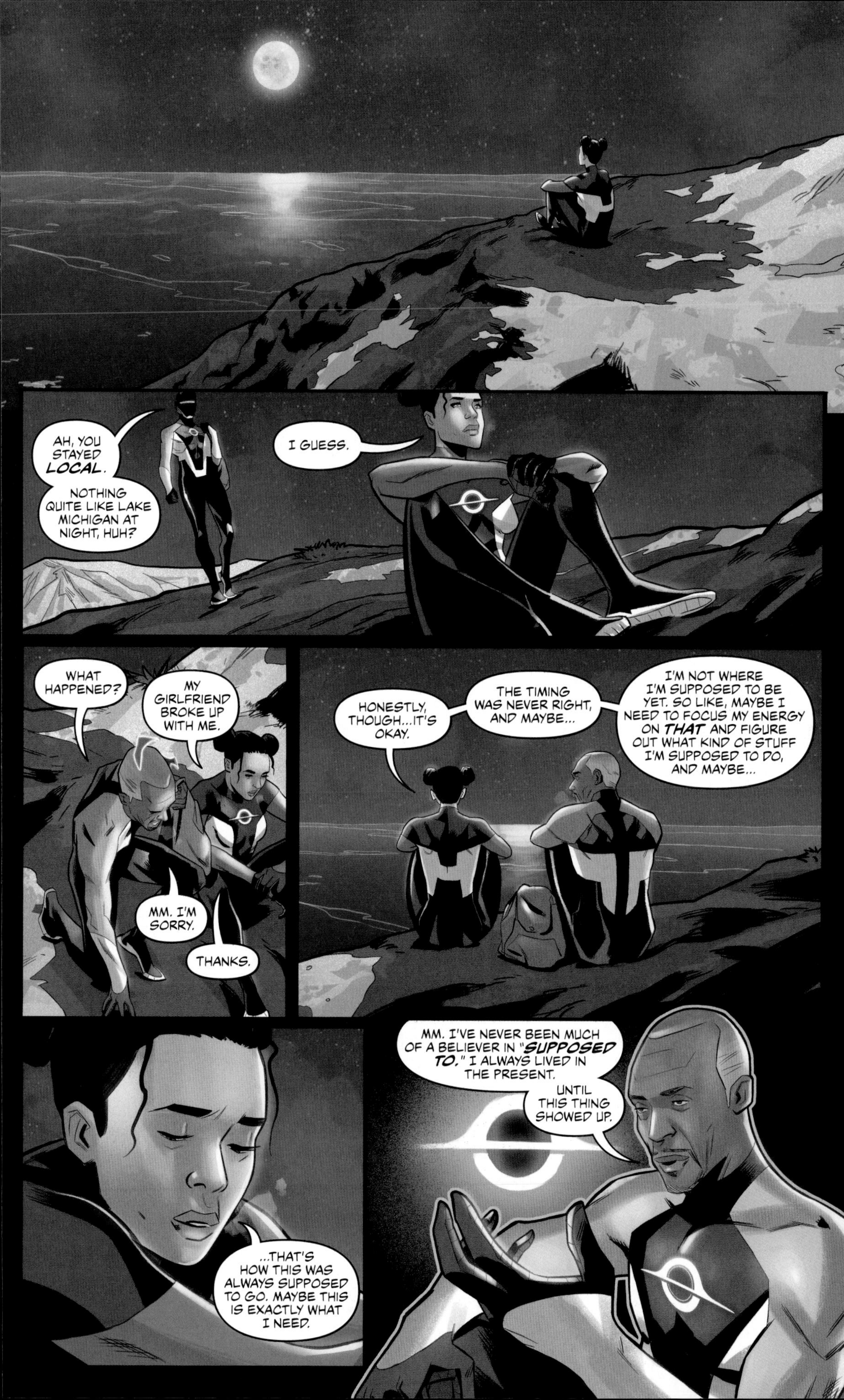
AH, YOU STAYED LOCAL.
NOTHING QUITE LIKE LAKE MICHIGAN AT NIGHT, HUH?
I GUESS.
WHAT HAPPENED?
MY GIRLFRIEND BROKE UP WITH ME.
MM. I'M SORRY.
THANKS.
HONESTLY, THOUGH...IT'S OKAY.
THE TIMING WAS NEVER RIGHT, AND MAYBE...
I'M NOT WHERE I'M SUPPOSED TO BE YET. SO LIKE, MAYBE I NEED TO FOCUS MY ENERGY ON THAT AND FIGURE OUT WHAT KIND OF STUFF I'M SUPPOSED TO DO, AND MAYBE...
...THAT'S HOW THIS WAS ALWAYS SUPPOSED TO GO. MAYBE THIS IS EXACTLY WHAT I NEED.
MM. I'VE NEVER BEEN MUCH OF A BELIEVER IN "SUPPOSED TO." I ALWAYS LIVED IN THE PRESENT.
UNTIL THIS THING SHOWED UP.

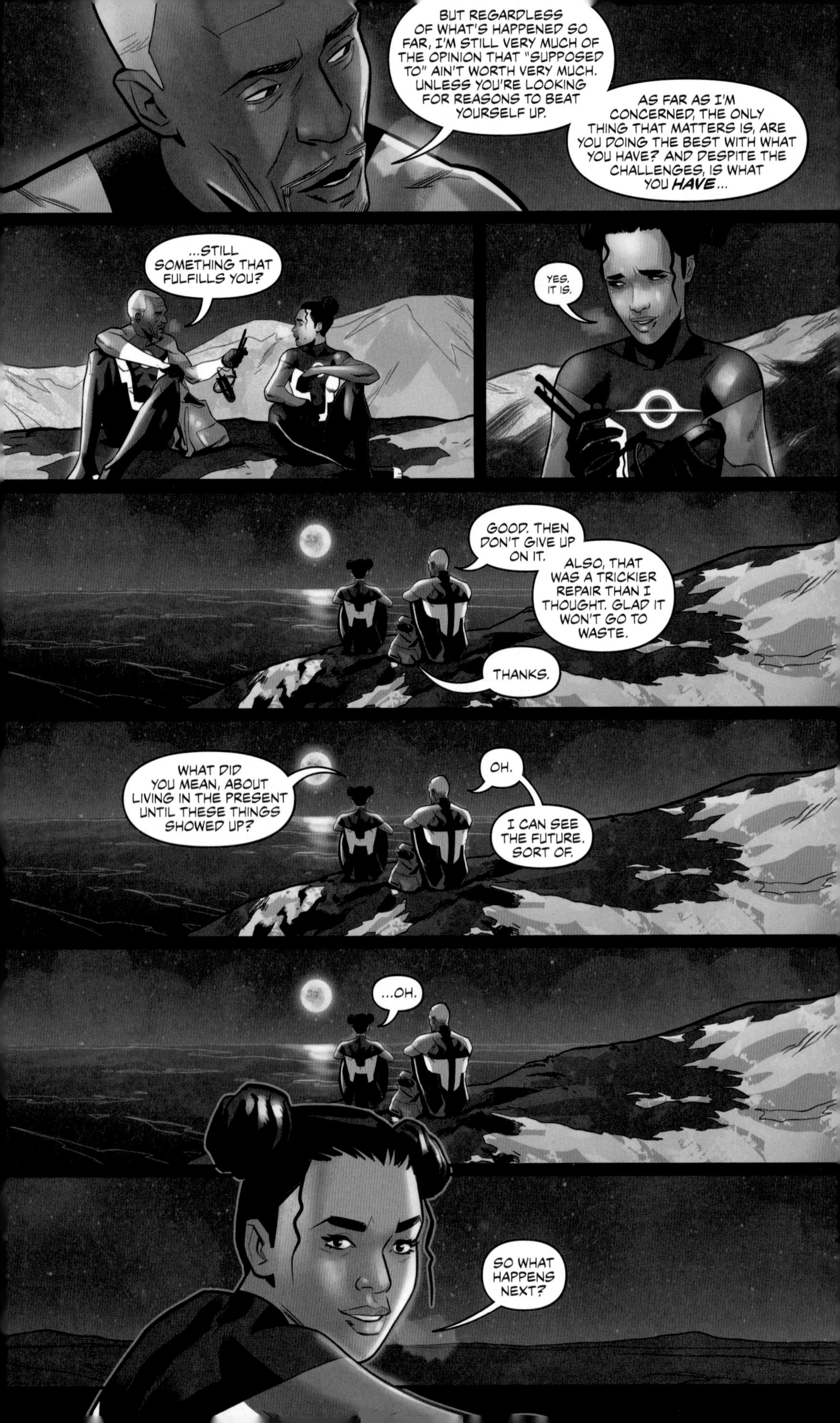
BUT REGARDLESS OF WHAT'S HAPPENED SO FAR, I'M STILL VERY MUCH OF THE OPINION THAT "SUPPOSED TO" AIN'T WORTH VERY MUCH. UNLESS YOU'RE LOOKING FOR REASONS TO BEAT YOURSELF UP.
AS FAR AS I'M CONCERNED, THE ONLY THING THAT MATTERS IS, ARE YOU DOING THE BEST WITH WHAT YOU HAVE? AND DESPITE THE CHALLENGES, IS WHAT YOU *HAVE*...
...STILL SOMETHING THAT FULFILLS YOU?
YES. IT IS.
GOOD. THEN DON'T GIVE UP ON IT.
ALSO, THAT WAS A TRICKIER REPAIR THAN I THOUGHT. GLAD IT WON'T GO TO WASTE.
THANKS.
WHAT DID YOU MEAN, ABOUT LIVING IN THE PRESENT UNTIL THESE THINGS SHOWED UP?
OH.
I CAN SEE THE FUTURE. SORT OF.
...OH.
SO WHAT HAPPENS NEXT?

COVER
GALLERY

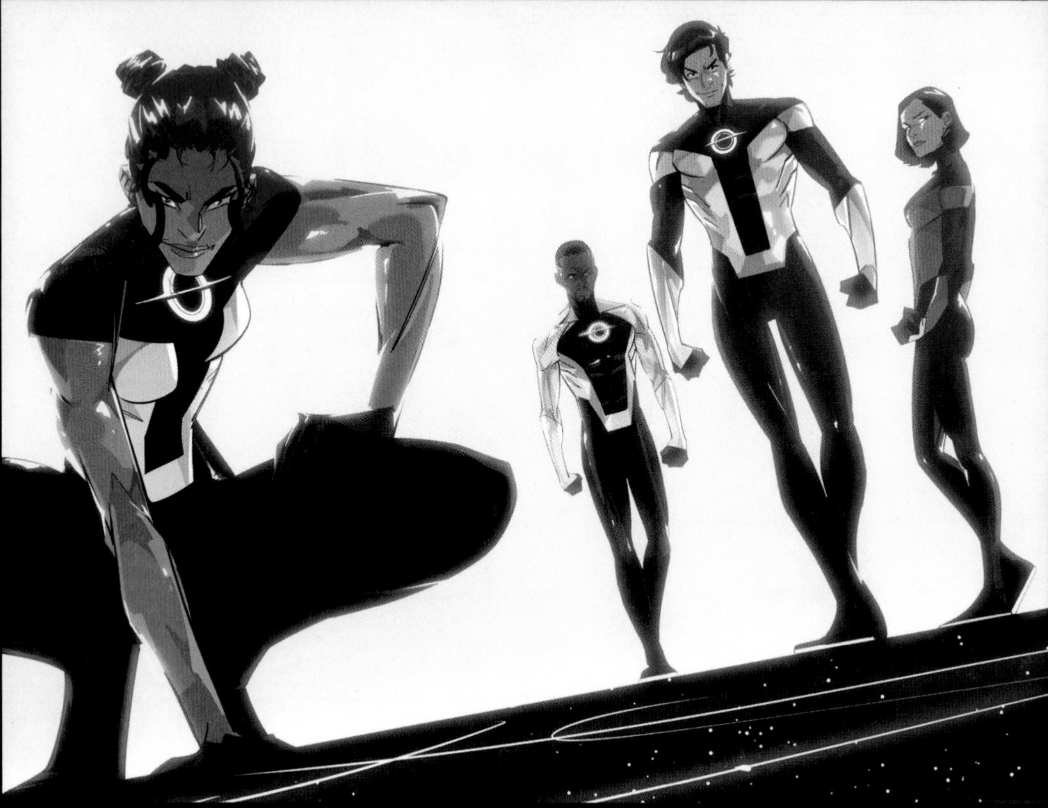

#07 [A]
Daniele Di Nicuolo w/ Walter Baiamonte

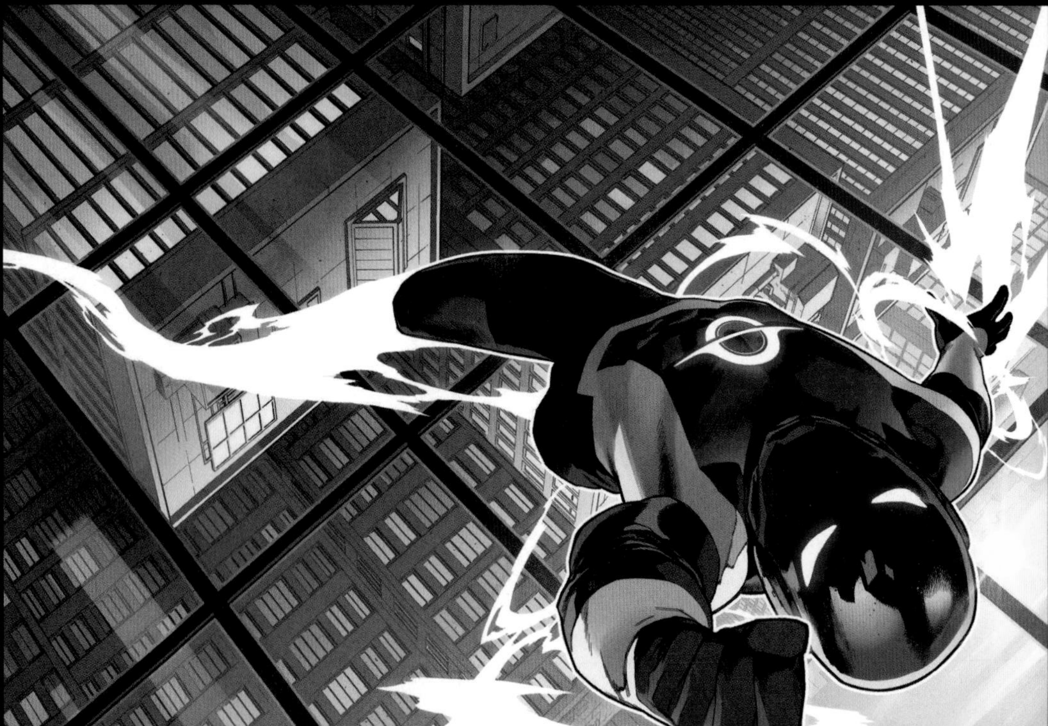

#07 [B]
Felipe Watanabe w/ Marcelo Costa

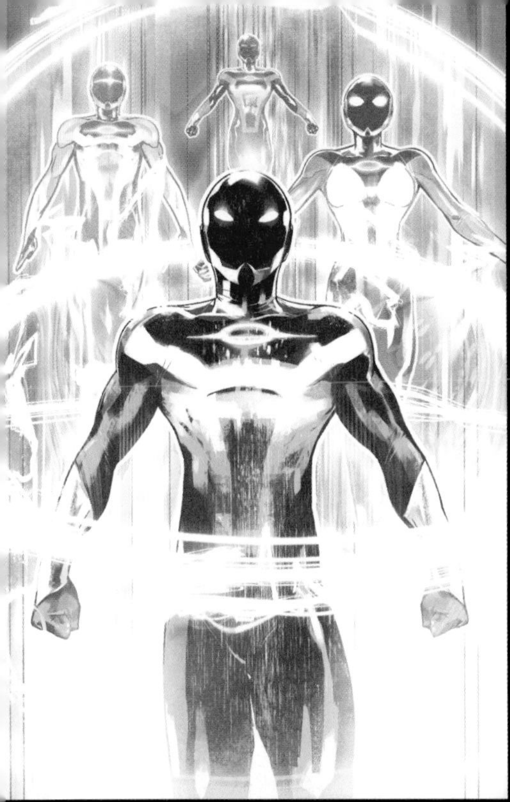

#07 [C]
Trevor McCarthy

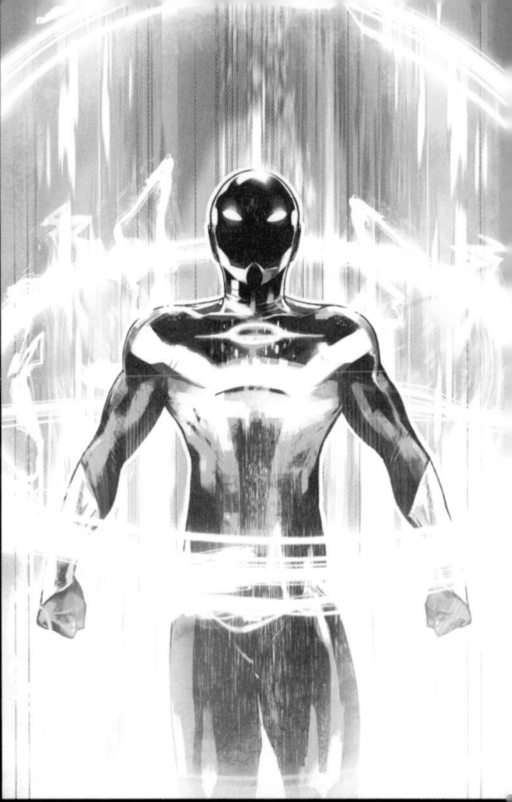

#07 [C] (Spoiler-Free)
Trevor McCarthy

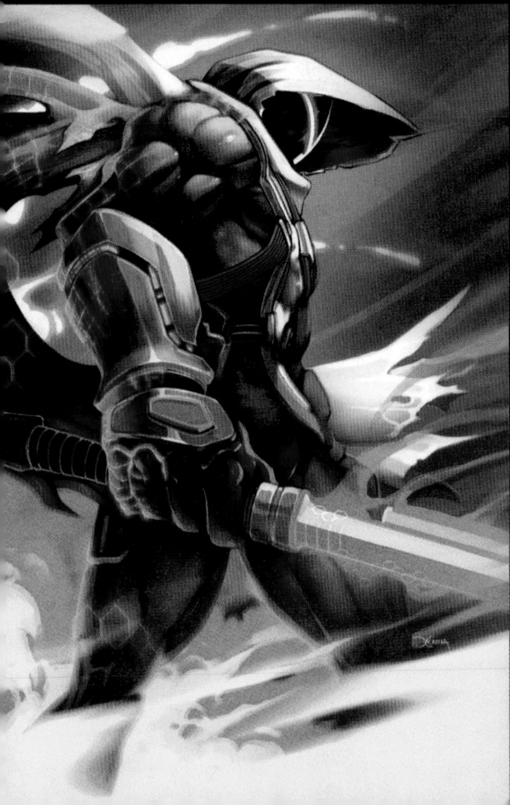

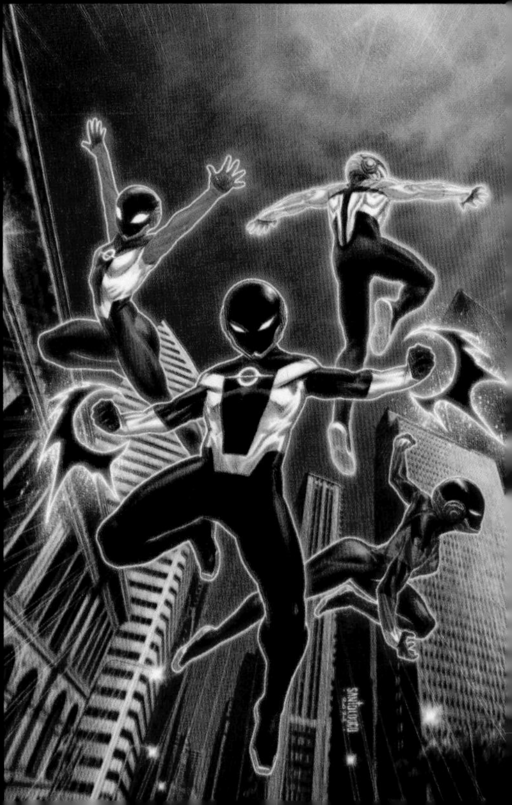

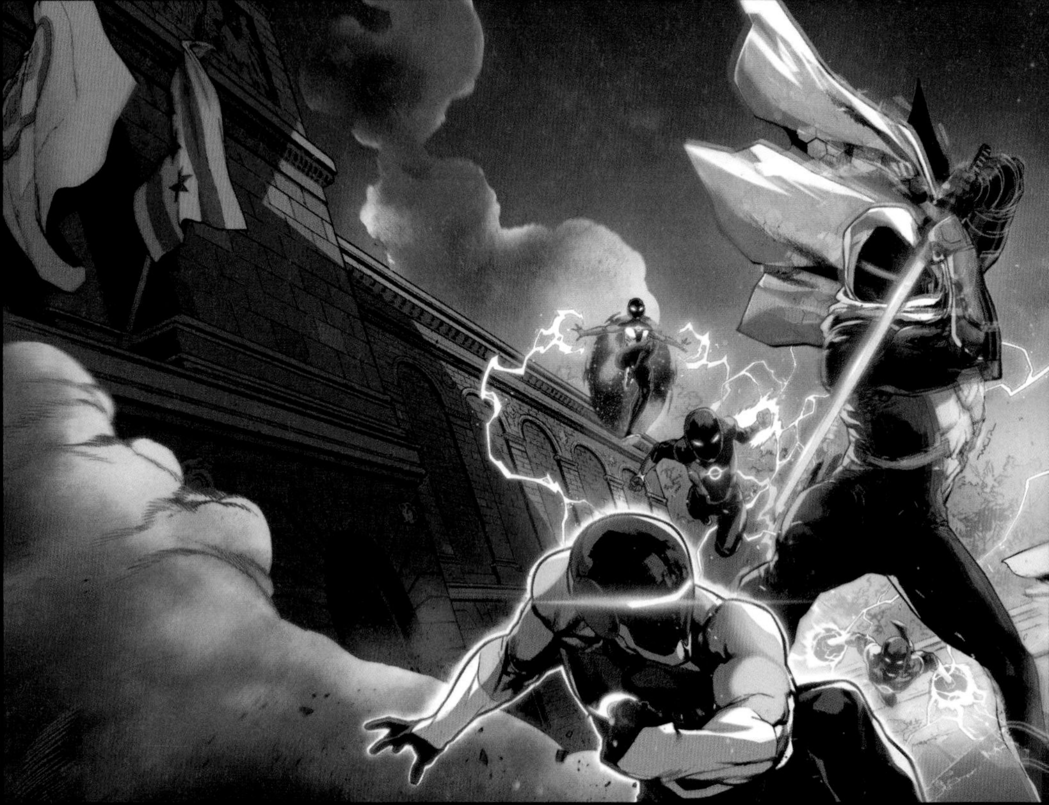

#08 [A]
Felipe Watanabe w/ Igor Monti

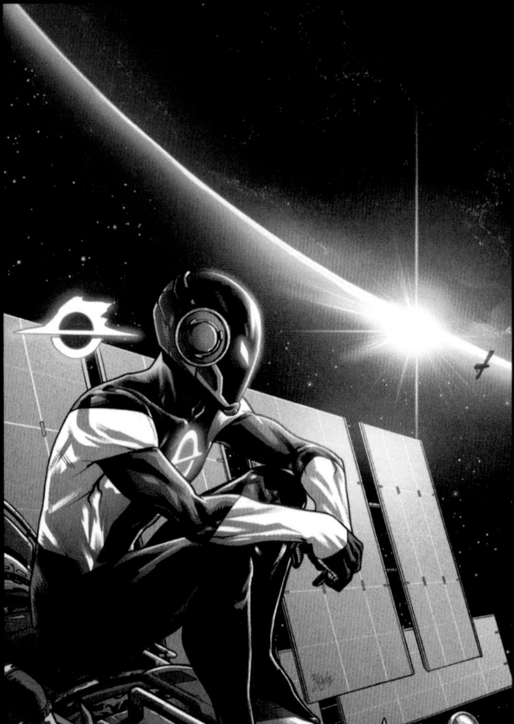

#08 [B]
Jose Carlos

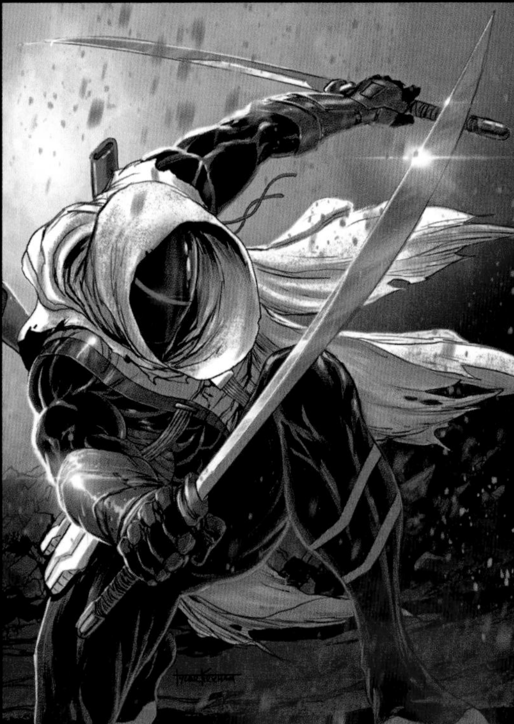

#08 [C]
Tyler Kirkham

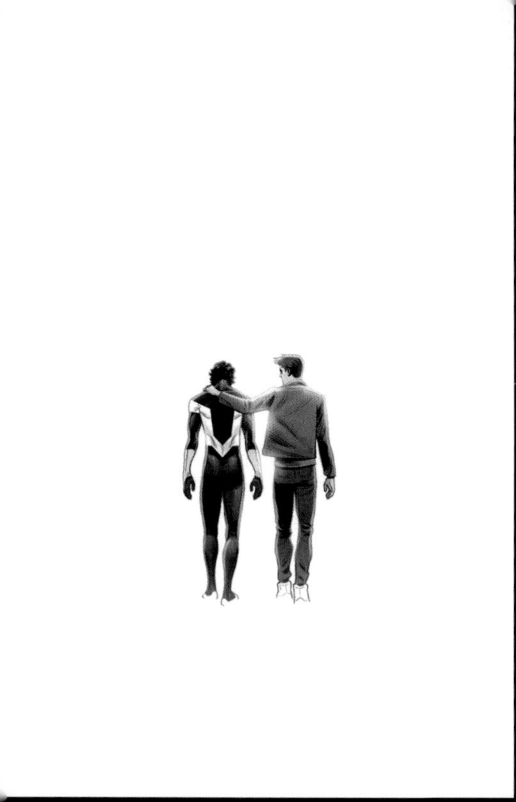

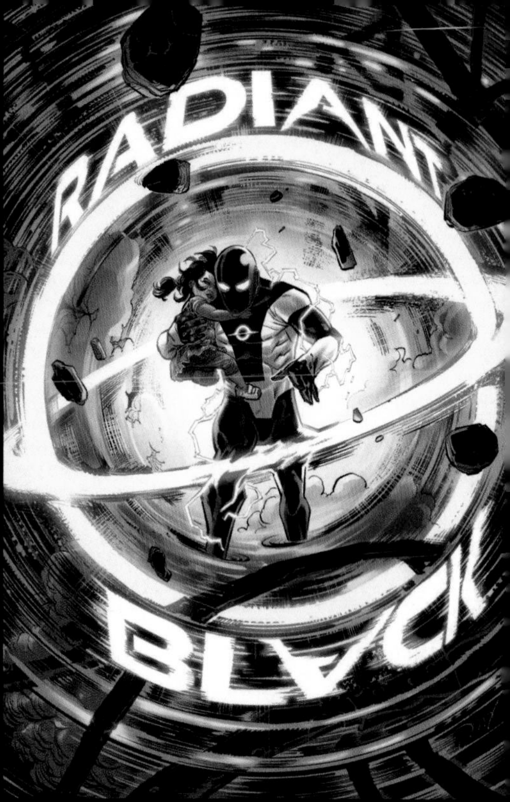
RADIANT
BLACK

#09 [A]

Marcelo Costa

#09 [B]

Danilo Beyruth

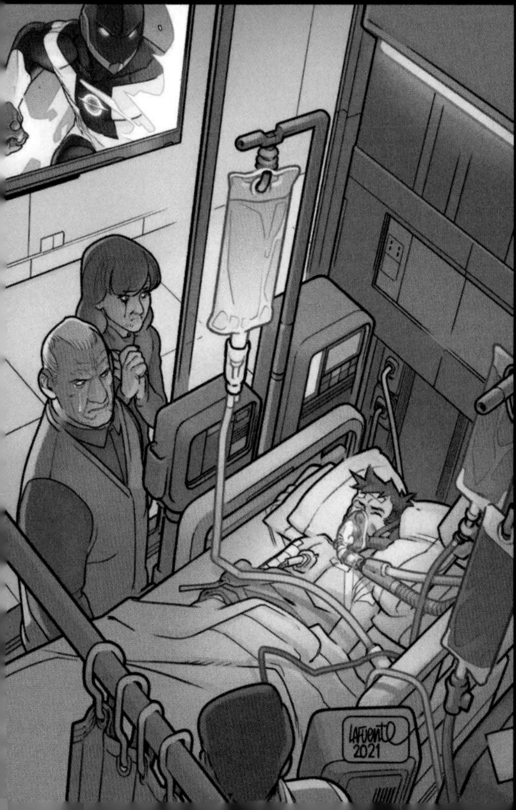

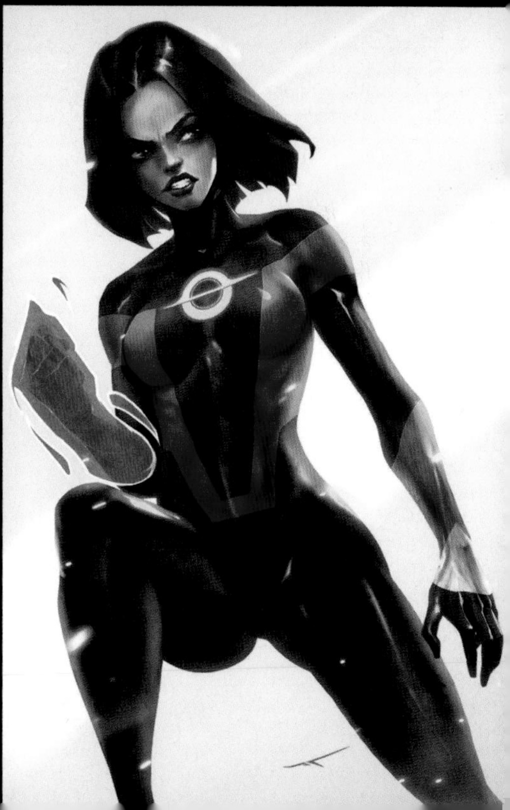

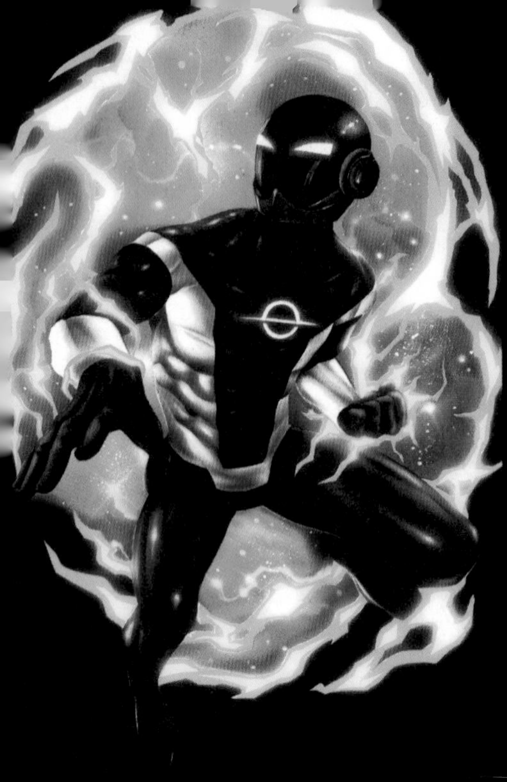

09 [B&S Comics]

artin Zavala

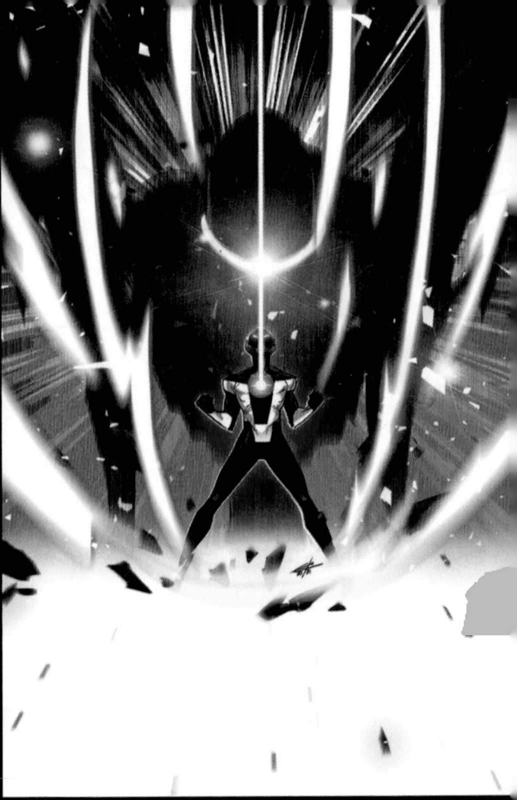

#10 [A]

Eleonora Carlini

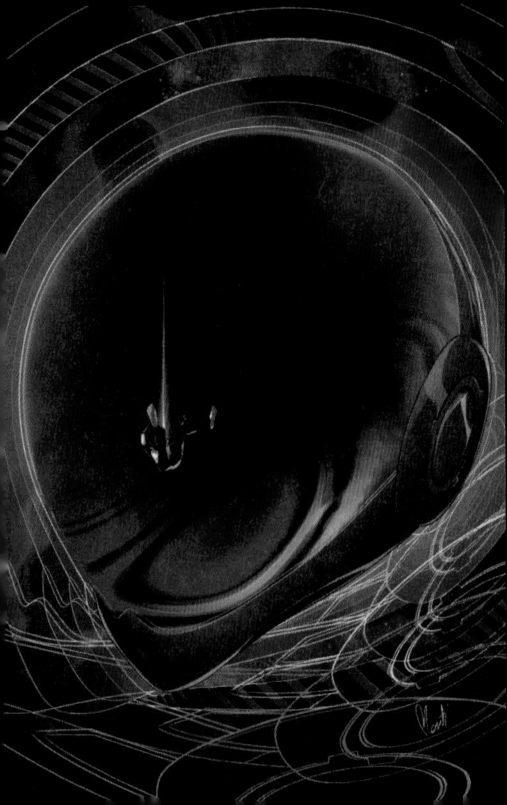

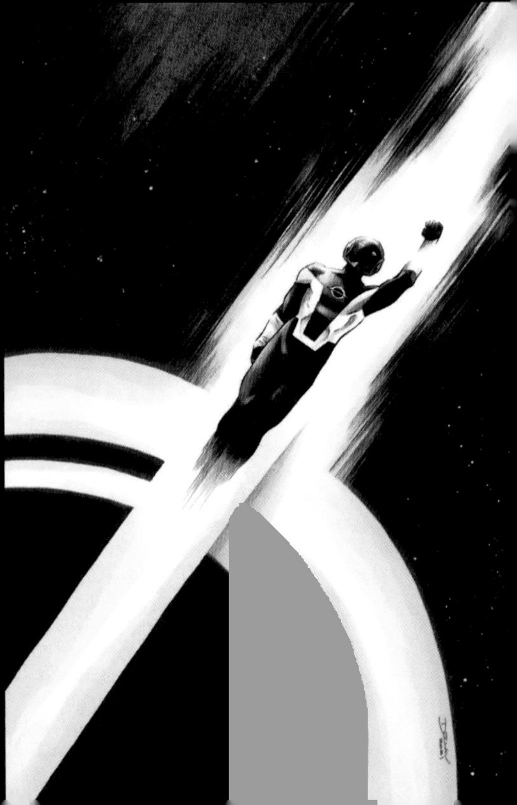

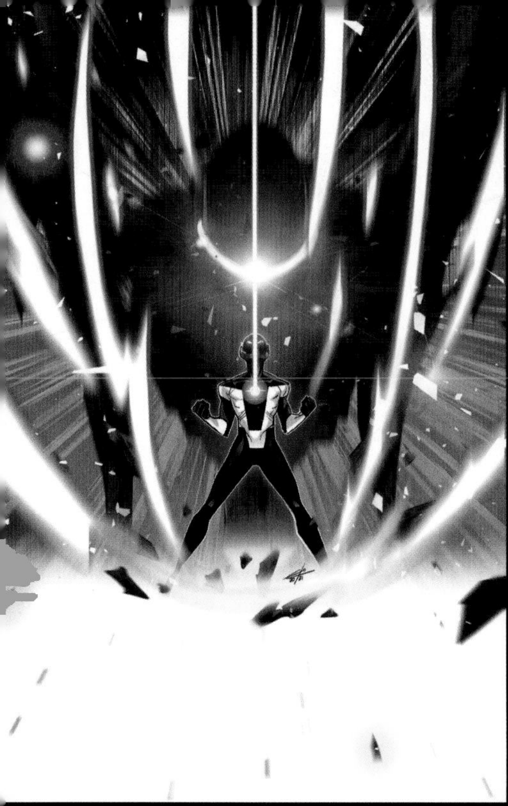

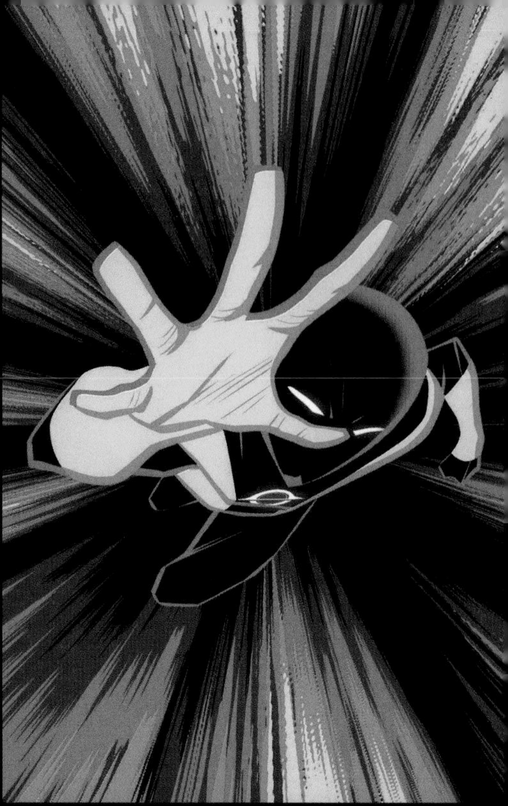

#10 Blacklight Edition [A]
Eleonora Carlini w/ Igor Monti

#10 Blacklight Edition [Black Market]
Marcelo Costa

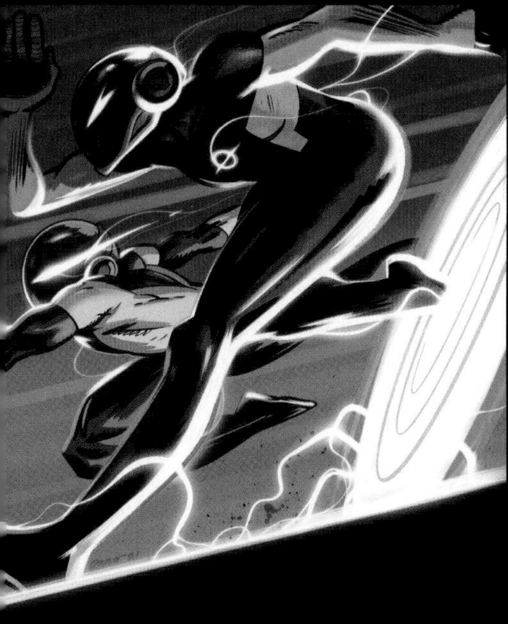

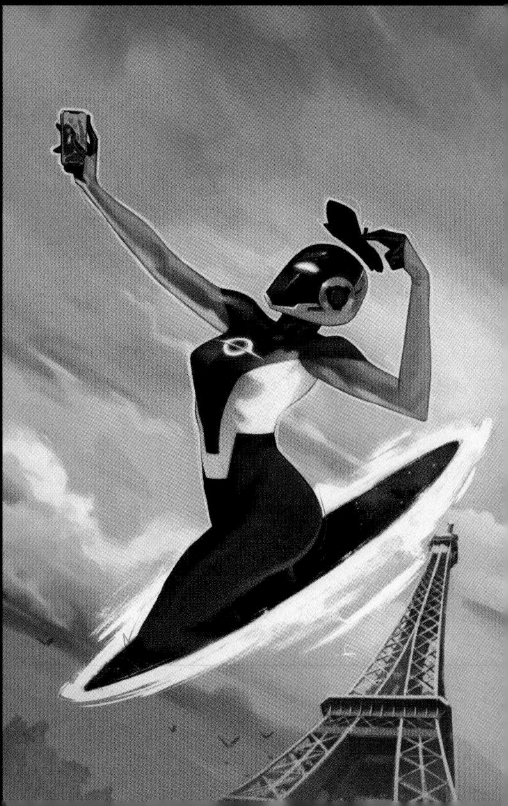

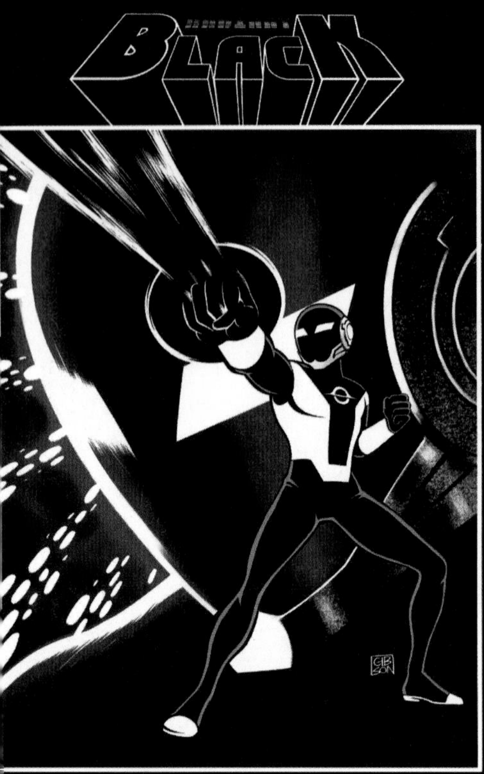
BLACK

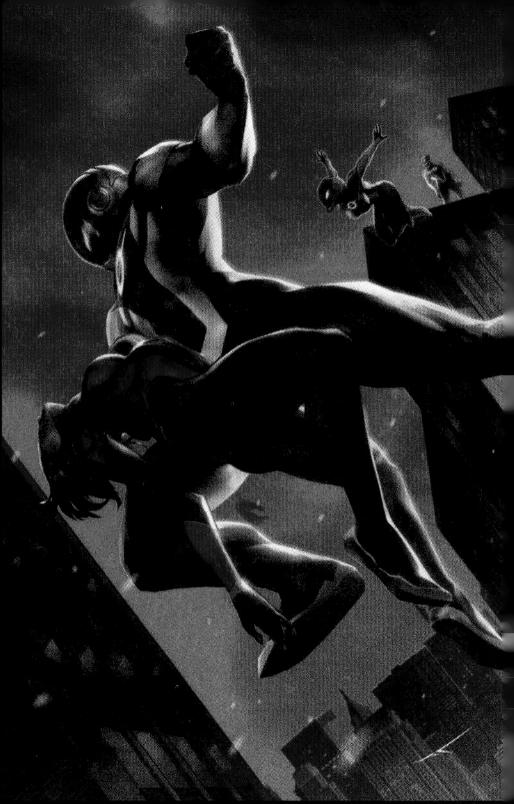

1 [C]

rdan Gibson

#11 [Mutant Beaver Comics]

Ivan Tao

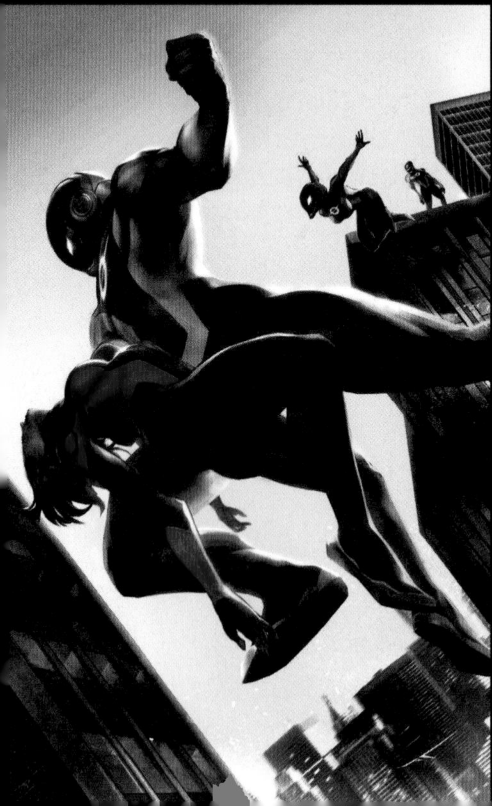

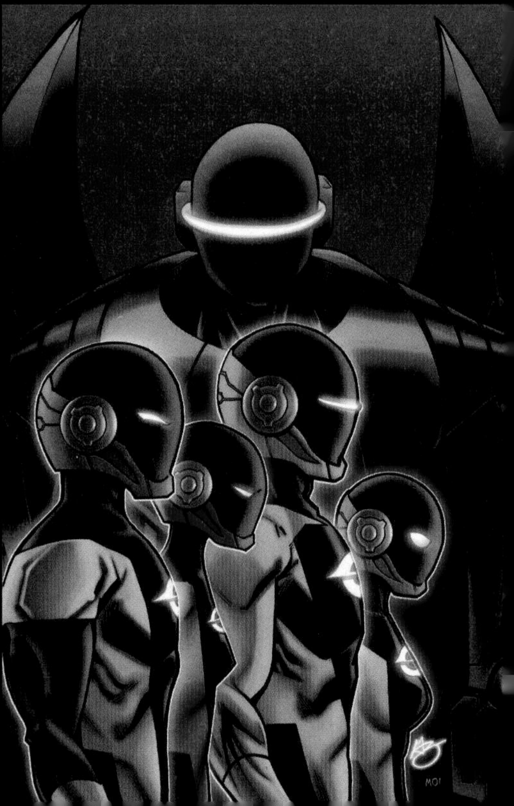

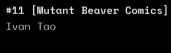

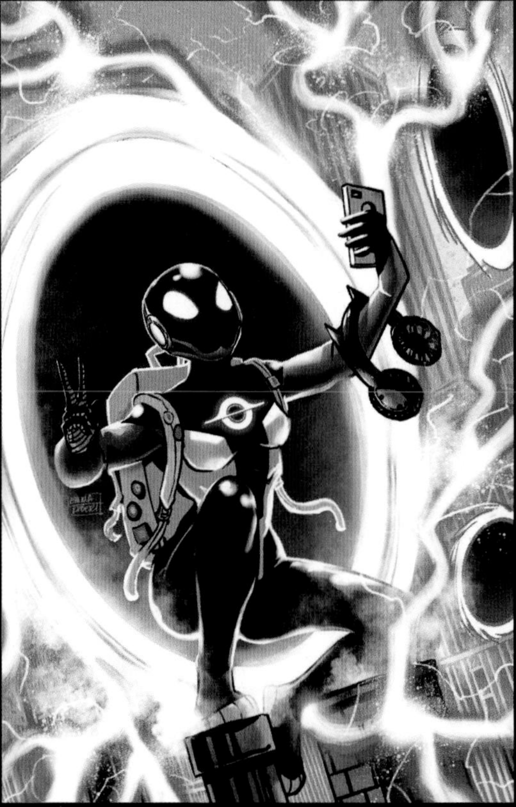

#12 [A]
Emma Kubert

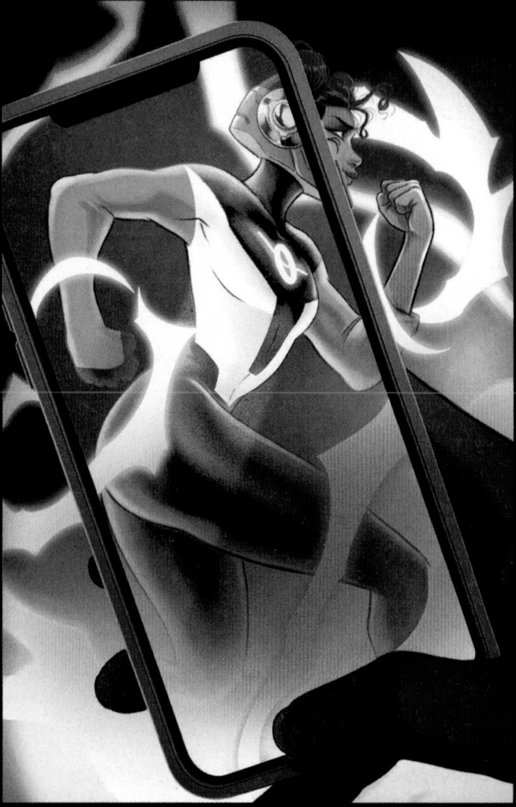

#12 [B]
Sweeney Boo

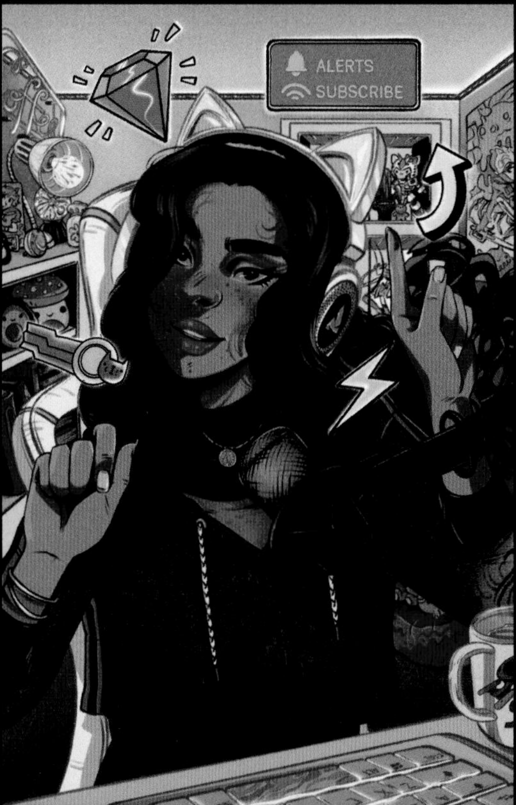
ALERTS
SUBSCRIBE

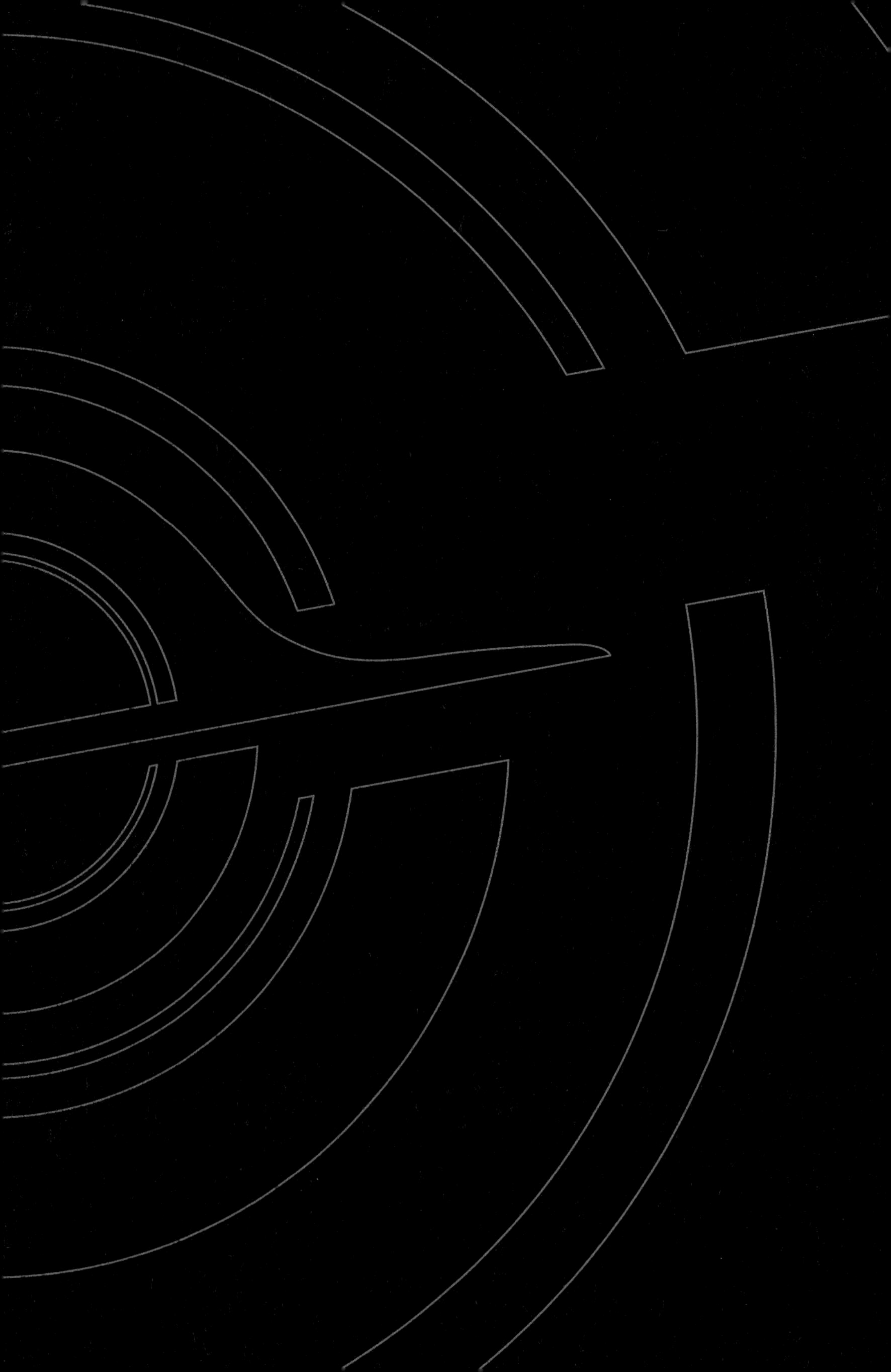

MARSHALL'S SCHOOL OF BUSINESS

Marshall's School of Business

The world's only accredited* business school based behind a video store counter.

*NOT ACCREDITED

W: Riley Trella A: Eduardo Ferigato C: Marcelo Costa L: Becca Carey

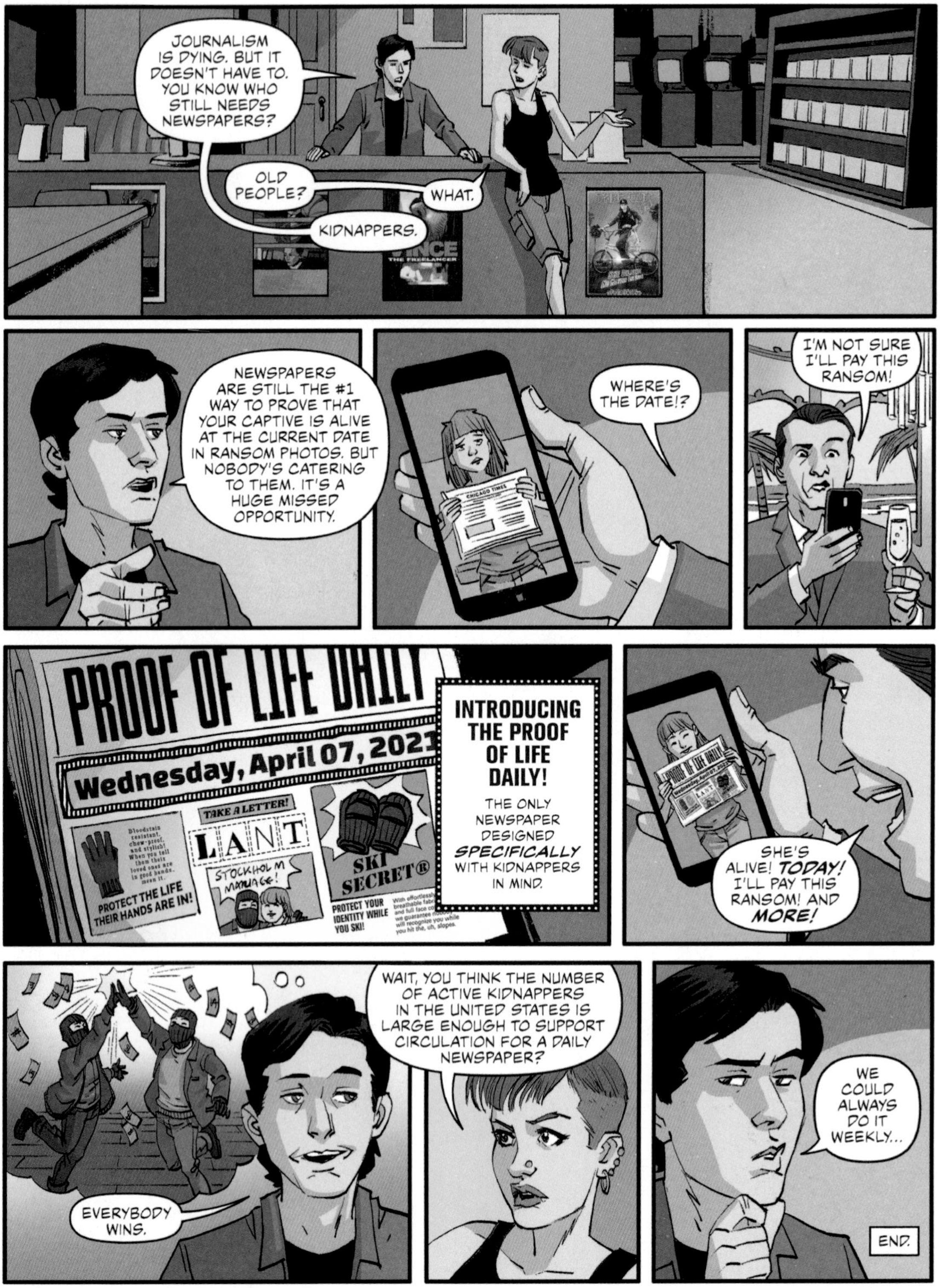
JOURNALISM IS DYING. BUT IT DOESN'T HAVE TO. YOU KNOW WHO STILL NEEDS NEWSPAPERS?
OLD PEOPLE?
WHAT.
KIDNAPPERS.
NEWSPAPERS ARE STILL THE #1 WAY TO PROVE THAT YOUR CAPTIVE IS ALIVE AT THE CURRENT DATE IN RANSOM PHOTOS. BUT NOBODY'S CATERING TO THEM. IT'S A HUGE MISSED OPPORTUNITY.
WHERE'S THE DATE!?
I'M NOT SURE I'LL PAY THIS RANSOM!
PROOF OF LIFE DAILY
Wednesday, April 07, 2021
Bloodstain resistant, chew-proof, and stylish! When you tell them their loved ones are in good hands, mean it.
PROTECT THE LIFE THEIR HANDS ARE IN!
TAKE A LETTER!
LANT
SKI SECRET®
PROTECT YOUR IDENTITY WHILE YOU SKI!
INTRODUCING THE PROOF OF LIFE DAILY!
THE ONLY NEWSPAPER DESIGNED *SPECIFICALLY* WITH KIDNAPPERS IN MIND.
SHE'S ALIVE! *TODAY!* I'LL PAY THIS RANSOM! AND *MORE!*
EVERYBODY WINS.
WAIT, YOU THINK THE NUMBER OF ACTIVE KIDNAPPERS IN THE UNITED STATES IS LARGE ENOUGH TO SUPPORT CIRCULATION FOR A DAILY NEWSPAPER?
WE COULD ALWAYS DO IT WEEKLY...
END.

W: Melissa Flores A: Joe Hunter L: Becca Carey

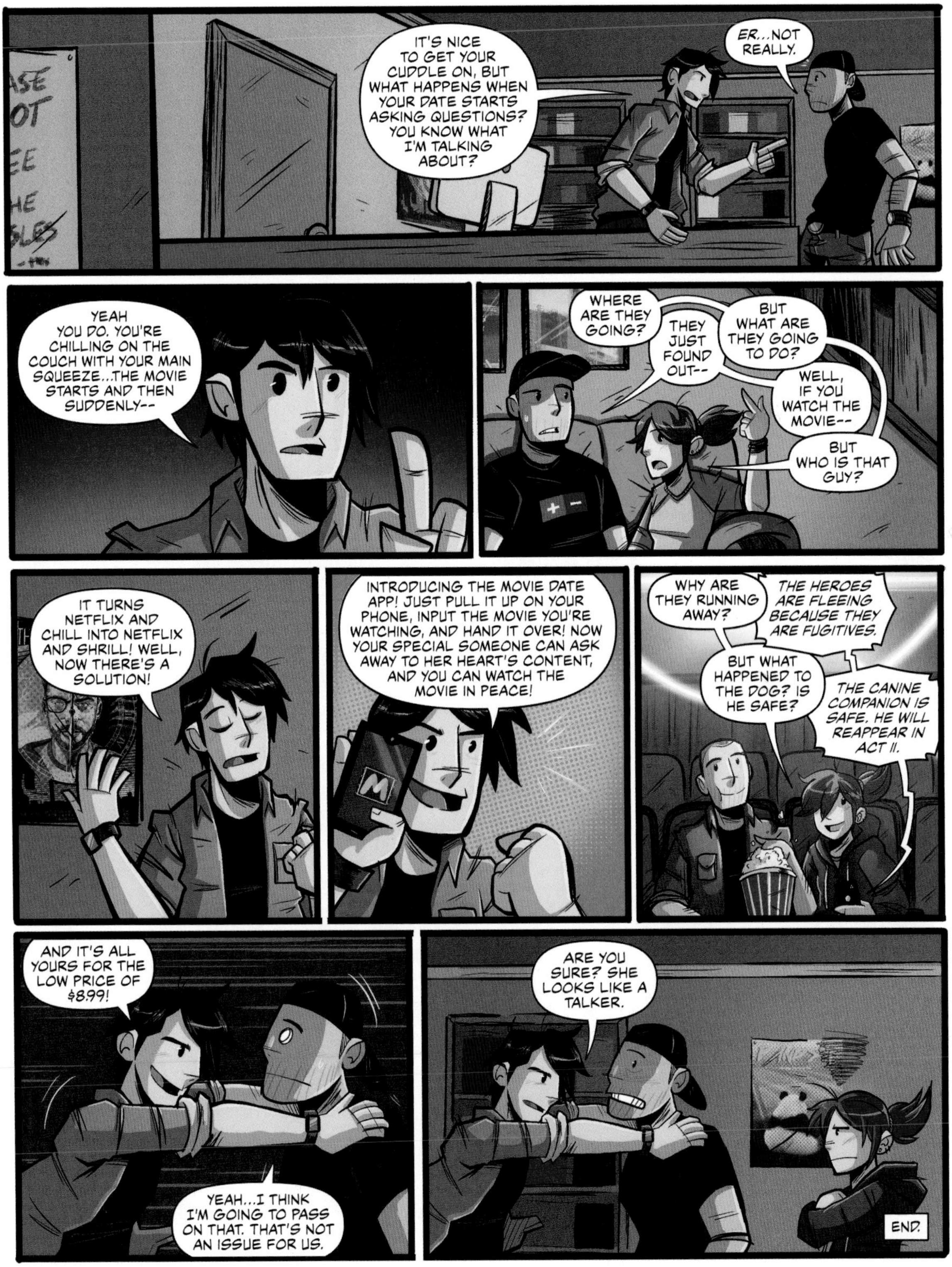
IT'S NICE TO GET YOUR CUDDLE ON, BUT WHAT HAPPENS WHEN YOUR DATE STARTS ASKING QUESTIONS? YOU KNOW WHAT I'M TALKING ABOUT?
ER...NOT REALLY.
YEAH YOU DO. YOU'RE CHILLING ON THE COUCH WITH YOUR MAIN SQUEEZE...THE MOVIE STARTS AND THEN SUDDENLY--
WHERE ARE THEY GOING?
THEY JUST FOUND OUT--
BUT WHAT ARE THEY GOING TO DO?
WELL, IF YOU WATCH THE MOVIE--
BUT WHO IS THAT GUY?
IT TURNS NETFLIX AND CHILL INTO NETFLIX AND SHRILL! WELL, NOW THERE'S A SOLUTION!
INTRODUCING THE MOVIE DATE APP! JUST PULL IT UP ON YOUR PHONE, INPUT THE MOVIE YOU'RE WATCHING, AND HAND IT OVER! NOW YOUR SPECIAL SOMEONE CAN ASK AWAY TO HER HEART'S CONTENT, AND YOU CAN WATCH THE MOVIE IN PEACE!
WHY ARE THEY RUNNING AWAY?
THE HEROES ARE FLEEING BECAUSE THEY ARE FUGITIVES.
BUT WHAT HAPPENED TO THE DOG? IS HE SAFE?
THE CANINE COMPANION IS SAFE. HE WILL REAPPEAR IN ACT II.
AND IT'S ALL YOURS FOR THE LOW PRICE OF $8.99!
YEAH...I THINK I'M GOING TO PASS ON THAT. THAT'S NOT AN ISSUE FOR US.
ARE YOU SURE? SHE LOOKS LIKE A TALKER.
END.

W: Melissa Flores A: Danilo Beyruth C: Dee Cunniffe L: Becca Carey

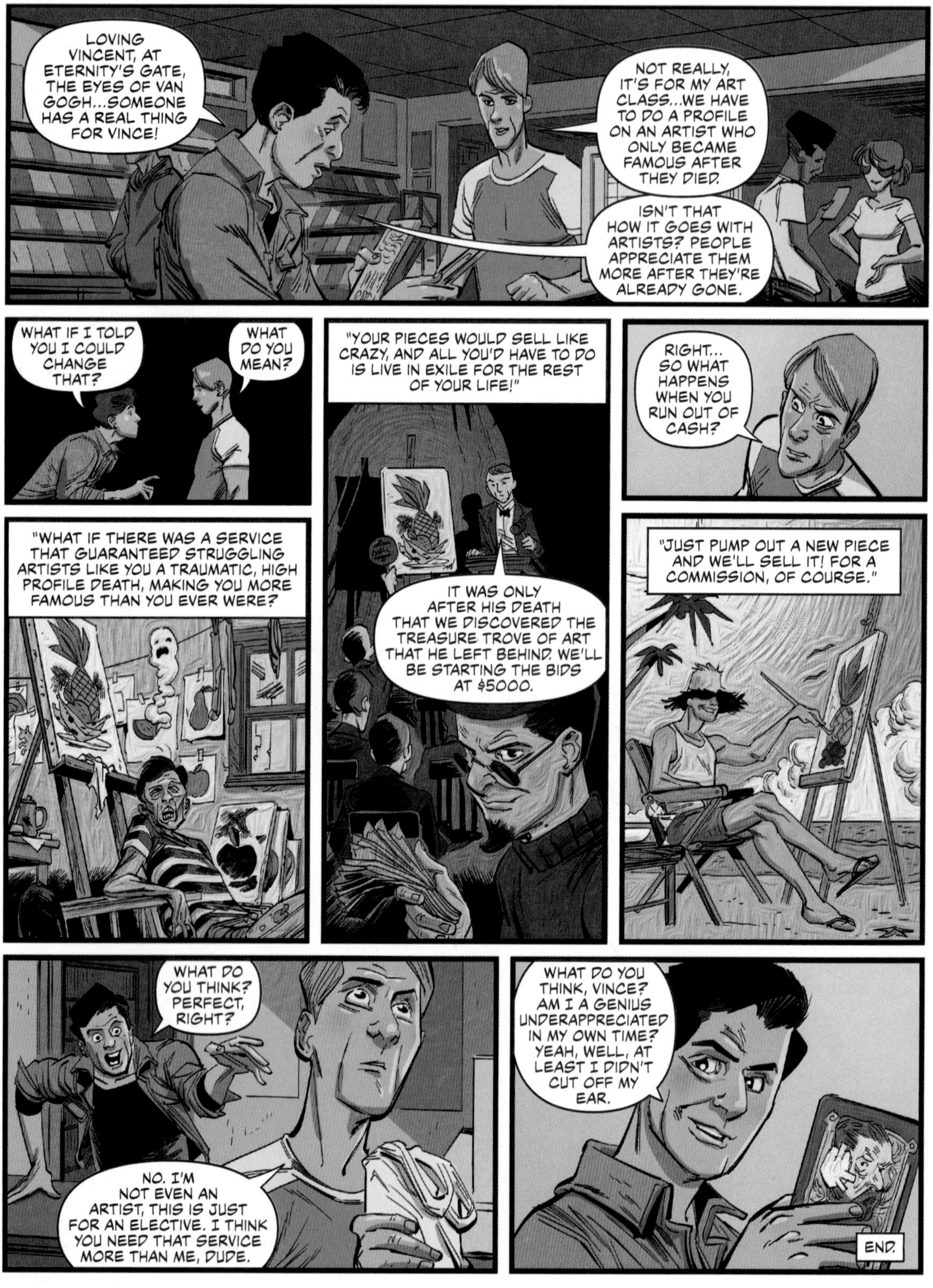
LOVING VINCENT, AT ETERNITY'S GATE, THE EYES OF VAN GOGH...SOMEONE HAS A REAL THING FOR VINCE!
NOT REALLY, IT'S FOR MY ART CLASS...WE HAVE TO DO A PROFILE ON AN ARTIST WHO ONLY BECAME FAMOUS AFTER THEY DIED.
ISN'T THAT HOW IT GOES WITH ARTISTS? PEOPLE APPRECIATE THEM MORE AFTER THEY'RE ALREADY GONE.
WHAT IF I TOLD YOU I COULD CHANGE THAT?
WHAT DO YOU MEAN?
"YOUR PIECES WOULD SELL LIKE CRAZY, AND ALL YOU'D HAVE TO DO IS LIVE IN EXILE FOR THE REST OF YOUR LIFE!"
RIGHT... SO WHAT HAPPENS WHEN YOU RUN OUT OF CASH?
"WHAT IF THERE WAS A SERVICE THAT GUARANTEED STRUGGLING ARTISTS LIKE YOU A TRAUMATIC, HIGH PROFILE DEATH, MAKING YOU MORE FAMOUS THAN YOU EVER WERE?
IT WAS ONLY AFTER HIS DEATH THAT WE DISCOVERED THE TREASURE TROVE OF ART THAT HE LEFT BEHIND. WE'LL BE STARTING THE BIDS AT $5000.
"JUST PUMP OUT A NEW PIECE AND WE'LL SELL IT! FOR A COMMISSION, OF COURSE."
WHAT DO YOU THINK? PERFECT, RIGHT?
NO. I'M NOT EVEN AN ARTIST, THIS IS JUST FOR AN ELECTIVE. I THINK YOU NEED THAT SERVICE MORE THAN ME, DUDE.
WHAT DO YOU THINK, VINCE? AM I A GENIUS UNDERAPPRECIATED IN MY OWN TIME? YEAH, WELL, AT LEAST I DIDN'T CUT OFF MY EAR.
END.

W: John Roy A: Breno Tamura L: Becca Carey

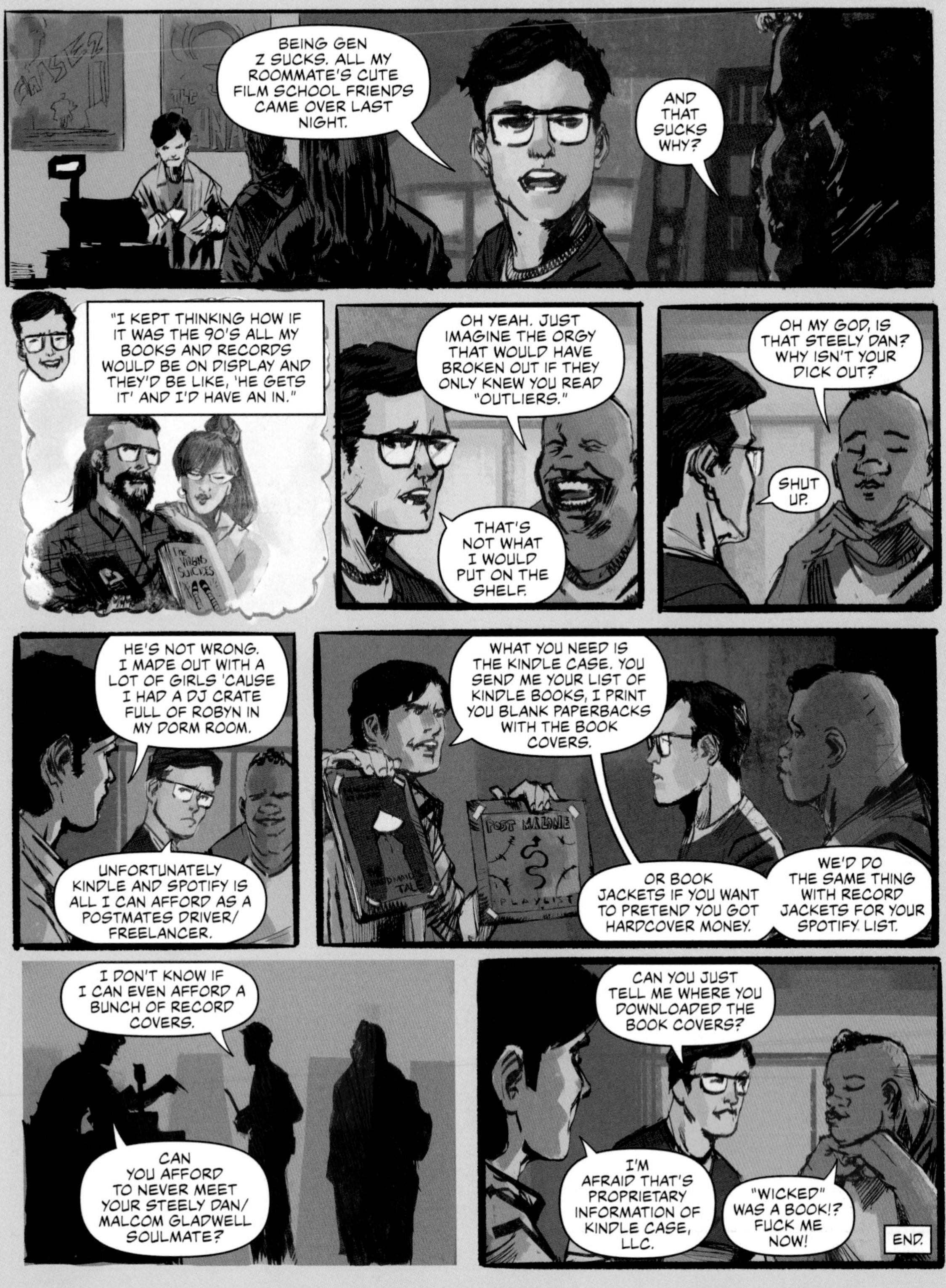
BEING GEN Z SUCKS. ALL MY ROOMMATE'S CUTE FILM SCHOOL FRIENDS CAME OVER LAST NIGHT.
AND THAT SUCKS WHY?
"I KEPT THINKING HOW IF IT WAS THE 90'S ALL MY BOOKS AND RECORDS WOULD BE ON DISPLAY AND THEY'D BE LIKE, 'HE GETS IT' AND I'D HAVE AN IN."
OH YEAH. JUST IMAGINE THE ORGY THAT WOULD HAVE BROKEN OUT IF THEY ONLY KNEW YOU READ "OUTLIERS."
THAT'S NOT WHAT I WOULD PUT ON THE SHELF.
OH MY GOD, IS THAT STEELY DAN? WHY ISN'T YOUR DICK OUT?
SHUT UP.
HE'S NOT WRONG. I MADE OUT WITH A LOT OF GIRLS 'CAUSE I HAD A DJ CRATE FULL OF ROBYN IN MY DORM ROOM.
UNFORTUNATELY KINDLE AND SPOTIFY IS ALL I CAN AFFORD AS A POSTMATES DRIVER/ FREELANCER.
WHAT YOU NEED IS THE KINDLE CASE. YOU SEND ME YOUR LIST OF KINDLE BOOKS, I PRINT YOU BLANK PAPERBACKS WITH THE BOOK COVERS.
OR BOOK JACKETS IF YOU WANT TO PRETEND YOU GOT HARDCOVER MONEY.
WE'D DO THE SAME THING WITH RECORD JACKETS FOR YOUR SPOTIFY LIST.
I DON'T KNOW IF I CAN EVEN AFFORD A BUNCH OF RECORD COVERS.
CAN YOU AFFORD TO NEVER MEET YOUR STEELY DAN/ MALCOM GLADWELL SOULMATE?
CAN YOU JUST TELL ME WHERE YOU DOWNLOADED THE BOOK COVERS?
I'M AFRAID THAT'S PROPRIETARY INFORMATION OF KINDLE CASE, LLC.
"WICKED" WAS A BOOK!? FUCK ME NOW!
END.

READ RADIANT

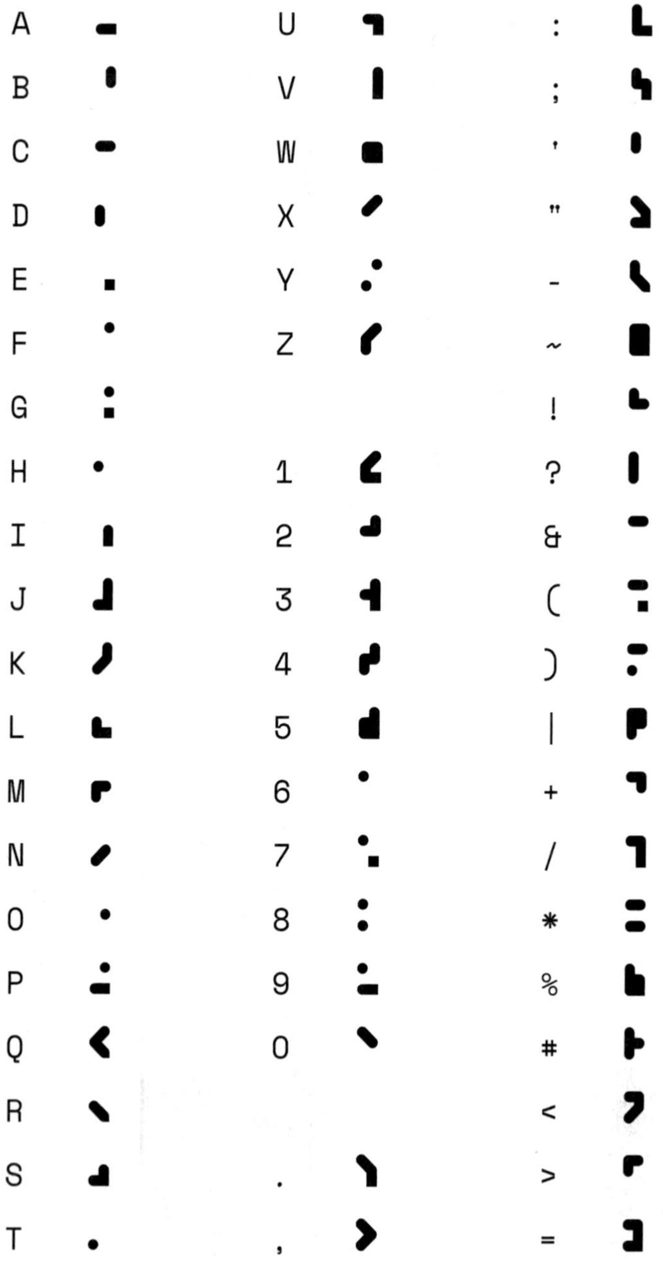
A
B
C
D
E
F
G
H
I
J
K
L
M
N
O
P
Q
R
S
T
U
V
W
X
Y
Z
1
2
3
4
5
6
7
8
9
0
.
,
:
;
'
"
-
~
!
?
&
(
)
|
+
/
*
%
#
<
>
=